D0080410

Language and Gender

Language and Gender is a new introduction to the study of the relation between gender and language use, written by two of the leading experts in the field. It covers the main topics, beginning with a clear discussion of gender and of the resources that the linguistic system offers for the construction of social meaning. The body of the book provides an unprecedentedly broad and deep coverage of the interaction between language and social life, ranging from nuances of pronunciation to conversational dynamics to the deployment of metaphor. The discussion is organized around the contributions language makes to situated social practice rather than around linguistic structures or gender analyses. At the same time, it introduces linguistic concepts in a way that is suitable for nonlinguists. It is set to become the standard textbook for courses on language and gender.

PENELOPE ECKERT is Professor of Linguistics, Professor (by courtesy) of Cultural and Social Anthropology and Director of the Program in Feminist Studies at Stanford University. She has published the ethnography *Jocks and Burnouts: Social Categories and Identity in the High School* (1989), the book *Linguistic Variation as Social Practice* (2000), and many linguistic articles.

SALLY MCCONNELL-GINET is Professor of Linguistics at the Department of Linguistics, Cornell University. Together with Ruth Borker and literary scholar Nelly Furman, she edited and contributed to *Women and Language in Literature and Society* (1980) and with linguist Gennaro Chierchia, co-authored *Meaning and Grammar: An Introduction to Semantics* (1990), which has recently been revised for a second edition.

Language and Gender

PENELOPE ECKERT

SALLY McCONNELL-GINET

CAMBRIDGE
UNIVERSITY PRESS

PUBLISHED BY THE PRESS SYNDICATE OF THE UNIVERSITY OF CAMBRIDGE
The Pitt Building, Trumpington Street, Cambridge, United Kingdom

CAMBRIDGE UNIVERSITY PRESS
The Edinburgh Building, Cambridge CB2 2RU, UK
40 West 20th Street, New York, NY 10011-4211, USA
477 Williamstown Road, Port Melbourne, VIC 3207, Australia
Ruiz de Alarcón 13, 28014 Madrid, Spain
Dock House, The Waterfront, Cape Town 8001, South Africa

http://www.cambridge.org

First published 2003
Fourth printing 2005

Printed in the United Kingdom at the University Press, Cambridge

Typeface Swift 10/14 pt   *System* LATEX 2_ε [TB]

A catalogue record for this book is available from the British Library

Library of Congress Cataloguing in Publication data

ISBN 0 521 65283 9 hardback
ISBN 0 521 65426 2 paperback

Contents

Illustrations

Acknowledgments

Our collaboration began in 1990 when Penny was asked to teach a course on language and gender at the 1991 LSA Linguistic Institute at the University of California at Santa Cruz, and Sally was asked to write an article on language and gender for the *Annual Review of Anthropology*. We decided to combine these projects into a joint effort to rethink approaches to language and gender, and particularly to bring together our work in quite different areas of linguistics. Penny's focus in linguistics has been on sociolinguistic variation, and she was employing ethnographic methods to examine the embedding of linguistic practice in processes of identity construction. Sally came to linguistics from math and analytic philosophy, and has divided her career between teaching and research on language and gender, especially the pragmatic question of what people (as opposed to linguistic expressions) mean, and on formal semantics. Both of us, in our individual writing and teaching, had begun to think of gender and language as coming together in social practice. Penny was then at the Institute for Research and Learning in Palo Alto, California, where she worked with Jean Lave and Etienne Wenger. Their notion of *community of practice* provided an important theoretical construct for our thinking about gender, about language use, and about how the two interact. We owe special gratitude to Jean and Etienne.

Each time we thought we'd finished working together, a new collaboration would come up. Our *Annual Review* article appeared in early 1992, and we presented a greatly abbreviated version as a talk at the Second Berkeley Conference on Women and Language. In 1993, we gave a public talk at the LSA Institute at the Ohio State University that grew into the paper in the volume edited by Mary Bucholtz (who was a student in our Santa Cruz course) and Kira Hall in 1995. Early in 1997, at the International Conference on the Social Psychology of Language, we participated in a session organized by Janet Holmes on communities of practice in language and gender research. With Miriam Meyerhoff, Janet edited a special issue of *Language in Society*, based on that session and including a paper from us.

At that point, we went off on our separate ways again. Various people had suggested that we try our hand at a textbook on language and gender, but we were both occupied with other projects, and were reluctant to take this one on. Frankly, we didn't think it would be much fun. We owe the turnaround to the exquisite persuasive skills of Judith Ayling, then the linguistics editor at Cambridge University Press. She has since left publishing to go into law, and we imagine she's a formidable lawyer. Andrew Winnard, who took over from Judith in 1998, is the one who has had to deal with us during the writing process. He has been wonderfully patient and supportive, and always a joy to be with. We also thank our capable and accommodating copy-editor, Jacqueline French.

The book took shape during a four-week residency at the Rockefeller Study and Research Center in Bellagio, Italy. Bellagio is a dream environment, and it gave us time to engage with one another with none of our customary home worries and responsibilities. The others with whom we shared our time there were enormously stimulating, and we are grateful to them all for their companionship, their conversation, and their bocce skills. And like everyone who experiences the magic of Bellagio, we are eternally grateful to the Rockefeller Foundation, and to the director of the Center, Gianna Celli, and her wonderful staff. We left Bellagio with drafts of most of the chapters in hand, but in the succeeding couple of years those chapters and the organization of the book have changed radically.

Sally has been teaching language and gender courses to undergraduates at Cornell during the years of working on the book, and their comments and questions as well as those of her graduate student assistants and graders have been very helpful in showing us what worked and what did not. Beyond that, Sally thanks her language and gender students over an even longer period, far too many to name individually, for thoughtful insights and imaginative and stimulating research projects. Cornell graduate students with whom Sally has worked on language and gender issues in recent years include Lisa Lavoie, Marisol del Teso Craviotto, and Tanya Matthews; all offered useful suggestions as the book progressed. Sociolinguist Janet Holmes very generously read and commented on the draft of this book that Sally used in her spring 2001 course and her keen eye helped us make important improvements. In the summer of 2001 Sally and Cornell anthropologist Kathryn March co-taught a Telluride Associate Summer Program for a wonderful group of high-schoolers on language, gender, and sexuality, using some draft chapters from this book; Kath and the rest of the TASPers offered acute and thoughtful comments.

Sally's first large language and gender project was *Women and Language in Literature and Society*, co-edited in 1980 with the late Ruth Borker, an anthropologist, and Nelly Furman, a literary theorist. Not only did she learn a lot from her co-editors (and from conversations with Daniel Maltz, Ruth's partner), but throughout this period she also corresponded with Barrie Thorne, Cheris Kramarae, and Nancy Henley, active figures early on in the field of language and gender. And she drew heavily on the expertise of colleagues from other disciplines in the Cornell Women's Studies Program. Co-teaching experiences with Nelly Furman, Ruth Borker, and Kathryn March stand out as particularly important. And Sally thanks Sandra Bem for many encouraging and enlightening lunchtime conversations and for her reading of the Spring 2001 draft of the book.

Penny came to the study of language and gender later than Sally, through the study of phonological variation in Detroit area high schools. In the course of her ethnographic work it became painfully (or perhaps joyfully) clear that gender had a far more complex relation to variation than the one-dimensional treatment it had been traditionally given. She owes her very earliest thoughts on this issue to Alison Edwards and Lynne Robins, who were graduate students working on this project at the University of Michigan in the early eighties. Since then, she has benefited from the probing minds of many sociolinguistics students at Stanford who have engaged together with issues of the relation between identity and language practice. She thanks most particularly the *Trendies* (Jennifer Arnold, Renee Blake, Melissa Iwai, Norma Mendoza-Denton, Carol Morgan and Julie Solomon) and the *Slicsters* (Sarah Benor, Katherine Campbell-Kebler, Andrea Kortenhoven, Rob Podesva, Mary Rose, Jen Roth Gordon, Devyani Sharma, Julie Sweetland, and Andrew Wong). In addition, undergraduates over the years in Penny's Language and Gender course at Standford have contributed countless examples, particularly from their often ingenious field projects. These examples have brought both color and insight to our thinking about language and gender, and many of them appear in this book. She is also particularly appreciative of her exhilarating lunchtime conversations with Eleanor Maccoby, whose probing mind and intellectual honesty have been a tremendous inspiration.

Both of us have learned much from conversations with scholars in other disciplines as well as from our contacts, casual and more formal, with colleagues in language and gender studies. Some of these influences are acknowledged in the text, but we want to express general appreciation for the intellectual generosity we have encountered over the past few years.

This book is very much a collaborative effort. Every chapter contains at least some prose that originated with Penny, some which came from Sally. We have worked hard to try to articulate a view that we can both endorse. The fact that 3,000 miles usually separated us made this close collaboration even more difficult, but we think that the result is a better book than either of us would have written on our own. It's been both more fun and more anguish than we'd expected. Our names appear in alphabetical order. Finally, our partners, Ivan Sag (a linguist) and Carl Ginet (a philosopher), have played a double role, not only supporting the project enthusiastically, but also offering us trenchant criticism at many different points. They are probably as happy as we are to see the end of this project.

We dedicate this book to the memory of Ruth Ann Borker, a pioneer in language and gender studies. Blessed with insight, imagination, and a formidable intellect, Ruth was passionate about ideas and about people, especially the students whom she loved to introduce to the unnoticed social and cultural complexities of everyday kinds of communication. This book aims to continue the lively conversations and debates about language and gender that she did so much to launch.

Introduction

In 1972, Robin Lakoff published an article entitled "Language and woman's place,"[1] which created a huge fuss. There were those who found the entire topic trivial – yet another ridiculous manifestation of feminist "paranoia." And there were those – mostly women – who jumped in to engage with the arguments and issues that Lakoff had put forth. Thus was launched the study of language and gender.

Lakoff's article argued that women have a different way of speaking from men – a way of speaking that both reflects and produces a subordinate position in society. Women's language, according to Lakoff, is rife with such devices as mitigators (*sort of, I think*) and inessential qualifiers (*really happy, so beautiful*). This language, she went on to argue, renders women's speech tentative, powerless, and trivial; and as such, it disqualifies them from positions of power and authority. In this way, language itself is a tool of oppression – it is learned as part of learning to be a woman, imposed on women by societal norms, and in turn it keeps women in their place.

This publication brought about a flurry of research and debate. For some, the issue was to put Lakoff's linguistic claims to the empirical test. Is it true that women use, for example, more tag questions than men? (e.g. Dubois and Crouch 1975). And debate also set in about the two key parts of Lakoff's claim – (1) that women and men talk differently and (2) that differences in women's and men's speech are the result of – and support – male dominance. Over the following years, there developed a separation of these two claims into what were often viewed as two different, even conflicting, paradigms – what came to be called the *difference* and the *dominance* approaches. Those who focused on difference proposed that women and men speak differently because of fundamental differences in their relation to their language, perhaps due to different socialization and experiences early on. The very popular *You Just Don't Understand* by Deborah Tannen (1990) has often been

---

1 This article was soon after expanded into a classic monograph, *Language and Woman's Place* (1975).

taken as representative of the difference framework. Drawing on work by Daniel Maltz and Ruth Borker (1982), Tannen argued that girls and boys live in different subcultures analogous to the distinct subcultures associated with those from different class or ethnic backgrounds. As a result, they grow up with different conventions for verbal interaction and interaction more generally. Analysts associated with a dominance framework generally argued that differences between women's and men's speech arise because of male dominance over women and persist in order to keep women subordinated to men. Associated with the dominance framework were works like Julia Penelope's *Speaking Freely: Unlearning the Lies of the Fathers' Tongues* (1990) or the earlier but more widely distributed *Man Made Language* by Dale Spender (1980).

Lakoff herself had made it clear that issues of difference and issues of dominance were inextricably linked. And many of the early studies of difference were clearly embedded in a dominance framework. For example early studies of interruptions, such as Zimmerman and West (1975), were based on the assumption that interruption is a strategy for asserting conversational dominance and that conversational dominance in turn supports global dominance. And underlying studies of amount of speech (e.g. Swacker 1975) was the desire to debunk harmful female stereotypes such as the "chattering" woman. But as time went on, the study of difference became an enterprise in itself and was often detached from the wider political context. Deborah Tannen's explicit "no-fault" treatment of difference (1990) is often pointed to as the most prominent example.

The focus on difference in the study of language was not an isolated development, but took place in a wider context of psychological studies of gender difference. Carol Gilligan (1982), for example, argued that women and girls have different modes of moral reasoning, and Mary Belenky and her colleagues (1986) argued for gender differences in acquiring and processing knowledge. Each case constituted a powerful response to male-centered cognitive studies, which had taken modes of thinking associated with dominant men as the norm and appraised the cognitive processes of females (and often of ethnic and racial minorities as well) as deficient. While all of this work ultimately emerged from feminist impatience with male-dominated and male-serving intellectual paradigms, it also appealed to a popular thirst for gender difference. And in the end, this research is frequently transformed in popular discourse – certainly to the horror of the researchers – to justify and support male dominance.

By the end of the seventies, the issues of difference and dominance had become sufficiently separated that Barrie Thorne, Cheris Kramarae, and Nancy Henley felt the need to counteract the trend in the introduction to their second anthology of articles on language and gender (1983). They argued that framing questions about language and gender in terms of a difference–dominance dichotomy was not especially illuminating, and urged researchers to look more closely at these differences. First of all, they argued, researchers needed to take into consideration the contexts in which the differences emerged – who was talking to whom, for what purposes, and in what kind of setting? For instance, do people speak the same way at home as at work, or to intimates as to casual acquaintances? They also argued that researchers should not ignore the considerable differences within each gender group – among women and among men. Which women are we talking about and which men? When do the differences within each gender group outweigh any differences between the groups? Considering difference within gender groups shifts the focus from a search for what is common to men and to women to what is the nature of the diversity among men and among women, and what are the tolerances for such diversity. In other words, how does diversity structure gender?

Another dichotomy that emerged in the study of language and gender is the one between how women and men speak, and how they are spoken of. It was often thought that the study of people's use of language was quite separate from the study of the embedding of gender in language. After all, the speakers did not make the language. This separation was supported by the academic linguistic canon, which viewed language as a system beyond the reach of those who use it. Thus the fact that expressions referring to women commonly undergo semantic derogation and sexualization – for example the form *hussy* once simply meant "housewife," *mistress* was just a feminine equivalent of *master* – was viewed as merely a linguistic fact. Once again, the specter of the paranoid feminist emerged in the seventies, as the Department of Linguistics at Harvard University made a public declaration that the use of masculine pronouns to refer to people generically (e.g. *every student must bring his book to class*) was a fact of language, not of society. Feminists' insistence that people should cease using *man* to refer to *humankind*, or *he* to refer to *he or she* was dismissed as "pronoun envy." But early on, scholars began to question this ahistorical view of language – as, for example, Ann Bodine (1975) traced the quite deliberate legislation of the use of masculine generics in English in the nineteenth century, as Sally McConnell-Ginet (1984) traced the relation between semantic change and the power dynamics of the everyday use of words, and as Paula Treichler (1989) traced the power dynamics involved in the inclusion of words and definitions in the great arbiter of linguistic legitimacy – the dictionary. All of this work made it quite clear that language and the use of language are inseparable; indeed, that language is continually constructed in practice.

As a result, there has been increased attention to what people do with language and how linguistic and other social resources can be transformed in the process. Deborah Cameron's 1985 *Feminism and Linguistic Theory* argued that the standard linguistic focus on a static linguistic system obscured the real gender dimensions of language. As Cameron (1998a) observed, the years since the early days have seen a shift in language and gender research from the search for correlations between linguistic units and social categories of speakers to analysis of the gendered significance of ongoing discourse. What we can call for short the "discourse turn" in language and gender studies emphasizes both the historical and dynamic character of language, and the interactive dimensions of its use. The "discourse turn" need not mean that we ignore linguistic units like speech sounds or words, but it does require that such units be considered in relation to the functions they serve in particular situated uses, and it also requires that the units themselves not be taken as fixed and immutable.

At the same time that discourse was becoming prominent on the language side, there was a shift in feminist theory and gender studies in thinking about gender. Rather than conceptualizing gender as an identity someone just "has," analysts began viewing gender as involving what people "do." In this view, gender doesn't just exist, but is continually produced, reproduced, and indeed changed through people's performance of gendered acts, as they project their own claimed gendered identities, ratify or challenge others' identities, and in various ways support or challenge systems of gender relations and privilege. As Erving Goffman (1977) pointed out, even walking into a public toilet – which is always saliently gendered – *does* gender. Judith Butler's philosophical work (esp. Butler 1990) was very influential, but there were also related precursors in the different traditions of sociology and anthropology (esp. Kessler and McKenna 1978) that drew attention to the centrality of gender performance. The "performance turn" has led many language and gender scholars to question familiar gender categories like *woman* and *man* and to explore the variety of ways in which linguistic performances relate to constructing both conventional gendered identities and identities that in one way or another challenge conventional gender norms. As we begin to separate "male" and "female" linguistic resources from "men" and "women," linguistic usages of transgendered people become of special interest.

By the time we began writing this book, language and gender studies had already been profoundly affected by both the discourse turn and the performance turn. Our earlier joint work and this book bring these two shifts in emphasis together theoretically by insisting that both language and gender are fundamentally embedded in social practice, deriving their meaning from the human activities in which they figure. Social practice involves not just individuals making choices and acting for reasons: it also involves the constraints, institutional and ideological, that frame (but do not completely determine) those individual actions. We attach particular importance to everyday social interactions in face-to-face communities of practice, groups that come together around some mutual interest or concern: families, workplace groups, sports teams, musical groups, classrooms, playground groups, and the like. On this conception, language is never "all" that matters socially, because it is always accompanied by other meaningful aspects of interactions: facial expressions, dress, location, physical contact, and so on.

Once we take practice as basic to both language and gender, the kinds of questions we ask change. Rather than "how do women speak?" or "how do men speak?" we ask what kinds of linguistic resources can and do people deploy to present themselves as certain kinds of women or men. How do new ways of speaking and otherwise acting as women or men (or "just people" or members of some alternative category) emerge? Rather than "how are women spoken of?" we ask what kinds of linguistic practices support particular gender ideologies and norms. How do new ideas about gender gain currency? How and why do people change linguistic and gender practices? The shift from focusing on differences between male and female allows us to ask what kinds of personae can males and females present.

The first two chapters of this book set out the background, focusing on gender and on linguistic resources respectively. The first chapter introduces the conception of gender as a "social construction" – that is, as the product of social practice. We discuss the relation between gender and biology, and the development of gendered identities and behaviors over the life cycle. We also introduce the notion of the gender order, examining institutional and ideological dimensions of gender arrangements. In the second chapter, we focus on the analysis of language, introducing our general take on the discourse turn, and the social underpinnings of linguistic practice. We then turn to the linguistic resources for gender practice, and discuss issues of method and analytic practice in language and gender research.

The remainder – the "meat" – of the book is organized around the different ways in which language participates in gender practice. We focus throughout on meaning-making. Gender is, after all, a system of meaning – a way of construing notions of male and female – and language is the primary means through which we maintain or contest old meanings, and construct or resist new ones. We begin in chapter three with an examination of verbal interaction – specifically with the organization of talk. Our main concern in this chapter is how people get their ideas on the table and their proposals taken up – how gender affects people's ability to get their meanings into the discourse. Getting to make one's desired contribution requires first of all access to the situations and events in which relevant conversations are being had. And once in those situations, people need to get their contributions into the flow of talk, and to have those contributions taken up by others. Gender structures not only participation in certain kinds of speech activities and genres, but also conversational dynamics. Since this structuring is not always what one would expect, we take a critical look at beliefs about conversational dynamics in this chapter.

Every contribution one makes in an interaction can be seen as a social "move" – as part of the carrying out of one's intentions with respect to others. After all, we don't just flop through the world, but we have plans – however much those plans may change from moment to moment. And these plans and the means by which we carry them out are strongly affected by gender. Chapter four focuses on speech acts and other kinds of meaningful social moves people make in face-to-face interactions. Chapter five follows on closely with a focus on linguistic resources that position language users with respect to one another ("subject positioning") and with respect to the ideas they are advancing ("idea positioning"). We consider such things as showing deference and respect, signaling commitment and eliciting others' support, speaking directly or indirectly.

In chapters six and seven, we discuss how people build gendered content as they interact in their communities of practice and elsewhere. All communication takes place against a background of shared assumptions, and establishing those assumptions in conversation is key to getting one's meanings into the discourse. Chapter six develops the idea that much of what is communicated linguistically is implied rather than strictly said. It examines some of the ways in which gender schemas and ideologies (e.g. the presumption of universal heterosexuality) figure as assumed background when people talk, and it explicitly examines strategies for the backgrounding or foregrounding of certain aspects of meaning. For example, although in many contexts men are presented as more "active" than women – as doing more – male activity and men's responsible agency are often downplayed in talk about sexual violence or other kinds of problematic heterosexual encounters. We discuss the powerful role of metaphor in making certain meanings salient: metaphors for talking about gender-related matters, and metaphors that use sex and gender to talk about other topics. We also discuss the question of who is engaging in making what kinds of metaphors and how are they understood.

The ultimate power, one might say, is to be able to dictate categories for the rest of society – to determine what racial categories are (and which people will be viewed as "having no race"), to determine where petty theft leaves off and larceny begins, to determine what constitutes beauty. The focus of chapter seven is on categorizing, on how we map our world and some of the many ways those mappings enter into gender practice. We consider how categories are related to one another and how social practice shapes and changes those relations; and why people might dispute particular ways of mapping the world. We discuss linguistic forms like generic masculines, grammatical gender, and "politically correct" language. The importance of the "discourse turn" here is that we connect the forms not only to the people using them but also more generally to the social practices and ongoing discourses in which their use figures.

In chapter eight, we turn from the things one says to the linguistic variety in which one says it. The variety that we use – our "accent" and "grammar" – is considered to be central to who we are, and it often plays a central role in determining our position on the social and economic market – our access to such things as employment, resources, social participation, and even marriage. In chapter eight, we examine language ideology in its relation to gender ideology, and then we turn to show how people use a wide range of linguistic features (especially small features of pronunciation) to present themselves as different kinds of women and men: as proper, as tough, as religiously observant, as urban and sophisticated, as rural and loyal to the land, and so on.

Chapter nine brings it all together, with a focus on the use of the various linguistic resources discussed in chapters three through eight in the production of selves. In this chapter, we talk about stylistic practice as the means by which people produce gendered personae. Style, we argue, is not a cloak over the "true" self but instantiates the self it purports to be. We consider some gender performances that might seem of dubious legitimacy and that flamboyantly challenge established gender ideologies and norms: phone sex workers in California, hijras in India, the 'yan daudu in Nigeria. And we look at other cases of gender performance that, while not perhaps so obviously transgressive, nonetheless represent new kinds of femininities and masculinities. We close this chapter and the book by noting that the possibilities for gendered personae are indeed changing and that changing linguistic practices are important in these changed possibilities. At the same time, we observe that changes always produce reactions and that there is no nice neat picture of eventual outcomes for language or for gender or for their interaction.

We have tried to write this book so that readers with no special expertise in either gender or language studies will find it accessible and engaging. We hope that it may also interest those who are already familiar with one of these areas, and that it may even offer something to our colleagues who have themselves done work on language and gender issues, or on other dimensions of the interaction of language with culture and society. Readers will not get answers to global questions about differences between the set gender categories "women" and "men." What they will get, we hope, is a taste for more interesting questions – questions about what makes someone a woman or a man, how language participates in making women and men, and how language participates in changing gender practice as well.

CHAPTER 1

Constructing, deconstructing and reconstructing gender

We are surrounded by gender lore from the time we are very small. It is ever-present in conversation, humor, and conflict, and it is called upon to explain everything from driving styles to food preferences. Gender is embedded so thoroughly in our institutions, our actions, our beliefs, and our desires, that it appears to us to be completely natural. The world swarms with ideas about gender – and these ideas are so commonplace that we take it for granted that they are true, accepting common adage as scientific fact. As scholars and researchers, though, it is our job to look beyond what appears to be common sense to find not simply what truth might be behind it, but how it came to be common sense. It is precisely because gender seems natural, and beliefs about gender seem to be obvious truth, that we need to step back and examine gender from a new perspective. Doing this requires that we suspend what we are used to and what feels comfortable, and question some of our most fundamental beliefs. This is not easy, for gender is so central to our understanding of ourselves and of the world that it is difficult to pull back and examine it from new perspectives.[1] But it is precisely the fact that gender seems self-evident which makes the study of gender interesting. It brings the challenge to uncover the process of construction that creates what we have so long thought of as natural and inexorable – to study gender not as given, but as an accomplishment; not simply as cause, but as effect. The results of failure to recognize this challenge are manifest not only in the popular media, but in academic work on language and gender as well. As a result, some gender scholarship does as much to reify and support existing beliefs as to promote more reflective and informed thinking about gender.

---

1 It is easier, though, for people who feel that they are disadvantaged in the social order, and it is no doubt partially for this reason that many recent theories of gender have been developed primarily (though not exclusively) by women. (In some times and places, women have not had the opportunity to develop "theories" of anything.)

Sex and gender

Gender is not something we are born with, and not something we *have*, but something we *do* (West and Zimmerman 1987) – something we *perform* (Butler 1990). Imagine a small boy proudly following his father. As he swaggers and sticks out his chest, he is doing everything he can to be like his father – to be a *man*. Chances are his father is not swaggering, but the boy is creating a persona that embodies what he is admiring in his adult male role model. The same is true of a small girl as she puts on her mother's high-heeled shoes, smears makeup on her face and minces around the room. Chances are that when these children are grown they will not swagger and mince respectively, but their childhood performances contain elements that will no doubt surface in their adult male and female behaviors. Chances are, also, that the girl will adopt that swagger on occasion as well, but adults are not likely to consider it as "cute" as her mincing act. And chances are that if the boy decides to try a little mincing, he won't be considered cute at all. In other words, gendered performances are available to everyone, but with them come constraints on who can perform which personae with impunity. And this is where gender and sex come together, as society tries to match up ways of behaving with biological sex assignments.

Sex is a biological categorization based primarily on reproductive potential, whereas gender is the social elaboration of biological sex. Gender builds on biological sex, it exaggerates biological difference and, indeed, it carries biological difference into domains in which it is completely irrelevant. There is no biological reason, for example, why women should mince and men should swagger, or why women should have red toenails and men should not. But while we think of sex as biological and gender as social, this distinction is not clear-cut. People tend to think of gender as the result of nurture – as social and hence fluid – while sex is simply given by biology. However, there is no obvious point at which sex leaves off and gender begins, partly because there is no single objective biological criterion for male or female sex. Sex is based in a combination of anatomical, endocrinal and chromosomal features, and the selection among these criteria for sex assignment is based very much on cultural beliefs about what actually makes someone male or female. Thus the very definition of the biological categories *male* and *female*, and people's understanding of themselves and others as male or female, is ultimately social. Anne Fausto-Sterling (2000) sums up the situation as follows:

> labeling someone a man or a woman is a social decision. We may use
> scientific knowledge to help us make the decision, but only our beliefs

about gender – not science – can define our sex. Furthermore, our beliefs about gender affect what kinds of knowledge scientists produce about sex in the first place. (p. 3)

Biology offers us up dichotomous male and female prototypes, but it also offers us many individuals who do not fit those prototypes in a variety of ways. Blackless *et al.* (2000) estimate that 1 in 100 babies are born with bodies that differ from standard male or female. These bodies may have such conditions as unusual chromosomal makeup (1 in 1,000 male babies are born with two X chromosomes), hormonal differences such as insensitivity to androgens (1 in 13,000 births), or a range of configurations and combinations of genitals and reproductive organs. The attribution of intersex does not end at birth – 1 in 66 girls experience growth of the clitoris in childhood or adolescence (known as late onset adrenal hyperplasia).

When "anomalous" babies are born, surgical and/or endocrinal manipulations may be used to bring their recalcitrant bodies into closer conformity with either the male or the female category. Common medical practice imposes stringent requirements for male and female genitals at birth – a penis that is less than 2.5 centimeters long when stretched, or a clitoris[2] that is more than one centimeter long are both commonly subject to surgery in which both are reduced to an "acceptable" sized clitoris (Dreger 1998). As a number of critics have observed (e.g. Dreger 1998), the standards of acceptability are far more stringent for male genitals than female, and thus the most common surgery transforms "unacceptable" penises into clitorises, regardless of the child's other sexual characteristics, and even if this requires fashioning a nonfunctional vagina out of tissue from the colon. In recent years, the activist organization, the Intersex Society of North America,[3] has had considerable success as an advocacy group for the medical rights of intersex people.

In those societies that have a greater occurrence of certain kinds of hermaphroditic or intersexed infants than elsewhere,[4] there

---

2 Alice Dreger (1998) more accurately describes these as a phallus on a baby classified as male or a phallus on a baby classified as female.

3 The website of the Intersex Society of North America (http://www.isna.org) offers a wealth of information on intersex. [The publisher has used its best endeavors to ensure that the URLs for external websites referred to in this book are correct and active at the time of going to press. However, the publisher has no responsibility for the websites and can make no guarantee that a site will remain live or that the content is or will remain appropriate.]

4 For instance, congenital adrenal hyperplasia (which combines two X chromosomes with masculinized external genitalia and the internal reproductive organs of a potentially fertile woman) occurs in 43 children per million in New Zealand, but 3,500 per million among the Yupik of Southwestern Alaska (www.isna.org).

sometimes are social categories beyond the standard two into which such babies can be placed. But even in such societies, categories that go beyond the basic two are often seen as anomalous.[5]

It is commonly argued that biological differences between males and females determine gender by causing enduring differences in capabilities and dispositions. Higher levels of testosterone, for example, are said to lead men to be more aggressive than women; and left-brain dominance is said to lead men to be more "rational" while their relative lack of brain lateralization should lead women to be more "emotional." But the relation between physiology and behavior is not simple, and it is all too easy to leap for gender dichotomies. It has been shown that hormonal levels, brain activity patterns, and even brain anatomy can be a result of different activity as well as a cause. For example research with species as different as rhesus monkeys (Rose *et al.* 1972) and fish (Fox *et al.* 1997) has documented changes in hormone levels as a result of changes in social position. Work on sex differences in the brain is very much in its early stages, and as Anne Fausto-Sterling (2000) points out in considerable detail, it is far from conclusive. What is supposed to be the most robust finding – that women's corpus callosum, the link between the two brain hemispheres, is relatively larger than men's – is still anything but robust. Men's smaller corpus callosum is supposed to result in greater lateralization, while women's larger one is supposed to yield greater integration between the two hemispheres, at least in visuo-spatial functions. But given that evidence for sex-linked brain differences in humans is based on very small samples, often from sick or injured populations, generalizations about sex differences are shaky at best. In addition, not that much is known about the connections between brain physiology and cognition – hence about the consequences of any physiological differences scientists may be seeking or finding. Nonetheless, any results that might support physiological differences are readily snatched up and combined with any variety of gender stereotypes in some often quite fantastic leaps of logic. And the products of these leaps can in turn feed directly into social, and particularly into

---

5 There are cultures where what we might think of as more than two adult gender categories are named and otherwise institutionally recognized as well: the berdache of the Plains Indians, the hijras in India. Although details vary significantly, the members of such supernumerary categories are outside the "normal" order of things, and tend to be somewhat feared or devalued or otherwise socially disadvantaged. Nonetheless, there is apparently considerably more tolerance for nonstandard gender categories in some societies than in the western industrial societies most likely to be familiar to readers of this book. An early discussion of social groups with more than two sex and/or gender categories is provided by Martin and Voorhies (1975), ch. 4, "Supernumerary sexes." More recent contributions on this topic from both historical and cross-cultural perspectives appear in Herdt (1996).

educational, policy, with arguments that gender equity in such "left-brain areas" as mathematics and engineering is impossible.

The eagerness of some scientists to establish a biological basis for gender difference, and the public's eagerness to take these findings up, points to the fact that we put a good deal of work into emphasizing, producing, and enforcing the dichotomous categories of male and female. In the process, differences or similarities that blur the edges of these categories, or that might even constitute other potential categories, are backgrounded, or *erased*.

The issue here is not whether there are sex-linked biological differences that might affect such things as predominant cognitive styles. What is at issue is the place of such research in social and scientific practice. Sex difference is being placed at the center of activity, as both question and answer, as often flimsy evidence of biological difference is paired up with unanalyzed behavioral stereotypes. And the results are broadcast through the most august media as if their scientific status were comparable to the mapping of the human genome. The mere fact of this shows clearly that everyone, from scientists to journalists to the reading public, has an insatiable appetite for sensationalist gender news. Indeed, gender is at the center of our social world. And any evidence that our social world maps onto the biological world is welcome evidence to those who would like an explanation and justification for the way things are.

To whatever extent gender may be related to biology, it does not flow naturally and directly from our bodies. The individual's chromosomes, hormones, genitalia, and secondary sex characteristics do not determine occupation, gait, or use of color terminology. And while male pattern baldness may restrict some adult men's choice of hairdo, there are many men who could sport a pageboy or a beehive as easily as many women, and nothing biological keeps women from shaving their heads. Gender is the very process of creating a dichotomy by effacing similarity and elaborating on difference, and even where there are biological differences, these differences are exaggerated and extended in the service of constructing gender. Actual differences are always paired with enormous similarities, never dichotomizing people but putting them on a scale with many women and men occupying the same positions.

Consider our voices. On average, men's vocal tracts are longer than women's, yielding a lower voice pitch. But individuals' actual conversational voice pitch across society does not simply conform to the size of the vocal tract. At the age of four to five years, well before puberty differentiates male and female vocal tracts, boys and girls learn to differentiate their voices as boys consciously and unconsciously lower their voices while girls raise theirs. In the end, one can usually tell whether even a very small child is male or female on the basis of their voice pitch and quality alone, regardless of the length of their vocal tract.

Relative physical stature is another biological difference that is elaborated and exaggerated in the production of gender. Approximately half of the women and half of the men in the USA (Kuczmarski *et al.* 2000) are between 64 and 70 inches tall. With this considerable overlap, one might expect in any randomly chosen male and female pair that the woman would run a good chance of being taller than the man. In actuality, among heterosexual couples, one only occasionally sees such a combination, because height is a significant factor in people's choice of a heterosexual mate. While there is no biological reason for women to be shorter than their male mates, an enormous majority of couples exhibit this height relation – far more than would occur through a process of selection in which height was random (Goffman 1976). Not only do people mate so as to keep him taller than her, they also see him as taller than her even when this is not the case. For example, Biernat, Manis, and Nelson 1991 (cited in Valian 1998) presented college students with photos of people and asked them to guess the people's height. Each photo had a reference item like a doorway or a desk, making it possible to compare the heights of people across photos. Although photos of a male of a given height were matched by photos of a female of the same height (and vice versa), the judges saw the males as taller than they actually were and the females as shorter than they actually were.

This book will focus on gender as a social construction – as the means by which society jointly accomplishes the differentiation that constitutes the gender order. While we recognize that biology imposes certain physiological constraints on the average male and female, we treat the elaboration and magnification of these differences as entirely social. Readers will come to this book with their own set of beliefs about the origins and significance of gender. They may have certain understandings of the implications for gender of biological and medical science. They may subscribe to a particular set of religious beliefs about gender. The notion of the social elaboration of sex is not incompatible with belief in a biological or divine imperative – the difference will be in where one leaves off and the other begins. All we ask of our readers is that they open-mindedly consider the evidence and arguments we advance. Our own thinking about gender has developed and changed over many years of thinking about these issues, and it will undoubtedly continue to change as we continue to explore gender issues in our research and in our lives. We have written this account of gender from a broadly feminist perspective. As we understand that perspective, the basic capabilities, rights, and responsibilities of women and men are far less different than is commonly thought. At the same time, that perspective also suggests that the social treatment of women and men, and thus their experiences and their own and others' expectations for them, is far more different than is usually assumed. In this book we offer evidence that these differences in what happens to women and to men derive in considerable measure from people's beliefs about sexual difference, their interpretations of its significance, and their reliance on those beliefs and interpretations to justify the unequal treatment of women and men.

Learning to be gendered

Dichotomous beginnings: It's a boy! It's a girl!

In the famous words of Simone de Beauvoir, "Women are not born, they are made." The same is true of men. The making of a man or a woman is a never-ending process that begins before birth – from the moment someone begins to wonder if the pending child will be a boy or a girl. And the ritual announcement at birth that it is in fact one or the other instantly transforms an "it" into a "he" or a "she" (Butler 1993), standardly assigning it to a lifetime as a male or as a female.[6] This attribution is further made public and lasting through the linguistic event of naming. To name a baby *Mary* is to do something that makes it easy for a wide range of English speakers to maintain the initial "girl" attribution. In English-speaking societies, not all names are sex-exclusive (e.g. *Chris*, *Kim*, *Pat*), and sometimes names change their gender classification. For example, *Evelyn* was available as a male name in Britain long after it had become an exclusively female name in America, and *Whitney*, once exclusively a surname or a male first name in America, is now bestowed on baby girls. In some times and places, the state or religious institutions disallow sex-ambiguous given names. Finland, for example, has lists of legitimate female and legitimate male names that must be consulted before the baby's name becomes official. Thus the dichotomy of male and female is the ground upon which we build selves from the moment of birth. These early linguistic acts set

---

6 Nowadays, with the possibility of having this information before birth, wanting to know in advance or not wanting to know can become ideologically charged. Either way, the sex of the child is frequently as great a preoccupation as its health.

up a baby for life, launching a gradual process of learning to be a boy or a girl, a man or a woman, and to see all others as boys or girls, men or women as well. There are currently no other legitimate ways to think about ourselves and others – and we will be expected to pattern all kinds of things about ourselves as a function of that initial dichotomy. In the beginning, adults will do the child's gender work, treating it as a boy or as a girl, and interpreting its every move as that of a boy or of a girl. Then over the years, the child will learn to take over its part of the process, doing its own gender work and learning to support the gender work of others. The first thing people want to know about a baby is its sex, and convention provides a myriad of props to reduce the necessity of asking – and it becomes more and more important, as the child develops, not to have to ask. At birth, many hospital nurseries provide pink caps for girls and blue caps for boys, or in other ways provide some visual sign of the sex that has been attributed to the baby. While this may seem quite natural to members of the society, in fact this color coding points out no difference that has any bearing on the medical treatment of the infants. Go into a store in the US to buy a present for a newborn baby, and you will immediately be asked "boy or girl?" If the reply is "I don't know" or, worse, "I don't care," sales personnel are often perplexed. Overalls for a girl may be OK (though they are "best" if pink or flowered or in some other way marked as "feminine"), but gender liberalism goes only so far. You are unlikely to buy overalls with vehicles printed on them for a girl, and even more reluctant to buy a frilly dress with puffed sleeves or pink flowered overalls for a boy. And if you're buying clothing for a baby whose sex you do not know, sales people are likely to counsel you to stick with something that's plain yellow or green or white. Colors are so integral to our way of thinking about gender that gender attributions have bled into our view of the colors, so that people tend to believe that pink is a more "delicate" color than blue. This is a prime example of the naturalization of what is in fact an arbitrary sign. In America in the late nineteenth and early twentieth centuries, Anne Fausto-Sterling (2000) reports, blue was favored for girls and bright pink for boys.

If gender flowed naturally from sex, one might expect the world to sit back and simply allow the baby to become male or female. But in fact, sex determination sets the stage for a lifelong process of gendering, as the child becomes, and learns how to be, male or female. Names and clothing are just a small part of the symbolic resources used to support a consistent ongoing gender attribution even when children are clothed. That we can speak of a child growing up *as a girl* or *as a boy* suggests that initial sex attribution is far more than just a simple observation of a physical characteristic. *Being a girl* or *being a boy* is not a stable state but an ongoing accomplishment, something that is actively *done* both by the individual so categorized and by those who interact with it in the various communities to which it belongs. The newborn initially depends on others to *do* its gender, and they come through in many different ways, not just as individuals but as part of socially structured communities that link individuals to social institutions and cultural ideologies. It is perhaps at this early life stage that it is clearest that gender is a collaborative affair – that one must learn to perform as a male or a female, and that these performances require support from one's surroundings.

Indeed, we do not know how to interact with another human being (or often members of other species), or how to judge them and talk about them, unless we can attribute a gender to them. Gender is so deeply engrained in our social practice, in our understanding of ourselves and of others, that we almost cannot put one foot in front of the other without taking gender into consideration. Although most of us rarely notice this overtly in everyday life, most of our interactions are colored by our performance of our own gender, and by our attribution of gender to others.

From infancy, male and female children are interpreted differently, and interacted with differently. Experimental evidence suggests that adults' perceptions of babies are affected by their beliefs about the babies' sex. Condry and Condry (1976) found that adults watching a film of a crying infant were more likely to hear the cry as angry if they believed the infant was a boy, and as plaintive or fearful if they believed the infant was a girl. In a similar experiment, adults judged a 24-hour-old baby as bigger if they believed it to be a boy, and finer-featured if they believed it to be a girl (Rubin, Provenzano and Luria 1974). Such judgments then enter into the way people interact with infants and small children. People handle infants more gently when they believe them to be female, more playfully when they believe them to be male.

And they talk to them differently. Parents use more diminutives (*kitty*, *doggie*) when speaking to girls than to boys (Gleason *et al.* 1994), they use more inner state words (*happy*, *sad*) when speaking to girls (Ely *et al.* 1995). They use more direct prohibitives (*don't do that!*) and more emphatic prohibitives (*no! no! no!*) to boys than to girls (Bellinger and Gleason 1982). Perhaps, one might suggest, the boys need more prohibitions because they tend to misbehave more than the girls. But Bellinger and Gleason found this pattern to be independent of the actual nature of the children's activity, suggesting that the adults and their beliefs about sex difference are far more important here than the children's behavior.

With differential treatment, boys and girls eventually learn to *be* different. Apparently, male and female infants cry the same amount (Maccoby and Jacklin 1974), but as they mature, boys cry less and less. There is some evidence that this difference emerges primarily from differential adult response to the crying. Qualitative differences in behavior come about in the same way. A study of thirteen-month-old children in day care (Fagot *et al.* 1985) showed that teachers responded to girls when they talked, babbled, or gestured, while they responded to boys when they whined, screamed, or demanded physical attention. Nine to eleven months later, the same girls talked more than the boys, and the boys whined, screamed, and demanded attention more than the girls. Children's eventual behavior, which seems to look at least statistically different across the sexes, is the product of adults' differential responses to ways of acting that are in many (possibly most) cases very similar indeed. The kids do indeed learn to "do" gender for themselves, to produce sex-differentiated behavior – although even with considerable differential treatment they do not end up with dichotomizing behavioral patterns.

Voice, which we have already mentioned, provides a dramatic example of children's coming to perform gender. At the ages of four to five years, in spite of their identical vocal apparatus, girls and boys begin to differentiate the fundamental frequency of their speaking voice. Boys tend to round and extend their lips, lengthening the vocal tract, whereas girls are tending to spread their lips (with smiles, for example), shortening the vocal tract. Girls are raising their pitches, boys lowering theirs. It may well be that adults are more likely to speak to girls in a high-pitched voice. It may be that they reward boys and girls for differential voice productions. It may also be that children simply observe this difference in older people, or that their differential participation in games (for example play-acting) calls for different voice productions. Elaine Andersen (1990, pp. 24–25), for example, shows that children use high pitch when using baby talk or "teacher register" in role play. Some children speak as the other sex is expected to and thus, as with other aspects of doing gender, there is not a perfect dichotomization in voice pitch (even among adults, some voices are not consistently classified). Nonetheless, there is a striking production of mostly different pitched voices from essentially similar vocal equipment.

There is considerable debate among scholars about the extent to which adults actually do treat boys and girls differently, and many note that the similarities far outweigh the differences. Research on early gender development – in fact the research in general on gender differences – is almost exclusively done by psychologists. As a result, the research it reports on largely involves observations of behavior in limited settings – whether in a laboratory or in the home or the preschool. Since these studies focus on limited settings and types of interaction and do not follow children through a normal day, they quite possibly miss the cumulative effects of small differences across many different situations. Small differences here and there are probably enough for children to learn what it means in their community to be male or female.

The significance of the small difference can be appreciated from another perspective. The psychological literature tends to treat children as objects rather than subjects. Those studying children have tended to treat others – parents, other adults, peers – as the primary socializing agents. Only relatively recently have investigators begun to explore children's own active strategies for figuring out the social world. Eleanor Maccoby (2002) emphasizes that children have a very clear knowledge of their gender (that is, of whether they are classified as male or female) by the time they are three years old. Given this knowledge, it is not at all clear how much differential treatment children need to learn how to do their designated gender. What they mainly need is the message that male and female are supposed to be different, and that message is everywhere around them.

It has become increasingly clear that children play a very active role in their own development. From the moment they see themselves as social beings, they begin to focus on the enterprise of "growing up." And to some extent, they probably experience many of the gendered developmental dynamics we discuss here not so much as gender-appropriate, but as *grown-up*. The greatest taboo is being "a baby," but the developmental imperative is gendered. Being grown-up, leaving babyhood, means very different things for boys than it does for girls. And the fact that growing up involves gender differentiation is encoded in the words of assessment with which progress is monitored – kids do not behave as good or bad people, but as *good boys* or *good girls*, and they develop into *big boys* and *big girls*.[7] In other words, they do not have the option of growing into just people, but into boys or girls. This does not mean that they see what they're doing in strictly gendered terms. It is probable that when boys and girls alter the fundamental frequency of their voices they are not trying to sound like *girls* or like *boys*, but that

7 Thorne (1993) and others have observed teachers urging children to act like "big boys and girls." Very rarely is a child told "don't act like a baby – you're a big kid now."

they are aspiring for some quality that is itself gendered – cuteness, authority. And the child's aspiration is not simply a matter of reasoning, but a matter of desire – a projection of the self into desired forms of participation in the social world. Desire is a tremendous force in projecting oneself into the future – in the continual remaking of the self that constitutes growing up.

Until about the age of two, boys and girls exhibit the same play behaviors. After that age, play in boys' and girls' groups begins to diverge as they come to select different toys and engage in different activities, and children begin to monitor each other's play, imposing sanctions on gender-inappropriate play. Much is made of the fact that boys become more agonistic than girls, and many attribute this to hormonal and even evolutionary differences (see Maccoby 2000 for a brief review of these various perspectives). But whatever the workings of biology may be, it is clear that this divergence is supported and exaggerated by the social system. As children get older, their play habits are monitored and differentiated, first by adults, and eventually by peers. Parents of small children have been shown to reward their children's choice of gender-appropriate toys (trucks for boys, dolls for girls) (Langlois and Downs 1980). And while parents' support of their children's gendered behavior is not always and certainly not simply a conscious effort at gender socialization, their behavior is probably more powerful than they think. Even parents who strive for gender equality, and who believe that they do not constrain their children's behavior along gender lines, have been observed in experimental situations to do just that.

Learning asymmetry

While it takes a community to develop gender, not all participants in the community are equally involved in enforcing difference. In research on early gender socialization, males – both children and adults – have emerged as more engaged in enforcing gender difference than females. In the research by Rubin *et al.* cited above, for example, fathers were more extreme than mothers in their gender-based misassessments of infants' size and texture. Men are more likely than women to play rough with boys and gently with girls, fathers use differential language patterns to boys and girls more than mothers, and men are more likely than women to reward children for choosing gender-appropriate toys. There are now books aimed at men who want to become more involved parents than their own fathers were. But the message is still often that parenting a girl is quite a different enterprise from parenting a boy. On a self-help shelf encountered at a tourist shop, *How to Be Your Daughter's*

Daddy: 365 Ways to Show Her You Care by Dan Bolin (1993) stood right next to *How to Be Your Little Man's Dad: 365 Things to Do with Your Son* by Dan Bolin and Ken Sutterfield (1993).

It is not only that male adults seem to enforce gender more than female. This enforcement is more intensely aimed at boys than at girls. Adults are more likely to reward boys for choice of gender-appropriate toys than girls – and fathers are more likely to do so for their own sons than for other boys. Boys, in turn, are more rigid in their toy preferences than girls, and they are harder on other boys than on girls for gender-inappropriate play styles. A study of three to five year olds (Langlois and Downs 1980) showed that while girls tended to be neutral about other girls' choices, boys responded positively only to boys with male play styles, and were especially likely to punish their male peers for feminine choices. The outcome is that while activities and behaviors labeled as *male* are treated as appropriate for females as well as for males, those labeled as *female* are treated as appropriate only for females. One way of looking at this is that female activities and behaviors emerge as *marked* – as reserved for a special subset of the population – while male activities and behaviors emerge as *unmarked* or *normal*. This in turn contributes to the androcentric (male-centered) view of gender, which we will discuss in the following section of this chapter.

This asymmetry is partially a function of the cultural devaluation of women and of the feminine. One way or another, most boys and girls learn that most boy things and boy activities are more highly valued than girl things and girl activities, and boys are strongly discouraged from having interests or activities that are associated with girls. Even where they do not encounter such views formulated explicitly or even find them denied explicitly, most boys and girls learn that it is primarily men and not women who do "important" things as adults, have opinions that count, direct the course of events in the public world. It is hardly surprising then that pressures towards gender conformity are not symmetrical.

This asymmetry extends to many domains. While females may wear clothing initially viewed as male, the reverse is highly stigmatized: western women and girls now wear jeans but their male peers are not appearing in skirts. Even names seem to go from male to female and not vice versa. There are girls named Christopher, but no boys named Christine. A girl may be sanctioned for behaving "like a boy" – particularly if she behaves aggressively, and gets into fights – on the grounds that she is being "unladylike" or "not nice." But there is a categorization of "tomboy" reserved for girls who adopt a male rough and tumble

style of play, who display fearlessness and refuse to play with dolls. And
while in some circles this categorization may be considered negative,
in general in western society it earns some respect and admiration.
Boys who adopt girls' behaviors, on the other hand, are severely sanctioned. The term "sissy" is reserved for boys who do not adhere strictly
to norms of masculinity (in fact, a sissy is a boy who does not display
those very characteristics that make a girl a tomboy).

A child who's told she has to do more housework than her brother
because she's a girl, or that she can't be an astronaut when she grows
up because she's a girl,[8] is likely to say "that's not fair!" A boy who is
told he cannot play with dolls because he's a boy, or that he cannot
be a secretary when he grows up, may find that unfair as well. But
the boy who is told he can't be a nurse is being told that he is too
good to be a nurse. The girl, on the other hand, is essentially being
told that she is not good enough to be a doctor. This is not to say that
the consequences cannot be tragic for the boy who really wants to play
with dolls or grow up to be a nurse. He will be deprived of a legitimate
sense of unfairness within society's wider discourses of justice, hence
isolated with his sense of unfairness. But gender specialization does
carry the evaluation that men's enterprises are generally better than
women's, and children learn this quite early on.[9]

Now there are some counterexamples to these general trends, many
of them prompted by the feminist and gay rights movements. Some
men are taking over domestic tasks like diaper-changing and everyday cookery that were once women's province. Others wear jewels in
their ears or gold chains around their necks, adornments reserved
for women when we were teenagers. But the dominant pattern that
restricts men in moving into what are seen as women's realms and
thereby devalued is by no means dead.

Separation

To differing degrees from culture to culture and community to community, difference is reinforced by separation. Boys play more with boys;

8 These examples may seem anachronistic, but such explicit messages persist. The first
is reported by some of the young women in our classes at Stanford and Cornell (though
certainly not by all or even most). And the second message was relayed to astronaut
Sally Ride in 2001 by a girl whose teacher had offered her that discouragement.
9 Even a child whose own mother is a physician is sometimes heard saying "ladies
can't be doctors." Of course kids sometimes get it wrong. An anecdote circulated during
Margaret Thatcher's time as prime minister told of a young English boy asked "do you
want to be prime minister when you grow up?" "Oh no," he replied, "that's a woman's
job."

girls with girls. And this pattern repeats itself cross-culturally, in nonindustrial societies as well as in industrial societies (Whiting and Edwards 1988). The extent to which individuals in western industrial countries grow up participating in same-sex playgroups varies tremendously, depending on such things as the genders and ages of their siblings and their neighbors. Some kids spend more time in same-sex groups at one stage of their lives, less at other stages. The fact remains that however much kids may play in mixed-sex groups, there is a tendency to seek out – and to be constrained to seek out – same-sex groups. This constraint is stronger for boys – girls who prefer playing with boys are tolerated, perhaps admired, while boys who prefer playing with girls are not.

Psychological research shows that many American children begin to prefer same-sex playmates as they approach the age of three (Maccoby 1998), which is about the age at which they develop a clear sense of their own gender, and this preference increases rapidly as they age. Eleanor Maccoby notes that this preference emerges in institutional settings – day care, preschool, and elementary school – where children encounter large numbers of age peers. On the same theme, Thorne (1993) points out that schools provide a sufficiently large population that boys and girls can separate, whereas in neighborhoods there may be less choice.

Even though children lean towards same-sex groups in these settings, they often maintain prior cross-sex friendships formed outside the institution (Howes 1988). It is important to note that the preference for same-sex play groups is not absolute, and that in fact children often play in mixed groups. Maccoby and Jacklin's study (1987) of individual children's choice of playmates in a preschool setting shows four and a half year olds playing in same-sex groups 47 percent of the time, mixed groups 35 percent of the time and other-sex groups (i.e., where the child is the only representative of her or his own sex in the group) 18 percent of the time. While these figures show a good deal of mixing, the same-sex groups are far greater than random playmate selection would produce. And at age six and a half, children in the Maccoby and Jacklin study were playing in same-sex groups 67 percent of the time. Maccoby (1998, pp. 22–23) suggests that the choice of playmates in school is a strategy for ensuring safety and predictability in an open setting, as children seek out others with a recognizable play style. This presupposes different play styles to begin with, presenting a complicated chicken-and-egg problem. For if sex-segregated play groups fill a need for predictable play and interaction styles, they are also a potential site for the production and reproduction of this differentiation. It has been overwhelmingly established that small boys engage in more physically aggressive behavior than small girls. However, experimental and observational evidence puts this differentiation at precisely the same time that same-sex group preference emerges. Maccoby points out that this play style reaches its peak among boys at about the age of four and that it is restricted to same-sex groups, suggesting that there is a complex relation between the emergence of gendered play styles and of same-sex play groups.

The separation of children in same-sex play groups has led some gender theorists to propose a view that by virtue of their separation during a significant part of their childhoods, boys and girls are socialized into different peer *cultures*. In their same-sex friendship groups, they develop different behavior, different norms, and even different understandings of the world. Daniel Maltz and Ruth Borker (1982) argue that because of this separation, boys and girls develop different verbal cultures – different ways of interacting verbally and different norms for interpreting ways of interacting. They argue, further, that this can result in *cross-cultural miscommunication* between males and females. Deborah Tannen (1990) has popularized this view, emphasizing the potential for misunderstanding. The separation of gender cultures does not necessarily entail male–female misunderstanding, although it describes the conditions under which such misunderstanding could develop. Certainly, if girls and boys are segregated on a regular basis, we can expect that they will develop different practices and different understandings of the world. The extent to which this actually occurs depends on the nature of the segregation – when, in what contexts, for what activities – in relation to the actual contact between boys and girls. In other words, to the extent that there is separation, this separation is structured – and it is structured differently in different communities. This structure will have an important bearing on the nature of differences that will develop. It will also have a bearing on the extent to which these differences are recognized.

The miscommunication model that Maltz and Borker proposed and that Tannen has further developed draws on John Gumperz's work with ethnically distinct subcultures (e.g. Gumperz 1982). It hypothesizes both that male and female understandings of interaction are in fact different, and, critically, that they are unaware of these differences, and believe that they are operating from the same understanding. It is the unawareness that may be the most problematic assumption for this approach to gender-based miscommunication (or conflict), since the gender beliefs that most kids are industriously acquiring in their peer groups and outside them emphasize difference, to the point sometimes of absurd exaggeration. Gender segregation in childhood almost certainly plays some role in the development of gendered verbal practice. But for understanding gender, separation is never the whole picture. Gender segregation in western societies is virtually always embedded in practices that bring the sexes together and that impose difference in interpretations even where there are great similarities in those actions or people being interpreted.

As we move farther along in development, the complexity of explaining gender differences increases exponentially. As kids spend more time with their peers, and as they enter into more kinds of situations with peers, not only does the balance between adult and peer influence change, but the nature of peer influence also changes. Peer society becomes increasingly complex, and at some point quite early on, explicit ideas about gender enter into children's choices, preferences, and opportunities. Whatever the initial factors that give rise to increasing gender separation, separation itself becomes an activity, and a primary social issue. Barrie Thorne (1993) notes that public choosing of teams in school activities constrains gender segregation, hence that games that involve choosing teams are more likely to be same gender, while games that simply involve lining up or being there are more likely to be gender-mixed. Separation can carry over to competitions and rivalries between boys' groups and girls' groups, as in elementary school activities such as "girls chase the boys" (Thorne 1993). These activities can be an important site for the construction of difference with claims that girls or boys are better at whatever activity is in question. In this way, beliefs about differences in males' and females' "natural" abilities may be learned so young and so indirectly that they appear to be common sense. It is not at all clear, therefore, to what extent differences in behaviors and activities result from boys' and girls' personal preference, or from social constraint.

The heterosexual market

Towards the end of elementary school, a highly visible activity of pairing up boys and girls into couples begins to dominate the scene. This activity is not one engaged in by individual children, and it is not an activity that simply arises in the midst of other childhood "business as usual." Rather, it is the beginning of a social market that forms the basis of an emerging peer social order (Eckert 1996). And with this market comes a profound change in the terms of gender separation and difference.

In childhood, it is primarily adults who attend to children's behavior. As the peer social order develops, it takes over much of this function as it develops the means to organize its own social control. Heterosexuality is the metaphor around which the peer social order organizes itself, and a heterosexual market (Thorne 1993) becomes the center of the emerging peer social order. While up until now, boys and girls may have seen themselves as simply different, and perhaps as incompatible, in the context of the heterosexual market, boys and girls emerge as complementary and cooperating factions.

The market metaphor is not frivolous, for the heterosexual market is the first of a series of social markets that the age cohort will engage in on the way to, for example, the academic market and the job market. It is here that both girls and boys will come to see themselves as having a place in a structured system of social evaluation. Kids participating in the heterosexual market can act as both commodity and as broker – they can be paired up, or they can engage in negotiating the pairing up of others. The matches that are made on this market are initially short-lived – a pair may remain "together" for a few hours, a few days, a week, sometimes longer. It is the rapidity of "trades" on the market that establishes individuals' value, and that establishes the nature of value. The rapt attention that the market attracts from those participating in it and even from many nonparticipating observers is part of the establishment of gender norms, as people's worth is recalibrated within the context of heterosexual attractiveness.

It is important to note that for most participants, this activity precedes active heterosexual activity – even dating – by a year or two, as these relationships have little to do with attachments between the members of a pair. The activities establish a system and hierarchy of desirability prior to the actual onset of overt heterosexual desire and activity. One's value on the market is a function of the matches that are made on one's behalf – not so much on the number of matches, but on the people with whom one is matched. The new and enduring status system that forms around this market constitutes the core of the emerging adolescent social order. In this way, the social order is – fundamentally – heterosexual, dramatically changing the terms of the cohort's gender arrangements. What was appropriate for boys and girls simply as male and female individuals now defines them with respect to a social order. Their value as human beings and their relations to others are based in their adherence to gender norms. And the differentiation of these norms intensifies as differentiation of male and female merges with engagement between male and female.

Readers who were developing gay male or lesbian identities during this stage of their lives may think that this account forgets about them. But the point is not that everyone is active in the heterosexual market, or that everyone who participates in this market is heterosexual. This market is the means by which the social order comes to *presume* heterosexuality, marginalizing and rendering deviant any who do not eventually participate. Sometimes there are alternative markets on which to claim worth and value – the academic market, for example – but the heterosexual imperative spreads its umbrella very widely, and because of its central place in the age cohort, it affects all – even those quite averse to any direct participation in it.

There are some cultural contexts where heterosexual coupling is not so early or so central a part of development. Even in the US the heterosexual market was not apparent among such young kids a couple of generations back. In almost all cultures though, eventual marriage is a central social goal that marks adulthood even in cases where the young people themselves do not play a very active role in forging heterosexual links. Most cultures have some kinds of institutions that focus on heterosexual desire among the young and are linked to plans for eventual marriage. The Tamang women of Nepal whom Kathryn March (2002) spoke with, often recalled with great fondness those youthful days in which they and their young female friends went to gatherings where they sang songs to groups of young males who responded with songs of their own. Part of the point of the lyrical exchanges was determining just who might be available marriage partners.

In the US, gender difference and heterosexuality are deeply embedded (and intertwined) in the institution of adolescence and in the formal institution of the high school that houses the age group. Heterosexual couples have a special status in high school – popularity is closely linked to heterosexual alliances, and "famous" couples gain extra visibility and provide theater for their cohort (Eckert 1989). Gender difference and separation are emphasized by such things as mock elections that have male and female counterparts for "most popular," "most likely to succeed," and similar categories. The message in these polls is that being successful or popular is different for males and females – that the terms of these statuses are themselves gendered. Meanwhile, the institutions of prom and homecoming king and queen emphasize the importance of heterosexual alliances, elevating such alliances to institutional status. And the classic pairing of the cheerleader and the football player emphasizes the role of the female supporting the male, as the latter upholds the honor of the institution.

Developing desire

Throughout gender development until the emergence of the hetero-sexual market, the emphasis has been on difference – on opposition. The heterosexual market brings an important change in the nature of dichotomous thinking, as suddenly, opposites are supposed to attract. Opposition gains the twist of complementarity, and where before male and female might have been in conflict, now they are collaborators. And with this comes the introduction to gender of the conscious element of desire.

Everywhere we look, we see images of the perfect couple. (For a still compelling discussion of the construction of male and female in advertising along these lines, see Goffman, 1976.) They are heterosexual. He is taller, bigger, darker than her. They appear in poses in which he looks straight ahead, confident and direct; she looks down or off into the distance, often dreamily. Standing or sitting, she is lower than him, maybe leaning on him, maybe tucked under his arm, maybe looking up to him. And from the time they are very young, most kids have learned to desire that perfectly matched partner of the other sex. Girls develop a desire to look up at a boyfriend. A girl begins to see herself leaning against his shoulder, him having to lean down to kiss her, or to whisper in her ear. She learns to be scared so she can have him protect her; she learns to cry so he can dry her tears. Girls put on large men's shirts to emphasize their smallness. This concentration of desire, or *cathexis* (Connell 1987), is an extraordinarily powerful force in the maintenance of the gender order. It leads one not simply to desire those in the other sex class, but to form oneself in a particular mold as an object of desire by those others. Girls come to want to feel small and delicate; boys want to feel big and strong. Or at least these are the dominant socially endorsed images of self, images that sometimes rest uncomfortably with such developments as the explosion of girls and women in competitive sports requiring strength and often height or weight. Even the athletic young woman, however, is instructed to work on making her body desirable to men, as is attested by advertising and features in such publications as *Sports Illustrated for Women*. Diets, hairstyling, shaving legs or heads, appetite suppressants, steroids, tattoos, body piercing, makeup: all these and more are in the service of the desired self.[10] Consumption of all kinds is driven by

---

10 Historian Joan Brumberg (1997) has chronicled the historical development of the contemporary extreme focus in the US on the need for young women to work hard at maintaining and improving their bodies (rather than their souls, which got at least as much or more attention in nineteenth-century America). Indeed, even men are

desire, and this desire is overwhelmingly gendered. Fashion, cosmetics, vehicles, homes, furnishings, gardens, food, leisure activities – are all extensions of the self, driven by desire.

We think of emotion and desire as natural, but in fact both are highly structured and learned. It is generally said that the taboo against men crying or showing fear requires men to learn to control their emotions. This is certainly true, and many boys and men can attest to how difficult such control can sometimes be. Following the tragic events of September 11, 2001, many Americans watched obviously brave and tough men from the New York City police and fire departments weeping unashamedly for their friends and colleagues and for the many others who died in the World Trade Center. Since then, news media have speculated that we are moving into a new era in which men no longer need to control their tears. Well, perhaps. More likely is that there will be more acceptance of men's tears in some contexts but there will still be gendered constraints on crying and other expressions of emotional vulnerability.

The focus on male control of emotion misses the fact that there is also a good deal of socialization involved in women's learning to display their emotions to others, learning when to cry or show fear to an audience. It is appropriate for women to shed public tears, for instance, upon the death of an acquaintance, and it is appropriate for women to show fear in the face of physical threat. In fact, it is appropriate for women to show these emotions in imagined situations, as they read novels or watch movies. There are situations in which girls and women push themselves to shed a tear for something that has not touched them as much as it "should" – and perhaps sometimes to convince themselves that it has touched them after all. Acting scared in action or horror movies can be an important female skill. Learning to be immune to fear in these situations, and learning to not be immune, are alternative possibilities – gendered alternatives. And the choice between these alternatives is further supported by the structuring of desire. People do not simply learn to have the appropriate emotional responses; they learn to want those responses, and to be the *kind of people* who have those responses. Girls and boys envision themselves in situations, and mold themselves to those situations. A

beginning to devote more effort to their bodies; there is an increase in plastic surgery among men as well as considerable attention to diet and exercise as urged by the recent spate of "men's" magazines. This is not to say that bodywork is no longer gendered: women and men continue to be steered in different directions in their "body projects," and most women still invest far more time and money in those projects than their male peers.

common scene in movie theatres is the teenage heterosexual couple on a date.[11] A sad or a scary scene sends the girl into her boyfriend's protective arms, hiding her head in his jacket. Perhaps he pats her head protectively or chuckles knowingly at her weakness. The movie provides the pretext for the girl and the boy to play out their gender roles, and to activate the complex links among romance, heterosexuality, gender, and the theme of fear and protection. We will return to these themes below.

Gender development does not end with childhood or adolescence. Gender continues to be transformed as we move into the market place – as we learn to act like secretaries, lawyers, managers, janitors. And it continues to be transformed as our family status changes – as we learn to be wives and husbands, mothers and fathers, aunts and uncles, sisters and brothers, grandmothers and grandfathers. As we age, we continue to learn new ways of being men and women: what's expected from the teenaged girl is rather different from expectations for a woman in her mid-forties and those expectations differ from those for a woman approaching eighty. Those not caught up in heterosexual alliances are not thereby rendered exempt from gender expectations. Personals looking for lesbian partners, for example, often specify that respondents should be "feminine" in appearance: no "butch" need apply (Livia 2002). And men who look or act "feminine" face discrimination in some gay male communities.

As we've seen above, learning to be male or female involves learning to look and act in particular ways, learning to participate in particular ways in relationships and communities, and learning to see the world from a particular perspective. We are inclined to see many of our habits, preferences, and beliefs as simply the result of our individual history – not as a result of our place in the social order. However, habits, preferences, and beliefs develop in response to experience, and to the extent that the social order structures our experience, there are likely to be patterns to who develops what. This does not mean that women or men are homogeneous groups: some men may cry readily, some women may never shed tears. Not everyone adopts the dominant script. How we develop, however, is never a matter of the straightforward unfolding of individual dispositions but always reflects exposure to norms, expectations, and opportunities that depend on gender and other social categories.

---

11 We thank Alejandra Kim for this example, offered in a class assignment at Stanford University.

Of course, gender is by no means the only aspect of social identity that one learns in this developmental story. Gender interacts with other hierarchies based in such socially constructed categories as class, age, ethnicity, and race: we find, for example, sexualized racism and racialized sexism. We could rewrite this entire section, focusing on how kids learn their socioeconomic status, their race, their ethnicity – even their body type and their reading abilities. And we could rewrite this entire section for each possible combination of gender, class, race, and all the other socially significant categories we might list – for of course, it is the combination that people experience, not the abstraction of any element.

The rewrites would, of course, bring out interesting and important differences between how gender and other categories are structured. Importantly, there is not really an analogue of the heterosexual market and the broader heterosexual imperative, or of the strong gender polarization and notions of gender complementarity it supports. Gender norms try to inculcate the desire for a partner of the other sex, whereas while there are cases in which race and class do structure aspects of family life, race and class norms do not operate in this way. Indeed, there are strong pressures towards finding a partner of the other sex who is of the *same* race or class; this is one way that gender and race or class interact. And gender and age are categories that systematically structure family life, whereas racial or class diversity within families is relatively rare. We could go on detailing such differences between gender and other principles of social division and inequality, but the important point remains that social hierarchies interact and inflect one another, making talk about any of them in isolation potentially very misleading.

This developmental narrative has raised several fundamental principles. First of all, it is clear that gender is learned. And because gender involves a restriction of choice – severe constraints on behavior for all, as well as asymmetries – it must be not just learned but taught, and enforced. This leads to the second principle, that gender is collaborative. It is common to think of gender in terms of individual attributes – an individual is male or female, more or less masculine or feminine, is fulfilling male or female roles. This focus on the individual obscures the fact that we cannot accomplish gender on our own. Gender is not an individual matter at all, but a collaborative affair that connects the individual to the social order. As we have noted, children learn gender initially by having other people do gender for them, and eventually take over the responsibility for their own performances and for supporting the performances of others. This support involves some direct coercion, but mostly gender is so built into our ways of doing things that simple actions and interactions usually call forth gendered responses in others with eventually little or no conscious attention to this gendering.

This leads to the third principle, that gender is not something we have, but something we do. Children often do gender quite consciously – it is clear to all that the swaggering boy and the mincing girl are engaged in gendered performances. As they get older, they get better at masking the raw performances they are engaging in, but more importantly, their gendered performances also become second nature. The fact remains that gender requires work, and when aspects of gender are not consistently performed at all levels of society they can wither away. It is this aspect of gender that led to Judith Butler's (1990) theory of *gender performativity*, which we will discuss further in chapters four and nine. Finally, gender is asymmetrical. However a person may feel about the current gender order, there is no question that male and female are not simply two equal sides of a coin. Inequality is built into gender at a very basic level. Indeed, Kate Bornstein (1998) has said that gender is just a system to justify inequality. In arguing for the universality of beliefs in male superiority, Sherry Ortner and Harriet Whitehead (1981, p. 16) put a similar point this way: "[a] gender system is first and foremost a prestige structure." In more recent writings, Ortner (1990, 1996) offers a more complex view of gender, observing that there are generally different axes of social value or prestige operative in a given society, with men ahead on some and women on others, but that some axes are more deeply embedded in social life and thought than others. A related important point is that power and influence do not always line up directly with prestige. A cartoon from the middle of the twentieth century brought out this point: a man is shown saying to his young son "I decide all the important issues like whether God is dead or whether the UN should admit Communist China and I let your mother deal with things like which school you should attend or which house we should buy." Learning gender asymmetries is not straightforward.

Keeping gender: the gender order

Gender does not simply unfold from individual biology, or from an individual predisposition to be a particular kind of person – it is not even an individual property. Gender is a social arrangement, and every individual's gender is built into the social order. For this reason, we turn to the nature of the gender order, and of individuals' connection to it, in preparation for investigating the role of language in maintenance and change of the gender order.

One thing that is overwhelming in our narrative of development is the ubiquity of gender. Children get gender from everywhere. Gender consists in a pattern of relations that develops over time to define male and female, masculinity and femininity, simultaneously structuring and regulating people's relation to society. It is deeply embedded in every aspect of society – in our institutions, in public spaces, in art, clothing, movement. Gender is embedded in experience in all settings from government offices to street games. It is embedded in the family, the neighborhood, church, school, the media, walking down the street, eating in a restaurant, going to the restroom. And these settings and situations are all linked to one other in a structured fashion. Gender is so intricately organized at every level of experience that there is something approaching a seamless connection between a girl's desire for a frilly party dress and the male control of the means of production. What we experience as our individual, perhaps whimsical, desires emerge within a far-reaching gender order – an order that both supports, and is supported by, these desires. It is this seamless connection that makes language so important to gender and vice versa. Our smallest interactions can be imbued with gender, and our continual performance in those interactions strengthens their role in supporting gender. Every time a little girl desires a frilly pink party dress, insists on having one, or wears one, she is performing a gendered act that renews the gendered meanings associated with pink, frills, dresses, and party clothes. The little girl who insists on wearing grubby overalls has a different effect. Interestingly, however, people often dismiss what they see as "exceptions" so that the actions of the nonconforming girl may have less ongoing effect.[12] The purpose of this section is to give some account of the connection between the pink party dress and the male control of institutions – an account of the structuring of gender ubiquity and of male domination.

We begin by reiterating that dichotomous gender is at the center of our social order because we keep it there. Our survival does not depend on males wearing blue and females wearing pink; humans are a reflective species, and we can talk to each other. The continual

---

12 Virginia Valian (1998) cites a number of psychological studies showing that we tend to give greater "weight" to what conforms to our expectations (not only in gender but also in other domains). Barrie Thorne (1993) reported that in her elementary school study she found herself initially focusing on both acts and individuals that seemed gender-typical.

differentiation of male and female serves not to guarantee biological reproduction, but to guarantee social reproduction – to reaffirm the social arrangements that depend on the categories *male* and *female*. These dichotomous categories are an ongoing human accomplishment, and for this reason, our study of language and gender will treat language not simply as reflecting pre-existing categories, but as part of what constructs and maintains these categories.

Convention and ideology

The gender order is a system of allocation, based on sex-class assignment, of rights and obligations, freedoms and constraints, limits and possibilities, power and subordination. It is supported by – and supports – structures of *convention*, *ideology*, *emotion*, and *desire*. These are so interwoven that it is often difficult to separate gender from other aspects of life. The power of convention, or custom, lies in the fact that we simply learn ways of being and ways of doing things without considering any reasons behind them, and without recognizing the larger structures that they fall into. And while convention changes continually, members of society often view individual conventions as timeless and necessary, and as key to order. An important property of convention lies in its apparent timelessness. Indeed, part of the process of conventionalization is an erasure of the actual circumstances under which the particular practice in question came into being. For example, we automatically say, "Mr. and Mrs. Jones" – not "Mrs. and Mr. Jones"; and "husband and wife" – not "wife and husband."[13] While this is a matter of convention, the convention was explicitly established that men should be mentioned before women on the grounds of male superiority. As early as the sixteenth century, grammarians argued that male should be mentioned before female: "let us kepe a natural order, and set the man before the woman for maners Sake" (Wilson 1560, p. 189; cited in Bodine 1975, p. 134), for 'The Masculine gender is more worthy than the Feminine" (Poole 1646, p. 21; cited in Bodine 1975, p. 134). Here is a case in which linguistic convention has been overtly determined by gender ideology and, in turn, supports that ideology at least implicitly.

---

13 There is a convention in English that orders word pairs according to phonological shape, and the first (but not the second) of these pairs conforms to that order. However, it has been shown (Wright and Hay 2002) that once phonological constraints have been taken into consideration, there remains a tendency to order male names before female names in pairs.

Ideology is the system of beliefs by which people explain, account for, and justify their behavior, and interpret and assess that of others. *Gender ideology* is the set of beliefs that govern people's participation in the gender order, and by which they explain and justify that participation. Gender ideologies differ with respect to such things as the nature of male and female, and the justice, the naturalness, the origins, and the necessity of various aspects of the gender order. Ideologies differ on whether difference is fundamental, whether it should be maintained, and whether it can – or should – be maintained without inequality. Some accept difference as given, and as justifying, or as the necessary result of, inequality. Some see difference as manufactured in order to support hierarchies. For some, the maintenance of the gender order is a moral imperative – whether because it is of divine origin or simply because it is embedded in convention. For others, it is a matter of convenience – a sense that "if it ain't broke don't fix it." Of course, the sense that it is or ain't broke depends on one's perspective.

"Essences" and the nature of the dichotomy

We begin our discussion of the gender order with a brief description of what we take to be some of the main features of the dominant gender ideology in our own society – the view of gender currently privileged in society at large, the terms in which the male–female dichotomy is publicly understood and frequently justified. Members of any western industrial society are likely to be able to produce the following set of oppositions: men are strong, women are weak; men are brave, women are timid; men are aggressive, women are passive; men are sex-driven, women are relationship-driven; men are impassive, women are emotional; men are rational, women are irrational; men are direct, women are indirect; men are competitive, women are cooperative; men are practical, women are nurturing; men are rough, women are gentle. (Note that some characterize men positively while others seem to tilt in women's favor.) The list goes on and on, and together these oppositions yield the quintessential man and woman – Superman and Scarlett O'Hara. While many (perhaps even most) individuals or groups reject some or all of these both as actual descriptions and as ideals to which to aspire, virtually all our readers will recognize that they are part of a pervasive image of male and female. The dominant ideology does not simply prescribe that male and female *should* be different – it insists that they simply *are* different. Furthermore, it ascribes these differences to an unchanging essential quality of males and females. This view is referred to as *essentialism*.

These oppositions are extremely powerful, both because of their place in gender ideology, and because of the ways in which their representations permeate society. First of all, the oppositions appear to come as a package, explanations for each lying somewhere in the others. When we examine the separate oppositions closely, they are not intrinsically linked, but the web of associations that constitutes gender has tied them together in the popular mind. The links among size, physical strength, and bravery may seem clear (to the extent that we limit our definition of bravery to bravery in the face of physical threat). But the link between strength and aggressiveness is not clear, nor is the link between either of these and emotionality, rationality, directness, and competitiveness – or, for that matter, among any of these. For example, the link between impassivity and rationality assumes an inability for an emotional person also to be rational, implying that emotionality involves lack of reason and control. What kind of view is this of emotionality? The reader would do well to study the possible relations among any of these oppositions, seeking their connections in the dominant ideology.

The ubiquity of the view of male and female as opposites is witnessed in the common English expression *the opposite sex*. Rarely do you hear an alternative expression, such as *the other sex,* much less *another sex.* Gender oppositions focus not simply on difference but on the potential for conflict, incomprehension, and mystification: the *battle of the sexes*, the *gender gap*. But as male and female become collaborating factions in the heterosocial enterprise, opposition is supplemented by a notion of complementarity. Embedded in expressions like *my better half*, the ideology of complementarity emphasizes interdependent characters and roles, suggesting a kind of ecological necessity. The notion of attraction (*opposites attract*)[14] and that one is necessary to the other suggests that it is this sharp gender differentiation that keeps society on an even

14 Psychologist Daryl Bem (1996) has hypothesized a fundamentally oppositional principle for sexual attraction – the exotic becomes erotic – to explain both cross-sex and same-sex desire. Girls and boys constructing themselves as heterosexual see others of the same sex as too like themselves to be desirable, whereas those who develop same-sex desires see themselves as sex-atypical and find sex-typical members of their own sex more desirable than members of the other sex because of the greater "exoticness" of those conforming same-sex individuals. Although Bem's theory has the virtue of trying to explain heterosexual as well as homosexual desire, it has been criticized on a number of grounds. The theory is hard to reconcile with the fact that sex-atypicality is only loosely correlated with same-sex desire. It also would seem to predict a much higher incidence of cross-racial and cross-class attraction than is found. (Stein 1999 offers a good discussion of this and other accounts of the origins of desire, especially same-sex desire.) But Bem's theory does fit with a long tradition of conceiving heterosexual attraction in terms of complementary opposites, each incomplete but together completing each other.

keel. The view that gender differences serve central social purposes – what social theorists call *functionalism* – is an important component of dominant gender ideology, and one that plays a powerful role in conservative gender discourse.

Gendered oppositions are ubiquitous, permeating our experience by appearing in all kinds of sites and in all kinds of forms. Earlier in this chapter, we commented on the social forces that exaggerate the statistical size difference between women and men, and on the role of images of the man towering over the woman in the media in instilling desire for a particular kind of mate. Although indeed the average height of women is somewhat smaller than the average height of men, the fact that in only a small minority of heterosexual couples is the man no taller than the woman attests to the ubiquity and the power of gender images.

Another way in which these oppositions are reinforced is in their potential for embedding. The opposition *larger–smaller*, for example, does not only differentiate male from female, but it operates within the male and female categories as well. Men who are small with respect to other men are viewed as less masculine; women who are large with respect to other women are viewed as less feminine. Susan Gal and Judith Irvine (1995) refer to this mirroring of the overall opposition within each component of the opposition as *recursiveness*. Recursiveness provides a particularly powerful force in gender enforcement, as people tend to compare themselves not with people of the other gender, but with people of their own. Men deemed feminine (or effeminate) are seen as inferior men. While women deemed masculine may sometimes be seen as inferior women, they are also seen as striving (if misguidedly) for what is in fact a valued persona. This is one reason that masculine behavior in women is often less stigmatized than feminine behavior in men. The association of gender and heterosexuality also leads to the association of gender-atypical behavior with homosexuality, especially for boys and men. Policing gender is tied very closely in modern western societies with policing sexual preference. The four-year-old boy may be steered away from flowers and towards stripes for his curtains because his dad doesn't want him to grow up gay.

Division of labor

The traditional gender oppositions listed in the above section are closely tied to a division of labor that permeates society at every level. This is not simply a division of physical and mental labor, but of emotional labor as well. Of course, no division of labor is simply a division

of activity, for activity determines such things as patterns of association, movement, and use of space. In turn, the division of labor tends
to call for, and even to instill, the gendered qualities that are the terms
of the oppositions. Those charged with caring for others' basic needs,
for example, can function well in their jobs only if they are other-
oriented, attending closely to signals from those others as to the state
of their minds and bodies. At the same time, a career of this kind of
work might well lead someone to become attuned to others and their
needs.

To the extent that some activities and spheres have greater power
and prestige than others, a division of labor can also be a division
of value. Across societies, the gendered division of labor involves differential power and status. Men's activities – those that are guarded
the most closely as men's domain – involve greater societal power,
through the disposition of goods and services and the control of ritual.
Males in most cultures have more access to positions of public power
and influence than females. While women sometimes wield considerable influence in domestic settings or in other nonpublic domains,
this influence is limited by the domain itself. Since the private sphere
is dependent on its place in the public sphere, the domestic woman's
ultimate position in the social order is dependent on the place of her
male relatives' positions in the marketplace. And her ability to exert
power and influence in the private sphere depends on how these men
allocate the goods that they gain in the marketplace.

The gendered division of labor in western society relies heavily on
the allocation of women's function to the domestic, or private, realm
and men's to the public realm. People often connect this division of labor to reproductive roles. Women, as bearers of children, are assigned
not only to delivering them, but to raising them, and to the nurturing not only of children but of entire families, and to the care of the
home in which families are based. If one were to imagine a division
of labor based on sex alone, women would bear and nurse children
and men would not. And women would likely be somewhat restricted
in their other activities while engaged in child-bearing and nursing.
But beyond that, a sex-based division of labor does not follow from reproductive function, which is either quite temporary or nonoccurring
within the life span of most women. Nonetheless, the sexual division
of labor in all kinds of areas is standardly justified in terms of the
different biological requirements for motherhood and fatherhood. Of
course, it is not just reproductive potential that is called on to justify the sexual division of labor: women were long kept out of certain
jobs because they were deemed too weak to perform them (sometimes

even when strength had long since become essentially irrelevant for job performance). Certainly, there might be different sex balances in the allocation of tasks that would emerge because of different sex balances in the attributes needed for success – certain tasks requiring unusual strength might, for example, fall to people of great strength, many of whom would be men but some of whom would be women. Yet societies around the world have elaborate allocations of activities and responsibilities purely on the basis of assigned gender, with no attention at all to actual reproductive activity or size. And the sexual division of labor in many areas bears little or no relation even to size or reproductive activity. Thus it should not be surprising that while the existence of a division of labor is universal,[15] the details of this division are not. What is considered men's work or role in one society may be considered women's in another.

In the division into private and public, women are generally in charge of caring for people's everyday needs – clothing, feeding, cleaning, caring for children – maintaining people and their living space on an everyday basis. Until recently, this division has kept many women out of the public workplace, and while nowadays most women in the west do work outside of the home, many of their occupations are extensions of their domestic role. Traditional women's jobs are in the service sector, and often involve nurturing, service, and support roles: teachers of small children, nurses, secretaries, flight attendants. There is also an emotional division of labor. Wherever they are, women are expected more than men to remember birthdays, soothe hurt children, offer intimate understanding. Men, on the other hand, are more expected to judge, to offer advice and expertise, or to "figure out" mechanical problems.

It is possible to continue this list ad infinitum: salesmen sell hardware, men's clothing and shoes, and computers. While men may sell women's shoes, they rarely sell dresses or lingerie; but women can sell any items of men's clothing. Saleswomen sell cooking utensils, lingerie, and flowers. Men construct things out of wood and metal while women construct things out of fiber. Men play contact sports; women play individual sports that do not involve physical contact. At home, women cook meals, clean homes, care for children; men do yard work, look after cars, and do house repairs. The reader could expand this list forever, both with current states of affairs and with stereotypes.

15 Nonetheless there seems to be much more flexibility in who does what in some societies than in others. See, e.g., Ortner (1990) for discussion of the Andaman Islanders, who seemed to have had little difficulty in men's taking on what were classed as women's jobs and vice versa.

More men cook and look after children these days than was the case when we were children, and plenty of women now change the oil in their cars and fix leaky toilets. But gendered divisions of labor are still deeply ensconced in patterns of opportunity. At some universities, administrators have opposed granting parental rather than maternity leave because they feared fathers would take the leave just to increase the time available for them to spend on their own research. Women still find considerable resistance when they try for jobs as mechanics or plumbers. And as we will see throughout this book, practices of talking about sexual difference, and especially of using beliefs about that difference to explain and interpret people and their activities, are key to making gender so powerful across society.

On close inspection, connections between the division of labor and the supposed male and female qualities supporting that division prove problematic. The attribution of "nurturing" seems to follow women's activities. A woman preparing food is seen as "taking care of" her family, while a man barbecuing is not seen in quite the same light. Just as women's activities are often viewed as nurturing even if their intent or effect might not be nurturant, men's activities can acquire prestige simply by their association with men, regardless of their inherent value. While most domestic cooks are women, men dominate in professional cooking – particularly in haute cuisine. This process of gendered assessment becomes evident when what were once men's jobs lose their associated power and prestige as women begin to occupy them. This was amply witnessed in the World War II era, during which military conscription cleared men out of many workplaces, and women were called upon to take their places. Women became bank tellers – a job reserved for men in the prewar era, on the assumption that only men were sufficiently responsible to handle large sums of money. After the war, women remained in teller jobs, which became "women's" jobs and came to be viewed as relatively menial, clerical work.

The domestic role also brings an interesting restriction of time. Feeding, cleaning and dressing others, and the other tasks involved in the day-to-day maintenance of a household, are continuously renewed, permeating time. Thus a woman's time is traditionally controlled by the continual needs of other people. The tasks that men traditionally do in the middle-class domestic sphere, on the other hand, are cyclical. Taking out the trash, tending the yard, doing repairs – these are things that can be scheduled in advance, to fit around the rest of one's activities. This difference in demands on their time then makes it more difficult for women to make the same commitment as men to activity in the marketplace.

The woman's domestic role commonly plays out in a restriction to private space, and a male domination of public space. It also extends to a common restriction of women's and girls' activities to the home, both in terms of space and activity, while men and boys have not only more tasks outside the home, but greater mobility and greater access to public places. The exclusion of women from public situations is one of the practices that have historically merged gender with class. In Victorian times in England, "nice" women didn't read the newspaper, go to speeches, or frequent places where public matters were discussed. *Nice*, in this case, is synonymous with *elite*. While the wealthier classes have always been able to leave part of their population idle, families in poorer situations tend not to discriminate in this way. Poor Victorian women went out in the street, worked in the market, knew what was going on in the public world. By virtue of their economic constraints, they were not "nice" by the standards set by the ruling classes. This is an example of what we mentioned earlier in this chapter – that gender does not exist independently of other salient social categorizations, in this case class. Of course, today women of all classes do participate in various ways in the public sphere. It is still the case, however, that they are frequently reminded that they do not belong there and that they should have men with them for protection.

The public/private dichotomy has consequences even in pursuits considered appropriate for women. While Victorian women were encouraged to pursue the musical and visual arts, they were encouraged to do so privately only. Linda Nochlin (1992), in a study of why there are so few "great" women artists, has shown that in an era in which the "great" artistic subjects were religious, and in which artistry was focused on the representation of the human body, only men were allowed into studios to train from human models (whether male or female). Women, therefore, were unable to develop the skills necessary to produce the kind of images that made Rembrandt famous. Later on, impressionist art focused on subjects in situations that women did not have access to as well – brothels, backstage at the ballet, bars. The two most famous female artists of this period, Mary Cassat and Rosa Bonheur, focused on domestic scenes – on women and children in their homes – for indeed these were the situations that they had access to. It can be no accident that just these themes were considered unworthy of "great art."

Ideology, belief, and dominance

People's beliefs and view of the world are based in their position in society: a woman born into the black working class has a very different life experience from, for example, a man born into the white upper middle class. With this different experience comes different knowledge, different opportunities, different views of the world. Pierre Bourdieu (1977b) uses the term *habitus* to refer to the set of beliefs and dispositions that a person develops as a result of his or her accumulated experience in a particular place in society. Depending on where people are in society, they will see and experience different things, know different people, develop different knowledge and skills. And they will engage in different conversations, hear different talk: they will participate in different *discourses.* Discourse is the socially meaningful activity – most typically talk, but non-verbal actions as well – in which ideas are constructed over time. When we speak of *a discourse,* we refer to a particular history of talk about a particular idea or set of ideas. Thus when we talk about a discourse of gender, or varied discourses of gender, we refer to the working of a particular set of ideas about gender in some segment or segments of society.

Just as each social position has its own perspective, each has its own interests. People's understanding of what is right and proper, what is good for them, for those around them, and for the world, are likely to differ. There is no "knowledge," "fact," or "common sense" that is not mediated by position and the interest that goes with it. The different experiences of a black working-class woman and a white upper-middle-class man are likely to lead them to have different understandings of the world, to participate in different discourses. We spoke earlier of ideology as a system of beliefs used to explain, justify, interpret, and evaluate people and their activities. For some (e.g. Foucault 1972), ideology and discourse are indistinguishable: both are projections of the interests of people in a particular social location. Others reserve the term *ideology* for a discourse that engages a central power struggle.[16] Terry Eagleton (1991, p. 8) argues that "A breakfast-time quarrel between husband and wife over who exactly allowed the toast to turn that grotesque shade of black need not be ideological; it becomes so when, for example, it begins to engage questions of sexual power, beliefs about gender roles and so on." But we slip quite readily from a discourse to an ideology in Eagleton's terms. Discourses of gender unfold not only in explicit talk about gender, but in talk about things (like burnt toast) that may be grafted on to gender. If enough people joke together continually about men's ineptness in the kitchen, women's role as cooks takes center stage, along with men's incompetence in the kitchen. The fact that these themes emerge in joking lends them an

16 For a thorough discussion of the use of the term *ideology,* see Eagleton 1991.

established status – a status as old information rather than as a new topic, naturalizing the relation between gender and kitchen activity. The consequences carry well beyond the home kitchen. In an office in which secretaries are expected to make coffee, a female secretary who makes bad coffee is likely to be considered more inept at her job than a male secretary. She will be seen as unable to carry out a "natural" function, while he will be excused on the grounds that he has been asked to carry out an "unnatural" task. A man who cooks at home often gets more "credit" (and more help from others) than a woman: she is just doing her job whereas he is seen as doing something above and beyond the expected.

Ways of thinking become common sense when we cease to notice their provenance – and this happens when they occur continually in enough places in everyday discourse. A discourse may have a privileged status in society by virtue of the power of the people who engage in it. It can be heard in more places, get more "air time" associated with voices of authority – and as it permeates institutions it comes to pass for "knowledge," "fact," or "common sense." Thus, by virtue of the position of its original proponents, a discourse can erase its history as it spreads, masking the fact that it is ideology.

An ideology can be imposed through the top-down exertion of power, as in the case of the Taliban government of Afghanistan, which made extreme subordination of women the law. But this kind of coercion is necessary only when significant parts of the general public recognize the conflict with their own ideologies. A dominant ideology typically owes its success not to brute power and conscious imposition, but to the ability to convince people that it is not in fact a matter of ideology at all, but simply natural, "the way things are." We refer to this process as *naturalization*. This use of the term *naturalization* does not necessarily refer to biological naturalness, but to people's sense of what needs no explanation.

Anton Gramsci's theory (1971) of *hegemony* focuses on this location of power in everyday routine structures, emphasizing that the most effective form of domination is the assimilation of the wider population into one's worldview. Hegemony is not just a matter of widespread ideas but includes the organization of social life more generally. Adopting and adapting Gramsci's notion, Raymond Williams (1977, p. 109) explains

> It is in [the] recognition of the *wholeness* of the process that the concept of "hegemony" goes beyond "ideology." What is decisive is not only the conscious system of ideas and beliefs, but the whole lived social process as practically organized by specific and dominant meanings and values.

Williams emphasizes that hegemony is never total, and Sherry Ortner (1990) draws on this nontotality to talk about "[t]he loose ends, the contradictory bits" of gender hegemonies that can be "examined for their short- and long-term interactions with and for one another."

In this introduction and elsewhere we will often gloss over the "loose ends, the contradictory bits" in order to sketch prevailing hegemonies in our own and similar societies. But the messiness is still there, and we will return to it at various points since it is crucial in challenging and transforming gender.

Institutions

Categories such as age, class, gender, and ethnicity exist on paper, because they are built into our formal institutions. We are asked to give information about them on paper, some of them determine our civil status, our rights and obligations. As society changes, some of the categories increase or decrease in importance, and the way they are inscribed in our institutions may change. Until recently the racial category *negro*, as defined by the supposed presence or absence of African blood, was an official category that defined one's legal status in parts of the US. While the specific status (as well as the name) of this racial category has changed over the years, it continues to have legal status in the monitoring of the population (e.g. the census), and it continues to have informal status throughout American society. This racial category is a social construction even less tied to biological criteria than sex/gender. One cannot identify "African blood," and the real criterion for racial assignment has always been physical appearance or knowledge of forbears' physical appearance. And of course, the identification of "African" physical characteristics is itself completely subjective. Yet race remains deeply embedded in our discourses of identity and personhood, and what matters is the experience of being "Black" or being "White" or being "Asian".

The *gender regimes* (Connell 1987) of global institutions such as corporations and government constitute a kind of "official" locus for the gender order. Until the last century, women's participation in both government and corporations was negligible. Women in the US did not vote until 1919, and as women gradually moved into the corporate workplace, they performed very low-level jobs. Even at the turn of the twenty-first century, women constituted only a tiny fraction of the Chief Executive Officers (CEOs) of America's Fortune 500 companies (in the year 2001 only 4 of the 500 CEOs were women), and women are vastly underrepresented in governmental positions of power. Large powerful US institutions, in other words, are dominated and directed by men. And though the details and extent differ, gender asymmetries in institutional authority are found around the globe, even where there are overt ideologies of gender equality.

Within major institutions, gender emerges not simply in institutional structure, but in the balances of activities that take place on a day-to-day basis. Who gives, and who takes, directives; who answers the phone, and what kinds of conversations do they have? Who leads meetings, who is expected to voice their opinion and who is expected not to? Whose opinions get picked up and cited approvingly by others? The oppositions of gender meanings are strongly embedded in workplace ideologies. The "rational" and "impassive" male has been seen as more suited to managerial work. At the same time, as women move into positions of corporate leadership, their value is viewed as based in the new qualities they bring to the table. Much is said about the value of bringing some of their "nurturing" and "cooperative" ways into corporate culture, and new buzzwords such as "emotional intelligence" are moving into the management consulting business. In other words, the value of women to business is viewed as directly related to their ability to change and improve the business culture. While it may be true that women are bringing new skills to the workplace that should be highly valued, the focus on "women's special abilities" genders certain skills and reinforces the gendering of women's place in organizations. Linking women's value to the workplace to the new skills they bring effectively erases women's ability to do what men have been doing all along. Educational institutions also reproduce the gender order in myriad ways. As prime sites for socialization, schools are key institutions for the construction of gender. Elementary schools not long ago were known for keeping girls and boys separate – lining them up separately to move about the school, pitting them against each other in competitions, separating them for physical education. More recently, schools have begun to enforce gender equity, often forbidding single-sex games on the playground, trying to downplay gender difference in the classroom, and sanctioning gender-discriminatory behavior on the part of students. This conscious attempt to foster gender equity is as gendered, of course, as earlier practices that fostered gender difference. Children are often made aware that the teacher has an explicit goal of fostering the mixing of boys and girls, which can have the effect of confirming their preference for same-sex groups.[17]

---

17 This is not intended as a critique of these attempts on the part of schools and teachers, but simply as an observation of the complex outcomes of social engineering.

Since schooling is accomplished primarily through talk, gendered verbal practices abound in schools. The gender dichotomy is emphasized each time teachers address a group of children as "girls and boys," and each time gender is used to teach the concept of opposites: black/white, good/bad, boy/girl. When gender is used as a metaphor for learning subject matter, the gendered metaphor is reinforced at the same time that it facilitates the new material. Some teachers teach children to distinguish between consonants and vowels by attributing masculine gender to consonants, feminine to vowels, reciting "Miss A, Mister B, Mister C, Mister D, Miss E" and so on.

Throughout the educational system, men are more likely than women to be in top administrative positions. But also, the gender balance of people in teaching positions changes dramatically as one moves from preschool through elementary and then secondary school, and on to university, with women primarily responsible for the education of small children, and men gradually taking over as the pupils get older. The view of women as nurturant is deeply embedded in the common belief that women are more suited than men to teaching small children. And current discussions of the need to increase the number of men in the elementary school classroom are commonly couched in the claim that children (especially boys) need a less nurturing and infantilizing environment. In a fashion analogous to women's entrance into corporate management, men can enter the female educational workplace not because they're capable of being nurturant, but because they can bring important *male* changes to educational practice. A similar gender shift occurs in educational institutions (and workplaces) as the subject matter gets more technical. Men in our society are more likely to teach science, math, and technology while women are more likely to teach humanities and – to a lesser extent – social science. Even within the sciences, women are more likely to be biologists than physicists. The metaphors "hard" and "soft" science bind this intellectual division of labor (along with consonants and vowels) to idealized gendered body and personality types – in this case, men's rationality comes to the fore. In this way, essentialist views of women as more nurturant, and men as rational are embedded in our institutions of knowledge and the ways we talk about them.

Attempts to foster gender equity in schools sometimes focus on supposedly gendered "ways of knowing" and learning, trying to get more appreciation for what is gendered female. See, e.g., Belenky *et al.* (1986) and Corson (2000). As with the valuing of "women's skills" in the world of work, such efforts have laudable motives but their effects may be problematic.

In addition to formal institutions, there are informal institutions that are established practices: baby showers, sweet sixteen parties, stag parties. The reader might consider how many such institutions are not gendered. Many institutions are informal but at the same time inscribed in formal arrangements. The practice of baseball, for example, is an American institution. And while it is pursued informally, it is also formally structured through leagues ranging from local parks to the professional leagues. The complex institutional status of the family is underlined by arguments about what actually constitutes a family. Some insist on marriage as the legal and moral foundation of a family. Marriage, on this view, officially sanctions heterosexual union between one man and one woman; it makes them responsible for rearing any offspring they might have, and the family is then the unit consisting of husband, wife, and children. Others argue that any adult or committed pair of adults living together along with children they might rear constitutes a family, while still others find the family among the very close friends with whom they share their lives though not necessarily their households. The issue of what constitutes the institution of the family is at the core of discussions of gender, since the family is the primary legitimized site for biological and social reproduction. Attempts in various parts of the US to extend marriage to same-sex couples (and resistance to those attempts) show how important formal institutions like marriage and the family are to the gender order.

Masculinities and femininities

Earlier in this chapter, we emphasized that generalizations about gender can all too easily erase the multiplicity of experiences of gender. Inasmuch as gender unfolds in social practice in a wide variety of communities, it is anything but monolithic. Male and female, masculinity and femininity, are not equally dimorphic everywhere. Nor are they experienced or defined in the same ways everywhere.

In his book *Masculinities*, Robert Connell (1995) counters the notion of "true masculinity," emphasizing that masculinity (like femininity) is not a coherent object, but part of a larger structure. Taking this structure as starting point, Connell locates, and elaborates on, two kinds of masculinities: the *physical masculinity* of the working class, and the upper-middle-class *technical masculinity*. Connell points out that working-class masculinity is associated with physical power, while upper-middle-class masculinity is associated with technical (scientific and political) power. This is not to say that physical power is

unimportant for upper-middle-class men – the masculine ideal throughout society involves physical power. However, physical power is fundamental to working-class masculinity, whereas the masculine power
that is embedded in the global market is only indirectly physical. While
global men are better off with a certain amount of personal physical
power, the more important fact is that they command the physical
power of other men – of men in the local market. Armies and work-
forces are the physical power of global men. Furthermore, the refinement needs of the global context place limits on men's physical power.
A global man has to look trim in a suit, his hands have to be clean
and uncalloused, and his movements have to be graceful. While these
two kinds of masculinity are age-old, the advent of high tech wealth
seems to be decreasing the connection between masculinity and physical power, as greater financial power is moving into the hands of those
who have notably defined themselves as living by their brains. There is
a similar class reversal for women. Women in the global market are expected to be small and delicate, with a carefully maintained body down
to the smallest detail. Just as physical strength is expected to some extent of all men, this delicacy is expected to some extent of all women.
However, since physical work and the ability to defend oneself are important to many women in the local market, both in the workplace
and out, there is less value placed on some aspects of physical delicacy. (An interesting combination of feminine delicacy and robustness
is found in current fingernail technology. Long nails have for centuries
symbolized abstention from physical labor. Those who engage in physical labor can now boast these symbols as well, with the help of acrylic
prostheses that will withstand a good deal of abuse.)

Ignoring the multiplicity of masculinities and femininities leads to
the erasure of experience for many people. For example, in a study
of girls attending the private Emma Willard School in the eastern US,
psychologist Carol Gilligan and her colleagues (e.g. Gilligan, Lyons, and
Hanmer 1990) found that as they approached adolescence, girls become
less sure of themselves, less assertive, more deferential, and generally
lost the sense of agency that they had had as children. This girls' *crisis
of confidence* has become a famous gender construct – a kind of developmental imperative for girls. Statistics show that indeed this kind of
crisis is common among white middle-class girls, like the ones who attend the school Gilligan *et al.* focused on. But this is a relatively small
segment of the population. What few statistics there are on African
American girls during this same life stage suggest that they do not
undergo such a crisis; on the contrary, they appear to gain a sense
of personal confidence (AAUW 1992, p. 13). We would argue that this

difference is a result of differences in European American and African American gender discourses, and particularly discourses of heterosexuality. European American girls – at least middle-class ones – are generally raised in a discourse of female subordination and material dependence on men, particularly in child-rearing. African American girls, on the other hand, are generally raised in a discourse of female effectiveness, with an expectation that they will take full responsibility for themselves and for their children (Dill 1979, Ladner 1971, Staples 1973). The age at which the Emma Willard girls begin to lose their sense of agency corresponds to the emergence of the heterosexual market (as discussed above). As kids begin to see themselves as agents in a heterosexual market, discourses of gender and heterosexuality begin to enter into their sense of their place in the world. Because of the discourses of heterosexuality that they grow up with, this can have a disempowering effect for middle-class European American girls, and an empowering effect for African American girls. In fact, educators are all too aware that African American girls become quite assertive during this period. But because assertiveness is not part of the dominant female gender script, they tend to associate this assertiveness not with gender, but with race. The assumption of an across-the-board gender experience makes it all too easy to generalize from one group's experience. And it is not coincidental that the girls whose experience is serving as the model are white and middle class; not African American, and not working class.

Just as some people's acts will have a more global effect by virtue of their placement in society, some people's gender discourses will as well. For this reason, girls suffering the preadolescent crisis of confidence that Gilligan describes actually define normative girlhood at that age – "nice" girls tend to be deferential, quiet, and tentative. As a result, the increasingly assertive behavior displayed by many African American girls at that age is viewed as inappropriate, and unfeminine. In schools, African American girls are frequently marginalized because white teachers interpret their behavior as antisocial. It is ironic that in a climate that is seeking to help girls counteract this now famous "crisis of confidence," it is not generally recognized that girls suffering this crisis should be emulating their African American sisters. Instead, there are people now creating programs for African American girls, to help them through one crisis that they may not in fact be experiencing.

In this way, African American girls and women are rendered invisible in totalizing discussions of gender. The construct of the preadolescent girls' crisis of confidence both erases boys' similar crises, and erases the African American experience that does not typically involve this particular crisis. And the picture of hegemonic femininity for this age group, one of a lack of confidence and a generally uncertain and self-subordinating demeanor, renders the behavior of many African American girls non-normative, so that it appears aggressive and threatening to some.

Although this book will focus on gender, we will try not to lose sight of its critical connections to other social categories. No one is simply female or male. No one is simply black or white. No one is simply rich or poor. No one is simply young or old. If we were to talk about gender as if it were independent of other categorization schemes and the systems of privilege and oppression they support, we would effectively erase the vast range of gendered experience, tending to focus on what we are most familiar with. As it is, this is always a danger, but a danger faced is always better than a danger ignored.

Gender practice

The force of gender categories in society makes it impossible for us to move through our lives in a nongendered way, and impossible not to behave in a way that brings out gendered behavior in others. At the same time, the maintenance of gender categories depends on reinforcement in day-to-day behavior. *Male* and *female* could not persist as structurally important social categories if we did not perform enough gendered and gendering behavior – if distinct groups of people did not continue to act like "women" and like "men." In other words, the gender order and the social categories – *male* and *female* – on which it rests exist in virtue of *social practice*.

We use the term *social practice* to refer to human activity when emphasizing the conventional aspect of activity and its relation to social structure. While structure constrains practice, it does not determine it. On the one hand, people may behave in ways that are compatible with existing structure – for example, a married woman may choose to stay at home to raise her children while her husband goes to work to support them financially. As people behave in this way, they *reproduce* the existing social order. On the other hand, a woman may go to work while her partner stays at home to mind the children, another woman may decide to have children on her own, a heterosexual couple may decide not to have children, or a homosexual couple may opt to have children. If only a few isolated people behave in one of these ways, what they are doing will have a negligible effect on social structure. As these life choices have become more common, they have come to constitute practices, recognized (though not necessarily endorsed) ways of doing things. The development of such nontraditional practices in recent years has contributed to changing the meaning of *male* and *female* and thus to changing the gender order, the social structures that in their turn shape gender practices.

Because structure and practice are in this dynamic and dialectical relation, there is always the possibility for change. One could say that the social order is in continual change – that even what appears to be stability is the result not of nothing happening, but of events of social reproduction. Every time a little girl minces in her mother's shoes, and every time a little boy swaggers, they are reproducing gender difference, the relation between gender and style of motion, and all of the implications of that relation. But the little boy pushing his doll and the girl with her truck are also part of the picture even though their actions may not be so widely adopted into social practice. Life and daily living are about change – about things happening, about creativity and intelligence at work in the space left open by the incomplete hold of ideologies and institutions. This book is about the changing gender order and especially the place of language in gender practices.

CHAPTER 2

Linking the linguistic to the social

Language is a communicative practice mediated by a linguistic system or systems. It is the systems, what we call *languages*,[1] that preoccupy most of the field of linguistics. The fields of linguistic anthropology and sociolinguistics, however, focus on communicative practice more broadly defined, and it is in this larger sense that we will be examining language and gender.

For many linguists, a speaker's *linguistic competence* is the knowledge underlying the ability to produce and recognize, for example, that *the cat chased the rat* is a sentence of English (with a certain meaning) whereas **cat the the rat chased*[2] is not. Sociolinguists and linguistic anthropologists, on the other hand, emphasize that knowledge of a grammar is not sufficient to participate in verbal practice – one needs to know the conventions by which people engage with each other in linguistic activity. People develop their linguistic competence in use, and along with the linguistic system or systems, they learn how to put the system(s) to work in social situations. What they develop, then, is not simply linguistic competence but also a wider *communicative competence* (e.g. Gumperz and Hymes 1972). In this chapter, we will introduce the reader to some concepts that will serve as the analytic basis for our discussions of language use: first the social locus of linguistic practice, then the linguistic system itself.

First, though, we would like to turn the reader's attention to the fact that neither language nor the social world comes ready-made, and neither language nor the social world is static. While it is often useful for analytic purposes to treat language and society as separate and stable systems, it is important to recognize that they are both

---

1 Philosopher David Lewis (1974) proposed using *language* as a count form (with an article or plural as in *the boat, boats*) to designate linguistic systems and using it as a mass form (with no article or plural as in *water*) to designate linguistically mediated communicative practices.
2 Linguists use an asterisk to mark a string of words that is not a possible sentence or to mark some other nonoccurring expression.

maintained – and maintained mutually – in day-to-day activity. And they change – mutually – as well.

Changing practices, changing ideologies

All we have to do is look at debates over women's rights at the turn of the twentieth century to see that the dominant ideology and linguistic conventions are not static. They are constructed, maintained, elaborated, and changed in action, and quite crucially in talk. Change does not happen in individual actions, but in the accumulation of action throughout the social fabric.

The fact that many business people have no equivalent of *sir* to use in addressing a female manager is not simply a static fact of language, but a result of the history of women in business, our talk to and about females, and our perceived need for such terms. We have not had many females in high institutional positions, so there has been no massive discomfort with the lack of a term. It may be that over time people will lose patience with using *sir* toward men. Or *sir* may be extended to women in positions of authority, as appears to be occurring at least occasionally toward police officers (McElhinny 1995). Or perhaps the widespread use of *ma'am* in the south and in the military as a term of respect directed to women will spread to other areas of society. It is foolhardy to predict what will happen, because there are many possibilities, each of which depends on a particular and complex set of events. Language has its effect on society through repeated use, through sequences of use, through the laying down of a history of use. And embedded in this history are not simply the things that have been said and done, but the identities and status of the people who have said and done them. An individual act, therefore, enters into a broader discourse – and its ultimate effect will be the result of its life in that discourse: how it gets picked up, and by whom, and how it mixes with what other people are doing and thinking.

In the late sixties, a concerted action on the part of US feminists introduced the social title *Ms.* into the lexicon of address forms. The purpose was to provide an equivalent of *Mr.* – a term that designates gender, but not marital status. This was felt to be particularly important because, unlike men, women were judged, qualified, and disqualified, included and excluded, on the basis of their marital status. Women were routinely expected to leave school and the workplace if they married; older women who were not married were considered personal failures; unmarried women with children were considered immoral. The emphatic use of *Miss* or *Mrs.* was often used to put women in their place (e.g. "it IS MISS, isn't it?"). Introducing this new term, therefore, was an act of rehabilitation for women, a move to increase gender equity. At the time, most English users thought this was a silly or futile act, and the use of the term was considered by many to signal only that the user was a feminist who rejected being defined by her marital status. *Ms.* did catch on, however, with the help of the advertising industry, not in the interests of female equality but as an alternative to offending women whose marital status was unknown to the advertiser. Day-to-day use, however, still reflects ideological difference and the flux that accompanies change. Most official forms nowadays give women the option to categorize themselves as *Mrs., Miss,* or *Ms.* What new information does *Ms.* offer? Is it equivalent to opting not to check a box for race or religion? Nowadays, most young women in the US use *Ms.*, but apparently some think they will switch to *Mrs.* if they get married. Older women still tend to interpret *Ms.* as connoting feminism and use it or the *Miss/Mrs.* alternatives depending on their political leanings; middle-aged divorced women, however, and professional women may use *Ms.* in their working lives even if they don't see themselves as making a political statement. This is certainly not the future that the feminists of the late sixties had in mind for their new term of address. While the outcome of this concerted action was change, the change took on a life of its own as soon as it moved beyond the communities of practice that initiated it.[3]

Another example of the fate of changes initiated within some communities is the current state of women's sports magazines. The considerable demand for magazines promoting and supporting women as serious athletes has yielded some publications that feature female athletes. However, they do not portray women as athletes in the same way that men's sports magazines portray men. They have quickly evolved into a kind of hybrid genre. In many ways they resemble traditional women's magazines, stressing beauty as well as athletic ability, and confounding fitness with thinness and the development and maintenance of a prototypically sexy female body. In other words, some women's desire for the promotion of their athletic lives emerged into a larger

---

3 Mary Vetterling-Braggin (1981) includes several discussions debating *Ms.* and its attempt to sidestep the marital status issue. Susan Ehrlich and Ruth King (1992) offer an account of how and why this and other feminist-inspired linguistic innovations did not accomplish what those proposing them had hoped for. Thomas Murray (1997) looked at attitudes toward *Ms.* in the American Midwest; Janet Holmes (2001) considers its use in New Zealand, and Anne Pauwels (1987, 1998) reports on Australian patterns. In Australasia, though the data are mixed, the use of *Ms.* may be decreasing, especially among the youngest women.

societal discourse of women's bodies and physical activities that yielded this hybrid portrayal.

In each of these cases, a concerted action on the part of an interest group introduced a change into communicative practice – in the one case into the language, in the other case into the print media. But each interest group could only perform their acts – get their acts onto the market. Once these acts were picked up on the market, they were subject to market forces. It is a useful metaphor to think of our contributions – in the case of language, our utterances – as being offered onto a market, in this case a market of meaning (and influence). This metaphor only works, however, if we do not lose sight of the fact that the value of an idea on the market is inseparable from the position of the person or group offering it.

The social locus of change

As we put linguistic and social change at the center of our analysis, we want to emphasize that change comes in subtle ways. At any historical moment, both the gender order and linguistic conventions exercise a profound constraint on our thoughts and actions, predisposing us to follow patterns set down over generations and throughout our own development. Change comes with the interruption of such patterns, and while sometimes that interruption may be sudden, it comes more commonly through infinitesimally small events that may or may not be intentional. We have seen in the preceding chapter that we perform gender in our minutest acts. It is by virtue of the accumulation of these performances that the gender order is maintained, and it is by virtue of small changes in these performances that the gender order can be restructured. Linguistic change in general, and change in the specific ways language enters into gender construction, come about in the same way, mostly through rather small shifts in how linguistic resources are deployed.

It will be the trip from a single variation of a repetition to societal change that will occupy much of our attention in the chapters that follow. As linguists, we are focused on the small day-to-day performances that have become part of our more-or-less automatic verbal routines. Connecting those routines to larger societal discourses requires that we think about how small acts ramp up into big ones. Above all, it requires thinking about how a single individual's verbal move could get picked up by others and eventually make it into public discourse. To do this, we cannot remain at a socially abstract level, but must focus on concrete situations and events. But just as we want to know how small verbal acts accumulate to have a large effect, we want to know how individual situations accumulate to produce and reproduce the abstract social structures we discussed in chapter one. How do we connect what happens at the Jones's breakfast table on Saturday to the gender order?

The speech community

Linguistic anthropologists and sociolinguists often locate the organization of language or linguistic practice in a social unit that they refer to as a *speech community*. Dell Hymes (1972, p. 54) has defined the speech community as "a community sharing rules for the conduct and interpretation of speech, and rules for the interpretation of at least one linguistic variety." This perspective emphasizes that knowledge of a language or languages, what Hymes calls a linguistic variety, is embedded in knowledge of how to engage in communicative practice – the two are learned together and while they are separable at the hand of the analyst, they are inseparable in practice. The difficulty of learning language in a classroom is testimony to this fact.

A particular language may participate in very different communicative systems from community to community. Thus speakers of the same language may have difficulty communicating if they do not share norms for the use of that language in interaction. John Gumperz (e.g. 1982) has focused on miscommunication among speakers of the same language – miscommunication between, for instance, English and Pakistani speakers of English in London – as a result of different ways of using language in service interactions. Gumperz found that differences ranging from intonation patterns to ways of requesting service could lead one participant to mistakenly find the other rude or unhelpful.

The notion of speech community can be slippery in actual practice, since in concrete situations it is unclear where one might draw the boundaries around a particular community (see, e.g., Rickford 1986). While Hymes (1972) limited the notion to quite specific face-to-face communities, the term has also been applied to more abstract collectivities. One might talk about the American compared to the British speech communities, since not only do the varieties of English differ, but so do some of the conventions of interaction. By the same logic, within the US, one might talk about New York and Detroit as separate speech communities as well, and within New York and Detroit it is common to speak of separate African American and European American speech communities. And if one were focusing on the linguistic practices of Italian Americans to the extent that they differ from those of other ethnic groups, one might define the speech community even more closely. In other words, the notion of speech community focuses on shared practices within communities that are defined both geographically and socially, but depending on the degree of specificity one seeks, the boundaries may be fluid. (As we will discuss briefly in chapter eight, a similar fluidity applies to the boundaries of languages.) For the purposes of our discussion here, we will think of speech communities in this flexible way, and keeping in mind the range of conventions that are shared within larger speech communities, we turn to more concrete social collectivities that are based in day-to-day practice.

Communities of practice

The people at the Jones's breakfast table, in Mrs. Comstock's Latin class, or in Ivan's garage band get together fairly regularly to engage in an enterprise. Whether the enterprise is being a family, learning (or not learning) Latin, or playing music, by virtue of engaging over time in that endeavor, the participants in each of these groups develop ways of doing things together. They develop activities and ways of engaging in those activities, they develop common knowledge and beliefs, ways of relating to each other, ways of talking – in short, practices. Such a group is what Jean Lave and Etienne Wenger (1991) have termed a *community of practice*. It is at the level of the community of practice that ways of speaking are the most closely coordinated. Of course, communities of practice do not invent their ways of speaking out of whole cloth, but orient to the practices of larger and more diffuse speech communities, refining the practices of those speech communities to their own purposes. Some communities of practice may develop more distinctive ways of speaking than others. Thus it is within communities of practice that linguistic influence may spread within and among speech communities.

It is through participation in a range of communities of practice that people participate in society, and forge a sense of their place and their possibilities in society. And an important link between each individual's experience and the larger social order is the structure of participation in communities of practice. Communities of practice emerge as groups of people respond to a mutual situation. A group of people start to play basketball in the park, a disgruntled group of employees come to engage in daily gripe sessions, a group of parents start a childcare cooperative, a group of nerds band together in their high school for protection – all of these groups of people come to engage in practice together because they have a shared interest in a particular place at a particular time. Thus communities of practice do not emerge randomly, but are structured by the kinds of situations that present themselves in different places in society. And categories like gender, class, and race emerge in clusters of experience – the clustering of kinds of communities of practice one participates in, and the forms of participation one takes on in those communities. Women are more likely than men to participate in secretarial pools, car pools, childcare groups, exercise classes. Working-class women are more likely than middle-class women to participate in bowling teams, neighborhood friendship groups, and extended families. Some communities of practice may be single-sex, some may accord different roles to each sex, or marginal roles to one sex or the other.

The community of practice is the level of social organization at which people experience the social order on a personal and day-to-day basis, and at which they jointly make sense of that social order. A group of high-school friends forms around some common interest – maybe they live in the same neighborhood, maybe they like the same kind of music, maybe they were thrown together by circumstances and decided to make the most of it. They probably aren't all equally good friends with each other – maybe there are little subgroups. Perhaps one of them has emerged as a leader, perhaps one of them is the joker, perhaps one of them is always looking to the others for advice or attention or comfort. Forms of participation develop as they engage together, as do mutual concerns and ways of engaging those concerns. They may develop little jokes, greetings, nicknames, funny ways of pronouncing things. Perhaps they have a specific table they sit at for lunch in the cafeteria, and from which they look out and consider themselves in relation to other groups at other tables. They go out to the mall, baseball games, rock concerts – and consider themselves in relation to the people they encounter in those settings, and to the activities they engage in. They develop their sense of a place in the social order – a place with respect to the school social order, and beyond the school with respect to class, gender, race, ethnicity – in the course of these encounters and their discussions of the encounters. And each member of the friendship group combines that with similar activities in her other communities of practice – her family, her softball team, her Latin class. Some of these may be more central to her construction of a self, some more peripheral, and she forges an identity in the process of balancing the self she is constructing across these communities of practice. This identity is inseparable from her participation in communities of practice, and each of these communities of practice can be defined only in terms of the interplay of the identities being constructed within it.

Face

This identity work is done primarily in face-to-face interaction. Face-to-face interaction is at the heart of social life, and everyday conversational exchanges are crucial in constructing gender identities as well as gender ideologies and relations. It is in conversation that people put their ideas on the table, and it is in conversation that these ideas get taken up or not – that they move on to be part of a wider discourse or just die on the spot. And it is in conversation that we work out who we are in relation to others, and who others will allow us to be. The individual connects to the social world at that nexus where we balance who we want to be with who others will allow us to be. Erving Goffman has dealt with this nexus in his important insight that social interaction always involves what he called *facework* (see esp. Goffman 1967).

Face is an intersubjective[4] enterprise. By Goffman's definition (1967, p. 5), face is "the positive social value a person effectively claims for himself by the line others assume he has taken during a particular contact." The ability to participate in the social enterprise requires some mutuality among the participants about what kind of people they are. Each individual, therefore, presents a self that he or she considers desirable, and that he or she figures others will be willing to acknowledge and support in the interaction. For face is something we can "lose" or "save" in our dealings with one another: it is tied to our presentations of ourselves and to our acknowledgments of others as certain kinds of people. As we engage with one another, we are always positioning ourselves and positioning each other in a social landscape, a landscape in which gender is often (though not always) a prominent feature. Different situations and participation in different communities of practice will call for different presentations of self. Facework covers all the many things people do to project certain personae and to ratify or reject other people's projections of their claimed personae. "Face," says Goffman, "is an image of self delineated in terms of approved social attributes – albeit an image that others may share" (1967, p. 5). Face, then, can be seen as the social glue that keeps people attuned to each other in interaction – it is what keeps them coordinating their actions closely.

Gender ideology and assumed gender identity enter into shaping both the face individuals want to project and the face others are willing

4 Itamar Francez (personal communication) has noted that Goffman presents facework in very individualistic terms that are culturally specific, and in conflict with some views of the self in relation to the collectivity. Indeed, Goffman presents the notion of face in an extreme way, but it allows us to examine what is at stake in resolving one's own actions with those of others, and does not deny the extent to which a given culture or community may endeavor to integrate that process.

to ascribe to them. One powerful force behind the maintenance of the gender order is the desire to avoid face-threatening situations or acts. A boy who likes purses may learn not to carry one into public situations rather than to risk public ridicule, an unpopular boy may learn not to try to interact with popular girls to avoid public rejection, a thirsty young woman may choose not to enter a bar in order to avoid unwanted sexual advances. A heterosexual man may speak in a monotone for fear someone will think he is gay, and a young woman may hedge her statements for fear someone will challenge her authority.

Linguistic resources

A language is a highly structured system of signs, or combinations of form and meaning. Gender is embedded in these signs and in their use in communicative practice in a variety of ways. Gender can be the actual content of a linguistic sign. For example English third-person singular pronouns distinguish between inanimate (*it*) and male and female animate (*she/her/her; he/him/his*). The suffix *-ess* transforms a male or generic noun into a female one (*heir; heiress*). Lexical items, as well, refer directly to male and female (as in the case of *male* and *female; girl* and *boy*). In other cases, the relation between a linguistic sign and social gender can be secondary. For example the adjectives *pretty* and *handsome* both mean something like 'good-looking,' but have background meanings corresponding to cultural ideals of good looks for females and males respectively, and are generally used gender-specifically – or to invoke male- or female-associated properties. Consider, for example, what *pretty* and *handsome* suggest when used with objects such as houses or flowers. And although it is positive to describe someone as *a handsome woman*, the description *a pretty boy* is generally applied with a derisive sneer. There are many means by which we color topics with gender – by which we invoke gender and discourses of gender even when we are ostensibly talking about something else.

We also use language to color *ourselves* as we talk. Linguistic resources can be used to present oneself as a particular kind of person; to project an attitude or stance; to affect the flow of talk and ideas. And these can involve gender in a myriad of ways. Tone and pitch of voice, patterns of intonation (or "tunes"), choice of vocabulary, even pronunciations and grammatical patterns can signal gendered aspects of the speaker's self-presentation. They can also signal the speaker's accommodation to, or enforcement of, the gender of other interactants in a situation. At the same time, the association of these linguistic devices with feminine or masculine ideals makes them potential material to reproduce – or to challenge – a conservative discourse of femininity or masculinity. For example, using a soft, high-pitched voice invokes the connection between female gender and smallness and fragility. Avoiding profanities, or using euphemistic substitutions such as *fudge* or *shoot*, invokes the connection between female gender and propriety.

For purposes of analysis, linguists divide the linguistic system into parts, or levels, each of which presents its own analytical and theoretical issues. In the following pages, we will set out these parts and briefly point out some ways in which they can be used to make social meaning. However, since there is no one-to-one relation between any part of the grammar and social function, we have not organized the following chapters around the types of linguistic resources so much as around the uses these resources are put to. Thus there is no single discussion of phonology or pronouns or expletives, for any of these may appear in more than one section. The book is not organized around aspects of gender either, or around theories of gender or of language and gender – it is not organized around dominance or difference, or power. Rather, it is organized around the practices in which language constructs and reflects the social order, just as it would be organized in a discussion of the construction of any other social categorization – race, class, ethnicity, or age. It is true that some parts of the linguistic system play a particularly significant role in certain kinds of practice, and thus there will be some clustering of discussion of parts of the grammar. To orient the nonlinguist reader, this chapter offers a quick preliminary tour of the linguistic system. Many examples offered in this chapter are discussed in greater detail later in the book.

Phonology

The phonological level of language structures the units of sound (or of gesture in the case of signed language) that constitute linguistic form. The phonological system of every language is based in a structured set of distinctions of sound (phonemes). The difference between the words *pick, tick, sick, thick,* and *lick* lies in the differences in the first segment of each, the consonant phonemes /p/, /t/, /s/, /θ/, and /l/. Phonemes do not themselves carry meaning, but provide the means to make distinctions that are in turn associated with distinctions in meaning. These distinctions are thus based not on the actual quality of the phoneme but on the oppositions among phonemes. The important thing about English /p/ is that it is distinct from /b/, /t/, and the rest. The actual phonetic quality of /p/, /b/, and /t/ can vary considerably so long as the distinctions are preserved among these sounds (and between these and others).

It is in the possibility for variation in the phonetic realization of a single phoneme that gender can be embedded. For example, the pronunciation of the first segment of *sick*, which involves turbulence as air is passed between the tongue and the front end of the roof of the mouth, can be accomplished by using the tip of the tongue or with the blade of the tongue. And the tongue can push against the back or front of the alveolar ridge (the ridge directly behind the teeth), or the teeth. The resulting sounds will all be quite different, but in English, they will all be recognized as /s/. Confusion begins to appear only if the tongue moves between the teeth, since at that point it crosses the line into the phonetic territory of /θ/ (*thick*, as in the classic case of a child's lisp). All the space within the territory of /s/, then, is free to be used for stylistic purposes, and all kinds of social meaning, including gender, are embedded in this kind of stylistic variation. While /s/ in North American English is generally pronounced with the tip of the tongue at the alveolar ridge behind the upper teeth, a pronunciation against the edge of the front teeth (what might be thought of as a slight lisp) is stereotypically associated with prissiness, with women,[5] and with gayness among men. Thus, the phonological system, while carrying no content in itself, is a potent resource for encoding social meanings.

Our perception of sound segments is hardly mechanical. We adjust readily to voices of different people and to different accents, something that designers of speech recognition systems have had trouble getting machines to do. And we do not adjust simply to what we hear but to what we expect to hear.

Joan Rubin (1992) reports on an experiment in which a tape-recorded lecture (by a native speaker of English) was played for two groups of undergraduates, and the students were shown a picture of the supposed lecturer. In one case, the picture was of a white woman, and in the other the picture was of an Asian woman. Some of the students who believed that the lecture was being delivered by an Asian woman reported that she had a foreign accent. And further, these students did worse on a comprehension test of the lecture material.

Phoneticians Elizabeth Strand and Keith Johnson (1996) used a similar technique to show that people's beliefs about the gender of a speaker actually affect the way they hear phonetic segments. The sibilant sound of /s/ can vary in frequency – and on average, women's pronunciation

5 In fact, there is evidence that on the whole women tend to pronounce this consonant closer to the teeth than men (Strand 1999).

of this phoneme does tend to have a slightly higher frequency than men's. This higher frequency brings the sound of /s/ as in *sin* microscopically closer to /ʃ/ as in *shin*. Strand and Johnson manipulated the acoustic signal of the word *sod*, so that the initial consonant ranged from [s] to [ʃ]. They then presented these randomly to subjects, in a videotape, sometimes matched with a picture of a female speaker and sometimes with a male speaker, and asked the subjects in each case to say whether they had heard *sod* or *shod*. They found that subjects perceived the boundary between [s] and [ʃ] differently depending on whether the perceived speaker was female or male – the boundary was at a slightly higher frequency when they perceived the speaker to be female, so that what sounded like *shod* in the mouth of a man sounded like *sod* in the mouth of a woman. In other words, speakers learn to perceive very small acoustic differences quite unconsciously, and use this information unconsciously in interpreting people's speech. Among other things, this shows that social effects like gender are completely integral to our linguistic knowledge[6] (see Strand 1999).

In addition to segmental phonology, prosody, which includes the tempo and the variations in pitch and loudness with which utterances are produced, is rich with social potential. Rhythm and tune (or intonation) clearly carry important gender meanings, and are certainly the objects of gender stereotype. The study of these aspects of phonology has intensified in recent years (see Ladd 1996), but has not yet reached a point where we can talk as confidently about intonational patterns as about segmental ones. Voice quality, as well, while not commonly studied as part of the linguistic system, is an obviously socially meaningful aspect of linguistic performance[7] and analysts (e.g. Mendoza-Denton forthcoming) have begun to investigate its gendered deployment.

Morphology

Morphology is the level of grammar at which recurring units of sound are paired with meaning. The meanings of *pick, tick, sick, thick,* and *lick* do not derive from the sounds they contain, but from a conventional association of meaning with a combination of sounds /pɪk/, /tɪk/, /sɪk/, /θɪk/ and /lɪk/. Some such combinations constitute entire words, as in these examples, while some other combinations do not. The forms *-ed, -s, -ish, -en, -ing*, for example, all have their own meanings. They must,

---

6 McGurk and MacDonald (1976) have shown that people regularly use visual information about the place of articulation of consonants in perceiving speech.
7 See Graddol and Swann (1989, ch. 2) for discussion of gender and voice quality issues.

however, occur affixed to stems – *picked, ticks, sickish, thicken, licking* – and they in some sense modify the basic meanings of these stems. The basic, indivisible combinations of form (sound) and meaning in a language are referred to as *morphemes*.

Lexical morphemes are what we usually think of when we think about words: they are content forms like *cat* or *dance*, and they only need to be used if one wants to speak about cats or dancing. *Grammatical* morphemes, in contrast, have very abstract meanings that can be combined in a rule-governed way with many different morphemes, hence they turn up more or less regardless of the topic. For example, the suffix *-ed* can be used with *pick* or *attack* or *thank* or almost any verb stem to signal the past tense.[8] Similarly, the suffix *-ish* can be used with almost all noun and adjective stems to form a mitigated adjective (in addition to conventional words such as *priggish* and *reddish*, one can, if one wants, coin new ones, such as "Now that I've fixed it up, my shack looks downright house-ish."). Not being bound to particular content areas, grammatical morphemes are ubiquitous and more productive, hence fundamental to the language. Speakers of the language are constrained to use many of these morphemes over and over, and some of the distinctions signaled by grammatical morphemes are required. The English morpheme *-ish* could readily be avoided but not the past tense *-ed*: English declarative sentences need tensed verbs, and regular verbs abound. It's not just in the verbal domain that grammatical morphemes may be required. In Standard English, the use of a noun like *goldfinch* or *idea* that can be pluralized or counted (with numbers or with *many* or *a few* or similar expressions) entails specifying whether it is singular or plural.[9] Not all language systems enforce the same distinctions. In Mandarin Chinese, for example, neither tense nor plurality has to be marked.

Gender in grammar

Some grammatical morphemes have gender as their content. And one of the most obvious ways in which language can reinforce gender is by

8 There are some differences in how the suffix is pronounced, depending on the final sound of the verb, and the *e* is dropped in writing if the verb to which the past tense form is attached ends orthographically with an *e*. Some verbs have "irregular" past tense: e.g. the past tense of *think* is *thought* rather than the "regular" *thinked*. Children as well as adults acquiring English often use regular past tense forms even for verbs that are "conventionally" ("correctly") associated with an irregular past tense.
9 This usually involves adding *-es* or *-s*. As with the past tense, the pronunciation of the plural suffix depends on the last sound of the word to which it is attached. And there are some irregular forms: nouns like *deer* or *sheep* that are the same in the singular and the plural and nouns like *woman* or *mouse* with the irregular plurals *women* and *mice*.

requiring the use of gender morphology – coercing the speaker verbally to point to, or *index*, the gender of various people involved in an utterance. In many languages, noun and verb morphology has explicit gender content. Classical Arabic has separate pronominal and verb forms in the second-person singular and plural, and in the third-person singular, dual, and plural, depending on whether a human addressee or subject is male or female:

katabta	'you (masc. sg.) have written'	katabti	'you (fem. sg.) have written'
katabtum	'you (masc. pl.) have written'	katabtunna	'you (fem. pl.) have written'
kataba	'he has written'	katabat	'she has written'
kataba:	'they two (masc.) have written'	katabata:	'they two (fem.) have written'
katabu:	'they (masc. pl.) have written'	katabna	'they (fem. pl.) have written'

In using a third-person singular pronoun to refer to a specific person, English also forces the speaker to index the referent's sex: to say *someone called but he didn't leave his name* is to ascribe male sex to the caller.

Linguists talk about grammatical gender when a language has noun classes that are relevant for certain kinds of *agreement* patterns. In Swahili and other Bantu languages, for example, there are gender classes that determine the form of plural suffixes and the form of adjectives modifying the noun as well as the form of a pronoun for which the noun is an antecedent. The general principles that sort nouns into classes have to do with properties like shape and animacy but not sex. In the Bantu languages, grammatical gender really has nothing at all to do with social gender.

But most of our readers are probably more familiar with one of the Indo-European languages with grammatical gender classes – for example German or Russian or French or Spanish or Italian or Hindi. In these languages, grammatical gender does have (complex) connections to social gender. Many words referring to women in these languages are feminine, many referring to men are masculine, and there are often pairs of words distinguished grammatically by gender and semantically by the sex of their potential referents. (Some of these languages also have a neuter gender.) Now even in these languages, there is nothing like a perfect correspondence between a noun's grammatical gender category and properties of the things or the sex of the people to which it can refer. For example the French words *personne* ('person') and *lune* ('moon') are feminine gender, while in German *Mädchen* ('girl') is neuter, not feminine, and *Mond* ('moon') is masculine, unlike its feminine counterpart in French. Facts such as these have led some linguists to suggest that grammatical gender in these languages is no more connected to social gender than it is in the Bantu languages. Here we will just mention a few ways in which grammatical and social gender are indeed linked in systems like those found in Indo-European, drawing most of our examples from French.

Nouns in French are classified as feminine or masculine. Grammatically, what this means is that articles or adjectives "agree" in gender with a noun that they modify. Pronouns that refer back to a noun (that have the noun as an *antecedent*) must agree with it in gender as well. Pronouns with antecedents are often called *anaphoric*. In the examples below, *maison* 'house' is grammatically feminine, while *camion* 'truck' is masculine.

> Regardez *la* maison. *Elle* est *grande*.   'Look at the house. It is big.'
> Regardez *le* camion. *Il* est *grand*.   'Look at the truck. It is big.'

This is a purely grammatical fact. The same pronouns and adjectives, however, must agree with the social gender of a person being referred to:

> Regardez Marie. *Elle* est *grande*.   'Look at Marie. She is big.'
> Regardez Jacques. *Il* est *grand*.   'Look at Jacques. He is big.'

And when the pronoun picks out Marie or Jacques, with no antecedent in the utterance, it is called *deictic* (i.e. pointing) rather than *anaphoric* and agrees with social gender:

> Elle est grande.
> Il est grand.

Most French nouns referring to women are grammatically feminine in gender, most referring to men are masculine, but, as we have noted, there is not a perfect correspondence. If for some reason a masculine noun – for example French *le professeur* 'the professor' – is used to refer to a woman in everyday colloquial speech, speakers tend to switch to a feminine pronoun in later references to the same individual. In Canada and to some extent in France, the move of women into new roles and occupations has led to the introduction of new feminine forms – for example *la professeur* or *la professeure* or *la professeuse*.[10] Similar changes are being launched also in countries using other Indo-European languages with grammatical gender (e.g. Spain, Germany, Russia, India), with varying degrees of success. An important impetus for this push to offer feminized forms of occupational terms is to create gender symmetry in occupational terms. But it also allows speakers to avoid conflict

---

10 King 1991 discusses this phenomenon in some detail.

between two different principles for selecting pronouns. Grammatical gender concord dictates that a pronoun should agree with an antecedent noun phrase. Conventions of deictic reference dictate that a pronoun should agree with the social gender – ascribed sex – of the individual to which it refers. Life is easier for speakers accustomed to grammatical gender if their lexicon offers them choices so that these two pronoun-selection principles do not conflict.

It is not only human beings for whom there is a tight connection between ascribed sex and gendered pronouns. In French, familiar or domestic animals (cats, dogs, cows, chickens) can (but need not) be distinguished by sex in deictic pronominal reference (that is, one can use the feminine or masculine pronoun depending on the sex of the particular animal rather than on the gender of the word designating that animal). There are other animals (such as mice, rats, and snakes) that are not so distinguished. Mice are always feminine, while rats and snakes are always masculine. (Even in English, which does not have a full-blown grammatical gender system, there is a tendency to ignore the sex of some animals but still refer to them with gendered forms; many speakers, e.g., use *she* indiscriminately for cats and *he* for dogs.)

And, as we have already noted, grammatical gender is not confined to animate beings. The rest of the French lexicon is divided into "masculine" and "feminine" as well (tables, anger, and schools are "feminine"; trees, circles, and hospitals are "masculine") even though the meanings of words in each grammatical gender category cannot be linked to social gender in any general way. (Recall that the word for moon is feminine in French, masculine in German.) Deictic uses of pronouns used to refer to things like tables or trees cannot, of course, rely on "natural" gender. What generally happens is that a gendered pronoun is chosen to agree with the noun most commonly used to designate that particular kind of thing. In English *it is big* can be used to say that something is big, whether or not the something being indicated is a table or a tree (or anything else). In French, however, *elle est grande* attributes bigness to the table, whereas *il est gros* does the same for the tree. There is some evidence that in the Indo-European languages, what are now gender agreement patterns arose as patterns of repeated sounds, rather than having anything to do with noun meanings.[11] Nonetheless, people continue to spin theories about the underlying meanings of feminine and masculine nouns, often revealing more about cultural preoccupations with dichotomous social gender than about how language is actually working.

11 See discussion in Corbett 1991.

We reiterate that there are connections of grammatical to social gender even if they do not seem to lie in any semantic unity of nouns in the different genders. We have already mentioned third-person reference to humans above, but the connections go further. To speak of oneself using the nongendered French first-person pronoun *je* and describe oneself using the copula and an adjective, the convention is to choose the feminine adjectival form if presenting oneself as female, the masculine adjectival form if presenting oneself as male. And even though the grammatical gender assignment of most nouns is not really rooted in social gender, grammatical gender provides a convenient link to social gender for thinking and talking about things. To speak of *la lune* in French and go on to talk about it, it is appropriate to use the pronoun *elle* (cf. Eng. 'she'), the same form that is used to point to someone and say something about them that assumes social female gender assignment. In German, *der Mond* is *er* (cf. Eng. 'he'), the form used to point to someone and assume assignment to the male gender class. Not surprisingly, personification of the moon by French and German poets proceeds quite differently. It is not only poets whose thinking about objects seems to be affected by the gender of the noun most commonly used to designate them. In carefully controlled experiments, psychologist Lera Boroditsky (forthcoming) showed that speakers whose dominant language is German assign "masculine" characteristics to tables, which are designated by the masculine noun *der Tisch*, whereas speakers whose dominant language is French assign "feminine" characteristics to the same object, which is designated by the feminine noun *la table*. In other words, whatever their origins, Indo-European grammatical gender systems are indeed now linked to social gender in a number of complex ways.

Another place where gender enters into morphology is in the existence of processes that transform a noun referring to a male human into its female counterpart. A familiar example is the English *-ess* (originally borrowed from French) as in *actress*, *waitress*, and *stewardess*. In general, the noun to which *-ess* is added implies, but does not specify, male gender. An actor and a waiter are still generally considered to be male (although many women in the acting profession are now calling themselves actors, for example), but a driver or a murderer can readily be male or female. (Note that we have conventions about the use of this suffix – we have murderesses, but not killeresses, driveresses or paintresses.) But while the underived noun can generally refer to either males or females, there is nothing ambiguous about *-ess*. A lioness can only be female.

Similar patterns will be seen over and over again in this book – forms that designate males can often be used generically, but forms that designate females generally cannot. (For example, *you guys* can be used to address a group of males and/or females. But *you gals* cannot.) Note, also, that other meanings associated with gender can bleed into the derived noun, affecting its ultimate meaning. Thus we find old word pairs in the lexicon that have taken on asymmetric gendered meanings related to the asymmetric social positions of males and females in society, such as *master* and *mistress*, *governor* and *governess*. In some cases, the terms were probably never fully parallel: for many centuries one has been able to become a *duchess* but not a *duke* through marriage.

By incorporating gender in linguistic forms, social gender is "called up." On occasion the language makes it difficult for a speaker to ignore gender, or to speak about specific people without reference to gender. Of course, while the grammar may make gender marking obligatory, speakers can construct their discourse in such a way as to choose, avoid, or emphasize their reminders of gender. One can plaster *his* and *hers* on towels or license plates. And one can use the masculine pronoun *he* as a generic or one can look for ways to avoid it.[12]

The use of the feminine suffix in *actress* invokes the fact that acting is gendered – that male and female actors generally portray different kinds of characters, and are expected to have different kinds of skills, and perhaps even that heterosexual relationships among male and female actors are salient to their professional lives. It may also be relevant that a few hundred years ago actors on the English stage were all male; the women who began to move into acting as a profession in the nineteenth century were often seen as having deplorably loose sexual morals.

We also often find feminine suffixes bringing their own additional meanings. For example, the feminizing suffix *-ette*, as in Ray Charles's *Raylettes*, merges gender and the primary diminutive sense of *-ette* (note words such as *pipette* or *cigarette*), suggesting that Ray Charles's background singers are not only female but small and cute. The trivializing effect of *-ette* is brought out quite vividly in a reference to *Barbie – the consumerette*, cited in Janet Holmes (2001). And there is a telling historical example. People working for women's suffrage, mostly but not exclusively women, were first called *suffragists*. The term *suffragette* was introduced by those opposed to women's having the vote. The aim seems to have been to make the movement for female suffrage seem less

---

12 Readers may notice that to avoid generic *he*, we sometimes use *he or she*, sometimes *she* and sometimes *they*. In using *they* in grammatically singular contexts, we follow a long tradition of English usage that includes such illustrious wordsmiths as William Shakespeare and Jane Austen but we do break with the "rules" our schoolteachers taught us, especially with a form like *themself* (which the word-processor "auto-corrected" to *themselves*).

serious and more frivolous (cf. the introduction of the term *women's lib* for *women's liberation* and *libbers* for *liberationists* in the late 1960s and early 1970s), something to be associated with those silly little women.

Lexicon

We use the term *lexicon* to refer to the inventory of lexical morphemes and words in a language. The lexicon is a repository of cultural pre-occupations, and as a result the link between gender and the lexicon is deep and extensive. The lexicon is also the most changeable part of language and an important site for bringing in new ideas. Because lexical items have content in different domains, different language users have access to somewhat different lexicons: linguists have their specialized terminology, and young pop music fans have theirs. The gendered division of labor is likely to produce gendered patterns in the precise lexical inventories speakers can access.

Grammatical morphemes like pronouns are more stable than lexical nouns or verbs, and come and go only very slowly (though they can and do change). The traces in a grammar of gender such as we discussed in the preceding section may reflect more the preoccupations of earlier eras than they do the culture of those currently using a particular language. Marks of gender in the lexicon are often more complex and multilayered than those found in gender morphology.

The lexicon is also a resource that different speakers may use differently as a function of gender. Not only will women be more likely to know words like *gusset* and *selvage* (from the domain of sewing) and men more likely to know words like *torque* and *tachometer* (from mechanics), there are also gender-linked norms for using certain lexical items. For example, men are expected to use profanity more than women, and they are expected not to use profanity around women. And there are in fact gendered differences in how and when people use this "taboo" part of the lexicon – but not precisely the differences dictated by prescriptive norms. In a study of the use of religious profanities in Quebec French, Diane Vincent (1982) found that while older men used more profanity than their female age mates, younger women and men used them at about the same rate.[13] In an examination of attitudes about these profanities, norms follow the age differences. Retired people were more likely than high-school students (84 percent) to believe that swearing is

---

13 This study was based on two tape-recorded corpora, totaling 165 hours of speech of a heterogeneous sample of speakers.

more "ugly" in a woman than in a man – and among the younger people, boys were more likely to hold this opinion (34 percent) than girls (12 percent). Furthermore, older women were more likely than anyone else to believe that women swear as much as men. An interesting twist is reports of parents' swearing. The retired people all claimed that their mothers had hardly used any profanity at all, while their fathers used very little. The high-school students, on the other hand, showed a sex difference in their observations – girls' reports of their mothers' swearing outdistanced that of boys. In other words, boys' views of their mothers conformed more than girls' to gender norms. Gary Selnow (1985) found a similar difference in reports of the use of sexual, religious, and excretory profanity among college students in the US. Both men and women reported that their fathers swore more than their mothers, but the women's estimates of their mothers' swearing were significantly higher than the men's.

Some gender indices are not grammatically obligatory, but are available when speakers wish to specify gender, such as *lady doctor, male nurse*. In this case, the speaker is not just indexing gender, but also invoking the presupposition that doctors are normally male and that nurses are normally female. While obligatory indices such as pronouns invoke male and female categories, optional ones such as these can invoke the content of these categories. And in invoking this content, the use of such devices serves to reinforce, or reproduce, the connection between gender and profession.

These linguistic resources seem to come ready-made. Like gender, however, they all have a history. Resources we deploy come to be embedded in language through use – sometimes over generations, sometimes almost overnight. *Monicagate* was coined, and everyone knew what it meant instantaneously because the social meaning of tawdry practices by politicians had already been brought into prominence with the use of *Watergate*. And it became widespread overnight because of its use in mass media. A word that did not appear until the twenty-first century is *dot-commer*, referring to a person who was accumulating unusual wealth working for a net-based startup. The term is rife with judgment – a dot-commer is looking for ways to spend money, wants to live lavishly but has neither the time nor the judgment to do so with taste. The term arose in Silicon Valley in a climate of resentment towards the new young wealthy who were associated with a prohibitive rise in the cost of living in the area. The term *dot-commer*, in turn, was made possible by the introduction in the 1990s of the term *dot-com*. And so it goes. The ability to introduce a new word or phrase is also the ability to introduce one's meanings. Terms like *dot-commer*, and related terms like *monster house* (the oversized homes that dot-commers built during their brief rise to wealth), came into being because of a charged social change, because the people who were coining these particular terms had visibility, and because enough people were concerned with these changes to adopt and use the terms.

What meanings end up encoded in language depends on who's doing what, and how they're talking about it. Some words never make it into widespread use or into the dictionary, because the concerns that they express are not widely shared. The term *ashy*, referring to surface dryness on skin that gives an ashy look, is used predominantly by African Americans. Though the physiological phenomenon is widespread, surface dryness shows up more prominently on darker skin, and the concerns of people with dark skin are commonly ignored by the wider community of American English speakers. As we noted with *Ms.*, some new forms are launched for very specific purposes. But just how their initial meanings fare depends on many factors. In the case of a number of feminist-inspired words and phrases, there is not just disinterest in the concerns expressed but considerable hostility towards them, hostility that leads to coinage of yet other terms (e.g. *feminazi*).

In English, we have masculine generics (*every man for himself*), pairs of words that reflect the social asymmetry of male and female (e.g. *master/mistress*, *fox/vixen*, *bachelor/spinster*), and even gender attributed to things (boats are *she*). But these meanings do not just appear in language; they come to be embedded in language through generations of use. And eventually some of them disappear from the language, or are modified, once again through changes in use. Political attitudes have been consciously pushing masculine generics out of use for several decades; and the term *mistress* is quietly falling out of use because the category of woman who is "kept" by a man she is not married to is losing relevance in the twenty-first century as the gender order itself changes.

Syntax

Syntax combines words into sentences – linguistic structures that express thoughts or propositions. Sentences describe events or situations and syntax indicates something about relations among the participants in those events or situations. For example, *Joan kissed John* and *John kissed Joan* are two sentences with exactly the same words. The difference in what they mean is indicated syntactically. In the first, it is Joan who initiates the kiss whereas John plays that role in the second. Joan is the subject of the first sentence and John is the object; those syntactic relations are reversed in the second sentence. With *kiss* and many other verbs, the subject in an active sentence is the star actor in the event whereas the object simply receives the action initiated by the subject. Linguists often say that the subject in such sentences plays the role of *agent*, and the object plays the role of *theme*. There is nothing inherently gendered about these syntactically-indicated meanings, but we find many English-language texts (e.g. primary school readers in the 1970s and syntax texts in the 1990s[14]) in which most of the agents or doers are men or boys, whereas women and girls, if present at all, are often themes to which things happen. Here the gendered meaning does not really come from single sentences but from more general discourse patterns, which we will discuss in the next section.

Syntax provides multiple ways to describe the same events: for example the passive sentences *John was kissed by Joan* or *Joan was kissed by John* express basically the same content as the active sentences above. The subject in these passive sentences is playing the theme role and the agent has been demoted to a prepositional phrase. In fact the agent may be missing altogether from passives in English and many other languages. So-called *agentless passives* can be very useful if the agent is unknown or is not relevant for the purposes at hand. For example, if we're only interested in the age of the house *the house was built in 1908* will do just fine. Linguist Julia Penelope (1990) suggests, however, that agentless passives are often used to deflect attention from male oppression of women. The report *she was raped* does not mention the rapist and, especially if coupled with a description of the revealing shirt and tight jeans she was wearing, may help shift the blame from the male rapist to the raped woman. When the content of a sentence has connections to gender or sexuality, syntactic choices may not only signal something about gender ideology but may also play some role in maintaining certain features of the gender order. This doesn't mean that the syntax itself maps directly into social meaning. The point is that messages about gender draw not just on the words used but on the syntactic structures in which they occur. Syntactic alternatives provide ways of conveying essentially the same message – describing the same situation or event – from different perspectives or with different emphases. Like other linguistic choices, they can help color messages with gender ideology.

Syntactic and related morphological choices can also help color speakers, entering into gender performance in a variety of ways. One

14 See Macaulay and Brice 1997 for syntax texts and references therein to textbook studies in earlier decades.

way in which this happens is in the opposition between "standard" and "nonstandard" grammar. Many speakers of English can choose between simple and multiple negatives, as in the Standard English *I didn't do anything* and the Nonstandard *I didn't do nothing*. The latter sentence has two negatives, but the second negative does not cancel the first. Rather the two negatives reinforce one another much as when one says *five cats* the *five* and the plural *-s* both convey more than one.[15] In French, multiple negatives that reinforce each other are quite standard. For example, in *je ne sais pas* 'I don't know' both underlined elements are negative but the English gloss has just one negative. At earlier periods, all varieties of English had reinforcing multiple negatives like French. The propositional meaning of the two English sentences above is the same, but the former is associated with education and, more generally, with middle-class status while the latter is associated with lack of education and with working-class speech. This opposition is central to language ideology, and relates in complex ways to gender ideology.

Many people alternate between standard and nonstandard forms of particular constructions. The difference between the two may be a matter of attitude, formality, or emphasis – and it may be not entirely a matter of choice, but a more automatic pattern (for example, a speaker may produce the former only when speaking with particular care). Sanctions for the use of nonstandard grammar permeate the parts of society that are dominated by the middle class – from disqualifying people from jobs to attracting stigma and even punishment in school. But nonstandard grammar is also associated with the positive aspects of working-class communities, and speakers may choose to use it for a variety of reasons – to signal rebelliousness, toughness, or solidarity. To the extent that such signaling is gendered, one can expect to find gender among the aspects of social identity that constrain speakers' use of forms like this. We have, for example, observed adolescent boys from well-educated, middle-class families use such nonstandard forms with their peers while generally using the standard forms at school and at home – even boys with sisters who never opt for the nonstandard forms. At the same time, there are also plenty of girls who make heavy use of nonstandard forms. The significance of all such choices is tied to how they fit into what is going on in particular communities of practice.

Other sets of syntactic alternatives may suggest slightly different stances towards what is said. A parent may ask a child about progress

---

15 The same words could be used so that the two negatives cancel one another. That might happen if *I didn't do nothing* is uttered in reply to someone else's accusing *You did nothing*. In this canceling use, primary stress or emphasis would probably be placed on the *didn't*.

with homework using any of three syntactic alternatives: "have you done your homework?" or "you haven't done your homework, have you?" or "you've done your homework, haven't you?" All of these query the same proposition, but the second and third also signal clear assumptions about the answer. While there is nothing in the differences among these forms that directly signals gender, it is possible that gender affects the ways in which people do such things as ask their children about their homework. And there are many more subtle distinctions associated with syntactic choices that we will discuss later.

Discourse

Linguists generally use the term *discourse* to refer to the study of structure and meaning that goes beyond the level of the sentence. In other words, discourse analysis focuses on the deployment, in the building of text, of the kinds of resources we've introduced above. While the levels of grammar discussed so far are themselves quite bounded, the move into the structure of their actual deployment brings us into a range of possibility that extends indefinitely. The study of discourse structure can be restricted to principles of combination in carefully bounded texts, such as the analysis of turn-taking in a single exchange, or the use of connectives to create coherence among sentences. It can include study of the gender of agents in a group of different textbooks as mentioned above. Or it can be expanded to take in the use of language in the building of a relationship over a lifetime. Utterances are sequenced and connected to produce a continually emerging text – whether spoken or written and whether individual or collaborative – that may be interrupted and extend for years, and may include ever-changing participants. The discourse context, therefore, expands indefinitely in time and social space. For this reason, while phonologists generally agree about the purview of phonology and syntacticians generally agree about what syntax includes, discourse analysts disagree quite markedly about how to define their enterprise.[16]

Discourse analysis in the more restricted sense focuses on patterns of syntactic combination which, like levels of grammar below the sentence level, can be studied without attention to meaning beyond what is actually being said in the bounded text itself. We can, for example, examine the productive uses of *so* or *but* as general linguistic strategies to connect propositions, without knowledge of the larger social context. In the following two sentences, the use of *so* and *but* signal different

16 Schiffrin (1994) lays out a number of different approaches.

relations between the two propositions *my car exploded* and *I walked away*. In the case of *so*, the connection is causal, whereas *but* signals that the second proposition is in some way unexpected given the first.

(1) My car exploded so I walked away.
(2) My car exploded but I walked away.

These relations between the two propositions would hold no matter what the speech situation and the speaker's attitudes towards the events described. Of course, one might expect utterance (1) to be uttered if the speaker had not been sufficiently close to the explosion to be in danger, whereas utterance (2) tends to suggest that the speaker had been in danger from the explosion. Notice that replacing *I walked away* by *I managed to walk away* sounds fine in (2) but rather odd in (1). In an attempt at bravado, a speaker might use utterance (1) when in fact (2) might better convey the fear-inducing nature of the event. But that does not change the meaning of *but* and *so*, or the nature of the connections between the propositions. The hearer will recognize the non-danger interpretation of (1), and may or may not recognize that the speaker was in fact in danger, and may or may not recognize that the speaker in using this utterance is attempting to construct themself as brave. Connectives like *but* and *so* are important to consider above the sentence level because they may join propositions expressed by different speakers. Consider a discourse in which the first speaker says "I hear your car exploded" and the second responds with (1') or (2').

(1') Yeah, so I walked away.
(2') Yeah, but I walked away.

Much the same things we said above about *but* and *so* when used in a single complex sentence produced by a single speaker will apply in this two-sentence and two-speaker discourse.

Some linguists define a discourse as just a sequence of sentences, which might or might not be produced by different speakers. Discourse analysis narrowly conceived adds to sentence-level analysis such matters as the basic propositional meaning that is imparted by the arrangement of sentences (e.g. their order, which can convey which event happened first) and by expressions like *but* and *so* that indicate connections among the propositions expressed by the individual sentences. This approach, while an important first step, does not address many questions important for understanding social meaning. One important omission in much of this work is the interactive nature of conversational discourse, which can, for example, lead sentences first entered into the discourse to be withdrawn under challenge. Nor have discourse analysts in this relatively narrow sense engaged much with questions of social power and ideology, which are at the heart of what is called critical discourse analysis.[17] Nonetheless, even this relatively abstract approach to discourse analysis can be made more socially sensitive.

The field of conversation analysis is another part of the more general enterprise of discourse analysis, and it has focused on the interactive and collaborative nature of conversation.[18] Speech interaction calls for reciprocity. A question calls for an answer, a *thank you* calls for a *you're welcome*, a move to interrupt coerces a speaker to stop speaking. For linguists, conversation includes not only the kind of talk engaged in at parties or during family mealtimes but also interactive talk in workplaces, schools, courtrooms, congressional committee rooms, doctors' offices, restaurants, stores. And though not face to face, the telephone and the computer now also offer important opportunities for conversation in the broad sense of communicative exchanges. Of course, people also deploy linguistic resources in contexts where linguistic interaction is not expected: they record song lyrics, write books, give formal lectures, post ads on billboards or TV. Even in cases like these where the back and forth of conversational interaction is absent, the impact of a person's words does not depend just on the words themselves and how they're uttered, but on reactions to that utterance. The language producer is always aiming words at an audience (even if only a later self). Audience response, which may or may not be available to the speaker or writer, is critical even though it may never be linguistically expressed; failure to reach any appropriate audience robs the uttered words of force, renders them effectively meaningless.

Conversation is basic analytically in part because it forces attention to audience response, to the fundamentally social character of verbal interaction. Many points we make about conversation apply to linguistically mediated communication more generally, and we will sometimes use examples that are not strictly conversational to illustrate our points. Conversation is basic experientially because it is so pervasive a part of human life. Except for those few individuals who are sealed off from others by some misfortune or some special resolve to isolate themselves from communicative interaction (hermits, for example), everyone past infancy participates in conversation of many different kinds. And in many cultures even infants whose linguistic skills are just beginning to develop are treated as conversational partners.

---

17 See, e.g., Fairclough (1987) for an accessible introduction to critical discourse analysis (CDA). And Mary Talbot (1998) has written an introduction to language and gender that is very much informed by the CDA framework.
18 Goodwin (1990) uses the methods and concepts of conversation analysis to look at gender construction in a particular community of practice.

When patterned by the gender of participants, conversational moves can coerce people into gendered roles. A compliment calls for a polite response – even when it is an unwelcome comment passed from a leering male to his female subordinate. And while a compliment offered to a woman on her appearance might be welcome, it is part of a linguistic practice by which women are regularly complimented on (i.e., judged on the basis of) their appearance while men are complimented on (i.e., judged on the basis of) their accomplishments.

We put our language to work in discourse, shaping our utterances to have an effect on our interlocutors, anticipating how they will react. Our interlocutors' responses, in turn, enter into the shaping of our next utterance. In this way, we use language to move our agendas along in the world – to pursue relationships, to engage in activities, to develop ideas. And in all of this activity we say things that we've never said before, and we say things in ways we've never said them before. All of this creativity is in the service of the flow of experience – our relationships, our beliefs, our knowledge, our interests, our tasks, our activities are all in progress. One could look at the social world as an extremely complex coordination of multiple works in progress.

Semantics and pragmatics

Readers familiar with the standard divisions of linguistics may wonder where semantics and pragmatics fit in our survey of linguistic levels. Semantics deals with how the meanings of grammatical morphemes and lexical items are combined to yield the propositional meanings expressed by sentences (and, sometimes, with the further question of how sentence meanings can be combined in discourse to produce yet more complex propositional meaning). Semantics also deals with the meanings of the basic units, the grammatical and lexical morphemes. As we noted, lexical morphemes have the closest ties to cultural concerns and are the most changeable. We will suggest in later chapters that word meanings are much less closely tied to a linguistic system than the meanings of grammatical morphemes and of syntactic structure. Basically, semantics offers interpretations of morphological and lexical units and of their syntactic combinations. In the case of lexical morphemes, these interpretations may be incomplete or relatively unspecific, and we rely on social context to fill in the meaning. This helps explain how social and cultural meanings enter the lexicon so readily. Thus semantics proper has less to say about word meanings because these meanings more often depend on language as used in social practice.

Roughly, semantics assigns the literal propositional content of utterances. Pragmatics enters the picture to augment the interpretations assigned by the semantic component of the grammar, to deal with the ways in which what is conveyed – what people succeed in meaning – outstrips what is strictly said.[19] How, for example, can *you throw like a girl* be understood as an insult? What is literally said is evaluatively neutral, but the derogatory message arises from background assumptions brought into play in interpreting the point of uttering those words in a particular context. The fact that communication goes beyond what the language system specifies is also part of the reason that language – which, remember, includes not just the system but everything involved in its use – enters so crucially into the social construction of gender (and other areas of social meaning).

Semantics and pragmatics play a central role in helping participants understand how language is being put to work in discourse, in particular in recognizing the content of what people are communicating to one another (sometimes overt, sometimes not). Semantic and pragmatic interpretation are assumed by discourse analysis, although they show only part of what is going on as people pursue their agendas through talk. Social meaning draws on much else. Some of the rest has to do with other aspects of the accompaniments of each utterance: tone of voice, phonetic detail, body language, and so on. Some has to do with connections to texts produced in other times and places, with patterns that emerge only when we look at the larger discourse picture. But we cannot ignore semantics and pragmatics in thinking about the role of language in constructing gender.

Analytic practice

The study of language and gender involves interpreting the use of the linguistic resources described above to accomplish social ends. What those social ends are, and how the linguistic form accomplishes them, are matters of interpretation, and because of the role of gender

19 There are many complications with drawing the semantics/pragmatics boundary that we will ignore. Like Christie (2000), we assume that pragmatics is indeed important for studying the contribution of language to the social construction of gender. As she notes, many investigators of language in social life disparage pragmatics, a field that originated with attention to rather asocial and quite abstract philosophical concerns, while at the same time drawing extensively in their own work on its concepts: speech acts, inferencing, deixis, presupposition, and so on. In this book (and in much of Sally's previous work on language and gender topics), we draw on pragmatic theory quite extensively to help illumine the social construction of meaning.

ideology in our thought processes, the analytic enterprise calls for con-siderable circumspection. The value of an analysis depends crucially on the quality of the analytic link between form and function.

People theorizing about the interactions between language and gen-der have tended to focus on particular issues – one issue at a time – often in response to one another. As a result, the theoretical litera-ture often appears to involve extreme stances, emphasizing power and male dominance on the one hand, gender separation and difference on the other. Each of these emphases points to important aspects of gender practice, but no single approach can tell the entire story, and a focus on one approach will miss important things, and thus distort the overall picture. A focus on difference, particularly of separate cultures and the distinct identities they produce, tends to dislodge dominance and structures of male privilege. A focus on dominance, on the other hand, tends to downplay the importance of difference in experience and beliefs. In the same way, a focus on social structure – whether one is talking about difference or dominance – tends to downplay the fact that gender is fluid, changing, and maintained in practice, while a focus on change and creativity can downplay the constraining weight of a system perceived as static in the very day-to-day practice in which change and creativity are accomplished. Similarly, a focus on the indi-vidual can mask the collaborative nature of gender, while a focus on the system can prevent us from thinking about individual agency. And any split between the social system and individual actions can prevent us from thinking seriously about the relation between the two.

Generalization is at the heart of research, and in the study of lan-guage and gender we ultimately seek global generalizations. But we need to exercise care in how we form those generalizations – how we move from observations of the behavior of particular people in partic-ular situations to broad societal patterns. In this enterprise we move from sets of real people (research "subjects") to categories of people, from real behaviors to patterns of behavior – and from patterns of the behavior of sets of people to generalizations about the underlying character and dispositions of those people and the categories we assign them to. For this reason, we turn now to issues of analytic method – to the consequences of taking broad leaps when careful steps are in order, and to the nature of those steps.

The hall of mirrors

Certain linguistic stereotypes are compelling to the person looking for gender differences, principally because they offer themselves up for ready-made gender-based explanations. Some are also compelling for the researcher who recognizes them as sexist stereotypes and seeks to refute them. As a result, there are a few putative gender differences in language use that have been studied over and over – frequently with inconclusive or negative results. Even when each individual researcher has made only modest claims on the basis of individual studies, the combination of the sheer volume of studies and the ambient belief that the results should be positive, have led to a general impression of robust findings. In the end, then, these stereotypes are accepted as scientific fact and become part of the background of general truth about language and gender. Shan Wareing (1996; cited in Cameron 1998a) used the term "hall of mirrors" to describe this phenomenon.

A couple of decades earlier, Ronald Macaulay (1978) had already pointed out the hall of mirrors effect in the literature on gender differences in language ability. It had been commonly claimed that research shows overwhelmingly that girls' language development is faster than boys', and that their language abilities are superior to those of boys. However, Macaulay found that the research results upon which these claims were based were anything but overwhelming.

The first problem in evaluating this research is assessing the value of the measures of language ability. It requires considerable ingenuity to measure small children's abilities, and investigators commonly have to rely on measures of behavior in familiar situations and with relatively little control. As a result, among reasonable measures, Macaulay also found such questionable measures of verbal ability as: "talked more frequently to other children," "appropriate verbalization during movie," "requests for information or evaluation from mother," "emitted fewer 'ah's'" (p. 354). One might argue that these touch on verbal style, but are of little value as measures of verbal ability.

But even assuming that the measures were impeccable, for a robust finding of female superiority in language ability, one would expect statistically significant gender differences in the same direction, in repeated studies. Macaulay's search of the experimental literature did not turn up this kind of consistency. Rather, he found a large number of measures that showed no gender difference, some that showed female superiority, and a somewhat smaller number that showed male superiority. In general, the measures that showed gender differences showed only slight differences, many of them not statistically significant, and many of them selected from a larger set of results that did not show this difference at all. On the other hand, he found that socioeconomic class was far more consistently and significantly correlated with verbal performance, and quite possibly accounted for some of the apparent gender differences. But in addition, Macaulay notes (p. 361) the claim (Johnson and Medinnus 1969, p. 159) that the gender of the tester influences scores on tests of language development. Inasmuch as the majority of researchers on child language development are female, it would be worth investigating the relation between research results and the gender of the tester.

The only truly robust gender difference in "language ability" is the finding that boys are significantly more likely than girls to develop language disorders such as stuttering. But language disorders represent interference of some sort, and do not necessarily indicate differences in initial capacity.

The fact is that if the results that Macaulay found for gender difference in language ability showed up in a study of the relation between eye color and language ability, that study would be dismissed. But since investigators as well as the general public are convinced that there must be gender differences, they approach their results with considerable bias, and as a result are willing to accept a considerably lowered statistical standard. To illustrate this, Macaulay cites the conclusion of a longitudinal study of language development up to the age of eight (Moore 1967). This study examined the performance of boys and girls on six linguistic measures, at ages studied (six months, eighteen months, three years, five years, eight years). Not all the linguistic measures were applied at all the age levels, but there was a total of sixteen possible sites for gender difference. Of these, Moore found only one significant gender difference, in performance on one of the six linguistic measures, and only at eighteen months. Nonetheless, his conclusion blossomed with gender claims:

> The little girl, showing in her domestic play the overriding absorption in personal relationships through which she will later fulfil her role of wife, mother and "expressive leader" of the family (Parsons & Bales, 1956), learns language early in order to communicate. The kind of communication in which she is chiefly interested at this stage concerns the nurturant routines which are the stuff of family life. Sharing and talking about them as she copies and "helps" her mother about the house must enhance the mutual identification of mother and child, which in turn, as Mowrer (1952) and McCarthy (1953) suggest, will reinforce imitation of the mother's speech and promote further acquisition of language, at first oriented toward domestic and interpersonal affairs but later adapted to other uses as well. Her intellectual performance is relatively predictable because it is rooted in this early communication, which enables her (environment permitting) to display her inherited potential at an early age.

The same thing happens in boys, but to a lesser extent because they cannot so easily share their interests. Their preoccupation with the working of mechanical things is less interesting to most mothers, and fathers are much less available. Probably too, effective communication about cause and effect presupposes a later stage of mental development than does communication about household routines. The small boy may be storing a great many observations, but his conversation tends to be limited to such remarks as *Train stop* until he is mature enough to ask *Why is the train stopping?* Only then can he begin to structure his accumulated experience with the aid of the explanations offered him, which he supplements for himself and progressively internalizes as Vygotsky (1962) describes. His language, less fluent and personal and later to appear than the girl's, develops along more analytic lines and may, in favourable circumstances, provide the groundwork for later intellectual achievement which could not have been foreseen in his first few years.

The girl, meanwhile, is acquiring the intimate knowledge of human reactions which we call feminine intuition. Perhaps because human reactions are less regular than those of inanimate objects, however, she is less likely to develop the strictly logical habits of thought that intelligent boys acquire, and if gifted may well come to prefer the subtler disciplines of the humanities to the intellectual rigour of science.

(Moore 1967, pp. 100–101; cited in Macaulay 1978, p. 360)

Few today would indulge in this kind of overt gender stereotyping. Indeed, most of the original authors had made only modest claims, or even dismissed the sketchy evidence they found of gender difference. It was later readers who inflated their results, who took them into the hall of mirrors and got back much larger-than-life reflections. And, though the language is somewhat more guarded these days, we still find such magnification of very limited data, magnification that always owes much to gender stereotypes and ideologies.

Accumulating nonsignificant results is not the only interpretive move that leads to dubious generalizations about gender. Many studies do show significant differences in the verbal behavior of males and females. But these differences are often generalized beyond the research situation in which they have been observed in such a way as to overextend their implications. One example of this overextension underlies the common claim that men interrupt in conversation more than women.

What would it take to prove this to be true? While we will discuss the issue of interruptions in greater detail in chapter three, we preview that discussion here as our second cautionary tale. As we will see in chapter three, the very notion of interruption is complex. What we wish to point out here is simply that the "well-established fact" of "man, the great interrupter" is perpetuated in spite of a long history of nonconfirming research.[20] In a detailed examination of studies of interruptions in the 25-year period between 1965 and 1991, Deborah James and Sandra Clarke (1993) found that there is no evidence of gender differences in speakers' general rates of interruption.

In total, James and Clark found thirteen studies that showed men interrupting more than women, eight in which women interrupted more than men, and thirty-four studies that showed no differences between men and women. This is hardly overwhelming evidence that men interrupt more than women. We should point out, though, that in these figures we have thrown together a variety of kinds of studies in such a way as to maximize our point. When broken down into studies of dyads as opposed to studies of larger groups, or studies of same-gender and mixed-gender groups, the figures show greater nuance. However, no matter how one breaks down the studies, there is no clear evidence that males interrupt more than females.

The hypothesis that men interrupt their interlocutors more than women is popular, no doubt because it appears to follow from the fact that men have greater power in society. It also fits into a view of women as peaceable and cooperative, in contrast to men's aggressiveness and competitiveness. This "women as lovely" view of gender permeates society and much of the literature on gender and on language and gender. It does not arise from analysis of language or of other aspects of social practice so much as it serves as the starting assumption for analysis. The hypotheses that people put forth tend to be based on components of opposing gender stereotypes. Do men interrupt more than women? Is women's speech more hesitant? More polite? More standard? Posed this way, the questions seek global differences. And inasmuch as the differences people seek are viewed as global (men ARE more competitive, women ARE more polite), particularistic conclusions are interpreted as global.

A matter of method

Stereotypes in language and gender research

> ...in every group of several words a woman will string together in a sentence, usually no two are spoken at the same pitch. This is what makes women's voices sound so "sing song." In fact, they ARE singing!

20 Deborah Cameron (1998a) cited this particular "result" as a prime example of the hall of mirrors phenomenon.

> Sometimes the stair steps go down to lower into that conspiratorial
> tone. Other times they go up to raise the emotional stakes. Often they
> rise and fall like sine waves to rush up under a phrase, then retreat like
> a wave on the sand. Speaking in stair step tonalities is best learned by
> listening to others, but it is learned, not intrinsic. Just like Dynamic
> Range, it is a function of conditioning rather than biology.

So goes Melanie Anne Phillips's online manual (1989–2000), offering instruction to male-to-female transgendering people on how to talk like
a woman. Our readers will recognize this as a stereotypic description
of female speech. What lies on the road between a stereotype and a
scientific finding? We might begin by asking whether women really do
have more "singsong" intonation patterns than men. And of course,
before we could approach such a question, we would have to ask what
might be the stickiest question – how would we define a singsong intonation linguistically so that we could identify one if we heard it?
And once we'd arrived at a technical definition of singsong intonation,
what women and what men would we compare? What kind of sample
of men and women would we have to examine to establish whether
women use a particular intonation pattern more than men?

What kinds of data would we use for this study? Individual interviews? Conversations in same-sex groups? Mixed-sex groups? Groups of
friends? Strangers? Recordings of meetings? Coffee klatches? Dinner
table conversations? What kinds of topics would we want people to
talk about? How do people use this pattern in actual interactions? Do
they use it all the time or for specific purposes? Does an individual's
pattern of use, or any gender balance in use, change according to the
circumstances?

What kinds of statistical results would we require to conclude that
the pattern counts as a *female* pattern? What other ways of categorizing
the users of this pattern might we examine – among and across women
and men? And how would we interpret the meaning of the pattern?
Is the pattern linked to regional or social dialects? How is it produced
and interpreted in different dialects?

Stereotypes are the starting point of much research on language and
gender for a reason. First of all, any research begins with a focus or
a hypothesis, and foci and hypotheses have to come from somewhere.
If gender stereotypes are part of our sociolinguistic life, they need to
be examined – not simply as possible facts about language use, but as
components of gender ideology. Our linguistic behavior is intertwined
with ideology, and stereotypes are not simply "lies" about language,
but exaggerations with a purpose. And that purpose is part of what
makes language tick. What does it mean for something to be *simply*

a stereotype? If it's out there and we can recognize it, then it has a life in social practice and it clearly has something to do with the life of language. First of all, our recognition of "singsong intonation" as a female pattern not only provides a resource for a person striving to lay claim to female status, but it foregrounds the difference between male and female. If women have singsong intonation, what do men have? We might ask what social purposes this stereotype serves. What role does it play in maintaining the gender order? Who invokes it and how? How is it used in humor and parody? How do people talk about it? What do they believe to be its connection to femininity? How does it function in an opposition to some male pattern?

After discussing the supposed "singsong" quality of women's speech, Phillips's manual continues:

> some words are more masculine or feminine than others. Part of this again derives from the brokering of power. For example, a man usually "wants" something while a woman "would like" something. "Want" means "lack" and implies "need" which further implies the right to have. This reflects the aggressive side of the power equation.
>
> On the other hand, "would like" states a preference, not an intent, and therefore runs the idea up the flagpole to see if anyone is against it before acting. This reflects the submissive side of the power equation.
>
> You can notice the difference in the way men and women will order at the speaker of a drive-through fast food restaurant. A man will say, "I want a Big Mac.", whereas a woman will say, "I'd like a salad, please."

Once again, we recognize the stereotype of the manifestation of power and entitlement in men's speech, and of submissiveness and deference in women's. Indeed, if a person wants to speak in a maximally "feminine" way, these are good stereotypic verbal behaviors to assume, along with a frilly pink blouse, long curly hair and high-heeled shoes. But an extreme application of these strategies will yield a hyperfeminine buffoon of a type that is rarely seen in the world. In the same way, if one were actually to stand at the MacDonald's counter and observe people ordering food, one would not find the polite orderers (of dainty salads) and brusque orderers (of giant burgers) falling out into neat male–female categories. And chances are that the orderer's behavior would have as much to do with the gender and the behavior of the person behind the counter as with their own gender.

In other words, there is considerable distance between the gender stereotypes that are available to us all, and the behavior of real people as they go about their business in the world. But the relation between stereotypes and behavior is in itself interesting, for the stereotypes constitute norms – rather extreme norms[21] – that we do not *obey*, but that we *orient* to. They serve as a kind of organizing device in society, an ideological map, setting out the range of possibility within which we place ourselves and assess others. For this reason, norms and stereotypes, and their relation to behavior, are central to the study of language and gender. Yet all too often, research on gender has taken these stereotypes as a starting point rather than as part of the object of study, taking for granted that they represent some kind of prototype – some kind of "normal" behavior, from which all other behavior is a deviation. But the study of gender cannot be based in popular beliefs about gender any more than the study of physics can be based in popular beliefs about motion. In issuing this caution, we are not denying the existence and the importance of gender stereotypes; on the contrary, we believe that they require serious study. But taking such stereotypes as a starting point for the study of behavior, even if the intent is to show that actual behavior fails to conform to them, contains serious pitfalls.

From observation to generalization

Consider the common claim that men are hierarchical while women are egalitarian (e.g. Tannen 1990). This generalization is based on a combination of interactional observations and claims from scientists interested in the (supposed) interaction of evolutionary biology and the social world.[22] To be hierarchical presumably means to view the world as hierarchically organized, and to attend to the self's place in that hierarchy. In particular situations, one will attend to one's own place in relation to other participants in the interaction. Competitive behavior, which focuses explicitly on the self's relation to other participants, can be said to indicate a hierarchical orientation. However, there is a

---

21 The term *norm* is used in two different ways in social science: on the one hand to refer to an average, on the other to refer to a standard expectation. We will be using it in the latter sense.

22 Sociobiology, very popular in the 1970s, has now mutated into the currently trendy field of evolutionary psychology. Unfortunately, in talking about gender difference, both fields have seemed to rely more on gender ideology and stereotyping than on actual careful observations of females and males of any species. We certainly do not deny that humans are biological creatures nor that reproductive demands for the species are likely to play a role both in individual lives and in evolution of the species. An important part of our biology, however, is that we are social and we are reflective creatures. It is also an important empirical fact that on virtually every property and capacity carefully studied there is considerable diversity within each sex and considerable overlap across the sexes.

lot of distance between such an orientation in a given situation and a more general hierarchical view. It is possible that the difference is not that men are more hierarchical than women, but that they are more licensed to be hierarchical, to expose their hierarchical orientation to public view. When we talk about "inner selves" or dispositions or characters, it is problematic to attend only to overt behavior. Interactional observations of men's hierarchical behavior come primarily from social psychological experiments in which single-gender and mixed-gender groups are given a task to do. Repeatedly, in single-gender groups, the men are shown to create hierarchies – certain men speak more while others recede into the background. The women, on the other hand, are shown to share the floor more. But what can one actually conclude from these experiments? Consider what has actually been shown. It has been shown that the men who participate in these experiments (mostly white middle-class students at American research universities) are more likely to create hierarchies in short-term interactions (that have been arranged, and are observed, by relative strangers) than are the women (mostly white middle-class students at American research universities) who participate in these experiments. This is a far cry from evidence that men are globally more competitive and hierarchical than women.

In fact, there is plenty of evidence that women can be every bit as competitive and hierarchical as men. The difference is not in whether men or women are hierarchical and competitive, but under what circumstances and in what ways. Marjorie Harness Goodwin (1990) observed preadolescent children living in a neighborhood in Philadelphia over a considerable period. During this time she observed, indeed, that the boys when working on tasks together (e.g. making slingshots) established clear hierarchies in each interaction. The girls (in this case making rings out of bottle tops), on the other hand, tended to be more egalitarian in their task-oriented interactions. However, over a period of weeks, the girls established clear and enduring hierarchies in their conversation outside of these activities. While the boys continued to play together in a consistent and egalitarian group, the girls were practicing elaborate systems of exclusion that not only created a hierarchy within the group but effectively isolated girls who were deemed unacceptable. Similarly, in her work in high schools, Eckert (1989) found that girls were more tightly constrained by hierarchies of popularity, while boys tended to compete over individual skills rather than global status. The evidence that males are more hierarchical, then, is restricted to immediate situations – whereas females may in fact be as hierarchical (and possibly more hierarchical) in the long run. The moral of this story is that the style of research may well be what determines the results. For example, experimental research will tell us only things that happen in the short term, while dynamics that unfold over time – and in situations that are not available for experimentation – will remain unobserved.

Since research questions tend to be posed in global terms, very specifically situated results tend to be interpreted as extending well beyond their actual scope. The research questions themselves often emerge directly from stereotypes – in an attempt to prove or disprove them. But such questions do not query the very purpose of the stereotype. It may be that males and females, at least in contemporary North America, establish hierarchies differently and perhaps even for different purposes. A reasonable research question would be, then, in what ways do different people construct and participate in social hierarchies? And what is the relation of gender to this enterprise?

There is yet another way in which gender differences in research can be overinterpreted. Beyond the collection of linguistic data is the rationale behind the interpretation of those data. While interruptions appear to be a prime example of a move to dominate the conversation and hence one's interlocutor, there are several steps between the observation of an overlap between two speakers and domination. Deborah Tannen (1989) has shown that many overlaps are, on the contrary, supportive conversational moves – and that the speech styles of some social groups abound with such overlaps. The relation between linguistic form and social function, in other words, is not as simple as one might think. But when the interpretation of social function stems from a gender stereotype, it is all too easy to overlook the crucial analytic work that must link form to function.

It might appear that we object to the study of gender differences in language use, or that we even deny their existence. Far from it. Our purpose is not to deny that differences exist, but to point out that the quality of research depends on the approach that one takes to finding and establishing such differences. Above all, one cannot assume that the most interesting differences will be in straightforward oppositions between the behavior of males as a group and females as a group. As we will show in the following chapters, gender often manifests itself in differences in the range of behavior among males and among females. And gender is not only about difference: it often manifests itself in similarities among certain males and certain females. Above all, gender is built on a lifetime of differentiated experience, and as a result is inextricably mixed with toughness, occupation, entitlement, formality, class, hobbies, family status, race, and just about any other life experience you can name. Separating gender from the other aspects of social life cannot be accomplished with a blunt instrument – and often as not it cannot be accomplished with the sharpest scalpel either. Gender must be recognized in its full glory – in its inseparability from the rest of life experience.

In the chapters that follow, therefore, we will address not only the question of how males and females use language, but also the question of how people use language to maintain the focus on male and female. How do we use language to construct and maintain the gender order? How do people deploy linguistic resources in the interests of their own gender ideologies? How are dominant ideologies reinforced in day-to-day talk, and how are rival ideologies furthered or squashed in talk? To examine language at the level of practice, we need to focus not simply on categories, but on the sites and situations in which these categories are made salient.

CHAPTER 3

Organizing talk

Human discourse is an ongoing project of meaning-making, and the extent to which an individual or a group or category of individuals actually contributes to meaning depends on their ability to get their contributions heard and attended to. The fate of a speaker's contribution is already at issue even before it is uttered – before one can put one's ideas on the floor, one has to be in the situation and the conversation in which it is appropriate to talk about certain things. And once one is in the situation, one has to be able to actually get the idea onto the floor – to make that particular utterance on a particular occasion. The very beginning of the analysis of language and gender, therefore, lies in the division of labor writ large. In the course of the day, who is present where particular situations unfold? What kinds of speech events and activities take place in these situations and who is thus present to participate in them? Who has the right and/or authority to participate in these events and in what ways? Who is entitled to speak and be heeded on what kinds of topics? How does one get one's contribution into the flow of speech? And who will be in a position to follow up that contribution in other situations? We begin our examination of language and gender, therefore, with aspects of the organization of talk that determine one's ability to get one's stuff into the discourse – the gendered structure of participation in speech activities.

For starters, speaking rights are commonly allocated differentially to different categories of people. In some cultures, children are expected to be silent, while in others they are left to express themselves freely. Gender quite generally figures in this allocation. For example, in the Araucanian culture of Chile, volubility figures prominently in gender ideology:

> Men are encouraged to talk on all occasions, speaking being a sign of masculine intelligence and leadership. The ideal woman is submissive and quiet, silent in her husband's presence. At gatherings where men do much talking, women sit together listlessly, communicating only in whispers or not at all.
> (Hymes 1972, p. 45)

Hymes goes on to say that when a new bride arrives in her husband's home, she must remain silent for some time. In other words, speaking rights are not simply allocated to categories of people, but to these categories in particular situations and activities. How women and men get their stuff into the discourse requires first and foremost an understanding of access to situations and of the structure of interaction in these situations.

Access to situations and events

In chapter two, we discussed the traditional linguistic notion of *competence*, and also the anthropologist's and sociolinguist's expanded notion of *communicative competence*. In his construction of a theory of language in which political economy plays a central role, Pierre Bourdieu (1977a) challenged traditional linguistics for its narrow focus on the speaker's ability to produce and recognize sentences, and its neglect of what happens to those sentences once they are put out in the world. Bourdieu equated linguistic competence with the ability not simply to produce utterances, but have those utterances heeded. But no matter how broadly it is defined, *competence* may not be the best word to describe a person's capacity to be communicatively effective. Individual knowledge and skill are only part of the picture. A person's contribution to an ongoing discussion is determined not simply by the utterance the person produces, but by the ways in which that utterance is received and interpreted by the others in the conversation. Beyond that conversation, the force of an utterance depends on what people do with it in subsequent interactions. Is it quoted? Is it ignored or disparaged? How is it interpreted? And where and by whom? The force of an utterance is not manifest in the utterance itself, but in its fate once it is launched into the discourse – once it begins its "discursive life."[1] And that fate is not in the hands of the initial utterer, but depends on the meaning-making rights of that utterer both in the immediate situation and beyond, and of those who might take up the utterance and carry its content to other situations and communities. It is this fate, all along the line, that determines what ideas will make it into common discourse.

1 Citation practices in scholarly discourse are one guide to the effectiveness of contributions to that particular discourse. McElhinney *et al.* (forthcoming) found, for example, that women in the fields of sociolinguistics and linguistic anthropology cite women at a significantly higher rate (about 35%) than men cite women (about 21%).

The right to speak depends on the right to be in the situation, and the right to engage in particular kinds of speech activities in that situation. In this way, the gendered division of labor and the public/private dichotomy presented in chapter one have important implications for the linguistic economy and the economy of ideas. In cultures where women do not speak in public places, their ideas will not get onto the table – at least not directly – in the situations in which public affairs are decided. Consider the role of public comedy in getting ideas into common discourse. Joking about men's impatience with discussing relationships has already made it to the top among discourses of gender, but joking about women's impatience with babies has not. One will often hear the former on late night comedy shows, but the latter kind of jokes generally do not make it beyond quite selected gatherings in which the recognition that child-care is not every woman's dream activity is part of everyday discourse. A 2002 automobile ad shows the male owner of a shiny new car looking around furtively, and then using his baby's diapered bottom to wipe off a speck of water. While a mother might be equally inclined to use her baby to polish her prized new vehicle, portraying her doing so in an ad is not likely to go over as well. Or at least so the advertisers seem to think. But if women were making car ads to appeal to female consumers, such a portrayal might in fact happen and might well be effective. Indeed, the emergence of women performing as stand-up comics may have a profound effect on discourses of gender as it is beginning to bring such humor into public discourse.

The gender balance in formal institutions has a profound effect on who constructs official discourse – who designs the world. Although their numbers have increased dramatically in the past decade, there are still very few women in the US Senate, House of Representatives, and the Cabinet. This means that most of the conversations in which US national policy is being shaped have few female participants, and many have none. Most technology is designed by men (and in this case, they often quite consciously design the technology for themselves), so the conversations that have taken place about what technologies should be developed and what features they should have involve virtually no women. Women's relative absence from the conversations that have determined medical practice and research has led over the years to a stunning lack of information about women's health, the responses to drugs and treatments of women's bodies, and similar issues.

In spite of considerable advances in women's access to positions of influence, it remains the case that it is primarily men who have the authority to engage in conversations that affect large numbers of people, and to perform speech acts that change people's civil status. In some cases, access to speaking roles is by virtue of gender alone – for example it is expected that women will not contribute to men's locker room talk because they are women, and women are not supposed to be in men's locker rooms. Only very recently have most private clubs in the US dropped rules barring women from dining or playing golf, opening at least the possibility of women's participating in exchanges at the club dining table or on the fairway.

Access to situations may also be a function of the gendered allocation of roles. Religious practices offer many examples. Women do not say mass in the Catholic Church because only priests can do so, and women cannot be priests. Interestingly, however, the Protestant ministry in some denominations in the US is increasingly feminized, so much so that, in recent years, women are relatively frequently heard giving sermons, baptizing infants, and performing marriage ceremonies. Judaism in the US offers a spectrum from orthodox congregations in which men are required for important prayers and women do not read aloud from the Torah, to reform groups with women serving as rabbis (a relatively recent development but nonetheless a significant one).

There are many cases in which gender structures access to speech events not because of formal prohibitions but because of histories of gender imbalance in certain positions. No woman has ever given a state of the union address in the US – not because women cannot now legally be president, but because they have not yet been president. Thus there is a continuum of access and participation, and there is ongoing change in how gender relates to that continuum.

Looking like a professor

A congenial man who frequents the "Collegetown" neighborhood near Cornell cheerily greets us as we walk to campus. "Hi, girls." He turns to Carl, Sally's partner, also a professor, "Hi, Professor." He doesn't know who any of us are, but one of us looks like the prototypical professor and the other two don't. We joke about it – it's trivial. We're used to being called "girls" – to having people assume that we're secretaries as we sit in our offices. But the fact remains that any small act has large potential. Fidell (1975) sent resumé summaries of ten fictitious psychology Ph.D.'s to 147 heads of psychology departments in the US, asking them to assign an academic rank to each resumé. The same dossiers sometimes had men's names at the top, sometimes women's. The respondents consistently ranked the same dossiers higher when they believed them to be men's than when they believed them to be women's. The only difference between the man on the street in College-town and these department chairs is the consequence of their asssumptions. In the end, it's all a matter of who looks more like a professor.

All this is to say that it is never just the language that determines if someone's stuff gets into the discourse. The effect of one's verbal activity depends, among other things, on one's apparent legitimacy to engage in that activity. The words of a person who doesn't appear to be a professor are less likely to be taken as authoritative than the same words coming from someone who does look like a professor. And, of course, being a professor in the first place depends on one's looking (and sounding) sufficiently like one to get the job.

The practice of a woman's putting her words into a man's mouth, then, should not be surprising. George Eliot is a famous case of a woman writing under a man's name in order to get published, read, and attended to. And there are many others. As the work of Ellis Bell, Emily Brontë's prose was read as strong and forceful; when the author's identity as a woman was revealed, critics found delicacy and gentleness in the works. So it is not only whether one's words are read or heard but also how they are judged that can depend on whether one is thought to be woman or man. The familiar claim that women are often very influential behind the scenes, through their influence on men, points out that some women do indeed have the opportunity to make their ideas known to some men, who in turn are moved by them. Nonetheless, it is the man who decides whether to take these ideas beyond the private realm, and what to do with them. And, of course, it is that man who will engage in the public deliberation, whose decisions about how to argue will determine the power of "her" words. Not surprisingly, the archetypal influential woman is the adored wife or lover of a powerful man. We let the reader consider the implications of this for who is getting her ideas across and how. But we also note that the level of grumbling about Hillary Clinton's potential influence on her husband was considerably higher than the level of grumbling about Joseph Kennedy's potential influence on his son John. Neither wife nor father was or had been an elected official, yet while both were interested and expert in particular aspects of public policy, the public seemed to have far more objections to the wife's potential influence. What is it about a wife's influence that is more suspect than a father's? And now that Hillary Clinton is herself a US senator, there has been no talk at all about her husband's influence on her.

It will often be said that women have not played a role in a particular decision because they did not *happen* to be present when the

decision was made. But it is important to take separately each element of the process of getting one's ideas into the discourse, and examine its relation to a larger whole, for it is all too easy to segment
experience – to focus on particular episodes without seeing recurrent
patterns – and attribute each segment to chance. Whether the women
were absent because they were not allowed into the conversation, or
because they did not hear about the conversation in advance, or because they were busy taking care of responsibilities that fell to them
because of their gender, or simply because they did not feel comfortable
in the situation, their absence was very likely structured by gender.

Networks

The division of labor works to allocate meaning-making opportunities
not simply in the formal sphere, but in the informal sphere as well.
Race, ethnicity, and gender all work to limit people's sources of information gained in informal situations, reinforcing a specialization of
knowledge among racial, ethnic, and gender groups. To some extent
this knowledge may be specific to the informal sphere – but segregation
of informal activities also has important repercussions for people's relation to formal institutions. Some of the most important institutional
knowledge is gained, not in the classroom or the workplace, but at
lunch, at dinner, in the carpool, on the squash court. The kind of informal exclusion that results from the fact that women tend to eat
lunch with other women and men tend to eat lunch with other men
can be both unintentional and invisible. But it is nonetheless real and
often consequential.

   The individual's professional network is a set of overlapping institutional, professional, and personal networks, and the way in which the
individual combines these networks is extremely important for success. Because of the overlap of personal and institutional networks, a
good deal of personal information flows in institutional networks, and
a good deal of institutional information flows in personal networks.
It is for this reason that one cannot afford to be ignorant of personal
ties, but also, and more importantly, personal networks become a key
locus for the flow of institutional resources. The fact that institutional
resources get exchanged in personal encounters creates an ecology in
which information of institutional importance, by virtue of spreading
in informal and private situations, may never come up in public situations. Influence also resides in private groups – many workplace problems have been resolved in bars, restaurants, poker games, people's
homes. And many of the important developments in the workplace

have their origins in regularly-interacting groups, as colleagues who interact regularly on an informal basis reinforce their mutual interests and negotiate ideas and plan strategy. Another informational need that arises from the combination of personal and institutional networks is personal information – who is friends or lovers with whom, who is married to whom, who doesn't associate with whom. This kind of information can be extremely valuable in navigating one's way through the professional world, and its lack can be dangerous. In short, one learns about the social structure of institutions by learning how the personal and the professional dovetail, and in order to be privy to much of this information, one must spend large amounts of time in casual and personal talk with the people who make up the network.

If it is apparent that the combination of personal and institutional networks maximizes the flow of career resources, it is also apparent that this combination puts women at a disadvantage for several reasons. If an individual's personal situation or activities are seen as incompatible with professionalism, the mixing of personal and professional networks can feed damaging information into the professional network. The threat of this is clearly greater for women than for men. Simply appearing in the role of homemaker or mother has often been damaging professionally for women. Appearing as the more powerless member of a couple is, needless to say, damaging. Appearing as a sexual being – whether in a conventional relationship or otherwise – is more damaging to a woman's professional image than to a man's, and certainly traditional norms for women make them far more vulnerable to the leakage of "negative" personal information. To the extent that a woman actually does participate in a male personal network she and her male friends tend to be vulnerable to sexual gossip and suspicion, which are generally more damaging to the woman. (Openly lesbian women as well as women who are old or physically unattractive sometimes find it easier than presumptively "available" heterosexual women to participate in personal networks with men. Of course that doesn't mean that such women lead generally easier lives!) A final difficulty for many women in the combination of personal and professional networks is that domestic responsibilities still frequently constrain women's social activities, preventing them from servicing their ties in the way that single people and most married men can. A woman with children, particularly if she is single, is prevented from building networks on a variety of counts: the fact that her motherhood may be seen as conflicting with professionalism is compounded when domestic responsibilities interfere with professional activities and networking.

Speech activities

Once in the situations where verbal exchange is taking place, our ability to get our words and ideas out depends on our ability to participate in the speech activities and events that take place in those situations. Every speech community, and every community of practice, engages in a limited set of speech activities: lecturing, sermonizing, gossiping, griping, talking dirty, joking, arguing, fighting, therapy talk, small talk. The reader could expand this list of activities, and could make a good deal of headway in describing the special characteristics of each one.

There are some speech activities that occur in all speech communities, while others may be specific to, or more common in, particular communities. And although a particular activity may occur in many communities, it may unfold differently across communities, and it may figure differently in ideology. Argument in an academic community might be quite different from argument at a family dinner table, and what is considered an argument in one culture or community of practice might be considered a fight in another. And while arguing might be highly valued in one culture (Deborah Schiffrin [1984], for example, talks about the value of arguing in Jewish culture), it might be avoided in another. People in Inuit communities, living a traditional subsistence life in the Arctic, avoided conflict talk in everyday interaction because of the threat that interpersonal conflict posed to the safety of the community in the harsh Arctic environment. Conflict is dangerous in a community that depends on cooperation for survival, and the Inuit organized their verbal interaction so as to work out conflict in safe, ritualized ways (Eckert and Newmark 1980).

Speech activities can be quite specific at the most local level. Some couples, for example, value arguing while others avoid it. Some friendship groups engage regularly in fast-paced banter while others are more deliberate in their conversation. Particular communities of practice may engage regularly in – or even be built around – gossip, exchanging salacious stories, mutual insults, talking about problems, complaining, reading aloud, praying. Others may eschew some of these activities. Scott Kiesling's research (e.g. 1997) on verbal practice in an American college fraternity shows how joking and ritual insults are commonly used in this community of practice to enforce heterosexuality.

Just how a particular speech activity is classified may itself be colored by gender ideologies. Highly similar exchanges in English are sometimes classified differently depending on who the participants are. John's "shoptalk" with his friends and colleagues may be pretty hard to distinguish from Jane's "gossip" with hers. Such gendering of speech activities is often used to reinforce gender hierarchies. Shoptalk is seen as something that professionals engage in, perhaps at inconvenient moments for others to deal with, but for laudable work and achievement-related goals. In contrast, gossip is seen as "idle talk; groundless rumour...tittle-tattle." To "discuss matters relating to one's trade or profession; business" (i.e., to "talk shop") is to do one's duty whereas to reveal the "private concerns of others" or "pass on confidential information" (i.e., to "gossip") is to raise questions about one's integrity. (The quotations here are taken from entries in the 1993 *New Shorter Oxford English Dictionary*, hereafter referred to as NSOED.)

Gossip reconsidered

A number of feminist analysts in recent years have revisited the concept of gossip, questioning both its heavy feminine gendering and its bad reputation. Much of what passes as shoptalk involves evaluative (and often critical) commentary on absent parties, characteristics often offered as definitive of gossip. (See, e.g., Wierzbicka 1987.) There are also many other situations in which men engage in speech activities that would count as gossip, using the standard criteria. Deborah Cameron (1997) analyzes the talk of some young men just "hanging out" in front of the TV in their living quarters in a small Virginia college. Some of this talk involved bragging about sexual conquests (and, at the same time, certainly speaking of what might seem to be "private concerns" of the women with whom they had "scored") and about their own capacity for holding alcohol. But also figuring prominently were comments about various other (absent) men. They were "homos," "faggots," "wimps," singled out for the frat boys' derision on the grounds that they seemed somehow "weird," not acting, dressing, or looking like the norms they endorsed for "real men." Seldom was there any real information on sexual preference or behavior of the men being criticized. Cameron argues quite persuasively that these young men were using homophobic discourse about absent others to establish their own (heterosexual) masculinity and to enforce certain norms of masculinity. And she also points out that the guys' disparagement of absent others certainly fits standard definitions of gossip – except for its gendering.

Some have taken the tack of trying to rehabilitate the concept of gossip, to show that women's gossip often has very positive social functions. Deborah Jones (1980) was one of the first to develop this approach. The word *gossip*, she notes, descends from Old English *god sib*, which originally meant something similar to godparent or supportive friend.

This later became specialized to female friend and further specialized to designate a friend invited to be present at a birth. Birthing among the English at this time (around the sixteenth century) was very much a female-dominated event, and Jones speculates that the picture of gossip as a nasty kind of feminine talk derived from men's fears of what unsupervised women might be saying to one another on such occasions. Women supporting one another raised the possibility of their challenging male authority or at least devising ways to resist it.

Others, too, have been willing to accept *gossip* as a characterization of much of women's talk while offering a nonstandard understanding of just what gossip is. Jennifer Coates (1988), for example, seems to suggest that any informal talk among close women friends counts as gossip whether or not it focuses on reporting and evaluating activities of absent parties. Coates (1996) offers transcripts and analyses of a number of conversations in which the women participating collectively explore topics that matter a lot to them in a supportive and positive way. Are these women gossiping? Not in many of the cases according to the criteria that most English speakers would probably say apply. But Coates's use of *gossip* to label speech activities that positively connect women astutely picks up on Jones's etymological observation. It is not only in the past that observers have been quick to assume that any women talking together in an "informal" and "unrestrained" way, "esp. about people or social incidents," must be up to no good, venturing into territory that is "none of their business." (The quoted phrases are further characterizations from the NSOED definition of *gossip*.) Women talking together over lunch in a formerly all-male faculty club are often approached by male colleagues with a joking "Well, who are you all laughing about?" or "What are you ladies up to?" or something similar that suggests a certain discomfort with what this group of presumptively "gossiping" (or perhaps "plotting") women might be up to.

Talk among women about absent others by no means always implies a focus on making absent others look bad. The talk may be very sympathetic and understanding. Observers, however, may still be quick to disparage it. Of course, like the fraternity brothers in Cameron's study, women can and sometimes do forge bonds with one another by sharing damaging observations or critical comments about absent others. In the absence of formal control of material resources or institutionalized political authority, women in certain European peasant societies have been argued to wield considerable influence through making strategic use of all kinds of information they gather through frequent informal talking with one another while washing clothes, shopping, preparing food. The threat of being the subject of the women's censure keeps some men in line. In a widely read essay about Oroel, a small Spanish village, Susan Harding (1975) argues that women's words enable them to exercise real power in local matters of some consequence. And it is not just what women do say to one another and to the men in their lives: it is also concern about what they might say that constrains both other women and men in significant ways. As Harding also points out, however, such power is limited in the domains to which it can apply. Women's words cannot really challenge the profoundly patriarchal character of the various institutions that shape the lives of the residents of Oroel: church, schools, courts, legislatures. Nonetheless, women's gossip here is hardly "idle" but does social work of many different kinds.

Arguing

Argument is another kind of speech activity that comes in many forms, and that is highly gendered. The NSOED offers this quote from Milton: "In argument with men a woman ever Goes by the worse." Milton's misogynistic line is offered to illustrate the following sense of *argument*: "Statement of the pros and cons of a proposition; discussion, debate (esp. contentious); a verbal dispute, a quarrel." Although *quarrel* appears in this definition of *argument* and we also find *argument* used to define *quarrel*, the two have very different flavors. Argument canonically involves giving reasons and evidence and using rational principles of inference to support a position. In contrast, quarrels are seen as more emotional, primarily a manifestation of "temper" and often leading to a rupture in friendly relations among participants. As Wierzbicka (1987, p. 138) puts it, "quarrelling has a more personal orientation in general, whereas arguing is essentially focused on the subject matter...quarrelling [involves] a struggle of wills and a display of tempers." To be argumentative is not necessarily a bad thing: it can suggest strong convictions and intellectual skill ("fond or capable of arguing," says the NSOED). Being quarrelsome, on the other hand, does not suggest any capabilities, just a propensity to engage in contentious "hot-tempered" speech. To label a dispute *bickering* is to trivialize it completely: *quarrel* is used to define *bicker* (along with *squabble* and *wrangle*) but *argue* is not.

Pitting reason against emotion is, of course, a staple of gender construction in most English-speaking countries. Men argue, women quarrel or bicker. That's why a woman "ever Goes by the worse" in arguing with men. She is doomed by her inability to engage with him on intellectual grounds, by being at the mercy of her emotions. Although Milton's view of matters is less likely to be overtly endorsed these days, disagreement and contentious speech activity remain important in gender construction. Whether a particular dispute is labeled an argument or a quarrel often depends less on how the dispute actually proceeds than on the labeler's assumptions about the intellectual capacities of the disputants and their relative interest in ideas versus feelings. And those assumptions are often strongly influenced by gender ideologies.

Argument is important in many different communities of practice. In communities focused on scientific and other scholarly practice, argument is typically quite central though the style can vary quite significantly. An adversarial style of argumentation is the norm in some such communities. Scholar A develops a position and presents it to her colleagues. Those colleagues see an important part of their job to be testing that position, exposing any weaknesses. They may criticize the kind of evidence A has given or the way she has argued from that evidence to her position. They may offer new evidence, which conflicts in some way with what A has presented. Such debates may be conducted face to face in a laboratory or over coffee or, with more onlookers, at a conference or public lecture. They may go on in print, with B responding to A's article and A replying in turn to B's critique in the pages of some academic journal. Others may join in, offering additional support for A's position or additional support for B's critique. B may go beyond critique to propose his own counterposition. And argument of this kind is, as Deborah Tannen (1998) has observed, overwhelmingly conceptualized as battle, as words gone to war. Philosopher Janice Moulton proposed some years ago that the striking absence of women from mainstream US philosophy departments was connected to the philosophers' embrace of this adversarial mode of argumentation (see Moulton 1983). Few women, she suggested, like to engage in this kind of verbal combat, which they often see as destructive of people's sense of self-esteem and ultimately more likely to promote individual advancement than real intellectual gain.

Like fisticuffs, verbal sparring can also be engaged in with a certain playfulness and certainly without aiming to hurt other participants. In some communities of practice, argument often functions as a kind of game or at least an activity that is seen as focused on the stuff of the argument and not on the arguers themselves. Cultural norms are quite variable. In many Italian-speaking communities of practice, for example, lively and loud arguments involving both women and men are frequent. Americans, whose main experience has been in communities of practice that work to minimize overt disagreement, are sometimes taken aback by the intensity and vehemence of these exchanges and even more surprised to see the "combatants" ending their encounter with laughter and embraces. In such contexts, argument can mark the strength of participants' connections to one another.

Speech situations and events

Speech activities as we've described them so far are unbounded. Just as every speech community and community of practice engages in particular speech activities, it has ways of structuring the pursuit of these activities. While arguing, dressing-down, lecturing, gossiping, and preaching are well-defined speech activities, they are further organized in *speech events*: an argument, a dressing-down, a lecture, a gossip session, a sermon. A focus on speech events allows us to consider the ways in which speech activity is embedded in situations – how a particular activity is initiated, how it is structured, how it ends.

In his programmatic article on the ethnography of speaking, Dell Hymes (1972) outlines properties that distinguish speech events within and across communities. He begins with the settings in which particular speech events can take place. Different social situations may call for or license different speech events. In one community, a wake might be a situation in which joke-telling is expected to occur – while in another community this may be completely inappropriate. A cocktail party calls for conversations, the co-presence of acquaintances at a bus stop calls for small talk. In Gwere culture (East Uganda), pre-menarche girls engage in sexual instructional talk with their female peers as they gather firewood (Mukama 1998). The link between the verbal activity and the situations in which it occurs has led the community to refer to these conversations as "collecting firewood" (*okutyaaba*[3] *enkwi*[2] is the Lugwere form).

Situations that call for speech in one culture may call for silence in another culture. For instance, Keith Basso (1972) reports that in the Apache community of Cibecue, Arizona, silence is a culturally specific way to deal with interpersonal uncertainty. He found that when children returned to the community from time away at boarding school, they and their parents observed silence for some time.

2 The superscript "3" indicates a linguistically significant tone.

This was because of the uncertainty posed by the fact that the children could be expected to have undergone change during their time at school. And because of the uncertain nature of the new romantic relationships, courting couples also maintained silence when they were together.

While silence is the appropriate Apache response to uncertainty, in European culture, talk rather than silence is often used to smooth awkward situations. Of course, there are vastly different community norms about how to go about using talk for this purpose. Is it inappropriate to strike up a conversation with a stranger at a bus stop? Or is it rude not to? When is small talk called for, and what are appropriate small talk topics? And what is an appropriate topic of conversation? The weather? The bus service? Your health? Your sex life? Can you tell a joke? And what kind of a joke? Can you ask the other person at a bus stop where they're going? Can you ask their name? And can a woman initiate small talk with a man she doesn't know? Are women more likely to engage in such talk together than men? Can others join in? How long can or should the small talk go on? Does it continue on the bus? These activities are governed by community-specific norms for the speech event *making small talk*. These norms dictate when a particular event can take place, and how it can be initiated. What may constitute a move to initiate a joking session in one community or situation, for example, may start a war in another. And they dictate how the event itself can unfold – who says what, when, and how.

Speech events may be more or less ritualized (invariant from one occurrence to another). The Inuit living a traditional subsistence life, for example, limited conflict talk to specific, and highly ritualized, events called *song duels*. Song duels were carefully planned formal events that brought together the entire community to participate – and adjudicate – as two parties worked out their conflict in the context of a "song contest," in which the parties engaged in a highly stylized exchange of accusations couched in elaborate metaphor. The ritual nature of this event, by bounding the conflict talk in time, space, situation, and verbal style, excised it from daily life and hence made it maximally safe for the community. Similar caution accompanies African American boys' ritual insult activity *playing the dozens* (Labov 1972b) but to a much smaller degree. Since real insults could cause serious conflict, these exchanges, like the Inuit song duels, are carefully excised from normal exchange by ritualized introductions (e.g. "your mother!"), stance, voice quality, and the actual content, phrasing, and development of the insults. Most important is keeping out of the insults material that might be construed as true. Even greetings, which do not necessarily entail further conversation and might seem quite simple, have a clear (often complex) structure that may well differ from community to community. There are differing norms about when a greeting is required, and who should greet first. Is it the outsider or the resident? Is it the people sitting in the café or the new person entering? What does one say in greeting? Judith Irvine (1974) describes the elaborate greeting conventions observed by the Wolof of Senegal. Not only does convention strictly determine when a greeting is called for, but the process of greeting itself is an elaborate negotiation of status with far-reaching consequences. On the other hand, it is common in European peasant communities, where people's paths tend to cross routinely in the course of the day, for greetings simply to mark the relation between activity and time of day. Penny observed a regular cycle of greetings in Soulan, a small village in the French Pyrenees: *as mingeach?* 'have you eaten?' *as mouilluch?* 'have you milked the cows?' *as barrach?* 'have you shut the barn?' – and in those off-moments, *oun bas?* 'where are you going?' will do. Rather than being a real request for information, this last is somewhat equivalent to the greeting sequence common nowadays from some segments of the US population: "whassup?" "not much." Communities of practice commonly have a set of speech events that they engage in on a regular basis, and these events can provide a repeated performance of gender scripts. Elinor Ochs and Carolyn Taylor (1992), for example, studied the speech situation provided by dinner table conversation in several families. They found a recurring speech event that they refer to as "father knows best," in which mothers prod children to recount events in their day for the benefit of their father. Fathers, then, are set up to comment on aspects of their children's (and their wives') activities. Daily engagement in this particular speech event casts the father on a continuing basis in a judge-like role, reproducing one piece of gender asymmetry in the dynamics of these families.

Frames

The same event can be construed as being about many things. What Jill thinks is a lunch meeting with her professor to discuss her dissertation, her professor may see as a date. Erving Goffman (1974) refers to the interpretive schemes that people apply to interaction as *frames*. Conversational frames are not gender-neutral, as people's assessments of situations are often transformed when the gender participation changes. In the year 2000, the *New York Times* reported that a young woman astronomer at a conference tried to join a conversation some men were having on a topic that happened to be in her area of expertise. Noticing her, one of them said to another, "oh, we must be boring this pretty young thing." The young woman was trying to join a speech situation framed as professional talk, but her male colleagues could not envision her in that frame, and when she joined them they reframed the situation as intellectually empty male–female banter. Intentional manipulation of the frame can transform a speech event. Western urban culture has a limited set of speech events that can take place between or among strangers in public places – events that arise from the mobility that characterizes these settings. Asking for public information – locations, directions, services, and the time – is generally allowed among strangers. However, the events in which these requests take place are closely defined and tightly regulated so as to keep them public, to protect the anonymity of the participants. When we need to ask directions on the street in a strange city or neighborhood, for example, we first need to identify a person who is "available." We are unlikely to approach a group engaged in intense conversation, a person sitting in a café reading a book, or someone who is obviously rushing. We are likely to seek out someone that we are certain will know the answer to our query – perhaps a police officer, but not a small child or someone sporting a camera and a guidebook. When we approach them, we first ascertain through a sequence of small moves (often somewhat unconscious moves such as eye contact and changes in gait) that they are indeed available and willing to engage with us. And we protect their anonymity and ours by not providing or seeking private information – we generally do not introduce ourselves or tell them why we need to go to the place they're giving us directions to (although in small communities where anonymity is anomalous, we may be expected to do just those things). Many people, however, can attest to the fact that some people on occasion will attempt to transform the public interaction into a private one by exploiting the state of talk to strike up conversation – perhaps to attempt a pickup. One agrees to engage in a public interaction on the basis of the trust that it is impersonal. But engaging in talk with another can be seen as obligating one to cooperate in conversation, and as the seeker of information takes advantage of the state of talk to move into more personal things – "Are you from around here?" "Are you in a hurry?" – the giver of information often experiences discomfort at challenging the move as a shift of frame. Sexual harassment often plays on the face-threatening character of talking explicitly about frame. It has been a common ploy for sexual harassers, when challenged, to claim innocently that they were just being friendly – or just joking.

Genres

Speech events may call for particular genres: coming out stories, song duels, novels, jump-rope rhymes, rap songs and conference papers. While our focus will be on spoken genres, writing of course also comes in many different genres: reflective essays, historical romance novels, science fiction, poetry, memoirs, self-help books, love letters, research reports, textbooks, newspaper headlines, shopping lists. Genres are conventional text types distinguished on the basis of typical content and internal organization. Particular genres may constrain verbal form or *style* in certain ways. For example, many scientific articles are written according to conventions that promote the use of agentless passives ("ten subjects were interviewed" doesn't say who did the interviewing) and strongly frown on first-person pronouns. Genres in which words and music are joined often make extensive use of repetitive refrains. Such genre-specific stylistic characteristics are closely connected not only to the aims of individual producers in a given genre but also to expectations and ideologies among both producers and consumers of that genre. There is an enormous literature on literary style and within that literature a substantial consideration of gendered authors (and, sometimes, their audiences). Sara Mills (1995) and Terry Threadgold (1997) discuss many of the relevant issues.

Each culture has its own genres. For instance, women's lamentations do important social work in a number of different cultures (see, e.g., Seremetakis 1991, Briggs 1992), but there is no directly comparable genre in most English-speaking societies. And what one might think of as the same genre may differ from one culture to another. A funny joke in France may not go off so well in the US and vice versa. Haiku is a genre of poetry that originated in Japanese culture, as the sonnet originated in England. And the same genre could occur in more than one event. For example, limericks constitute a genre – five-line poems with a closely defined structure of metre and rhyme. Some communities have speech events that are limerick contests, in which individuals vie to compose the best limerick on a particular topic (or more likely, about a particular person). But a limerick may also constitute a single act in a conversation, a joke session – or even an argument. Genres, like the events and the situations they occur in, are differentially available to people on the basis of gender. When women first entered academics, they encountered resistance to their right to deliver lectures. Gender also structures access to written genres and affects their prestige and the kind of social and cultural impact they have. Virginia Woolf offered one account of why women writers were more visible as novelists than as poets:

> A novel is the least concentrated form of art. A novel can be taken up or put down more easily than a play or a poem. George Eliot left her work to nurse her father. Charlotte Brontë put down her pen to pick the eyes out of the potatoes. And living as she did in the common sitting-room, surrounded by people, a woman was trained to use her mind in observation and upon the analysis of character. She was trained to be a novelist and not a poet.
>
> (Woolf 1966; reprinted in Cameron 1998b, p. 49)

Cora Kaplan has suggested that beyond such material constraints, the very conditions of psychosexual development in western societies leave women in an uneasy relation to language, their access to public discourse at best limited. To become a poet, to deal in "the most concentrated form of symbolic language," Kaplan suggests, a woman has to break taboos inculcated very early on (Kaplan 1986; reprinted in Cameron 1998b, p. 63). When Penny was teaching high school, she learned that the head of the English department had censored a very gifted female student for writing love poetry. Labeling it slutty and inappropriate for a young girl, he effectively drove her poetry writing underground.

Some recent feminist scholarship considers the gendered consumption and reception of particular genres. The readers of historical romances, for example, are overwhelmingly women, and works in this genre are often condescendingly dismissed as "escapist trash" that serves to blunt women's critical faculties and to put a false romantic glow on gender arrangements in which women are subordinated to men. Feminist scholar Janice Radway ([1984] 1991), however, argues that women reading historical romances are not simply anaesthetized cultural dopes, but that they use their reading as a form of resistance and also as a way of expanding their knowledge.

Gender-structured access to genres can have quite unforeseen consequences. In tenth-century Japan, only men learned Chinese well enough to produce the kind of serious and recondite literary works in Chinese that were then valued in Japan. Some women, however, wrote tales in everyday Japanese, stories that were thought of as light fare for consumption by women, children, and others who lacked the language and intellectual skills required for appreciating the men's more learned works. But tastes and evaluative criteria change. Today, Lady Murasaki's *Tale of Genji* is still read and is widely considered an extraordinary literary achievement, whereas the works of her more learned male contemporaries have long since been forgotten.

As we define speech situations, events, and genres, we hasten to emphasize that they are not static categories. Like the rest of language, they change over time and new ones arise, while some old ones disappear. A hundred years ago in Soulan, a village in the French Pyrenees, men used to sit around the café and compose raucous, insulting songs about each other. These events, along with the genre that defined them, have disappeared along with the setting that housed the events. While there is still a café in Soulan, it long ago stopped being the exclusive, intimate territory of a local and long-standing community of Gascon-speaking peasants. Coming out stories, on the other hand, emerged fairly recently as a genre (Wong 2001), along with the politicized gay and lesbian communities that legitimate them. Richard Bauman (2001) shows how street vendors in a Mexican market adapt their sales cries to new situations, for example creating more internally elaborate cries for the sale of luxury items. While sermons, university lectures, and parliamentary debates were almost exclusively male events a century ago, they are now more commonly female events as well – and quite possibly transformed as a result.

The pursuit of conversation

Once we have access to the interactions in which important things happen, getting our stuff into the discourse is, of course, not just a matter of blurting out the words. Although we tend to think of the actual pursuit of talk as automatic, conversation is, in fact, a highly structured activity. The structure of talk allows complete strangers to enter into conversations without negotiating how to go about exchanging words; on the other hand, it leaves room for strategy galore – for people to trick and foil each other, to support or undermine, to give each other the floor or to rob each other of words. For this reason, conversational practice has been intensely examined in the study of language and gender. And many a hall of mirrors has been constructed on the conversational terrain. Communicative conventions include conventions to regulate turns at talk. Conventions govern how many people can talk at once and what kinds of talk can take place simultaneously. They govern when it's appropriate to speak and how long it's appropriate to speak. And they include ways of letting others know that one wants to speak – ways of getting the floor. These conventions do not simply provide rules for appropriateness; they provide the material to develop and carry out strategies – ways to get heard, ways to get others heard, and ways to keep others from being heard.

Conversational conventions have been the subject of considerable study for several decades, under the rubric of *conversation analysis*. In English-speaking communities of the northern hemisphere, the prevalent norm for conversation is a sequencing of turns, alternating among speakers, with a minimum of silence between adjacent turns (see, for example, Sacks *et al.* 1974). This norm does not tolerate substantive simultaneous talk in a single conversation, nor does it tolerate long silences. This means that speakers have to be able to manage the alternation between speakers without the use of noticeable silence. Conversational conventions handle some of this work by providing routines for such things as initiating and ending conversations and for signaling that one is coming to the end of one's turn – that one is at a "transition-relevant" place, a point where there might be transition to another speaker (Schegloff 1972, Schegloff and Sacks 1973). Video research (Duncan 1972, 1974) has shown that speakers use a complex and almost imperceptible set of cues to show that they are coming to the end of their turn, and people waiting their turn have a similarly subtle set of cues that show that they wish to take the floor. People thus can orchestrate their conversation in such a way as to avoid serious overlaps or long silences.

For many English-speaking children, the norm of one substantive stream of speech at a time is strongly inculcated. They have it drilled into them not to interrupt, and not to talk all at once. Teachers in school will commonly tell their classes that they can only hear or understand one voice at a time. The truth of this is limited, of course – people in restaurants routinely carry on conversations while eavesdropping on the conversation at the next table. Indeed, a certain amount of simultaneous talk is required in many communities. People are expected to provide evidence that they are attending to the main stream of speech, not only with nods, but with vocalisms: *uh-huh, yeah, really?, no kidding*, etc. This kind of reinforcement is called *backchanneling*, and although it is universally expected in the English-speaking world, the amount and kind expected varies considerably. In general, though, not to provide backchanneling leaves an interlocutor high and dry, wondering if they're being listened to or understood, or if they've said something wrong. Several American studies have found women providing more backchanneling than men (Bilious and Krauss 1988, Roger and Nesshoever 1987, Edelsky and Adams 1990). Why this is so remains unclear. It has been claimed (Maltz and Borker 1982) that women and men use backchanneling differently – specifically that women use the minimal responses *yeah* and *uh-huh* to signal attentiveness, and that men use them to signal agreement. It is further claimed that in male–female conversations, therefore, men tend to mistake women's attentiveness for agreement. While this is an interesting idea, there is, to our knowledge, no evidence beyond the most anecdotal that this particular gender difference really does exist.

Turn-taking conventions are particularly ripe for the study of gender differentiation because they are at the more conscious end of linguistic practice. Turn-taking is regulated from the time one is small – being told not to interrupt, being interrupted, having difficulty getting the floor are all foregrounded for children. Inasmuch as getting the floor is fundamental to having a say in the world, conversational strategies are a fundamental locus of the exercise of power in language.

Interruptions

As we mentioned in chapter two, it is common belief that men interrupt more than women, and that women get interrupted more than men. The first problem in examining interruption in conversation is defining it. In their early study of gender patterns in interruption, Don Zimmerman and Candace West (1975) distinguished between an interruption and an overlap. An overlap occurs when a second speaker begins speaking before the first finishes, but at a point that might be mistaken for a transition-relevant place – for example during the final syllable of what could be a complete sentence. In other words, the overlap anticipates a new turn. An interruption, on the other hand, violates turn-taking conventions, specifically by taking place at other than these "transition-relevant" places. Deborah Tannen (1994) points out that such a definition of interruption, to say nothing of the more mechanistic operationalizations of this definition in various subsequent studies,[3] tends to put a variety of distinct social moves into one category. More particularly, Tannen argues that overlap is often a supportive conversational strategy, enhancing rather than violating a speaker's right to the floor. In her study of ethnic styles in conversation, Tannen (e.g. 1981, 1984) has coined the term "high involvement" to describe a style in which simultaneous talk is the norm. Among people practicing such a style, a person who is allowed to talk "uninterrupted" may feel frozen out rather than supported. The norms of conversation analysis describe white middle-class Anglo-American talk, and are an

---

3 For example, Esposito (1979) established as the criterion for an interruption the cutting off of more than one word.

interesting point of departure for considering other conversational systems. Reisman (1974), for example, observes that conversations on the
island of Antigua commonly involve multiple simultaneous speakers.
A West African man once told Penny that when he went to England to
university, it took him some time to become accustomed to the British
turn-taking system. At the beginning of his studies, he continually felt
as if his peers were uninterested in what he had to say, because they
never joined in while he was talking.

Thus interruption and overlap can be strategies for supporting the
contributions of others, and studies of women's conversational style
(e.g. Coates 1996) have shown that women make considerable use of
this strategy in informal conversation. There has not been enough examination of equivalent men's conversation to establish whether this
constitutes a gender difference, but what evidence there is suggests
that it might be. But it is not only in talking among themselves that
some women make considerable use of overlap. Carole Edelsky (1981)
looked at mixed-sex conversations during faculty meetings and found
both women and men participating roughly equally in very informal
portions of the meetings where there were simultaneously multiple
speakers "on the floor," whereas women's participation was significantly less than men's when the meeting was proceeding in the more
canonical single-speaker at a time fashion.

While overlap can clearly be supportive, it is also true that one person
might interrupt another solely for the purpose of showing dominance.
Models of dominance tend to focus on the dominator, so the actual
overlap is seen as a dominating move. But as Tannen (1994) emphasizes, an interruption takes more than one participant. An interruption
is not complete until the first speaker ceases talking. For a pattern of
interruption to persist, not only does someone have to persist in starting to talk while another is still in the process of getting their ideas
on the table; the interlocutors have to persist in ceding. Such patterns
can develop in relationships and in extended interactions, and if so,
the nature of those interruptions will tell us whether the interruptor
is in fact wielding power over the interruptee.

Certainly there are relationships in which the exercise of conversational power is striking. Pamela Fishman's study (1983) of the private
conversations of several graduate student heterosexual couples stands
as a landmark in the study of male conversational dominance. This
study depicted men dominating their partners through the strategic
use of both silence and interruption. These men not only interrupted
their partners during conversation; they also did not take up their
partners' topics in conversation. The result was that women often failed

in trying to start a conversation on a topic of their choosing. The numbers were viewed as particularly overwhelming in the light of the fact that these couples were selected for the study because of both partners' overt espousal of feminist ideals. While this seems shockingly contradictory at first, one might consider the nature of heterosexual and family relationships. These "private" relationships are a central locus of the gender order, and one might say that all of one's cathected patterns of interaction come to roost in them. Patterns learned from one's parents may surface without the participants even noticing. And worse yet, one's desire for such patterns may hover somewhere in the unconscious. But there is another twist. While the study was published in 1984, the actual tape-recordings were made in the seventies, and these couples were in the vanguard of the new "liberated" generation that was making a concerted effort to move towards equality. But the focus was no doubt on the pairs' pursuit of professional equality – a very highly charged arena – and it is worth considering that the tensions of social change in the professional sphere may have been displaced into the private sphere. Or looking at it slightly differently, it is possible that the couples' private lives lent a feeling of "normalcy" to external arrangements that were still quite anomalous. Kollock *et al.* (1985) found that in heterosexual couples in which the woman had greater professional or class status than the man, the man tended to talk more nonetheless. They attributed this to their finding that men were more resistant to reversals of status hierarchies. In this vein, one might also consider the considerable contradictions in the famous long-term relationship between Jean-Paul Sartre and Simone de Beauvoir. Author of the monumental feminist philosophical work *The Second Sex* and a highly respected participant in the intellectual community she and Sartre inhabited, de Beauvoir nonetheless submitted to an overwhelmingly unequal personal relationship with Sartre. There have been few studies of private interaction of the sort reported by Fishman, and it would certainly be interesting to pursue this line of work (although there are serious questions of research ethics raised by such observations of private lives). The fact remains that in the large preponderance of studies of more public behavior, men have not emerged as interruptors. (See James and Clarke 1993 for a review.) On the other hand, this does not mean that men do not dominate public conversation. People who never get their words in are powerless. People who interrupt constantly, on the other hand, may not necessarily become powerful – but they render (at least temporarily) powerless those they interrupt. The raw display of power in interruption, though, is a very immediate form of domination, and as such is easily recognized. And with recognition comes a loss of that very power. The person with greatest power is the person who does not "have to" interrupt – the person to whom others cede the floor willingly, and interruption can suggest not so much dominance itself but a need to establish dominance. As it turns out, men tend to dominate conversation relatively effortlessly.

The relation between power and conversational dominance is not one-way. In her observations of fifth- and sixth-grade classrooms, Penny noted that the emerging popular crowd produced its own dominance in the classroom by colluding to give its members more quality air time. They listened intently when their members had the floor, laughed at their jokes, answered their questions, responded to their performances. And the members who had the floor called on other members, and so it went. Those with lowly social status, on the other hand, had a harder time getting the floor, and once there received less attention and cooperation. Having the floor, as a result, became less attractive for those without social status, and some tended to gradually slow down in volunteering. Indeed, their status could only be lowered by persisting with the face-threatening unsuccessful attempts to claim public attention. What is important about this observation is not simply that status determines who gets more quality air time, but that the allocation of such air time is central to the actual construction of status – and that that construction is unwittingly a collaborative affair. In the beginning of fifth grade, there was not much of an organized social hierarchy, but as the cohort matured, so did its peer-based social order. And to a great extent, that social order was constructed through the collaborative differential allocation of visibility to those who would emerge as "popular." For many of the kids in the class, the knowledge of the emerging social hierarchy came through observation of this allocation.

Who does all the talking?

Quantity of speech is a dimension of verbal behavior that appears to be socially salient across cultures. As we have seen above, it is common for conventions in speech communities to allocate volubility to particular social situations, or to social categories, and for perceptions of volubility to figure in perceptions of difference among communities. We are all familiar with stereotypes about gender differences in speech quantity in western societies, where women are commonly portrayed as talking excessively and trivially. But does this stereotype actually hold up?

In 1975, Marjorie Swacker did an experimental study in which men and women were given a line drawing of a room to examine, and were then asked to describe the picture from memory. She found two differences in the responses of the male and the female subjects. One item in the picture was a bookcase with a number of books on it. Although the men and women were equally inaccurate in saying how many books were on the shelves, the men were more precise in their statements, for example "there are seven books on the shelf" while the women tended to hedge, for example "there are about seven books on the shelf." The other difference was that the men talked overwhelmingly longer than the women, on occasion having to be stopped by the experimenter as the tape ran out. How are we to interpret this difference in amount of speech? The desirable interpretation at the time, in response to the overwhelming claim that women are blabbermouths, was that it is in fact men who are blabbermouths. But there is also the possibility that men and women respond differently to test situations – that the men felt they were expected to speak at length whereas the women felt they were expected not to. It is possible that the men, in the absence of feedback about the accuracy of their performance, felt constrained to continue in order to improve their performance while the women were less expectant of positive feedback. This line of interpretation does not come simply out of the blue, but out of consideration of the kinds of encouragement that boys and girls get for verbal displays. Penny recalls running into some acquaintances with their small son in an airport. As they waited for their delayed flight, the parents called upon their son to tell them all about dinosaurs. The boy rattled on and on, displaying quite a prodigious knowledge of flying, hopping, and plundering prehistoric creatures. What was more striking than the knowledge, however, was the parents' encouragement of this display – and the observers' relative certainty that this kind of display is far less encouraged in small girls. If this is true, then boys and girls would tend to grow up with different understandings of what is expected of them in conversational situations.

Research on amount of speech shows that not only do men talk more overall than women, but that women and men tend to talk more in different kinds of situations. In a review of the literature on amount of speech, Deborah James and Janice Drakich (1993) found that out of 56 studies of adult mixed-gender interactions, 34 (61 percent) showed males talking more than females overall, while only 2 studies showed females talking more overall. The remaining 20 studies showed either no gender differences (16) or sometimes males and sometimes females talking more (4). The studies that provided these data differed in the nature of the speaking tasks that the subjects were asked to perform. In keeping with the constraints on observation and experimentation, the preponderance of the studies involved formally structured interactions. In 24 of the studies, subjects were given a formal task to accomplish collaboratively. Sixteen of the studies focused on formal situations, such as meetings and classes, with no specific task to accomplish beyond the general business of the encounter. And the remaining 16 studies were based on informal interaction. Male domination of talk was concentrated in the two formal types of situation: men talked more than women in 16 (67 percent) of the task-oriented situations and in 12 (75 percent) of the formal situations, but in only 6 (38 percent) of the studies of informal situations.

James and Drakich account for men's dominance of the formal situations in terms of the social psychological *status characteristics theory* (Berger *et al.* 1977), which offers an account of interaction in terms of the participants' perceptions of their relative social status. Those with greater status will expect – and be expected by others – to perform better. Hence the various parties to the interaction will contribute to the dominance of those mutually believed to have greater status. Status, of course, can be attributed on a variety of bases – global categories such as gender and race – but also on the basis of more specific and locally relevant characteristics. Thus James and Drakich cite a study (Eskilson and Wiley 1976) in which gender difference was neutralized when the experimenter told the participants that a particular one of them had done better on a (bogus) test. (This was not a study of amount of speech, but of leadership in the accomplishment of tasks.) The result was that the designated "experts" spoke more than others regardless of their gender.

One study that focuses not only on amount of speech but on the rhythm or shape of speech shows a dramatic difference in a formal situation. A study carried out at Harvard University (Krupnick 1985) found that in classes taught by men and with a majority of male students, male students spoke two and a half times longer than female students. Female students' participation tripled in classes taught by women. But even when women participated in class discussion, their turns were short – what the author describes as "bursts." Particularly interesting was the observation that men and women tend to speak in "runs," in which long periods of predominantly male talk were followed by short bursts of all-female talk. Lynn Smith-Lovin and Dawn T. Robinson (1992) also found that in mixed-sex group discussions in experimental situations, men tended to take longer turns than women.

Myra Sadker and David Sadker (1985), observing a hundred public school arts and sciences classrooms, found that boys spoke, on average, three times as much as girls, and that boys called out answers eight times as often as girls. They also noted that the teachers were more likely to tolerate calling out from boys than from girls. Inasmuch as behavior in the classroom is under the control of a teacher, it is reasonable to figure the teachers' behavior into any examination of classroom dominance – as well as the behavior of the other students in the room. In what ways is the boys' dominance supported by the overall classroom system? To address this question, Joan Swann and David Graddol (1988) examined videotape of an extended discussion in each of two elementary school classrooms. In both cases, they found boys speaking almost twice as much as girls – in both number of turns and total number of words. This appeared to result in part from two interesting teacher–student dynamics. First, Swann and Graddol found that the teachers' gaze was more regularly on the boys than on the girls. They also found that the teachers were more likely to shift their gaze from girls to boys when a boy's hand went up, than vice versa. It is generally recognized that at least some of the attention boys get in school is a response to their greater likelihood to require control. The teachers' gaze, which may well be part of a possibly unconscious practice of selective surveillance and control, ultimately resulted in the boys' being noticed and called on more often. Additionally, Swann and Graddol found that teachers tended to call more readily on kids whose hands went up early and enthusiastically – and those hands tended to belong to boys.

In her observations of fifth- and sixth-grade classrooms, Penny noticed something that could account for this latter fact. As the cohort moved into preadolescence, they observed new gender norms for public performances. It became "childish" for girls to engage in public clowning – to make raucous jokes, perform funny walks, and do "stupid" things. Boys, on the other hand, continued to gain status for skill in such things. Raising one's hand without knowing the answer, or in order to give a silly answer, was one such antic. As lack of cooperation, and even academic ignorance, was beginning to signal independence for boys, it did not have the same value for girls. Girls, as a result, became unlikely to raise their hands unless they were certain they had a correct answer, which led them to be a bit slower in putting their hands up. It cannot be said that the girls were less confident academically than the boys, but that they were less brash as the social order tolerated less incompetence from them.

Table 3.1. *Average number of contributions to discussion by male and female college students in same- and mixed-sex groups*

	males	females
same-sex groups	25.7	26.8
mixed-sex groups	31.4	24.8

In other words, men in general get their stuff into mixed-sex conversation more than women, at least in most of the kinds of situations studied so far. In same-sex conversations, however, the disparity disappears. Table 3.1 shows data from an experiment reported by Lynn Smith-Lovin *et al.* (1986), in which white college students were given a gender-neutral task to undertake together. In same-sex groups of six participants, males and females made the same average number of contributions. In mixed-sex groups, however, the males contributed more and the females contributed less than in the same-sex groups.

In other words, both male and female participants modify their behavior in the direction of gender-appropriate participation rates when they move into mixed-sex interactions. But what happens once these contributions are put on the floor? There is a general feeling among women in the professions that women's ideas do not get taken up in mixed-sex interactions at the same rate as men's – and that when they are taken up they tend to be attributed to men. There is, in fact, some experimental evidence that this is so. Katherine Propp (1995) organized experiments in which mixed-sex groups of college students were given the task of making a judgment about a custody case. Information about the case was given to the participants, and then they were asked to discuss the case and come to a decision. The experiment was designed so that not everyone in the group had the same information, hence participants were called on to offer up information in the course of the discussion. The experimenters found that new information offered up by male participants was far more likely to be taken into consideration than new information offered by female participants.

What all this adds up to is that in the institutional settings in which official knowledge and decisions are being made, men talk significantly more than women – and their talk is more likely to be taken up. But what of informal situations? Do women make up for their relative silence when they're engaged in the normal give and take of less official conversation? Apparently not. James and Drakich found that in five out of sixteen studies of conversation in informal settings, men were found to speak more than women, while women spoke more than men in only one of these studies.

Speech and silence

It is often said that women are silenced. And we can certainly point to reams of prose through the ages extolling the virtues of silence in women (and their status-mates, children). But silence is not always or only an absence of expression. Speech is, among other things, an absence of silence, and in the interplay between speech and silence, each frames the other. Silence in social situations is never neutral. We talk about awkward silences, ominous silences, stunned, strained, awed, reverent, and respectful silences. Silences take on meaning because in Anglo-American culture, we expect social exchange to involve fairly continuous talk. (Scandinavians, on the other hand, can feel comfortable with extended periods of silence and often find the constant talk expected by American friends quite wearing.) A protracted silence between turns at talk, therefore, signals something unusual. But exactly what it means depends on its discursive history. If Mary is in a conversation with Ellen, and says, "I believe that gender is socially constructed," and Ellen says nothing, how will we interpret her silence? It could mean that she considers the statement so outrageous that she is indicating that she is "speechless." On the other hand, it could mean that she considers the statement so obvious that she is "speechless." It could mean that she is so unfamiliar with the topic that she doesn't know what to say next. Or it could be that she is so overwhelmed by the brilliance of Mary's utterance that she is leaving an awed silence. It could even mean that she's tuned out of the conversation or that she wants to let the topic drop. To know what Ellen's silence means, it helps to know something about the background of the conversation – what Ellen's beliefs about gender are, what has already been said, and so on. Or observation of how the conversation progresses may retrospectively shed light on the significance of that particular silence.

It is not only the right or obligation to speak that is significant for the making of meaning, but also participation as an addressee, or even overhearer. An addressee can be cast simply as a receiver of knowledge and information; or the addressee can be cast as an adjudicator. Norma Mendoza-Denton (1995) has argued that silence was used in the Clarence Thomas hearings to lend weight and drama to Thomas's account of his interactions with Professor Anita Hill, who was accusing him of having sexually harassed her while she was his employee. Examining videotapes of the hearings, Mendoza-Denton measured the

gaps left between Thomas's and Hill's utterances and the following utterance by a committee member. She found a statistically significant
difference in average gap length of 1.386 seconds after Thomas's utterances, and 1.045 after Hill's. These differences were not evenly spread
out throughout the hearings, but used strategically to add weight to
Thomas's utterances, while shorter gaps and rapid changes of topic
kept Hill off-balance. Senators sympathetic to Thomas, according to
Mendoza-Denton, left long pauses after Thomas's dramatic answers,
lending weight and sympathy to these answers. For example (p. 60):

> Thomas: Senator, there is a big difference between approaching
> a case subjectively and watching yourself being lynched.
> There is no comparison whatsoever.
> [gap: 2.36 seconds]
> Heflin: Ah yes [sighs]
> [gap: 1.12 seconds]
> Hatch: I may add that he has personal knowledge of this as well,
> and personal justification ... for anger.

The senators' silence not only contributed weight to Thomas's utterances, but reaffirmed their own authority to accord speech or silence.

Thus, while getting the chance to speak is fundamental to getting
one's ideas into the discourse, sheer amount of talk is not a sufficient measure of the extent to which one's ideas are entered into
the discourse. People with sufficient power will have others speaking
their ideas for them. One measure of status and power is having a
spokesperson – presidents, senators, corporations, and corporation
heads have spokespeople, presumably because they themselves are
spending their time talking to other important people and do not
have time to do the telling. Among the Wolof of Senegal (Irvine 1989),
there is a specific caste whose responsibility is to speak for the nobles.
Known for their high-pitched, fast-talking verbal prowess, the lowly
griots do the verbal work of others but are themselves relatively powerless. Erving Goffman (1974) distinguishes three distinct roles, often
subsumed under the single rubric of speaker: principal, author, and
animator. The principal is the person or persons responsible for what
is being expressed, the author determines the precise wording (ghost-
writers for celebrity authors, speech-writers for busy public figures),
and the animator is the one who actually speaks or writes the words
for audience consumption (spokespeople reading out words provided
by their bosses, actors playing a role, calligraphers inscribing an invitation). The griots are authors and animators for their noble clients,
who are the silent principals.

As we noted earlier, it has often been said that women in traditional cultures get their ideas into public discourse through the men in their families. There certainly are women in history who are famous for having wielded power by commanding the ears of famous men. They might be viewed as principals for whom the men with whom they are intimate act as authors and animators. But there are important differences between, say, a Victorian wife and a Wolof noble. The economic fate of the griot depends on success in representing the noble's ideas; the Victorian husband was under no such constraint. Nor was the Victorian wife credited for her ideas: unlike the Wolof noble, she was not publicly recognized as the principal, the ultimate source of what was said. Indeed, often even the husband or lover voicing her ideas had conveniently forgotten their source. Even today many women in the professions and business report that their contributions in meetings are often ignored until some man repeats them as his own, presenting himself as principal and author when in a real sense he is only animator (though he also becomes principal by putting the force of his own authority behind what he says). And many women continue to exercise their influence mainly out of public view, allowing others to think that they have few ideas of their own. One reason for this behind-the-scenes focus may be that these women recognize that ideas seen as originating with some authoritative man often have more impact than those from a source less fully respected.

Miyako Inoue (forthcoming) has pointed out a conversational participant role that is not normally discussed – the person who subjects the talk of others to an invisible gaze. Phone tappers, peeping Toms, observational researchers and clinicians, people watchers – all are engaged in discursive practice, for they do not simply observe, but enter what they observe into discourse. Inoue discusses, particularly, male Japanese researchers' covert observations of schoolgirls at the beginning of the twentieth century. Because of their status, these observers were able to deliver these girls' behavior to the scholarly and public gaze, and to thereby construct the very social category of "schoolgirl." The normal give and take of conversation engages people in a co-construction of meaning. But as nonparticipants, these men never had to subject their interpretations of the girls' utterances to the test of conversation. Yet the weight of their social status allowed them to enter those interpretations into the public discourse.

The fact that until recently almost all researchers, clinicians, journalists, and writers have been men means that women, like children, have been particularly subject to the non-participatory gaze. It is overwhelmingly men's interpretations of women's behavior and of their words that have found their way into public discourse. This is one important reason why Simone de Beauvoir dubbed women *the second sex.*

Conversational styles and conversationalists' character

Research on gender and conversation among English speakers has tended to emphasize women's strategies for cooperative, supportive talk. Women pick up and build on each other's themes (Kalčik 1975, Coates 1996), they engage in supportive overlap (Eckert 1990, Coates 1993), they provide plentiful backchanneling (Bilious and Krauss 1988, Roger and Nesshoever 1987, Edelsky and Adams 1990). This style has been contrasted with a male style that is said to be competitive rather than cooperative. Men's conversation has been found to involve competitive banter, and to foster hierarchy (Kiesling 1997). Elizabeth Aries (1976), for example, in a longitudinal experimental study of conversation in same- and mixed-gender groups of college students, found that the men established a hierarchy of conversational dominance in their interactions, and maintained that hierarchy in subsequent sessions. Women, on the other hand, spread the talk around more, and if a dominance pattern was established in one session, it was reversed in subsequent sessions. The topics they discussed were also different, and appeared to correspond to the style of talk:

> [M]ales engaged in dramatizing and story telling, jumping from one anecdote to another, and achieving a camaraderie and closeness through the sharing of stories and laughter. Females discussed one topic for a half hour or more, revealing more feelings, and gaining a closeness through more intimate self-revelation. The findings from the content analysis and who-to-whom scoring similarly reflect the themes of intimacy and interpersonal relations for women, and themes of competition and status for men.   (Aries 1976, p. 13)

From the looks of it, the differences between men's and women's conversations are overwhelming. But this needs to be put in perspective. First of all, the data on men's conversation is sparse, and gathered in what one might call ritual situations that may make men feel called upon to render masculine performances: for example, experiments in the case of Aries, and a college fraternity setting in the case of Kiesling.[4] Similarly, one might think women's rap groups such as Kalčik studied

---

4 Kiesling emphasizes the importance of the competitive and hypermasculine environment of the fraternity in the structuring of the interactions he has studied.

Table 3.2. *Women's and men's reports of topics discussed with close friends*

	Discussed frequently		Discussed infrequently	
	Women (%)	Men (%)	Women (%)	Men (%)
personal problems	45	14	50	73
doubts and fears	46	16	49	60
family problems	47	26	51	56
intimate relations	26	8	45	44
sports	18	45	42	40

represent a hyperfeminine environment. And Coates bases her work on women's conversation (e.g. 1996) on recordings of groups of close friends over a long period of time. The result may well be polarized performances from the two gender groups.

Focusing on difference can also have the effect of erasing similarities. Aries and Johnson (1983) emphasize this in their study of adult friend-ships. In this study, Aries and Johnson asked male and female adults to reflect on the topics they discussed on a regular basis with their same-sex best friend. They found that male and female close friend pairs in general discussed the same topics: religion and morals, reminiscences, family activities, personal finances, friendship, social and political is-sues, secrets about the past, community and civic affairs, and work. And men and women alike reported talking little about sex and sexual concerns. The differences came in the stereotypically gendered topics. Women reported discussing personal problems, doubts and fears, fam-ily problems, and intimate relationships more than men, while men reported discussing sports more than women. Women also reported discussing personal problems in depth more than men. These are real differences, but they constitute only the margin of these people's self-reports. Focusing on what's different between women and men, ignor-ing the large preponderance of behavior that is the same, gives the impression that men's and women's concerns and conversations are overwhelmingly different. But it elevates what is a proportional differ-ence at the margins to something resembling an overall difference. As Table 3.2 shows, the difference is not in what men and women talk about, but in how much time they devote to those topics.

The topics that people choose may well reflect their particular responsibilities – and even preoccupations – in the world. And the gendered expectation of such topics may be part of policing these pre-occupations (and may influence the reports people give of themselves).

It appears that women in general do spend more time than men talking with their friends, while men in general spend more time engaging in other activities with their friends. Aries and Johnson (1983, p. 1187) found that the women in their sample were far more likely than men to have phone conversations with their best friends. Half of the women, and only 19 percent of the men reported daily or weekly phone conversations of more than ten minutes. And one quarter of the women and 14 percent of the men reported such conversations at least once a month. And in these conversations, there is some difference in the balance of topics. It is generally said that these differences show women to be more affiliative than men – to seek connection and intimacy. In contrast, these differences are said to show that men are more individualistic and competitive.

The observation that men tend to spend more time with each other engaged in activities other than conversation should not be surprising, given gender norms in our society. Inasmuch as men are rewarded for accomplishments, while women are rewarded for aspects of their "personhood" – their looks, personality, moral qualities – it stands to reason that women will be compelled to talk about, and work on, their personhood while men will be compelled to talk about, and work on, their accomplishments. This in turn speaks to the issues of competition and affiliation.

As discussed in chapter one, a man's personal worth is primarily based on the accumulation of goods, status, and power in the marketplace. A woman's worth, on the other hand, has traditionally been constructed in the domestic realm and has rested on her ability to maintain order in, and control over, her domestic realm, and to develop personal influence. Deprived of public power, women have had to develop personal influence through the construction of moral authority. Thus women's influence has often depended primarily on the accumulation of symbolic capital (Bourdieu 1977b): on the painstaking creation and elaboration of an image of the whole self as worthy of authority. This is not to say that men are not also dependent on the accumulation of symbolic capital, but that until recently symbolic capital has been the only kind that women could accumulate with impunity. While men can justify and define their status on the basis of their accomplishments, possessions, or institutional status, women still often must justify and define theirs on the basis of their overall character, and the kinds of relationships they can maintain with others. Even women who hold high-status positions and who are accumulating material capital for themselves face expectations that they should be "nicer" people than men in equivalent positions, that they should care more about their personal relationships. Women, therefore, unlike men, are frequently obsessed with being the perfect spouse, the perfect parent, the perfect friend. Professional women still often shop for the perfect gift, send the perfect card, prepare the perfect meal.

If men compete for their place in society, so do women, even when that place is conceived of as in the personal realm. However, although women's situation is indeed competitive, they cannot overtly compete in the construction of good personhood. Since good personhood is supposed to be an inherent property, its possession specifically excludes competitiveness or the need for competition. Norms against women's competitiveness stem from two sources, therefore: competition in the marketplace violates men's cultural prerogative, and competition in the personal realm contradicts the underlying definition of personal worth.

While the marketplace establishes the value of men's capital, women's symbolic capital must be evaluated in relation to community norms for women's behavior. The establishment and maintenance of these norms requires regular monitoring, and since it is women who must compete in relation to these norms, it is they who have the greatest interest in this monitoring. To the extent that they can control norms, women can increase their competitive edge. Conversation among women can be said to serve this purpose. While it may forge ties among women, it also works out (and helps enforce) social standards for women.

Interestingly, for many women such talk activity – which not only creates ties but also rankings and exclusions – begins in girlhood around the time that they enter the heterosexual market. In Eckert (1996), Penny describes how two fifth-grade girls she was observing gave up games on the playground to sit aside – very visibly – and "just talk." At first they did not know what to talk about but eventually their talk focused on the developing saga of girl–boy relations. Marjorie Harness Goodwin has detailed some of the verbal activities in which preadolescent and adolescent girls develop cliques, gang up on one another, and shun certain individuals. Girls police and sanction one another's behavior in "he-said-she-said" discussions (Goodwin 1990), and they use clever insults as they shun undesirables (Goodwin 2000). These girls are not constructing a tolerant egalitarian social order but one of peer-based social control in which some are "in" and others are "out."

We emphasize competition in this discussion, not because we believe that women are overwhelmingly or fundamentally competitive, but because we believe that they are every bit as driven to compete as men. Only the domain in which they compete, and the means and form of competition, are different.

There is plenty of evidence that in most US populations there are ways in which women and girls are more hierarchical than their male peers. As boys approach adolescence, they tend to become extremely competitive about a range of things – strength, athletic skill, certain kinds of knowledge, and for some, academic skills. Their competition commonly takes the form of overt one-upping. Girls, on the other hand, move away from these forms of competition, and become extremely competitive about different kinds of things. They develop social hierarchies, manipulating exclusivity through the establishment of cliques, and through active participation in the heterosexual market. This kind of hierarchy is not about particular things, but about global worth on the social market. The behavior constructing this market and the hierarchical rankings on it is not overtly competitive, but consists in a set of activities such as discussion, arguments, and dramatic friendship incidents. These hierarchies are developed over time in discursive practice. Because girls are often not overtly competitive, the resulting rankings emerge in roundabout ways. Rarely, for example, will a girl claim to be prettier than another; but her friends will do it for her.

Popularity, in high school, is the ultimate competitive sphere. Eckert (1990) examined an extended conversation among six high-school girls that ranged from relationships to religion. These were girls who had been good friends in junior high school, but gone their own ways to some extent in high school, and looked upon this conversation as, among other things, a way to catch up with each other. The conversation had all the markings of the "cooperative" style of conversation that has been observed in women's conversations, and the topics covered appear to involve a good deal of self-revelation. In each topic, the girls put their opinions on the floor, and carefully negotiated a common ground – which was necessarily quite often very abstract. For example, given the considerable religious differences in the group from nonbeliever to devout Catholic, the ultimate resolution of the discussion of religion was that everyone must decide what's right for them. But does this consensus-building mean that these girls were trying to forge connections? And if so, what was the purpose of the connections? And does this style of conversation mean that these girls were being noncompetitive? Penny described their engagement as "cooperative competition," concluding that while this conversation may in fact have allowed these girls to touch base and to retrieve some of the closeness of their past relationship it also helped them negotiate their individual symbolic capital. In fact, after the conversation, these girls saw no more of each other than they had before.

As we will see in the next two chapters, it is not just conversational style overall but preferred kinds of speech acts and stances toward what is said that have led many to describe male speech as competitive and individualistic, female speech as cooperative and other-oriented. The implication is often that competitiveness and cooperativeness are fundamental (and sharply opposed) features of male and female personalities or characters, respectively. We have already seen above that some of what is said to mark female connectedness can be understood in a less flattering light as serving to create and maintain social hierarchies. Similarly, what might seem on the face of it to show male competitiveness can sometimes be better understood as fostering positive social connections among members of a group. Comparing girls' and boys' narratives in single-sex playgroups in Reading, England, Jenny Cheshire (2000) found the boys' stories more "collaboratively" constructed than the girls' stories. Boys asked for and got more input from the rest of the group; more than the girls, they spoke in ways that marked their connections to other members of the group, for example recalling shared experiences. As Cheshire puts it, the boys tended to emphasize the telling, whereas the girls tended to focus on the tale, seen more as the property of the individual teller than as a group product. Noting that the same individual might sometimes adopt a "cooperative" and sometimes a more "competitive" style, she observes that "[c]ontradictions and challenges can be labeled as competitive strategies, but this misses the point that, like co-construction, they allow more than one person to join in the telling" (p. 250). Her point is not simply that individuals vary or that gender generalizations are often too hastily drawn. She is questioning the utility of such broadstroke oppositions to illuminate the place of talk in constructing gendered selves and relations. "The idea that women are more inclined to seek connection through their talk with friends whereas men seek separateness ... masks the complexities of conversational interaction" (p. 259).

It may well be that women in many communities are constrained to cloak competition in the guise of cooperation, whereas men are often under pressure to present their search for intimate connections in the form of independent self-aggrandizement. Thus surface style may indeed often look highly gender-polarized (at least in certain kinds of situations). But the deeper substance of people's aims and motives cannot be read off so easily, nor is it likely that aims and motives will prove neatly dichotomized.

We have emphasized that influence in the world depends on getting one's ideas into the discourse, and that ideas get into circulation, and speech patterns become conventionalized, in the course of day-to-day exchange. What kinds of things can be done with words (the subject of the next chapter), by whom, and with what consequence, depends among other things, on who actually gets to talk when, and who attends to this talk. The issue of getting one's words into the conversation, therefore, is a primary one, and it is certainly foremost in many people's minds. However, it is altogether too easy to take a simplistic view of the relation between talk and influence, and to focus on the form of conversation with little attention to the substance (and the effect). If we do this, furthermore, with gendered expectations already governing our observations, we are already well on our way down the hall of mirrors.

CHAPTER 4

Making social moves

When people converse with one another, they are making various kinds of social moves. As we saw in the preceding chapter, this is why conversational access is so important and also why it can be problematic. In this chapter we will look in more detail at different kinds of linguistically mediated social moves, what analysts call *speech acts*. Speech acts are firmly embedded in social practice. Each particular utterance enters into the discourse and into the plans being developed in that interaction and, in turn, into a larger landscape of social practice, including gender practice. The work each utterance does is not a matter simply of its form, its linguistic properties. Each utterance is part of the social situation in which it occurs, and its significance unfolds in the emergent history of the discourse and interaction that it enters. We have seen that gender structures people's access to participation in situations, activities, and events, hence to their opportunity to perform particular speech acts legitimately. In this chapter, we will see how the acts themselves accomplish gender.

Talk is often thought of as quite distinct from action. "He is a man of action, not words." "She's all talk, no action." (The pronouns here reflect language and gender ideologies familiar to many English speakers.) A sharp dichotomy between talk and action is, however, problematic. It is true that simply to say "Let's have lunch together sometime soon" need not result in any lunchtime meeting. Perhaps the utterance is in some way a figure of speech, the overt literal proposal to have lunch not really intended to lead to a lunch but just to indicate that the relationship between the interlocutors should be seen as continuing to be cordial. Even in such pro forma cases, however, the words do something. What precisely those words do on any particular occasion of their utterance depends on the social relations of the people who are talking and on what they are doing together, both during this interaction and more generally. Perhaps one reason that people are sometimes tempted to identify talk with inaction is that words alone really do not do anything. Their often considerable force derives from their being embedded in social practice. Not surprisingly, that force is implicated in gender practice in complex ways.

A speech act is a move in a continuing discourse among interactants. Like other acts, it moves their relationship along one more step, moves their mutual connection to ideas and ideologies, and it moves their accomplishment of things in the world as well. A move can be a compliment, a complaint, an insult, a request, a command, a criticism, a question, a one-up, an exclamation, a promise – these are some of the kinds of speech acts that linguists and philosophers have discussed. We will sometimes refer to them as *social moves* in order to emphasize their place in a larger discourse and as part of socially-oriented plans and strategies. But we also refer to them as moves because there are meaningful interactive moves, such as waving, raising one's eyebrows or handing someone a pen, that do not use language and are thus not speech acts as ordinarily understood. As we saw in the last chapter, conversational conventions can make silence a meaningful social move. It might insult or compliment. It might or might not be accompanied by meaningful facial expressions or other bits of "body language" (which also, of course, can accompany speech). Sometimes we will talk about speech acts when we really mean communicatively significant social moves more generally. That is, our interest is in meaningful interactive moves that often – perhaps canonically – involve speech but may also be made in other ways. The gendered division of labor can mean that certain kinds of speech acts are seen as more the province of one sex than the other or that particular ways of performing them enter into gender practice, or that their effect is different depending on who performs them.

Repeated moves of a particular type can grow into an activity – a series of one-ups can become a competitive conversation, a series of complaints can become a gripe session, a series of criticisms from one person to another can become a dressing down, a series of statements on some topic uttered by the same person can become a lecture.

Speech act theory

Philosopher J. L. Austin (1962) initiated the systematic study of *speech acts* in his well-known exploration of "how to do things with words." To undermine the view that speech and action are opposed to one another, Austin drew attention to what he called *performative* utterances. A person with the proper institutional authority, he pointed out, can say "you're hired!" and *thereby* give a job to the addressee. The utterance itself, given the proper institutional setting and a speaker authorized to produce it, brings it about that the addressee has indeed been hired. Those words start a chain of events that will, if the addressee accepts the offer, lead to the addressee's showing up for work and getting a paycheck some time thereafter. Hiring and firing, naming boats and babies, pronouncing judgments in a courtroom, marrying two people or joining them in a domestic partnership: verbal performances are central to doing such things. And, of course, we have already observed in the last chapter that gender often affects which people will be institutionally empowered to bring off particular kinds of verbal performances. Although Austin (like most analytic philosophers of his era) generally spoke of individual speakers as if their social identities and relations to one another were irrelevant to their status as speakers (or, more generally, as actors), he spoke of overt performatives like *promise* or *christen* as "trouser words,"[1] gendering the notion of performativity at its birth.

As we noted in chapter one, gendering people can be thought of as accomplished through a series of acts, many of them linguistically mediated. "It's a girl," pronounces the medical professional at the moment of birth, and indeed it is thereby made a girl and kept a girl by subsequent verbal and nonverbal performances of itself and others. In developing the performative theory of gender mentioned in chapter one, Judith Butler (1990) draws inspiration (and nomenclature) from Austin's theory of performative utterances. Butler develops Austin's important insight that performativity is not just a matter of an individual's wanting to do something by saying something. Verbal as well as other performances come off, acquire their meaning, and do their work, because they draw on discourse histories of similar performances, reiterating elements that have worked similarly in the past. In that reiteration, however, there is the possibility of individuals going beyond the constraints of the social or linguistic system they have inherited, perhaps ultimately thereby contributing to changing it. As Butler (1990, p. 145) puts it, "In a sense, all signification takes place within the orbit of the compulsion to repeat; 'agency', then, is to be located within the possibility of a variation of that repetition." (We will return to Butler's ideas about performativity in chapter nine.) Austin focused on the speaker's agency but later work has emphasized that what speakers can do with their words is constrained (though not fully determined) by linguistic and other social conventions.

---

1 Trousers were at that time very much masculine apparel and symbolized authoritative action. Compare "she wears the pants in that family," a line often used in the same era to criticize a woman who wielded what the speaker saw as inappropriate authority in her household, usurping the place of the legitimate pants-wearer, the man of the house.

Not all utterances affect the world as dramatically as overt performatives like "I hereby pronounce you husband and wife" (when uttered by a person licensed by the state to perform marriages). Nonetheless, Austin observed, all utterances are indeed actions. He distinguished three different kinds of acts involved whenever someone says something. There is a *locutionary* act. The speaker produces an utterance – a stream of sound or hand gestures or marks on a page or computer screen – *as* a particular linguistic expression with a particular structure and (literal) meaning. The locutionary act sets the stage for the *illocutionary* act, what is done *in* saying whatever has been said. Have you claimed something or inquired? Have you promised or threatened or warned? Invited or implored or commanded? Expressed your anger or your pleasure? Praised or criticized? Apologized or empathized or complained or teased? In saying something and meaning something by it, a speaker always performs one or more such illocutionary acts. There will also be *perlocutionary* acts accomplished *by* saying something. You may persuade someone of your views, frighten or annoy them, cheer them up or comfort them, move them to some kind of action of their own (e.g. to follow your suggestion or respond to your request), impress them with your wisdom, fan their love of you.

The literature on speech acts (e.g. Searle 1969) generally focuses on illocutionary acts (e.g. promising or requesting). If we just pay attention to illocutionary acts, however, the social character of speech acts may be underrated. To come off, to work, it looks as if an illocutionary act needs only to be comprehended (assuming that certain preparatory conditions are met). So, for example, if the speaker is giving a party at some future time and says "Please come to my party," then the addressee who understands what is said is thereby invited to the party. The addressee does not have to welcome or to accept the invitation, but it has successfully been issued. Comprehension is not trivial, of course. The speaker cannot always guarantee that the interpreter will figure out the illocutionary point of what has been said: whether, for example there is just a report offered by "I'm thirsty" or a further request for a drink. But generally, if the illocutionary point is understood, then the illocutionary act has been performed. (This assumes that the speaker is indeed empowered to perform the illocutionary act in question, not always a safe assumption.) Perlocutionary acts, however, are inescapably social: their coming off as the speaker intends requires very active participation from the addressee – for example the addressee's coming to the party or getting a glass of water for the speaker. Perlocutionary acts have to do with effects that go far beyond simple understanding. It is obvious that gender and other aspects of social standing will affect success in performing intended perlocutionary acts. It is less obvious but also true that gender and other social attributes of speakers may enter into success in getting particular locutionary and illocutionary acts to come off as intended.[2]

In our everyday taxonomies, illocutionary and perlocutionary acts are not so sharply distinguished as this discussion might suggest. For example, a threat and a promise are two different kinds of illocutionary act. But they both commit the speaker to some future course of action. They are distinguished only by whether or not the addressee is presumed to be negative or positive about the speaker's commitment. The person who aims to threaten intends to scare the addressee in contrast to the promiser, who aims to please. Scaring and pleasing are distinct desired perlocutionary effects. The same words may be a threat addressed to one person and a promise addressed to another. You cannot tell if someone is threatening someone else by simply observing what words are uttered. And indeed a speaker may be neutral as to whether the addressee will welcome the commitment made, simply expressing the commitment with no intention to scare or to please. English words for speech acts often convey information about both the kind of illocutionary act and the perlocutionary effects the speaker hopes to produce.

There is a large literature on apparently gendered speech acts or speech act types: for example compliments, apologies, insults, one-ups. As we observed earlier, research in this area has probably raised at least as many questions as it has answered. To try to sort out some of the issues involved and think about how research might usefully develop, we find it useful to see speech acts as kinds of social moves that are part of larger, socially accomplished plans of action. We will expand this idea below. First, however, we want to talk about interactional purposes and effects at a very general level.

Functions of talk and motives of talkers: gender oppositions

In chapter one, we saw that gender is overwhelmingly conceptualized in terms of oppositions and in the preceding chapter we looked at

2 Inequality of various kinds among speakers can affect interpretation so that even if comprehension is all that is needed it might not be forthcoming in some situations (e.g. from someone who thinks that the speaker is not fully competent linguistically or is ignorant of some fact relevant for interpretation). The importance of interpretation and its social character are central themes throughout this book.

gender-polarized characterizations of conversational style: cooperative or other-oriented versus competitive or individualistic. The same or closely related oppositions are also advanced to describe gender differentiation in linguistic politeness and, more generally, speech-act usage. Thus women are said to be more polite – to use more polite language – than men; and this is said to be because they are more other-oriented, more collaborative, more affective. Such oppositions are in many ways an advance over views of women as simply ineffective speakers who deviate from the (effective) norm set by men's speech. But these polarized oppositions, however appealing we may find their more flattering view of women, are ultimately as problematic as the deficit views of women's speech that they replaced. And from a linguistic perspective, notions such as politeness and affectiveness are completely undefined. How do we identify them in our linguistic data? Is the utterance *thank you* always a polite speech act? How about when it is uttered as a response to the refusal of a favor?

Politeness

Penelope Brown and Stephen Levinson (1987) have developed a theory of politeness that builds on Erving Goffman's (1967) ideas about face-work (discussed in chapter three), and that has been very influential in work on gender and politeness. What Brown and Levinson are trying to do is articulate a theory that will shed light on general principles of politeness while also showing how it can differ cross-culturally and offering a framework for doing comparative work on politeness. Each individual, they argue, has ongoing interests in promoting their *positive* face: projecting a self that is affiliated with others, that is liked and identified with, part of a "we." Each individual also cares about their *negative* face: projecting a self that is a separate individual, someone deserving of respect and freedom from imposition, someone whose own interests have intrinsic value.[3] An individual's positive face needs have to do with need for approval from others, for a sense of being liked by others, of being connected to them. Negative face needs have to do with a need to make a place for oneself, a need to pursue one's own projects without interference from others, a need to have one's own distinctive individuality recognized and respected. Positive and negative face needs are in tension with one another. The more closely

---

3 Brown and Levinson's labels "positive face" and "negative face" are inspired in part by Durkheim's (1915) positive and negative rites, along with insights derived from Goffman.

connected we are and the more like one another we see ourselves as, the harder it may become to protect our own and others' needs for separateness and independence of action. The more respect we receive, the more recognition of our autonomy, the more difficult it may be to forge intimate bonds linking us to similar others. Brown and Levinson suggest that people typically have a better chance promoting their own face interests if they also attend to others' face interests. Although they don't put it this way, it may be most important to *seem* to care about helping others preserve and enhance their face needs, whether or not one in fact does care.

What Brown and Levinson call *positive politeness* involves addressing positive face needs: showing that you like or empathize with someone, that you include them in your "we," your "in-group." Commiserating with one another about common problems (interfering parents or a shared obnoxious boss), admiring the other's taste in clothes by commenting approvingly on their attire, friendly joking and playful banter marked by profanity and familiar terms of address (*sweetie, you old sonofabitch*): such speech moves can exemplify positive politeness.

Much of the behavior that ordinary folk call polite, however, is a matter of what Brown and Levinson categorize as *negative politeness*: showing respect or deference, avoiding imposing or offending, acknowledging "rights." Apologies, for example, often try to correct a social wrong done to another, thanks typically acknowledge that another has been willing to extend themselves for one's own good, greetings and farewells offer formulas to ease the strain created for face by the beginning and ends of interactions. Such speech acts and other linguistic practices such as the use of relatively formal modes of address and reference (*sir, madam, professor*) often convey negative politeness.

Although certain kinds of speech acts do tend to be used to promote positive face and others to protect negative face, the connections are not as straightforward as they might at first seem. Brown and Levinson emphasize that politeness does not lie simply in forms as such but in what speakers use those forms to do. Of course, forms are not irrelevant to politeness. There are, for example, often verbal formulas that are used to mark speech as conventionally "polite": many a child acquiring English has learned the magic powers of "please" as an accompaniment to a request. "Please" conventionally signals recognition that the request imposes on the addressee, that the speaker cares about this potential harm to the addressee's negative face and wants to mitigate the imposition. Politeness formulas are often aimed at least as much at promoting the speaker's face as protecting the addressee's. Following relatively rigid conventions for how one should speak in particular kinds of situations can be an important part of establishing one's own right to respect, showing that one is in the know on social norms. Similarly, flouting conventions can be a way to show that one is not socially controlled by those who promote those conventions. For example where certain politeness routines have been associated with mothers and women teachers, boys may avoid them as part of presenting themselves as independent of that female authority.

On the basis of extensive ethnographic fieldwork in Tenejapa, Mexico, Brown (1980, 1990) argued that the women of Tenejapa did more to promote others' face needs, both positive and negative, than did the men. Brown had not expected much negative politeness from women to other women because in Tenejapa women's subordination to men in general and to the particular men in their own households was strongly institutionalized. But she describes women's relations to one another as far more complex than she had predicted. She hypothesized that the women needed to show both negative and positive politeness to one another because of their extreme vulnerability to one another, their heavy reliance on the good will of other women in their household and in the village.

It is not always easy to classify speech acts as promoting positive or negative politeness or neither. Brown and Levinson's distinction is not exactly the same as one between that which aims to make another feel good and that which aims to lessen the bad feelings someone might have, to repair actual or potential damage to someone's face. There is also a further socially crucial distinction between saying and doing things to promote one's own face needs and saying and doing things to promote someone else's. Frequently, of course, the same action is intended to play both roles, perhaps even promoting one's own face needs by means of promoting the other's. But *considerateness* requires attention to the other's face needs, whereas politeness as often discussed in the literature may or may not. What looks like the same kind of act – for example a compliment – might be positively polite in one context but not in another. Sometimes it might be a considerate move to make, other times not. (Presumably, when a move is not considerate, it is not really positively polite.)

Drawing on her own and others' research on gendered distribution of a number of different kinds of speech acts, Janet Holmes (1995) argues that women tend to be more (linguistically) polite than men. She found, for example, women complimenting (and also being complimented) more than men. She also found women apologizing (and also being apologized to) more than men. Compliments she treats as positively polite, apologies as negatively polite. In other words, compliments are seen as aimed at making someone feel liked by others, connected to them. Apologies are seen as making someone feel that due attention has been given to their interests and rights, that others respect them. Holmes and her New Zealand colleagues had observers listen as they went about their affairs and write down the first twenty instances of utterances they heard as speech acts of the designated kind. This method represents a considerable advance on earlier studies in the US that relied on questionnaires rather than observation of naturally occurring speech acts. Although we can ask on what grounds observers decided that a compliment or an apology had been proffered (recall from chapter one how a baby's cries can be heard differently, depending on whether one thinks it is a girl or a boy), Holmes's results and those of a number of other investigators whose work she discusses strongly suggest that women predominate as both initiators and recipients of certain kinds of "polite" speech acts among the populations studied (mainly New Zealand and US middle-class people of European descent). Can we conclude that these women are more considerate than the men with whom they live and work? More interested in strengthening social ties, in promoting solidarity? More concerned to be seen as "nice"? Less "sincere"? Even if we assume that the data represent communicative patterns among these groups fairly accurately, accounting for the observations is not so straightforward.

What sort of self a person presents in a particular kind of situation and how they ratify the other's self-presentation will often be implicated in constructing gender. Holmes takes the fact that men apparently direct more instances of conventionally "polite" acts towards women to indicate their recognition that women value these acts more highly than do men. An alternative explanation might be that (at least some) men want to project a masculinity that takes a "protective" stance towards women, constructing women as especially vulnerable creatures in need of special handling. And, of course, both kinds of motives might be involved, sometimes even for the same man.

Unlike the work by Holmes and her colleagues, much earlier studies of politeness in service interactions in The Netherlands (Brouwer *et al.* 1979 and Brouwer 1982) found no difference linked to the speaker's sex (as judged by the data collector). Like Holmes's work, however, the Dutch studies did find significant differences linked to the sex of the addressee. But the results go in the opposite direction from those found in the New Zealand studies. Brouwer and her colleagues looked at what people said to ticket-sellers in a large train station and in this public service context found significantly more polite speech to male ticket-sellers than to female from customers of both sexes. Notice that differences which depend on the addressee's sex, however they are to be explained in particular cases, do point dramatically to the very social character of gendered facework, which is always framed in relation to the other participants in an interaction.

To evaluate research on gendered patterns of politeness, it is critical to see how each researcher has operationalized the notion of politeness. Is it a matter of the incidence of particular forms? Are the forms in one study comparable to those in another? In what kinds of social contexts are observations being made?[4] If it is a matter not of forms as such (e.g. *please, thank you*) but of speech act types like compliments or apologies, then it is important to understand how those act types are identified and in what circumstances they are produced as well as the form they take. Essentially the same kind of act can be performed very differently in different situations or by different people. And, like other features of conversational practice, politeness cannot be understood by looking just at isolated individual moves or speech acts. Compliments and apologies, for example, ask for responses from their addressees. Responses offer important evidence of the kind of facework accomplished by the speech acts eliciting them, a point that Robert Herbert (1990) emphasizes in his treatment of complimenting in gender practice.

Each community of practice develops its own expectations about the facework participants will do on their own behalf and for the other members of the community, often allocating differential responsibility for facework to different members of the community. There may also be expectations about the kinds of means chosen to do that facework and how to balance the demands of facework with the other kinds of things done in talking. What kinds of performance are possible? The "separate cultures" view of gender discussed in chapter one proposes that many people spend significant and formative periods engaged in single-sex communities of practice. These separate contexts for developing expectations about what is expected in the way of facework are then thought to explain gender-differentiated patterns emerging in mixed-sex communities of practice. Certainly gender separation at critical developmental stages is likely to be significant for various kinds of expectations people have of themselves and of others. In the case of

4 The Dutch study looks only at exchanges between strangers in service transactions, whereas many other studies have included exchanges between acquaintances and even intimates. Wolfson (1984) proposes that facework is done most between acquaintances and is far less consequential between intimates, whose relation is presumably settled, and between strangers who do not expect to encounter one another again. There is, she argues, a "bulge" in politeness at the middle distance. Holmes (1995) suggests that Wolfson's bulge model fits better with her observations of women than of men.

gender separation within a community, however, we have to keep in mind that those in each group are very much aware of the existence of the other group. Even more importantly, they are typically exposed to gender ideologies and gender-differentiated allocations of rights and responsibilities in mixed-sex communities of practice (e.g. many families) during the same period that they are gender-segregated for many peer activities. Differences that might emerge in "politeness" expectations for women and for men (and in tolerance of failure to meet expectations) almost certainly have multiple sources and implications for gender practice far beyond mere marking of "difference."

Affective and instrumental talk

Janet Holmes, who has done a lot of empirical work on gendered ways of talking among English speakers, associates women's putatively greater attention to (politeness-oriented) facework with a greater interest in the *affective* function of talk. The affective function of talk covers both the overt expression of emotion ("How sad," "Damn it," "What a sweetie/bastard he is") and everything that has to do with the maintenance of social relations. It is generally contrasted with the *referential* or *instrumental* function, conveying information (presumably about things other than emotional states) or trying to establish "facts" or get things accomplished. As Holmes recognizes, virtually all utterances serve both affective and referential functions. Indeed, these functions interconnect in many intricate ways. Making you feel good by complimenting your attire may be a move that is part of my strategy to elicit certain information I need from you in order to clinch a business deal. Or, conversely, reporting to you on certain facts may be a way to strengthen my social bonds to you, to convey that I like you.

The affective/instrumental split has long been associated in the US and many other English-speaking societies with a female/male division of labor not only in talk but also in many other kinds of social activities. Interestingly, however, people often ignore negative affect (e.g. anger) in endorsing this gendered view of social life. They often also ignore certain kinds of instrumental activities, especially what Eva Feder Kittay (1998) calls "dependency work": caring for small children, the sick and elderly, and others who require near constant assistance. This work is frequently seen not as work but as just the outpouring of love; not surprisingly, it is also seen as women's bailiwick. Caretakers have to pay great attention to getting things done: cleaning up after the incontinent elderly, bathing screaming (and slippery) babies, changing sickbed sheets. Although affection for their charges may keep them going, caretakers' primary focus very often must be instrumental, how to accomplish the tasks before them. Viewing women as "naturally" more concerned with affective matters and men with instrumental not only tends to devalue women's social contributions but also to steer people towards kinds of activities on the basis of gender rather than talents or inclination.

Not surprisingly, (male) instrumentality is associated with reason and (female) affect with emotion. But along with the mind–body dichotomy, the reason–emotion split has been challenged in recent philosophical and neuropsychological work.[5] Affect seems to play a particularly important role in moral reasoning and in social cognition. Although it is less clear that it usefully enters into debate in mathematics and the natural sciences, there is some evidence that it may usefully suggest lines of scientific inquiry and testing, as Evelyn Fox Keller (1983) has argued in her widely read biography of the Nobel prizewinning biologist, Barbara McClintock. In other words "a feeling for the organism" or some other "feeling" may help one find evidence to use in arguing for a completely new view in a particular arena. This does not mean that science is "about" scientists' feelings. It does suggest, however, that the image of the scientist as the "man of pure reason" is problematic for a number of reasons.

Of course, there are some clear cases of speech acts whose primary function is to express or affect someone's emotions ("Oh, shit!") and others whose primary function is to transfer information about some practical matter or to bring about some practical end ("Fire!"). In general, however, the affective and instrumental are closely intertwined, making the distinction of somewhat dubious value in mapping gendered patterning in speech. Nonetheless, a number of analysts have endorsed this or similar characterizations of gendered ways of doing things with words.

Intimacy and autonomy, cooperativeness and competitiveness

As we mentioned in chapter two, Deborah Tannen (1990) is one of the most widely read accounts of the gendered division of the work done by talk. Tannen characterizes women as most interested in promoting *intimacy* with others, in strengthening affiliative bonds among people, in promoting solidarity. Men, in contrast, are seen as most interested in establishing their independence from others, their *autonomy*. Although it is clear that many men want considerable intimacy and many women considerable autonomy, it is also clear that many women and men think that these stereotypes represent some kind of norm that they probably "ought" to fit. This is one reason that Tannen's and similar oppositional frameworks resonate so well for lots of readers. And it is probably one reason that we do find women and men favoring certain ways of doing things with words.

Once again, we enter the hall of mirrors. There is a powerful normative view in western industrial societies that women are (or should be) interested in connections to others and in promoting warm feelings all the way around (positive "affect"). And men are normatively disinterested in other people and in feelings. Men are supposed to focus instead on their individual aims and accomplishments, what they can do on their own. So women in these societies have powerful motives to appear affiliative and eager to promote the right kind of warm fuzzy feelings, to downplay their individual aims and ambitions. Men, in contrast, have powerful motives to appear strong and impassive, to mask emotions other than anger and to hide quests for intimacy with others. But appear to whom? Normative gendered appearances are produced not only for others but also for oneself. These norms also link directly to other features of the gender order: distribution of social responsibilities and of kinds of prestige and power.

As we mentioned in the preceding chapter, Tannen and a number of other analysts (e.g. Coates 1996) have also suggested that women work to constitute an egalitarian social world, one where horizontal ties predominate. In discussing this claim critically, we cited work of Marjorie Harness Goodwin that makes it clear that girls do indeed engage in many verbal activities that function to make and enforce social divisions. Yet it is Goodwin's ethnographic work with working-class African American children in Philadelphia (1980, 1990) that is probably most frequently called on to support claims that males engage in speech acts that build hierarchies whereas females speak in ways that build egalitarian societies. Goodwin did find boys engaged in a task-oriented activity both commanding ("gimme . . .") and seeking permission ("can I . . ."): hierarchy was being constructed during that particular activity though the rankings created often vanished with the end of the particular activity. The girls she observed in a similar activity with one another were far less likely to speak from either a commanding or a subordinate position. They more often framed directives as suggestions or proposals for joint action ("Let's . . . ," "Why don't we . . ."), rather than as commands. And the girls seldom requested permission from one another. Some girls did indeed lead more often than others, but their relatively greater influence (which might persist over many encounters) was not reflected in the form of directive exchanges between them and the other girls. Interestingly, however, the girls did issue downward-directed commands in some of their interactions with boys, showing clearly that their failure to do this with one another was not a matter of the absence of such moves from their repertoires. But among themselves hierarchy could not be so overtly manifested. Many have picked up on the striking gendered difference in directive form Goodwin uncovered and ignored the rest of the story that she and others have elaborated, establishing that American girls do indeed contribute at least as much to creating social hierarchy as their male peers.

Nor do all girls avoid overt competition or confrontation. African American communities of practice tend to place high value on skills in verbal jousting. In chapter three, we mentioned the African American ritual insult event *playing the dozens*, which is engaged in primarily by boys. While women and girls may not engage in protracted insult events, they do engage in a variety of confrontational exchanges. *Signifying*, or using a variety of types of indirection to make a point, is a common verbal strategy used by virtually everyone in the African American community. And many women do not shrink from the kind of spirited exchanges that can emerge with signifying – exchanges that would intimidate the average "nice" white girl. Claudia Mitchell-Kernan (1972) writes about an illustrative interaction between herself and an unknown man:

| Man: | Mama, you sho' is fine |
| Mitchell-Kernan: | That ain' no way to talk to your mother. |

The significant point of this illustration is that Mitchell-Kernan (and, by implication, many black women), rather than shrinking from the man's advance, engaged in repartee that resisted his advances without shrinking from them. Mitchell-Kernan (1969) also discusses *loud-talking*, in which someone raises their voice to make someone else's "business" public. African American girls and women can commonly be seen employing this strategy for humorous purposes, as well as for the purpose of sanctioning inappropriate behavior. Marjorie Harness Goodwin (1990) looked at the verbal activity of *instigating* in which conflict between young African American girls was initiated through talk to third parties. African American girls and women do get significant experience in various kinds of competitive interactions (not always arguments) that manage to stay fairly self-contained. In contrast, many

American girls and women who are not of African descent find that competition and confrontation – even where clearly engaged in as play (e.g. sports) – tends to threaten personal relations and feelings beyond the arena in which it originates.

Amy Sheldon's (1992) examinations of young middle-class European American children engaging in a struggle during their play together found the girls making attempts to negotiate, to recognize others' needs while at the same time still pressing their own position, for which they often offered reasons. In contrast, the boys tended to engage in physical tussles over possession rights, raising their voices rather than looking to reasons to persuade the others of their position. Sheldon describes the young girls she observed as skilled in a "double-voice" discourse which recognizes both the speaker's agenda and that of her interlocutor and that attempts to offer courses of action that might satisfy both. Together with Diane Johnson, she suggests that organizations might look to these girls for models on how conflicts among adults might best be handled (Sheldon and Johnson 1994). Parents often describe the boys as troublesome and argumentative and the girls as "nice," fostering practices among the girls of lots of repair work for any possibly damaged feelings. Focusing on repair can, paradoxically, increase the chance that bad feelings persist. And some women reach adulthood having constructed themselves as "nice girls," where being "nice" is incompatible with trying to "win" over someone else – or at least with appearing overtly to be doing so. Even the women who don't so construct themselves risk having such norms applied to them. As a number of feminist commentators have observed, Hillary Clinton has been often reviled for her "ambition" while there is a notable absence of similar comments about men with comparable goals.

We would suggest that girls who are not of African descent might have a lot to learn from their African American sisters about confidence and standing up for themselves. But girls' confrontational activity gets ignored because the egalitarian/hierarchical divide fits so well with the contrast between a focus on the well-being of others and a focus on one's own projects and achievements. Observers stand ready to interpret women's activities as showing their cooperative and egalitarian natures, men's as demonstrating their competitiveness and their capacity for leadership. And girls and boys, women and men, are eager to project themselves in socially approved modes. But as we noted in the preceding chapter, careful analysis of actual conversational interactions suggests far more polarization in interpretation and in superficial form of social moves than in underlying aims or characters of female and male speakers.

There are cultural contexts where neither the affective/instrumental division of linguistic labor nor the related gender polarities like cooperative/competitive would ever have seemed gendered in the ways so many investigators of English speakers have found appealing. Among the Malagasy of Madagascar, Elinor Ochs Keenan (1974) found that it was men who were seen as attending to other people's sensibilities. The men observed proprieties in speaking even when doing so might make it hard for them to say what was needed for practical purposes. Women's speech was seen as blunt and to the point, effective for certain purposes (e.g. interacting with westerners) but lacking in finesse and tact.

Speech acts embedded in social action

For some time now, speech act theorists have talked about speech acts as parts of larger plans for collaborative social action.[6] Our everyday taxonomies of speech acts take account of both content and form conditions. A promise must convey something about a future action of the speaker (or of someone over whom the speaker can assume control). One canonical promise form is to say "I promise to...," but uttering countless other forms with the right kind of content can do the trick of making the required commitment (in appropriate circumstances). "I'm baking a cake tonight" or "You'd better eat lightly at lunch because there'll be cake tonight": these or a host of other utterances might count as a promise to provide the addressee with cake before another day rolls around.

Beyond content and form there are also overtly intended effects on the interactants. A promise represents a commitment undertaken by the speaker with the overt aim of benefiting the addressee. Sometimes the future commitment is undertaken in order to avoid doing what the addressee wants at the present time. "I'll give you a cookie after you finish your sandwich," says the parent who is trying to get some nourishing food into the recalcitrant child screaming for a cookie. In these circumstances, this utterance would probably count as a promise. (Of course, it might also be described as a bribe!) The promise fits into the larger pattern of the parent–child interaction.

---

6 There is a large literature on speech acts as components of plans, much of it developed in conjunction with work related to artificial intelligence. See, e.g., Thomason (1990). There has been little contact in either direction between this quite abstract and theoretical work on speech acts and the tradition of empirical investigations of language in social life.

Once made, the parent's promise becomes one of the child's interactional assets. "You promised!" can be an effective protest from the child if the sandwich is eaten and the cookie is not forthcoming. Exactly what effects any particular move of promising might have will depend on many other features of the particular interaction and also on how such moves are viewed more generally.

Compliments are one kind of "named" speech act type in English that is widely seen as gendered. We use them to illustrate some very general points about the gendering of speech acts and social moves. Like all kinds of social moves, compliments have a host of different social functions and possible motivations. These functions and motivations may not always easily coexist and can often be interpreted quite differently by interactional participants. Compliments are also loaded with cultural values and associated with cultural norms that are by no means uniform across the English-speaking world.

What is a compliment?

Compliments are social moves that live in a landscape of evaluation. They convey, explicitly or implicitly, positive appreciation of some thing or action for which the addressee may apparently be credited: appearance, achievements, possessions. Criticism and insults inhabit the negative area of this same landscape. In the positive neighborhood, we find not only compliments but also such moves as praise and approval. Unlike praise or approval, however, compliments are not offered solely as evaluative moves. Compliments are also presented as moves that take good care of the target's positive face, as "stroking" in American vernacular. This explicitly other-directed affective function is why compliments are generally addressed to their targets. One can praise but not compliment absent third parties who are not expected ever to learn of the praise. Compliments must at least ostensibly try to make addressees feel good about themselves, their tastes or their skills or their general attractiveness.

Compliments do not only evaluate or appraise. Their positive appraisals are presented as intended to please addressees, to enhance their sense of themselves as admirable or likeable or successful people. Kerbrat-Orecchioni (1987, p. 15) describes a compliment as "un cadeau verbal," a verbal gift. Compliments are to be understood as doing facework on behalf of the addressee. What links the appraisal and the facework is the assumption that the addressee has earned the high marks bestowed. (Evaluation itself does important facework, as we will see in the next section, but the facework it does may or may not be assumed to be on behalf of the addressee.) The compliment credits the addressee for the positive evaluation, and receiving such credit is assumed to be something that will warm the addressee's heart.

Of course, what warms the heart varies situationally. A compliment is inappropriate if it conveys a positive evaluation in some domain that the addressee does not want to appear to care about in the particular context in which the evaluative move is made. Even one's nearest and dearest ought not to comment publicly on one's appearance as one is talking to colleagues about a scientific experiment. An athlete waiting to get into the game may not be particularly happy to hear polite words about the excellent paper she or he just handed in to the English teacher. Inappropriate compliments are moves that might do wanted facework for the addressee in some situation but do not do the face-work called for in the utterance context. Parents often embarrass their children by offering compliments that significantly damage the face-work the children are attempting to do with their peers.

Compliments that accomplish wanted facework are often presented as canonical examples of positively polite social moves. Notice, though, that supporting or building up the self apparently being presented by the addressee in the utterance context may or may not function to increase solidarity between the interactants, to create or strengthen ties of liking or affection or affiliation. Like other "gifts," compliments extended can put the complimentee in debt to the complimenter, and that debt may in some cases be resented. In some cultures, compli-menting a person on a possession obliges the owner to offer it to the complimenter as a gift. Also, when a person with few assets compli-ments a person with many, the compliment reminds both interactants of their different assets and of the complimenter's envy. The com-plimentee might or might not find this reminder upsetting, but it certainly seems unlikely to enhance solidarity between the two. One reason a common response to a compliment is a return compliment is that complimentees are often much happier if they can repay imme-diately the debt they have incurred.

Insults are much the same kind of move as compliments but with the opposite overt orientation. Insults offer a negative appraisal and attack the addressee's positive face through implicit blame, announcing their spirit-lowering aims. Insults and compliments are not perfectly coun-terposed: in many (perhaps most) communities of practice, the default assumption is that people want to (appear to) look out for one another. Particular situations may throw that assumption in doubt and some communities of practice may be organized around antagonism, but, for example, the absence of a compliment is far more often interpretable as an insult than is the absence of an insult construable as a compliment. This difference in defaults and the implications they generate is connected to the difference in ritualization and conventionalization. As we have already noted, there are communities of practice that engage in ritual insults.[7] Ritualization of compliments is, however, probably more widespread and will be discussed below. We will not discuss insults in detail but will occasionally point to some of their potential functions in constructing gendered identities and relations.

We can see the components of compliments – evaluation and stroking through crediting – by considering the different kinds of circumstances under which interactants deny that their moves should be construed as compliments. One illustration comes from Penny's fieldwork with Detroit-area high schoolers (see Eckert 1989 for the primary ethnographic report). Penny was initiating a discussion of popularity with a girl who was, by everyone's account, very popular. When Penny observed that the girl was popular, the girl denied it. Penny then pointed out that in saying that the girl was popular she did not intend to compliment her but simply to state an obvious fact that she would like to discuss. At that point the girl accepted the utterance and continued with the discussion. What Penny did was deny that describing the girl as popular was intended to credit her for a positive evaluation. At the least, she suggested that ascribing popularity can be nonevaluative – "simply" descriptive, based on widely agreed upon "objectively" applicable criteria. In offering the fact of popularity outside of a compliment, Penny was relieving the addressee of the need to acknowledge that Penny was in a position to evaluate her popularity, that she found popularity desirable, and – in accepting the compliment – that she believed she was popular.

In a somewhat different vein, consider the following exchange, variants of which are often heard.

A: I liked your paper about X.
B: Thanks for the compliment.
A: It's not (just) a compliment. I REALLY liked it.

In denying that the first utterance was (just) a compliment, A denies that making B feel good is what (primarily) motivated that utterance.

7 See, e.g., Labov (1972b) for an interesting discussion of "playing the dozens" in some African American communities and Dundes *et al.* (1972) for ritual insults among young Turkish boys; the function of verbal "battles" as substitutes for physical violence is explicitly addressed by some of the rappers quoted in Newman (2001).

A says: my liking your paper did not result from my liking you but from the quality of the paper. A also implies that when making the other feel good is the main thing at stake, complimenters frequently misrepresent or at least overstate their actual evaluation, exaggerate the degree of positiveness. (We'll return to this point below.)

Not surprisingly, the same words may sometimes be uttered as a compliment, sometimes not. This is true even if we set aside ironic or sarcastic utterances, which we will discuss later. What Penny said to her interviewee (something like "You're very popular") might have been a compliment if uttered in different circumstances. "You've lost so much weight" can be uttered as a compliment if directed towards someone known to think of themselves as weighing too much and wanting to lose weight. It might, however, be an expression of anguished sympathy if the addressee is someone who has lost weight because of a serious illness. Sometimes compliments are overtly presented as such: "let me compliment you on this amazing cake – it's so delicious it's practically sinful." Or: "please present my compliments to the chef." But compliments generally don't announce themselves explicitly. Exclamations frequently are pressed into service to compliment: "what a great dress that is!" or "how I wish I could sew like you" and often surface when people are trying to think of possible compliments. They were not, however, terribly common in the corpus of compliments collected in New Zealand by Janet Holmes and her colleagues (and were even less common in men's than women's mouths). Even imperatives can be used to impart a compliment: "Turn around so that I can really see that wonderful dress."

Indeed, virtually any sentential form, given the right circumstances, can be used to compliment. Many verbally expressed compliments do, however, fall into certain patterns. The bulk of the compliments collected by Janet Holmes and her colleagues included a positive evaluative adjective that was predicated of a nominal designating what was being admired ("That dress is nice," "That's a nice dress," or "Nice dress." More often than not the positive adjectives were *good*, *nice*, *great*, *beautiful*, *pretty*, which might or might not occur with an intensifier ("That's a really great dress"). "I like/love/admire/enjoy/ . . . X" was also a fairly common compliment, somewhat more common from women than from men (and in Herbert's 1990 study involving American college students, both much more frequent overall than in the New Zealand studies and significantly more skewed toward female speakers). In general, the formulaic expressions Holmes identifies are very similar to those found in empirical studies of compliments produced by American English speakers (in addition to Herbert, see Manes and Wolfson 1981, Manes

1983, Wolfson 1984). This similarity of form may have something to do with how data were collected. In most cases, researchers had to identify and record compliments "on the fly" as they observed or participated in real-life interactions, and the positive evaluative adjectives certainly attract attention readily. It probably also has something to do with the routinization/ritualization of complimenting, which we will discuss below.

Classifying a move as a compliment is a matter of situating the move-maker and the other participants in a larger social landscape.

Evaluation as facework

People's evaluation of one another is central to social interaction and to the construction and enforcement of social norms. Compliments and other evaluative moves create and sustain not only affiliative social ties but also hierarchical distinctions. Our social personae and statuses feed on evaluation, both explicit and implicit, both positive and neg-ative. In their study of some dinner table conversations of relatively affluent European American families in Los Angeles, Elinor Ochs and Carolyn Taylor (1995) argued that the fathers in these families were the primary evaluators of the other family members but that fathers were themselves only rarely the targets of others' evaluative comments. Interestingly, it was often mothers who directed conversations so that fathers would be positioned as family judges: "Tell Daddy what you did this morning, Jennifer."

Anything other people say about us or our things or our activities can be seen as potentially evaluative. Someone in Natasha's kitchen ob-serves: "I see you are stirring that sauce in a clockwise direction." Why has the observer mentioned this? Mentioning it suggests it is "men-tionable," something that might matter. Does stirring direction affect the texture of the sauce? Is Natasha being prodded to monitor it? Does it reveal something about her social origins? (Of course, if the observer is trying to learn to cook from Natasha, then Natasha is probably being constructed as the authority on stirring direction, and she will be un-likely to take the observer's comment as evaluative.) Entering the living room, the guest exclaims: "I see you have a purple couch." Are purple couches "in" or "out"? Does the guest like or loathe them? Does the guest admire or look down on people with purple couches? Of course, Natasha may be projecting a persona unconcerned with home decor or cooking habits, in which case she may be less likely to assume that her visitor's observations constitute implicit evaluations. Or her opinion of the visitor may be such that she accords little or no weight to the observations offered and thus ignores any possible evaluative import.

In making a complimenting move, the agent assumes the "authority" to appraise whatever is being complimented. Authority can depend on expertise or on the nature of the social relation between complimenter and complimentee. Compliments can flow down a socially asymmetric relationship (bosses can easily compliment employees, adults can readily compliment children), but compliments given up the hierarchy are often classified as "flattery" and thought "inappropriate." When they do occur, the recipient is far more likely to be a woman and the complimenter a man (which might suggest that the gender hierarchy can sometimes trump other principles of rank). Given that compliments are supposed to do facework on behalf of addressees, complimenters also presume that their "crediting" addressees for the things or achievements being noted in these situations should please the addressees. So, for example, to compliment a person's looks is to imply that one's opinion of the person's looks should matter to that person, at least a little. It also implies that how they look is (or should be) an important component of the face they are trying to project in the situation where the compliment occurs. Compliments instruct their recipients in what others might value about them. In communities of practice where compliments on certain properties are quite frequent, the absence of such compliments may be as eloquent as their presence. Young children seldom compliment (as opposed to admiring). Penny observed an eruption of complimenting behavior among girls in sixth grade as part of the evaluative practice that established norms in the heterosexual market. Sincere compliments confer worth, while insincere compliments (e.g. "nice hair" to a person with a bad case of bed head) detract. In both cases, they establish and reinforce norms.

In the English compliment corpora that have been collected, both women and men compliment women most often, and appearance is the dominant topic of the collected compliments, especially when women are the addressees. These corpora have fewer men giving compliments overall; those they do give are more often than women's focused on abilities or achievements of the complimentee. It is tempting to see in these patterns another confirmation of men as active subjects, women as passive objects to be looked at: "Women are, men do." It is perhaps more illuminating, however, to explore how compliments and other evaluations construct normative expectations that looks and likeability will matter a lot to women and that talents and active projects will matter more to men. Compliments are important in constructing and regulating the gender order. Adults early on compliment the bravery of boys and the beauty of girls, boys' toughness and girls' niceness.

And preadolescent girls' use of compliments is clearly important in instructing and enforcing social norms.

A young woman Sally knows was working during the mid-1980s on the clean-up crew of one of the dining halls at her college. Her boss, a man around sixty, greeted her daily with some kind of compliment about her attire or some other aspect of her appearance. He never tired of telling her how pretty she was. Not surprisingly, he never offered analogous comments to the male employees, an asymmetry that she pointed out to him. His compliments certainly did facework but not the facework the young woman wanted. He was able to continue, probably never understanding her annoyance, because he had so firmly bought into a cultural view of women as always appraisable on grounds of their appearance. His behavior was not quite like that of the construction workers who make appreciative comments about their bodies to women just walking by.[8] The young woman he complimented was not a stranger to him. Nonetheless, his compliments were at best inappropriate. Even women in high-level professional positions sometimes encounter similar inappropriate preoccupations of colleagues with their looks. Goffman 1979 includes a story about President Nixon's closing a press briefing with a compliment to senior reporter Helen Thomas on her attire. If compliments on appearance go in all directions (e.g. if the woman whose male colleague has just complimented her dress can respond with a similar compliment on his apparel), then their role in regulating the gender order is somewhat diminished. Notice, however, that it is not only men who emphasize appearance in their compliments to women. So do other women.

Both Tannen and Holmes have proposed that women compliment and are complimented more than men because for women complimenting is primarily about (positive) affect, about strengthening solidarity with others in one's communities of practice. For men, in contrast, complimenting is supposed to be primarily about asserting one's authority to evaluate the other and therefore carries potentially greater face threat (suppose that the claim to authority is rejected). In our view, compliments can be somewhat risky or face-threatening for both women and men. For complimenters, there's the risk of raising questions about their evaluative authority, both in terms of their capacity

---

8 Gardner (1980), Kissling (1991), and Kissling and Kramarae (1991) all discuss the phenomenon of "stranger compliments" from men to women. Although frequency of such comments may have lessened in the past couple of decades, our students report that such street remarks are still heard, sometimes with racist as well as sexist overtones. There is, however, the occasional reversal, with women yelling out numbers as men walk by ("Hey, you're at least a 9") or appreciative comments on the men's bodies ("Love those abs").

to appraise and their "right" to foreground the particular properties being praised. For complimentees, there are potential challenges to their capacity to regulate the impressions they create in others, the kind of persona they are able to project in the complimenting situation. And there is also the obligation implicit in any acceptance of a gift. At the same time, for both women and men, receiving a compliment can not only increase self-esteem but can also increase warm feelings toward the complimenter (and deepen confidence in the complimenter's warm feelings toward them).

Responses to compliments often indicate ambivalence. In many English-speaking communities of practice, simple thanks is a common response (suggesting at least the appearance of appreciation for the stroking) or some other token of agreement: "Yeah, I like this dress myself." Basically half the responses from both sexes fell into one of these categories in the New Zealand corpus. Outright rejection or disagreement was relatively infrequent from both women and men whereas some kind of deflection or evasion was fairly common from both sexes. Credit could be given elsewhere ("my husband bought it for me"), for example. Sometimes the compliment was simply ignored. Not infrequently, the recipient reciprocated by offering a compliment in the other direction, thus "repaying" the favor. Recall the overt rejection of the assumed compliment by Penny's interviewee. For her, there was probably an overriding concern to project herself as someone who is "nice" and suitably "modest," who is not "stuck-up" or "conceited." (See Eckert and McConnell-Ginet 1995 for discussion of the widespread view in high schools of popular girls as "stuck-up.") There was probably also concern to make her ascendancy in the heterosexual market look uncontrived, look as if it simply followed from her inborn merits. Compliments are social moves that give rise to other social moves, and we cannot look at the (putative) compliments without also considering responses to them.

Both women and men find negotiating the evaluative terrain and more specifically compliments a potentially worthwhile but also a sometimes risky business. One kind of risk has to do with the trustworthiness of compliments and complimenters, which we will discuss in the next section.

"Do they really mean it?" What's the key?

With any speech act or other meaningful social move, questions arise about what interactants are trying to do, whether they straightforwardly mean what their words say or whether something else is at stake. Are they being serious, honest, playful, sarcastic, joking, offhand? In what "key" is this song being played?[9] Of course what purports to be sincere might be sarcastic, what seems to be serious might be a joke. Compliments can be suspect on several different grounds, each of which we will discuss.

Complimenting is often *routine* and *formulaic*. Dictionary definitions of *compliment* often mention politeness, courtesy, and also formality. Some compliments use hyperbolic language: "I *love* that dress" or "Those are *fantastic* earrings." Both complimenter and complimentee know that the extravagant language is just that, but they may well accept it as part of complimenting practice. The person who said "It's not just a compliment – I REALLY liked the paper" is acknowledging that compliments sometimes go beyond the bounds of literal truth in the interest of marking goodwill and presumably increasing solidarity. For many communities of practice, there are certain situations in which compliments are expected and are routinely given, often in hyperbolic form. These compliments need not thereby be *insincere*. Rather they are conventional acknowledgments of social obligations among community members, of norms that enjoin members to show their willingness to give positive "strokes" to one another. They are like the "How's it going?" or "How are you?" that function as conventional greetings and not "really" inquiries into the state of the other's life. The use of intensifiers (e.g. *very*, *so*) and other "boosting" devices (e.g. *love* rather than *like*) draws attention to the social move being made, to the courtesy that one enacts. Such predictable language can help make manifest that the speaker's intention is to compliment and not simply to evaluate. Although what is said may go beyond the bounds of what the speaker would assent to literally, its effectiveness as a routine compliment depends in part on its not being wildly divergent from the speaker's actual views – e.g. not praising something the speaker actually finds quite awful, to be shunned. Exaggeration is OK but serious distortion moves us beyond the routine into the territory of deception, discussed below.

In some situations, routine compliments just show "good manners." Good manners are, of course, associated with maintaining class

---

9 Hymes (1972) introduced the metaphor of "key" for this aspect of an utterance: roughly, the nature of the utterer's stance toward the overt content of the utterance. It is part of what we call "idea positioning" in the next chapter. Goffman (1974) speaks of the key as what unlocks the utterer's stance, what transforms meanings from initial or apparent framing. He uses the term "footing" for something like the utterer's stance or positioning. There are many complexities that we cannot pursue here, but the important point is that we need to consider some of the variety of ways speakers can position themselves toward the literal content of what they say.

hierarchies. These conventions of behavior are also frequently gendered feminine in several senses. They are to be specially adhered to by women and they should be specially followed by men in the presence of women. They are also normatively policed by women (e.g. mothers, teachers of the young, and others seen as etiquette experts). Conventionally courteous complimentary utterances are likely to be the easiest to hear/code as compliments so it is not too surprising that many observers in English-speaking societies have heard compliments most in women's mouths and most often with women as recipients (whether the complimenter is female or male).

It is important to realize that just because a compliment is routine and in that sense not fully "meant" does not mean that it cannot make the recipient who recognizes its routine status feel good. The complimenter may be seen to have made an effort that is clearly supposed to be for the benefit of the complimentee, and that effort is often appreciated, even when the complimenter is uttering words that go beyond the bounds of what either interactant would judge literally true. Herbert suggests that men's compliments are accepted more often than women's because they are heard as nonroutine and thus as more trustworthy. Perhaps, but compliment responses indicating acceptance may be simply one of many contexts in which men continue to benefit from (subtle but still prevalent) cultural devaluation of women.

A routine compliment is very different from a *sarcastic* compliment. Sarcasm and irony are possible with any kind of speech act or social move though they are much more common in some communities of practice than in others.[10] The (openly) sarcastic compliment does something like mime an apparent compliment in order to mock it. It insults by appearing to compliment but making obvious that the putative positive evaluation in this situation is judged laughable, absurdly off the mark. There are sometimes vocal cues that an utterance is sarcastic, but not always. Sarcastic intent is easy to miss, especially since the existence of sincere hyperbolic compliments means that the mere inapplicability of the literal content of an expressed evaluation does not in itself signal sarcasm. (Alternatively, someone may mistakenly take a sincere but hyperbolic compliment as sarcastic.) Often, however, sarcastic

10 Rebecca Clift (1999) offers a study of conversational irony and proposes a theory of irony that links verbal and nonverbal cases, drawing on Goffman's notion of footing, which is similar to Hymes's concept of key. She argues that irony involves a shift in footing that makes interactional frames visible. "The ironist...effects a shift in footing from committed participant to detached observer" (p. 532). She draws insights from earlier theories that saw irony as echoic (Sperber and Wilson 1981), pretense (Clarke and Gerrig 1984), or theatrical (Haiman 1990) but argues that none of them applies as well as her account to different forms of irony.

compliments do indeed hit – and hurt – their targets. As we have noted earlier, young girls use them as one weapon when they work to exclude certain other girls from their group. Sarcastic compliments attack positive face.

Finally, there is the *deceptive* compliment. In this case, it is not only that the complimenter does not believe the literally expressed positive evaluation (which is also true in the sincere hyperbolic case and in the sarcastic case). Deceptive complimenters are usually primarily self-interested. They want to enhance complimentees' good opinions of them; enhancing complimentees' good feelings about themselves is not an end (as it is in the sincere hyperbolic case) but simply a means. People who are seen as deceptive complimenters may be described as "sucking up" to others, as "flatterers." They can also be seen as simply calculating – as the waiter who routinely compliments her customers, not in the hopes of making friends, but in the hopes of increasing her tips. If they are complimenting apparent equals or inferiors, they are likely to be classed as "phonies."

The line between sincere routine compliments and deceptive compliments is not always clear, especially since people often have rather mixed motives. You may genuinely want to make someone else feel good but, of course, you may also want to make them feel good about you. But if the other-directed motives are as strong as we expect them to be in order for us to find you "sincere," they will forbid you from, for example, making clear to third-party observers that you didn't "really mean" those pretty words you spoke. It obscures the genuinely positive functions of routine compliments to conflate their deviations from truth with those involved in sarcasm or in deception.

Are compliment "keys" gendered? Herbert contrasts "solidarity-building" with "more sincere" compliments, suggesting that Americans generally, and American women in particular, favor the solidarity-building use of compliments. By this he seems to mean what we have called routine compliments. Others have made similar suggestions that American women and men follow different "rules" for complimenting: women compliment to build solidarity, men to rank and evaluate. Why do both sexes seem to compliment women more than men? Because they recognize that women enjoy compliments? (This would mean that men do indeed recognize "solidarity-building" as an important compliment function, even if limited to making women feel good.) Because people generally feel freer to evaluate women, especially in the arena of appearance?

Women's greater use of routine compliments (and other apparently "solidarity-building" moves) could be partly connected to their learning that being seen as thoughtful, as "nice," is very important to their success in life, often more important than being seen as capable or industrious. For men, making others feel good is not so highlighted as central to the personae they learn to project, and they are expected to give significant attention to such matters as appearing strong and competent.[11] Of course, such suggestions are far too simplistic. Nonetheless, rather than saying that there are gendered "rules" for complimenting (or other speech acts) or gendered "characters" that orient people differently towards compliments, it is useful to explore some of the ways linguistic practices such as complimenting (and doing so in particular "keys") help produce gendered personae.

Beyond conversation

Social moves are not made only in face-to-face conversational interactions. Mass media are important, and there is an increasing literature on gender issues raised in magazines, TV, and films.[12] Information technology and the increased commercialization of "communication skills" also connect to gender in important ways.[13] Although we do sometimes mention other uses of language, this book emphasizes throughout making meaning in face-to-face interaction. It is in such interactions that children enter communities of practice and that adults lead much of their lives. In considering how such interactions matter for gender, we raise a number of points that apply to linguistic practice more broadly. Indeed, other kinds of linguistic practice often draw on practices found in face-to-face encounters. For example, Mary Talbot (1995) notes that some of the writing in girls' magazines works by mimicking certain features of such conversational moves as an older sister or trusted friend giving advice. There are, however, many special features of nonconversational communicative circumstances that we will not be able to consider, and we urge readers to explore other communicative modes for themselves.

11 Keep in mind that there are different femininities and masculinities, and these normative expectations do not function in the same way or with the same intensity for everyone or in every English-speaking community of practice. Some women stay away from such routinized compliments, some men employ them frequently.
12 Mary Talbot (1998) offers some discussion of print media; Marita Sturken and Lisa Cartwright (2001) offer a feminist-informed introduction to visual culture.
13 Susan Herring (1994) focuses on computer-mediated communication, whereas Deborah Cameron (2000) emphasizes such arenas as telemarketing.

CHAPTER 5

Positioning ideas and subjects

As we talk to one another, we express certain viewpoints, propose certain plans, query certain ideas. We not only "make moves," we also "take positions." In the next couple of chapters we will consider the content of discourse, the substance of the positions to which we commit ourselves as we speak. In this chapter we will examine some of the complexity of positioning and repositioning ourselves as discourse progresses.

There are two distinct but intertwined aspects of discourse positioning. On the one hand, we position ourselves vis-à-vis meaningful content that we and others first express. We push ideas and projects with more or less force, we modulate them in response to actual or anticipated reactions of others, we embrace them passionately, we explore them seriously, we mock them disdainfully, we play with them and with the linguistic forms we use for expressing them. On the other hand, we position ourselves vis-à-vis the others with whom we are developing and elaborating a meaningful discourse. We attend to the others' ideas and feelings and we assess their capacities, their institutional status, their stance towards us. Not only do we modulate and modify our own ideas and feelings, we also place one another in particular (and changing) discursive positions. These positions are many and varied. Some kinds of positions recur: facilitator, pupil, tutor, partner, leader, assistant, competitor, expert, novice, judge, plaintiff, defendant, supporting witness, clown, advisor, sympathetic friend, playmate, storyteller, hero, coward. Such discursive positions are tied to cultural contexts and social situations, and they are seldom completely gender neutral. A person may also occupy more than one position at a particular point in time. What we will see throughout this chapter is that these two different kinds of positioning – for convenience we'll call them idea positioning and subject positioning – are inextricably linked to one another.[1] Many linguistic resources play a role in both, often even at the

---

1 "Idea" may seem to suggest a focus on passive beliefs and opinions but as noted above we include much else: e.g. active interest in and commitment to various courses

same time. It is important also to note that positioning is not just the accomplishment of individual speakers: positioning is accomplished interactively and involves not just the aims of speakers but also the interpretations of, and effects on, other conversational participants.

"Women's language" and gendered positioning

Although not conceptualized in quite the way we are proposing, the insight that idea and subject positioning are interconnected and are both implicated in gender construction is really what launched language and gender studies. In the early 1970s, American linguist Robin Lakoff proposed that American women were constrained to soften and attenuate their expression of opinion through such devices as

- tag questions ("this election mess is terrible, **isn't it**?")
- rising intonation on declaratives (A: "When will dinner be ready?" B: "Six o'clock?")
- the use of various kinds of hedges ("That's **kinda** sad" or "it's **probably** dinnertime")
- boosters or amplifiers ("I'm **so** glad you're here")
- indirection (saying "Well, I've got a dentist appointment then" in order to convey a reluctance to meet at some proposed time and perhaps to request that the other person propose an alternative time)
- diminutives (*panties*)
- euphemism (avoiding profanities by using expressions like *piffle, fudge,* or *heck*; using circumlocutions like *go to the bathroom* to avoid "vulgar" or tabooed expressions such as *pee* or *piss*)
- conventional politeness, especially forms that mark respect for the addressee

There were other elements in the picture she painted of "women's language," but the main focus was on its "powerlessness," seen as deriving from the "weak" stance or position those women (and others) were assuming. (See esp. Lakoff 1975.)

Overall, Lakoff proposed, a distinctive part of speaking "as a woman" is speaking tentatively, side stepping firm commitment and the

---

of action. "Subject" deliberately evokes the "subject position" terminology of postmodern theorists and others who find the traditional notion of a unitary and coherent self problematic. Although our own thinking is informed by feminist and postmodern theorizing, our focus as linguists is on grounding the abstract notions of discourse and of subject positions in concrete linguistic practices. Finally, we adopt the term "positioning" because it brings together stance towards ideas and towards others. Goffman's notion of "footing" (1979) is very similar to what we're calling idea positioning.

appearance of strong opinions. Women are disempowered by being constrained to use "powerless" language, ways of speaking that simply are not very effective in getting others to think or do what the speaker wants them to. She was arguing that in positioning themselves as women, in taking up a certain place in the gender order, those who made use of the various resources she identified were also positioning themselves as powerless, were rejecting positions of authority from which they might successfully launch their meanings into discourse with a reasonable hope for their success.[2]

Reading Lakoff's work, many drew the moral that women could be empowered by changing their modes of speech, assuming more authoritative positions as speakers. As Mary Crawford (1995, ch. 4) explains, lots of people jumped on the "assertiveness bandwagon" during the late 1970s and the 1980s, proposing to train women to speak more assertively, to move away from the positions Lakoff had identified as constitutive of powerlessness and of "women's language." But as Crawford and others have argued, such moves wrongly assume that it is deficits in individual women that explain their relative powerlessness. Promoting compensatory training for individual women, they suggest, obscures the social arrangements that keep women's wages far below men's (in the twenty-first century, US women still earn less than three-quarters of what their male counterparts do) and assign disproportionate social and political power to men.[3]

Other readers of Lakoff pointed to the fact that the positioning devices she described as constitutive of "speaking as a woman" are actually multifunctional. Many resources that she characterizes as evincing a weak position for the speaker, a lack of force behind the main message, may do other things. A tag, for example, can both indicate a willingness to entertain alternative positions beyond that which the

2 Do men speak more "authoritatively" than women? Elizabeth Kuhn (1992) examined university professors' use of their authority on the first day of classes to get students to do what the professors wanted them to. Kuhn found male professors displaying more authority than women in both American and German universities but also found the differences smaller in the US than in Germany. Of course, a decade after Kuhn's study German universities still have fewer women than US universities at the highest levels in the academic hierarchy. And in both the US and Germany, men still predominate as the recognized authorities in academic and other domains.
3 Lakoff herself did not assume that women could automatically gain power by speaking in a different style. She pointed to a "double-bind" that penalized women if they eschewed "women's language" yet prevented them from interactional effectiveness if they did indeed so speak. A. H. Gervasio and Mary Crawford (1989) found that people reacted quite negatively to women speaking as assertiveness trainers had coached them. Some of this was due to the sociolinguistic naiveté of the advice given, but Cameron (1995, ch. 5) highlights the more central moral: how an utterance is interpreted does not depend solely on the linguistic forms used but on the interpreter's view of the utterer.

main clause conveys (thus, the absence of unshakeable conviction) and also serve to connect the speaker more firmly to others. Establishing such connections may ultimately strengthen a speaker's position by enlisting social support for the speaker and their ideas and projects. As we have already stressed, the multifunctionality of linguistic forms is an important theme in language and gender research of the past couple of decades. The work on tags and on intonation that we discuss below centers on the point that forms that can be interpreted as signaling the speaker's position with respect to the content expressed, can also position the speaker with respect to other folks: not only those directly addressed but often also overhearers or those spoken of.

Lakoff's proposals had the salutary effect of directing attention to a host of linguistic minutiae that usually are at best minimally noticed in the flow of conversational interaction. A flurry of studies followed, producing somewhat mixed results. William O'Barr and Kim Atkins (1980), for example, looked at courtroom testimony and found that speakers' overall social status as well as their familiarity with the courtroom setting better predicted use of many of these devices than speakers' sex. They suggested that what Lakoff had identified as "women's" language really was "powerless" language in the sense of being used by those with relatively little power, but it was not necessarily gendered. They also tested Lakoff's claim that many of these linguistic strategies might render language "powerless" in the sense of rendering it ineffective. They played alternative versions of essentially the same testimony for mock jurors and found that jurors were more likely to believe that testimony if it were delivered in the more direct, less hedged, style associated with people in authority. (Men in this study were overall heard as more credible than women.)

It is easy to criticize Lakoff's specific claims about gender and the use of particular forms, but her pioneering work had the important effect of directing attention to the critical issues of power in the interaction of language and gender. She also focused attention on some kinds of linguistic resources that might be central to constructing gendered identities and relations and, most importantly for our present purposes, gendered discourse positions. In the remainder of this chapter, we will say something about how gender interacts with the production and interpretation of these and other positioning resources.

Showing deference or respect?

To acknowledge others' rights and claims is at the heart of negative politeness, of showing respect, and negative politeness very often enters into gendered norms for language use. Showing respect generally looks very much the same as showing deference. Deference, however, involves not only respect: it also implies placing others' claims above one's own, subordinating one's own rights to those of others. Often what is offered as simple respect may be interpreted as deference, especially if the respect-giver does not overtly press their own position. If the recipient interprets the respect as deference and thereby assumes a position of advantage, then the respect-giver who does not challenge this assumption ends up in effectively the same position as the person who defers. But ritual deference, marking the other's position as higher than one's own or assuming a lower position, is one way to show respect and does not necessarily involve giving up one's own status claims. A bow lowers the bower vis-à-vis the other, but mutual bowing shows mutual respect.

As we noted in the preceding chapter, all forms of negative politeness or respect-giving tend to sit uneasily with positive politeness, which signals familiarity or solidarity. Sometimes to show solidarity is to fail to show respect and vice versa. Forms that show solidarity or familiarity when used reciprocally by equals show disrespect or condescension when used nonreciprocally, and forms that show respect between equals show deference or subordination if their use is nonreciprocal. Again and again, there are norms enjoining the use of respect forms to status superiors and countenancing the use of familiar forms to status inferiors.

In this section, we will discuss three kinds of linguistic resources that explicitly mark relative social location – distance and hierarchy – of the speaker and addressees and thus can directly show respect or familiarity. Positioning subjects can be accomplished through choice of forms of address (we use English examples), through second-person choices for referring to addressees (we use French), and through a more thorough-going system of honorifics (we use Japanese) that spreads positioning of subjects far beyond the marking of expressions that directly speak of or to the subjects who are being positioned.

Addressing

Address forms are sensitive indicators of how speakers are positioning their addressees, those to whom they are speaking.[4] In English, forms like *sir* or *ma'am* or social titles like *Dr.*, *Mr.*, or *Ms.* preceding a surname

---

4 For much more extensive discussion of how address and also forms for referring to addressees and others can enter into constructing gender, see McConnell-Ginet (1978, forthcoming) and references in both these papers.

assign a high position to the addressee, express the speaker's respect for the addressee. By simply acknowledging the addressee's claims, they may also express social distance and the absence of solidarity between the speaker and the addressee. Used nonreciprocally, they can express deference from a social subordinate (a young person or someone positioned as inferior on some other grounds). Another option in English, the use of first name only, indicates familiarity or solidarity. Used nonreciprocally, it can express power or condescension, lack of respect. Dr. Alvin Poussaint, an African American psychiatrist, tells of being accosted by police and asked, "What's your name, boy?" to which he replied "Dr. Poussaint," "No," the cops responded, "what's your *first* name, boy?"[5] Both the insistence on a first name and the use of *boy* as an address form showed that adult black men were being consigned to the lowly status of children, denied the respect accorded their white peers.

First names are now very widespread in most communities of practice using American English, and they mainly mark familiarity, with the use of titles growing increasingly rare (a major exception being address from children to adults outside their families).

Although the office with executive *Mr. Jones* and his assistant *Mary* on the nameplates is fast disappearing, American English address does still continue to mark hierarchies upon occasion, many of them gendered. Two professors recently called the same office at their university for information, identifying themselves by first name plus surname but also giving the person answering the phone the information that they were professors. The man was addressed as Professor X, the woman by her first name. The woman answering the phone was certainly positioning the male professor higher than the female, but she may also have been trying to position the other woman as closer to herself than the man, seeing herself as friendly rather than disrespectful.

Talking about addressees

Unlike contemporary English, many languages incorporate in the grammar itself resources for showing respect to, or marking solidarity with, one's addressee. Readers may be familiar with one or more of the European languages that have two second-person pronouns for talking about an addressee. In French, for example, one refers to addressees one knows fairly well as *tu*, reserving *vous* for those who are unfamiliar. Because *tu* is grammatically singular and *vous* is grammatically plural,

---

5 This incident is recounted in Brown and Ford (1961).

the choice between them also has implications for verbal agreement. In the case of an imperative where there is no overt pronoun we still find the contrast: *mange*, for example, directs a familiar addressee to eat, and *mangez* does the same for an unfamiliar addressee (as well as for a group of addressees).

Several generations ago, hierarchy was more important than it is now in the *tu/vous* choice, with *tu* used to social inferiors (which included younger people of the same social rank as the speaker) and very familiar equals, and *vous* to social superiors (including elders of the same social rank as the speaker) and those whom one did not know very well. In general, as a relationship became more familiar, the superior in an unequal relationship was supposed to initiate any switch to *tu* from an initial mutual *vous*. But the man was supposed to ask the woman for permission to use *tu* as their relationship developed into something more intimate. This did not mean that women were being seen as socially superior to men but that certain ritual courtesies were enjoined towards women. In other cases of differential status, the lower-status person was not supposed to request a switch to *tu* but to wait for the higher-status person to initiate such a switch, perhaps asking (as the man was supposed to with the woman) in order not to flaunt the status advantage. In a number of cultures using European languages with this T/V pronominal distinction,[6] sexual difference was interpreted as social distance, especially among those who might be potential sexual partners. Paul Friedrich (1972) notes the Russian comment: "Petya's grown-up now; he says *vy* [the Russian equivalent of French *vous*] to the girls." Petya was, of course, not deferring to the girls but marking their (new) social distance from himself by showing them respect, refraining from claiming familiarity with them.

As with English address options, however, the European second-person pronouns now mark familiarity far more than hierarchy. As Roger Brown and Albert Gilman (1960) put it, the power semantic has been giving way to the solidarity semantic. And ideologies of gender equality have also considerably lessened the gender-inflected uses of the power semantic of hierarchy and distance. The power semantic is by no means dead, however. It is still customary for the hierarchically superior person to initiate a switch to *tu*, and children's lesser status is still marked by their universally being called *tu*, and ideologies of egalitarianism are called forth as many students and leftists uniformly

---

6 Following Brown and Gilman, analysts often use "T/V" to designate any pronominal contrast between a familiar form like *tu* and a more formal form like *vous*, whether or not the pronouns in question actually begin with "T" and "V" respectively.

use *tu* to adult strangers as well as familiars. In Sweden, the move to national socialism brought about a public repudiation of this distinction and the adoption of the solidarity semantic. The constraints for the use of T/V are tied to the language itself. In bilingual communities in France, Occitan languages that retain a power semantic live side by side with French, which has a solidarity semantic. A person who is called *tu* in French may be called *bous/vous* in Occitan, and speakers may switch their pronoun usage as they switch languages even in mid-sentence.

Several centuries ago in English, the originally plural and respectful *you* won out over the originally singular and familiar *thou* for almost all kinds of address and addressee reference. The major exceptions were certain very special contexts such as prayer (in which the addressee is a deity, here seen as too close to be distanced by the nonfamiliar form). But members of the Society of Friends, the Quakers, continued to use the familiar forms to people, rejecting the deferential flavor of the plural form *you* for relations among humans and reserving it for addressing God, the one being to whom it was deemed appropriate to show deference. Among most users of English, however, leveling was to the originally respectful and deferential form rather than to the originally familiar and solidary form that seems to be gaining the upper hand these days in most European languages.

Systems for speaking of addressees show clearly the tensions between the power semantic of respect and deference and the solidarity semantic of familiarity and closeness. Within each of these poles, we also see the opposing demands of social equality and hierarchy. To enforce but not give respect is to require deference. To extend familiarity without inviting it in return is to claim social superiority, to show disrespect or condescension. And forms for speaking about addressees show the complex ways in which gender inflects the meanings of hierarchy and social distance.

Honorifics

Marking social status is tightly integrated into the grammar of Japanese, and showing respect or deference is a central component of so-called women's language in Japanese. Through its complex system of honorifics, the Japanese language constrains speakers to signal hierarchical social relations in a variety of places in their utterances, not only when using second-person pronouns or other address forms. The honorific system encodes relations among participants, both present and absent, in the discourse situations – that is, among the speaker, the addressee, and those spoken of. In a discourse situation that includes only the speaker and the addressee, speakers who wish to signal respect or deference to their addressees may use a respect form to refer to the addressees or things and actions associated with the addressees, raising the addressees with respect to themselves; or they may use a humble form to refer to things and actions associated with themselves, lowering themselves in relation to the addressees. It is also possible to choose a neutral form to avoid such raising of the other or lowering of the self. But while such avoidance does get the speaker out of an explicit commitment to relative status, the actual choice itself cannot be neutral, signaling as it does that the speaker has chosen to avoid honorific choice. The possible use of honorifics is virtually always hovering in the background, always highly salient. This contrasts, say, with the possible use of a respect address form like *sir* in English, which is occasionally there but certainly often quite irrelevant. And even French second-person pronouns and verbal inflections, though more often at issue than English address forms, do not have such a global presence as honorific choices in Japanese.

When the topic of the discourse includes people other than the speaker and the addressee, the choice is complicated by the relations not only between the speaker and the addressee, but by relations between those two and the referent and even among referents. The speaker may wish to show respect and token deference to the person being spoken of, but in doing so may be seen as implicating the hearer in that show of deference. This is particularly a factor to the extent that the person being spoken of is seen to be associated with the speaker or the hearer, what is generally referred to as "in-group" (*uti*) or "out-group" (*soto*) relations. Thus an assessment of whether the person being spoken of is a member of the speaker's in-group in relation to the hearer, or of the hearer's in-group in relation to the speaker, is necessary. Speakers may, for example, use humble forms to refer to the actions of their own family members, and honorific forms to refer to the actions of the addressees' family members. Not just families but companies, friendship groups, schools, and other groups may be relevant, making negotiation of appropriate honorific usage a very complex matter.

It is well beyond the scope of this chapter to outline all the possibilities for honorific usage. Sachiko Ide (1982) and Janet Shibamoto Smith (1985) provide thorough discussions of these forms and their normative uses. For the purposes of our discussion, a few examples will illustrate the resources that speakers of Japanese have at their disposal. Some common verbs have separate stems for humble, neutral, and respect usage:

Verbs	Humble	Neutral	Respect
'be'	oru	iru	irassharu
'go'	mairu	iku	irassharu
'do'	itasu	suru	nasaru
'say'	mōsu	iu	ossharu

It is also possible to use a gerundive with *be* as an auxiliary, in which case the three forms of *be* (as shown above) will carry the honorific meaning:

Humble	yonde oru	'I am reading'
Neutral	yonde iru	'I, you, he or she am/are/is reading'
Respect	yonde irassharu	'you, he or she are/is reading'

The nominal prefix *o-* (or *go-* in the case of words of Chinese origin) can signal respect for the person or people associated with the noun:

Neutral	watakushi no kangae	'my idea'
Respect	sensei no o-kangae	'the teacher's idea'

Similar choices can be made in the use of personal pronouns and address terms as well. While all Japanese deploy honorifics, women's place in the social hierarchy constrains them to "honor" others in their speech more than men. But in addition, inasmuch as the use of honorifics demonstrates that the speaker is attending to standards of respect, honorific usage signals propriety. Because of its complexity and its attention to the fine points of social intercourse, honorific usage is itself considered an art, and is consequently associated with refinement. In this way, by virtue of the fact that it expresses propriety and refinement, honorific usage indexes femininity.

There is another use of the nominal prefix *o-/go-* (see above) that extends conferring honor in the interest of highly elaborated and hierarchical social relations to a more general ability to beautify. Thus the use of this prefix with the word referring to an ordinary item, and particularly with an item or word that is considered vulgar in some way, can achieve a kind of social resurrection. Not surprisingly, verbal beautification like flower arranging is very much a feminine art. The "excessive" use of this prefix, particularly with words that are considered not to "need" beautification, is labeled *hypercorrect*. Ide (1982) relates this kind of hypercorrectness to ignorance and upward mobility, showing the tight connection of femininity and class hierarchy.

Can a Japanese woman assume authority while adhering to "feminine" norms for honorific usage and the apparent deference they entail? Yukako Sunaoshi (1994, 1995) and Miyako Inoue (forthcoming) note that in some contexts a woman can deploy the honorific system to mark social distance and to carve out her own position for wielding power effectively.

Backing down or opening things up?

Women's speech has often been interpreted as indicating uncertainty or unwillingness to take a stand. In this section, we discuss two linguistic resources in English that have been so interpreted when associated with women's speech: tags and rising intonations on declaratives ("uptalk"). Careful examination of their use, however, shows that the story is much more complex. These same resources can also be used to open up the conversational floor to other participants, to provide a space for others' contributions. And their gendering may have at least as much to do with how others interpret them as with differences in who produces them.

Tags

Lakoff focused on what linguists studying English sometimes call *tag questions*, which append what looks like a fragment of a question to an ordinary declarative clause. These tags contain an inverted auxiliary form, determined by the auxiliary in the main clause, and a pronoun that agrees with the subject of the main clause: "the weather's awful, **isn't it**?" or "your friends couldn't come next week, **could they**?" In both these examples the polarity of the main clause is reversed in the tag: a positive main clause gets a negative tag, a negative main clause gets a positive tag. (Positive tags can occur with positive main clauses, but matched tags have somewhat different functions than the polarity reversed ones: "she would like me to come, **would she**?") Intonation affects interpretation of these tags, although there are also other factors, some of which we will discuss below. English also contains *invariant tags*, as do many other languages. As the name suggests, the form of the invariant tag is the same no matter what kind of main clause it attaches to: "we've got a reservation at eight, **right**?" or "you'll write up the final section, **okay**?" Although their functions are related, the different kinds of tags do each have their own particular range of uses.

Betty Lou Dubois and Isabel Crouch (1975) conducted one of the first empirical studies of Lakoff's claims about tag questions. Using interactions taped at an academic conference, they found more instances of men using these tags than women. They raised questions about

Lakoff's claims that women were the primary users of tags and also that tags expressed a speaker's insecurity or lack of commitment. But then McMillan *et al.* (1977) found women using more tags in task-oriented exchanges among American students. Other studies in less formal contexts also came up with conflicting results; for example Lapadat and Seesahai (1977) reported men using more tags (by 2 to 1) whereas Fishman (1980) had women in the lead in tag use (by 3 to 1). Early tag studies had numbers of methodological flaws (see the critique in Holmes 1984); for our purposes what is most important is that they did not really attend explicitly to the functions of the tag question forms they observed.

Subsequent studies tried to sort through some of the complexities of tag functioning and its relation to gender construction. Researchers such as Holmes (1982) and Cameron *et al.* (1989) pointed out that tags have a range of quite different functions: they can indicate uncertainty and ask for confirmation from the other (their *epistemic modal* function: "he was behind the three-point line, wasn't he?") but they can also be *facilitative, softening*, or *challenging*. (This terminology is from Holmes 1995.) A facilitative tag invites the addressee to make a conversational contribution and is often found at the beginning of an encounter or from those like teachers or talk show personalities who are trying to elicit talk from others. Think, for example, of saying "great performance wasn't it?" to the friend you meet on the way out of the theater or "she doesn't look old enough to be his mother does she?" to someone with whom you're chatting about the bridegroom's family at a wedding reception. A softening tag attenuates or mitigates the potential negative impact of something like a criticism: "you were a bit noisy, weren't you?" Challenging tags often elicit defeated silence or reluctant admissions of guilt: think of an angry parent uttering "you thought you could pull the wool over my eyes, didn't you?" or "you won't do that again, will you?" or the cross-examining lawyer saying "Your friend Jane promised to pay my client a lot of money, didn't she?" Intonation on the tag can help signal which functions are primary in a given utterance (an epistemic modal tag often has a rising intonation, a facilitative tag a falling one) but intonation interacts with many other factors.

Even if we exclude the challenging uses of tags (as Lakoff did), there are reasons other than powerlessness or unwillingness to take a strong stand that might explain a particular use of a tag. Facilitating others' entry into the conversation or softening a blow both have to do primarily with connections among people, with facework and social relations. Epistemic modal uses of tags, on the other hand, signal the speaker's stance toward the content of the main clause and generally invite the addressee to help in appraising that content. One reason may simply be interest in having that content confirmed or rejected by another party. Seeking a judgment from someone else, after tentatively proffering one's own view, can happen when one thinks one's evidence is a bit shaky – for example one has trouble seeing and makes a guess on whether the shot was from behind the three-point line, turning to the other who may have had a better view. Such uncertainty lies behind paradigmatic epistemic modal uses. Such uses, however, are explicitly excluded by Lakoff as not the kind that position a speaker as "weak." Why not? Presumably because the uncertainty at issue is fully "justified"; given a player shooting from the general vicinity of the three-point line, anyone who can't see very clearly SHOULD be uncertain about whether the shot was a three-pointer or not. What Lakoff counts as problematically weak are tags appended to sentences that express something the speaker seems perfectly well positioned to appraise for herself. Lakoff seems to imply that what is problematic here is the speaker's being unwilling to take full responsibility for the content of what she's said, turning to others to certify her appraisal. (The female pronouns here reflect Lakoff's judgment that such "weak" uses of tags are part of "women's" language.)

Was Lakoff thinking of the kind of tags that Holmes has classified as (primarily) facilitative or mitigating? The answer is not clear, especially given her use of examples like "This war in Vietnam is terrible, isn't it?" or, for a more up-to-date example, "The September 11 attacks on the World Trade Center and the Pentagon were terrifying, weren't they?" A primary reason for such utterances is to initiate discussion of the war or the suicide-bomber attacks rather than to seek confirmation or rejection of the stated (very general) opinion. They are simply somewhat more substantive conversation openers than "It's a beautiful day, isn't it?", steering the conversation in a particular direction, and thus such uses certainly seem primarily facilitative. As Cameron and her colleagues observe, even a tag that clearly does seek confirmation of what the main clause expresses may also be used to soften an otherwise potentially face-threatening utterance. Their example, drawn from texts in the University College of London's Survey of English Usage, is "You weren't there last week, were you?" They classed this utterance as (epistemic) modal, since it really did seem in context to request confirmation. They noted, however, that either the bald declarative "You weren't there last week" or the straight interrogative "Were you there last week?" might have seemed more like accusations and thus threats to the addressee's face. Arguably, the tag here was a softener or mitigator as well as a request for confirmation. As Cameron's group concludes, it is not just that different utterances of tags serve different functions: a single utterance of a tag may itself be multifunctional. The possibility of coexisting functions in a single utterance is what some analysts call *polysemy*. Deborah Tannen (1994) notes widespread polysemy of indicators of power and solidarity. Polysemy contrasts with *ambiguity*, which allows multiple meanings of a single form in a single utterance only with a "punning" effect, a kind of joke. In everyday usage, however, we often call polysemous forms ambiguous: the important point for present purposes is that tags and many other multifunctional forms we will consider can readily serve different functions in a single utterance.

Overall, though, both Holmes and Cameron and colleagues found a higher proportion of tags uttered by women to be (primarily) facilitative or mitigating and a higher proportion of those from men to be (primarily) confirmation-seeking – that is, what more recent discussions by Holmes call epistemic modal. In one of their studies, however, Cameron's group examined tags used in overtly asymmetric encounters: teacher–student, doctor–patient, parent–child, employer–employee, interviewer–interviewee. What was especially interesting was that the relatively powerless individual in these unequal encounters was the one more likely to produce epistemic modal tags and the relatively powerful was the one more likely to produce facilitative or softening tags. Indeed, this study found absolutely no instances of facilitative or softening tags from the lower status participant in the unequal exchanges examined. In the case of softening, it is easy to see that criticism or other potentially face-threatening social moves (like compliments) come down the hierarchy overwhelmingly more than up. Thus it is the person higher in the hierarchy who is far more likely to offer potential threats to the other's negative face and therefore to place themself in a position where the question of softening might arise. And when the question does arise, those threatening another's negative face will often opt for mitigation even if they are clearly ascendant in a situationally relevant hierarchy. This is especially true in communities of practice where raw displays of power over another are frowned upon, where there are overt ideologies of mutual respect and of (basic) egalitarianism that conflict with actual asymmetric distributions of rights and responsibilities. In the section below on indirection we return to the issue of mitigation.

It may not be immediately obvious why the person with greater power in a particular interaction should so overwhelmingly make facilitative use of tags. The term *facilitate* sounds as if what the facilitator is doing is basically helping the other(s) achieve their goals. Although facilitative tags certainly are often used to provide wanted opportunities for another to participate in a conversational exchange, eliciting the other's explicit response can also be an exercise in wielding power. The unprepared pupil may not really want to say anything to the teacher, and the child seeking freedom from parental monitoring might prefer on a given occasion not to engage at all with the parent. The tag not only invites another into an exchange: it makes it very difficult for the other to refuse the proffered "invitation" even should they want to do so. Even facilitative tags can coerce.

In contrast to the (primarily) facilitative and softening tag uses, the (primarily) epistemic modal uses came from both the powerful and the powerless, but more often from the powerless. Interestingly, however, Cameron's group found significant difference in the uses of the epistemic modals from people positioned differently in the hierarchy: the powerless tended to use them to seek reassurance whereas the powerful tended to use them to sum things up (and often then to close off an exchange). As they point out, the medical and classroom contexts are both ones where reassurance is often sought from the one in charge, a fact that might explain the higher use of tags from the powerless in this study.

What's going on here? We have (primarily) facilitative and softening uses of tags statistically associated with women in casual conversation among acquaintances and with the more powerful in asymmetric exchanges. We have (primarily) epistemic modal uses of tags statistically associated with men in peer exchanges and with the less powerful in asymmetric exchanges. Does this mean that it is really women who are socially powerful and men who are powerless? There are many other contextual factors that are relevant, but Cameron and her colleagues make the important point that we need not suppose an (implausibly) inverted gender hierarchy to reject the automatic association of women's utterances with powerless utterances. They ask:

> whether the role of conversational facilitator, which appears to favour the use of some types of tags in both casual conversation and unequal encounters, is a subcultural norm of all-female groups, a burden shouldered by subordinate speakers, or a strategy used to control ongoing talk – or, of course, whether it is all of these things at different times and in different settings. The possibility that women's more frequent use of facilitative tags could be a marker of control over conversation rather than one of responsibility for "interactional shitwork" [Fishman 1978's characterization of women's role in the conversations among intimates she analyzed] may appear to go against the grain of feminist studies.... No feminist would dispute that women are a subordinate group; but subordinate groups do after all negotiate and struggle against the conditions of their oppression. Certain aspects

of their social behaviour might profitably be analysed not as a simple
demonstration of those conditions, but as a complex way of coping with
them, or even a mode of resistance to them.

(Cameron *et al.* 1989, 91–92)

There are many reasons why women might often position themselves
as conversational facilitators. After all, conversational facilitation is,
on the surface, "nice" cooperative behavior, thus offering a socially approved mode for women's coping and resistance in particular social
contexts. There certainly are many complexities. One may adopt an apparently tentative stance toward content for primarily social reasons of
the sort Lakoff suggested: for example in order to construct the other as
authoritative and to demur from assuming authority oneself. Yet much
the same effect is produced by someone who is trying to construct the
self as non-arrogant, respectful of others and open to their potential
contributions. Is the speaker positioning themself as deferential to the
other or simply as an equal who is willing to listen to the other? Is the
speaker insecure or open-minded? Or perhaps both? Speakers trying
to assume a position of openness and tolerance may be interpreted as
adopting weak and vulnerable positions, as being unable or unwilling
to support their own positions. Yet enlisting others in one's projects,
and facilitating their active participation in talk may actually enhance
one's own effectiveness. Sometimes an air of entitlement and assumption of authority does indeed impress others, convince them that the
authority projected is legitimate and should be attended to. But not
always. Those who do not look like professors often have a harder
time endowing their utterances in certain situations with real force
than those who do, but they do sometimes succeed. Nonetheless, look-
ing/sounding authoritative enters into gender construction in many
ways: division of labor that leads to male dominance in many public arenas, heterosexual eroticization of female "weakness," systematic
devaluation and undermining of, for example, women's intellectual
capacities.[7]

Noting the complex multifunctionality of forms does not excuse us
from attending to the particular details of the use of different forms.
A tag question, for example, cannot readily be appended to a main
clause whose content is obviously not such as to allow input from the
addressee. Note the peculiarity of #*I have a headache, don't I?*[8] or #*You*

---

7 Men's caring and communicative capacities are also undervalued; Cameron (2000)
notes that this disadvantages them in access to certain (low-paying) phone bank jobs
that demand lots of (apparently) sympathetic talk to strangers.
8 The # signals that the utterance that follows is peculiar.

remind me of your mother, don't you? or even #*It's snowing, isn't it?* if uttered
to someone who's been for hours located in a windowless indoor room
with no communication from the outside by someone who's just come
inside and is shaking snow off themself. If there is some special context
where, for example, you might have some insight into my having a
headache that I myself lack, then such utterances might be usable. The
tag question is closely related to the direct question: there must be at
least the appearance of the possibility that the addressee's response on
the matter of the main clause might matter to the ongoing discourse.
In contrast, invariant tags don't always require the plausibility of some
input from the addressee on the matter broached in the main clause.
Here's a plausible discourse. A: "Turn down that hi-fi". B: "Why?" A: "I
have a headache, OK?" An invariant tag like *OK* may or may not be construed with respect to the main clause to which it is attached whereas
a tag question is always tied in to the main clause. So although there
are many commonalities among the different kinds of tags and various
other discourse positioning devices, they do need to be distinguished
and will enter into gender construction in somewhat different ways.[9]

At the same time, we will see important recurring patterns throughout this chapter. As we have seen in preceding chapters, the authority
to make meanings and have them taken up by others is generally at
stake as people engage with one another to create discourse. Linguistic resources that allow speakers to articulate a position toward some
idea or plan – an "epistemic" function – will almost always also play
a role in their positioning themselves toward other discourse participants (as well as towards others outside the immediate interaction) –
a social function. This should not surprise us. After all, constructing
discourse – launching meanings and having them taken up, collaboratively refining views of the world, and collectively planning projects –
is an intrinsically social project.

Uptalk

Along with tag questions, Lakoff identified the use of a "question" intonation on sentences that are not questions as a central component of
the style she characterized as both "women's" and "powerless" or "weak."
The "question" intonation has a high-rising tone at the end of the
sentence. What Lakoff called "inappropriate question intonation" has

9 See Miriam Meyerhoff (1992) for an account of the New Zealand invariant tag *eh*,
associated with Maori speakers, especially men, and with young women of European
descent, a group known as Pakeha in New Zealand.

more recently been dubbed "uptalk" by the media. We have already mentioned her often quoted example (1975):

Husband: When will dinner be ready?
Wife: Six o'clock?

McConnell-Ginet (1975), an early review of Lakoff (1975), noted that there were many possible reasons for the wife's use of the high-rising terminal (HRT) in such an exchange other than insecurity about whether the time suggested was "right" or unwillingness to commit herself. She might be asking any one of a number of questions whose content is not explicitly given in the utterance: why do you want to know? are you listening to me? didn't I tell you already? do you have plans you haven't told me about? are you proposing that we go out for dinner instead of eating here at home? Or she may simply be indicating that she is open to continuing the exchange. Notice that the HRT is really quite different from the tag here: the wife would only reply "(it'll be ready at) six o'clock, won't it?" if she is not herself directly responsible for determining when it will be ready – maybe one of the kids is cooking tonight and she thinks the expected time has already been announced and is (perhaps gently) reminding her husband that he's already been given the information. Similarly, asked where one was born, only someone with a shaky hold on their life history (an adoptee, an amnesiac, a very old person suffering some dementia) would reply with a tag whereas the HRT is often used in such contexts (and more often if, e.g., the birthplace is not assumed to be familiar to the addressee – Ithaca, New York, rather than Boston, Massachusetts, for example). Requests for someone's name also often get HRT responses but not tags, with the likelihood of the HRT increased if the name is a relatively unusual one.

   McConnell-Ginet (1983) (a slightly revised version of McConnell-Ginet 1978) reports pilot results from a small-scale study that Sally and some of her students conducted in the late 1970s on the Cornell University campus. Investigators approached people outside a major campus building and asked, "what building is this?" Both sexes sometimes answered "Olin Library" with a rising intonation but women did this more frequently than men.[10] Sally and the students who worked with her thought it quite implausible that any of the respondents had any

---

10 The study distinguished the HRT from a "low rise," which was interpreted as ending the utterance more decisively, as less "open" than the HRT and much less like a question. Both kinds of final rise were heard more from women, but Lakoff seems to have had the HRT in mind.

doubts about the building's identity or were in any way insecure about what they had said. As with the dinnertime scenario, there are implicit questions possible in the context: is this really what you want to know? is this answer comprehensible to you? why did you ask me (rather than some other available addressee)? Ladd (1980) argued that rising finals simply mark incompleteness, lack of finality. Indeed, in a study of preadolescent boys' narratives, Andrea Kortenhoven (1998) found that almost every utterance in the development of the narrative carried the HRT, whereas the introduction and the conclusion never did.

Treating the HRT as having the basic meaning of "nonfinal" is consistent with understanding its use in response to questions as an implicit question and also as conveying "I'm open to continuing this exchange." There could be many reasons women might be somewhat more likely than men to find it advisable not simply to close off the interaction with a falling final tone. For example some research suggests that this falling final is heard as "self-centered" in contrast to the "sociability" of a rise (see Edelsky 1979). Women's construction of themselves often gives sociability a central role, whereas appearing self-centered is particularly problematic for women. Similarly, a woman might well be somewhat more wary of a stranger's approaching and speaking to her than would a man, and the strategy of the implicit query about the stranger's motives could be a very useful one. However they were positioning themselves, both women and men in the Cornell study sometimes answered with the HRT. In some contexts men lead in answering questions with HRT. In a fast-food kiosk on the Stanford campus, cashiers take orders and then add "your name, please?" A class project done on parents' weekend found that the overwhelmingly greatest use of HRT in response came from older (father-aged) men. The goodwill mission atmosphere of parents' weekend may well dispose society's more powerful to make special efforts to show their sociability.

A high-rising final on a declarative is heard far more often among speakers of American English now than when Lakoff's analysis first appeared, especially among younger speakers. And even before the notable increase in HRTs of some kind among young American English speakers, a similar (though not phonetically identical) pattern had been widely observed among speakers of Australasian English.[11] In the US, the phenomenon of a significant rise at the end of a declarative utterance has become so commonplace that, as we have noted, the media have picked up on it and dubbed it "uptalk." Uptalk figures in the (highly disparaged) stereotype of "Valley Girl" speech (note the

11 See Guy *et al.* (1986) for Australia, and Britain (1992) for New Zealand.

gendering) and is part of a number of other styles associated especially with young females and devalued by most media commentators.
Although uptalk is by no means absent from the speech of young men
(on opposite coasts of the US, both of us hear it fairly often from our
male as well as our female students, even from young men who seem
to exemplify hegemonic "straight" masculinity), it is still often characterized as both feminine and insecure, lacking in confidence. HRT is
widely viewed as a "weakening" usage, characteristic of the powerless,
with powerlessness and the feminine being closely linked. What is less
clear is whether it is interpreted in the same way when heard from a
man as from a woman.

Cynthia McLemore (1992) conducted a detailed study of intonational
usage in a sorority at the University of Texas. The young women in the
sorority used HRT frequently, but it certainly did not always or even
primarily signal lack of power. Indeed, it was often used by sorority
leaders in presentations at group meetings. One function was to indicate that the speaker was not yet ready to cede speaking space to
someone else – that she was still engaged in her turn. In some contexts HRTs were used by speakers to facilitate others' participation in
the ongoing discourse or to elicit cooperation in work tasks. But at the
same time that they used and interpreted HRT as interactionally useful
and unproblematic, the young women in the sorority recognized that
HRT – along with other features of the tunes of their speech to one
another – was devalued by those in the wider world, heard as evidence
of wishy-washy empty-headedness. Another double bind. To position
themselves with some authority outside the walls of their sorority, they
had to monitor and modify the intonational strategies they used so frequently and effectively for constructing themselves as competent and
likeable within its walls, strategies mainly not selected at a conscious
level. This is one case in which one might like to talk about different
male and female verbal cultures. But in contrast to the generic view
of misunderstanding put forth by Maltz and Borker (1982), we are not
talking about women's and men's intonation, but about intonation conventions in a particular female community of practice – a community
of practice that is quite aware of the ways in which its "inside" speech
differs from that of the "mainstream."

Who cares?: intensity and engagement

Women's speech is often seen as excitable, emotionally engaged but in a
trivializing way. Lakoff described women as "speaking in italics," trying
to strengthen but ultimately weakening their contributions. Men, she

said, use profanity to add emotional intensity and real force to their words. In this section we look more closely at how these two different kinds of linguistic resources for expressing engagement actually work in communicative practice and at their gendering.

Vocal and verbal italics

What does it mean to speak in italics? And what might someone do by so speaking? The most obvious interpretation of vocal italics invokes the ups and downs, the singsong quality and use of vocal accenting, that Melanie Phillips (see chapter two) advised male-to-female transgendered people to adopt in order to sound suitably feminine.

Sally McConnell-Ginet (1983), reviewing a number of studies of people reading passages out loud, claimed that English-speaking men heard as hegemonically masculine showed much less variation in fundamental frequency and that they shifted frequency less often than women or men whose speech was heard as effeminate. Rather than "singsong," she described the speech of women and men judged effeminate as relatively "dynamic." Fundamental frequency – how fast the vocal cards are vibrating – is associated with perceived pitch, what we hear as relatively high or low. Phonetician Carolyn Henton (1989) reminded readers that perceived pitch varies exponentially with fundamental frequency rather than linearly. For example the pitch interval between frequencies of 100 and 200 hertz (hz) per second is equal to that between 200 and 400. Correcting for this, it is by no means clear that English-speaking women as a group in the studies available do use a wider pitch range than English-speaking men. Nor is there adequate data of the role of intonational range in male speech judged "effeminate." (See Gaudio 1994 and Podesva *et al.* 2002 for discussion of phonetic characteristics of speech of men positioning themselves as gay; judging speech "effeminate" is, of course, not the same thing as positioning its producer as "gay".)

Another and perhaps more important aspect of intonational dynamism is relatively frequent pitch shifts. More frequent shifts highlight or accent a larger proportion of syllables – such liberality in giving special prominence to syllables certainly must be at least part of what Lakoff had in mind when she said women "speak in italics." Again, there is still relatively little data on actual usage available. The point that does stand – and that Lakoff first made – is that dynamism is often called on for assuming a feminine gendered position.

A flat monotone delivery is at the other end of the scale of intonational dynamism from speaking in italics. The extreme positions are the stuff of caricature, completely unengaged utter boredom pitted against off-the-charts excitability and excitement: Mr. Too-Cool-for-Words meets Ms. Bubbly-Congeniality-Gone-Wild. The extremes are, of course, available when parody is what's called for, and they are certainly gendered. In her video *Adventures in the Gender Trade*, Kate Bornstein reports on her visit to a speech therapist during the time she was making the transition from a male to a female identity. Swooping up and down the scale (and with lots of breathiness) and beautifully illustrating the singsong voice Melanie Phillips described as typical of women, Bornstein says "She wanted me to talk like THIS." Restraining the dynamism (and breathiness), she goes on: "But I didn't want to be that kind of woman."[12]

There are many speaking positions that make much subtler use of tonal accenting than the extremes of variability or monotonicity. Drawing on Judith Butler's work, Tom Delph-Janiurek (1999) argues that voices "are a form of 'drag'," performed by speakers against a backdrop of gendered expectations. They are interpreted by taking account of "roles" that speakers may be performing (e.g. teacher or student) and their perceived gender. At least for men, he suggests, voices that sound lively and engaged are sometimes heard as marks of nonheterosexuality, perhaps even overriding other cues to claimed sexual identity. Dynamism is one important voice feature he mentions.

A number of studies associate greater intonational dynamism with (perceived) greater emotional expressiveness, suggesting that dynamism can do "affective" work of a certain kind. Sharing one's feelings with the other and expressing caring interest in them are among the aims that heightened intonational dynamism may help serve. Of course this can make it useful in situations where a speaker's aim is to create the illusion of such bonding. Deborah Cameron (2000) reports on research among employees at a large phone bank center. These jobs require many hours of talking on behalf of a company to customers of that company, prospective or perhaps disgruntled. The employees' charge is to present the companies they represent as "caring" about the customer on the other end of the phone line. To this end, they are often instructed to "put a smile in your voice." The "smiley" voice is intonationally dynamic and also has various other phonetic features often associated with "feminine" speech. As several employees observed to Cameron, women are thought to be "naturally" good at this kind of talking. This reflects not only the belief that women "naturally" care

12 Throughout her work, Kate Bornstein questions gender dichotomies and gender categories more generally. Like the video mentioned in the text, her *My Gender Workbook* (Bornstein 1998) makes many important points about gender with intelligence and humor.

about others' well-being (even when the others are complete strangers). It also reflects the belief that intonation itself is largely "natural," an audible signal of the inner emotional state of the speaker. Both of these beliefs are deeply problematic.

Another kind of phone job in which an animated voice is important for creating the illusion of interpersonal bonds is that of the operators who respond to calls to 900 adult sex services. As Kira Hall (1995) makes clear, these operators draw on many of the elements of Lakoff's "women's language" to create phone personalities that male callers find appealingly "feminine" and sexually arousing, personalities that the male customers incorporate in their own sexual fantasies. In both kinds of phone work, the people engaged are quite self-consciously manipulating intonation and other vocal qualities as part of projecting a certain kind of stance toward the person on the other end of the line. In both instances, it is important that the sense of engagement and caring projected by the phone worker seem unfeigned, "natural."

Many workplaces require a very different "economy of affect," the phrase used by Bonnie McElhinny (1995) in talking about her work with women who have entered the traditionally masculine realm of policework. "I don't smile much anymore," reported one woman, and a persistent theme was that to be appropriately professional, police officers had to learn to control expressions of sympathy or similar kinds of personal involvement in their official encounters with members of the public. They had to seem "uncaring," interested only in their own responsibilities as law enforcers. To position themselves as capable professionals these women had to position themselves as unaffected by the plight of those whom they spoke with in the course of duty and thus to deny any affiliative ties with those people. Positioning oneself as cool, collected, and unaffected by the other's troubles will almost certainly involve dampening intonational dynamism, removing the vocal italics. The woman who doesn't "smile much anymore" will also probably refrain from offering reassuring pats on the shoulder, avoid certain kinds of eye contact, reduce her level of backchannel encouragement, regulate her facial expressions of disgust or horror, and so on. In addition, of course, the semantic content of what she says will be monitored: in particular, words expressing sympathy (whether explicitly or implicitly) will tend to be censored. In practice, of course, police officers of both sexes do indeed sometimes offer sympathy, though often only when they can "frame" it as outside the official interaction. In practice, it is also quite possible that sympathy is differentially withheld, with race and class and age and gender all potentially relevant. The important point is that to position themselves as impartial – disinterested in one sense of that word – the women police officers found it important to position themselves as uninvolved, unengaged – disinterested in another sense. Intonational "control" is one resource on which they draw, along with others.

Other things being equal, relative dynamism can attract and hold listeners' attention. Thus those who cannot depend on others' positioning them as worthy of attention may turn to verbal italics to try to improve their discourse position. Relative dynamism is one feature of "motherese," a speech register so named because it is associated with the speech of adult caretakers to young children. (And note that such speech is treated as "feminine.") Those who are trying to engage young children may often need extra help in doing so. Of course people are often also unable to assume the automatic attention of the adult audiences they address, whether in small group informal conversation or in more public forums. Intonational dynamism is part of what makes for a "lively" delivery, helping position a speaker as someone worth listening to.

Other things seldom are equal, of course. Perhaps those already positioned as respected authorities or otherwise particularly valued speakers can more readily afford to sound relatively unengaged or uninvolved with the listeners, whose interest and attention come at little or no extra "cost" to the speaker. But even for those who might seem to be authoritatively positioned, some effort may be advisable. Drawing on university students' remarks about the voices of some of their senior male lecturers, Delph-Janiurek (1999, p. 147) comments: "Cohering with the dictates of how hegemonic masculinity is vocally performed is clearly detrimental to the task of instructing, in that dreary, expressionless lecturing voices make for dreary lectures that do not hold the attention of student audiences, let alone interest or enthuse them." Speaking in italics is not required to elicit interest (and is indeed, given its extreme nature, probably counterproductive) but some vocal indicators of engagement are certainly needed.

There are, of course, many ways of taking a fully engaged discourse position, of trying to endow what one says with real force. Vocal (or printed) italics are one way. Relying on them does, however, render the speaker vulnerable to being interpreted as unable (or unwilling) to assume a subject position that will itself suffice to give the ideas expressed real weight. Talk of conversational "insecurity" or self-imposed "weakness" is no longer much encountered among language and gender scholars. In the wider US culture, however, it remains popular to attribute lack of influence or impact of what is said by a woman (or by anyone who does not occupy an authoritative position) to deficiencies in their speech. This idea gets support from an ideology of a meritocratic society, where failure to achieve is due to failure of talents or effort or both. The "insecure" speaker is seen as rendered unable (or unwilling) by a psychological (or character) flaw to position herself (or sometimes himself) effectively. That inability or unwillingness, some concede, might be induced by social norms she encountered growing up that warned her of the "unfemininity" of such positioning. Yet as Fishman (1980) argues, overall "insecurity" as an account of reliance on such attention-getting devices as "talking in italics" or asking questions misses the fact that such devices are used to (try to) solve specific interactional difficulties. Many of these difficulties arise in the context of social structural facts that render some discourse positions (virtually) inaccessible to people occupying certain gender, race, class, or occupational positions.

Other "boosting" devices such as the (liberal) use of intensifiers like *so, incredibly, awfully*, and their exaggerated kin can be thought of as verbal italics (and they are often delivered with tonal highlighting), and they face similar difficulties. Although ostensibly such devices indicate a "stronger" move than would be made without them, their actual effect is sometimes just the opposite because of how others respond to the speaker's choices. In a recent study of the Longman corpus from 1995 of conversations among friends and family, Kristen Precht (2002) did indeed find women using two of these amplifying forms (*so + adjective* and *so much*) significantly more than men, but there were no significant differences in the use of any of the other amplifiers she examined (e.g. *totally* or *really* + verb or adjective). Like tonal accents, these amplifiers can construct an engaged and enthusiastic speaking position. And they sometimes do. Others can, however, use them to position a speaker as lacking in "real" authority, as drawing on these resources in an attempt to divert attention from lack of institutional status or socially conferred prestige that would enable "plainer" words to do what's needed.

"Strong" language

What about profanity and other kinds of interjections that can express extreme intensity? Swearing is widely considered an expression of very strong emotion: anger at specific others or simply deep frustration, often manifest as anger directed at the closest available target. It is viewed as potent language and can indeed sometimes achieve impressive effects. Profanity is also considered unsuitable for women and children. As we mentioned in chapter two, there is considerable evidence that young women are using taboo language in large numbers these days (e.g. Vincent 1982) but also that many men and some women still express discomfort at hearing tabooed words from women's mouths or in mixed company. There are still laws on the books in parts of the US prohibiting the use of "foul" language in the presence of women and children: a Michigan man was indicted and convicted under such a statute in the summer of 1999.

Lakoff and others have seen gender privilege in access to profanity as depriving women of resources they need. In many contexts a woman using obscenity positions herself rather differently from a man speaking the same way. Recognition of this different positioning is part of what leads some women to seek substitutes for the tabooed forms. Euphemisms like "oh, piffle!" (reported by one of Sally's students as erupting from her mother at a moment of extreme frustration and anger) may sound silly to others but may enable those using them to vent without crossing over into the dangerous arena opened up by taboo language. Precht (2002), the recent corpus study of conversations recorded in 1995 that we mentioned in the preceding section, did find the men recorded saying *shit* significantly more than the women and the women saying *gosh* significantly more than the men. But there were no significant sex differences in the use of *damn* or *god* or, for that matter, of the positive interjections *wow* and *cool*.

Anger is the emotion most expected and tolerated (in some contexts even encouraged) from men. Raised voices and abusive insults are part of expressing anger: they can be frightening and thus function in social control. Anger is seen as heightening someone's power, their capacity to get others to respond as they want. The power of anger, including the power of some swearing, probably arises primarily from its capacity to produce fear, to intimidate. Of course, anger does not always intimidate. Women's anger is often repositioned as frustration or emotional "upset," framed as nonthreatening and, indeed, as rendering its subject vulnerable. "You're so cute when you're mad." Women's increased use of obscene language in expressing anger can represent a repositioning that challenges male dominance and that claims authority. Of course, whether such a repositioning is indeed accomplished depends on many factors: the woman whose anger and verbal abuse targets others (often women) not responsible for the inequities that enrage her is not engaging in feminist politics, no matter how much she draws attention to her disavowal of certain traditionally "feminine" positions. Anger directed at appropriate rather than simply available targets can be effective, but identifying such targets is generally difficult and often impossible. Of course, anger need not target individuals but can fuel action aimed at changing social structures.

Profanity probably does have a much wider range of uses in positioning and repositioning than its euphemistic substitutes. Along with ritual insults, many of which also involve taboo language, interjections like *fucking* are often liberally used in contexts where there is not even the pretense of anger or attempted intimidation. Kuiper (1991) and Kiesling (1997) have both examined male-only social contexts that are characterized by such "dirty language." As they and others have pointed out, this kind of talk often plays an important role in social bonding in such groups. It signals shared freedom from the control of those who have criticized such language in the past: mainly, mothers and schoolteachers (mostly women). Its connection with anger and intimidation often remains relevant, however. Exposure to such language in play helps prepare people to position themselves effectively to deal with more serious situations. Surface playfulness often coexists with the possibility, perhaps not explicitly acknowledged, that the mock abuse and pretend intimidation might erupt into real violence, verbal or otherwise. "Trash talk" on the basketball court is indeed intended to intimidate though, of course, the intimidation is in the service of a game, a ritual context for displacing many "strong" emotions. Finally, as has often been observed, profanity often draws on metaphors of gender and sexuality that evoke misogynistic or homophobic attitudes and practices. Not surprisingly, this can make its use problematic for those who are consciously trying to counter such attitudes and practices. (We discuss metaphors in discourse in the following chapter.)

Calibrating commitment and enlisting support

In the preceding section we saw that women's language is often seen as implicitly weakened by their turning to intensifiers or vocal indicators of emphasis. But women are often also accused of positioning themselves as less than completely committed to the content of what they have said, thus apparently explicitly weakening or mitigating the force of their utterances. Lakoff, for example, suggested that women speaking English tended to "hedge" their bets with qualifiers such as *sorta* or *probably* and also discourse particles like *you know*, *of course*, and *like* that do not contribute much to the content that is conveyed but in various ways solicit sympathetic interpretation and perhaps ultimate support from the listener. And in Japanese there are sentence-final particles signaling degree and kind of commitment of the speaker that are central to the picture of Japanese women's language. We will discuss first some English resources and then the Japanese. Just as apparent strengthening may sometimes weaken or mitigate, so apparent weakening can sometimes strengthen, and what seems to be empty can serve important communicative functions.

Discourse particles and hedges

Classic examples of "hedging" modifiers like *probably, sorta, kinda*, and *fairly* and also discourse particles like *you know* and *of course* and *like* (in certain of its uses) serve in many contexts to position their users defensively.

Kristen Precht's recent corpus study also looked at some of the hedging modifiers; she included forms like *kinda, sorta*, and *pretty* (as in "I'm **pretty** tired") not as hedges but as what she called downtoners. In both these categories, the only significant differences Precht found were ones where men were in the lead.

Discourse particles are generally not syntactically integrated into the main utterance, and they don't generally contribute to content as much as to positioning.[13] They are sometimes said to be "empty" or mere "verbal fillers." Some examples: "Her family's filthy rich, **you know**" or "**of course** most women expect to become mothers" or "I was *like* blown away by what he said to me". But neither hedging modifiers nor "empty" discourse particles serve always to "weaken" the speaker's position: as with other resources, these forms have many other (sometimes cooccurring) functions.

Carolyn Houghton (1995) examined a group therapy session conducted among young women, mainly Latinas from an economically marginal community, who were (involuntarily) living in a therapeutic institution. Although in the particular utterance she highlights *you know* does not technically occur as a discourse marker (because it is syntactically integrated into the sentence produced and thus not grammatically parenthetical), its use by the young woman "client" and the therapist's response to it shed considerable light on the discourse particle use of *you know*.

> Client: You know how that is when you just want to have a baby, just something that is yours and belongs to you...
> Therapist: No Mirna, we don't know what it is like. Please tell us, but don't say "you." It is *your* experience, not ours, so you need to say "I" instead of "you." "That is how *I* feel when *I* see a baby."
> Client: Okay. I.   (Houghton 1995, 123–124)

---

13 Schiffrin (1987) is a useful source for some of the most commonly used discourse markers in American English.

You know can serve to position addressees as sharing the speaker's out-look, as forming a collectivity with her. It is precisely this attempted positioning of the others as a source of potential support that the therapist challenges and tries overtly to prevent. Notice also that the therapist's *we* positions her as spokesperson of the group being ad-dressed, a group made up mainly of the young client's peers, other young Latinas who almost certainly do not share the therapist's out-look and who indeed are very likely to share the expressed perspective on having babies. Erecting obstacles to forming such collectivities is part of a (therapeutic) strategy to change the young women's attitudes towards early parenthood and to direct them into paths seen as socially more acceptable. Of course, the therapist and the state and other in-stitutions for which she works may well see themselves as working for the young women's best interests. Nonetheless, the stricture against *you* talk is a socially coercive move.

As *you know* illustrates, the functions of the discourse particles can draw on their meanings in other contexts (where there are such uses). Discourse particles are seldom as "empty" as they might seem. In a num-ber of contexts investigators have found women using more *you knows* than men and using it more often for subject positioning – especially connecting themselves to the others – rather than for idea position-ing.[14] As with other moves to position oneself in alliance with others (classified by some analysts as facilitative or affective), interpreters of *you know* may instead (unlike the therapist) position the speaker who uses it as lacking conviction and needing reassurance. Presumably just how it is interpreted depends at least in part on how the interpreter already views the speaker's position(s).

The discourse particle *like* seems to work semantically more like the so-called hedging modifiers. Muffy Siegel (2002) has recently argued that *like* loosens meaning criteria for the expression following it: "he has, like, six sisters" is to be interpreted as true, according to Siegel, even if he has only five sisters. In her study of actual use of *like* among middle-class Philadelphia-area adolescents (all of whom were inter-viewed by their friend, Siegel's daughter), Siegel did find girls using the particle more often than boys. Interestingly, she also found a striking correlation of *like* with rapidity of response to the interviewer's ques-tion (the interviewer asked for responses to the quite abstract question, "what is an individual?"). On this basis and also on the basis of other in-formation she had about the respondents and their general capacities

14 See Holmes (1986) and the summary of this and other research on *you know* in Holmes (1995), ch. 3.

and demeanor, she rejects the popular media explanation of *like* as positioning its user as at least insecure and probably also unintelligent, an "airhead." Rather, she suggests, its use reflects a willingness among these girls to produce speech as it is being planned online, with more spontaneity and less editing than she found in the speech of most of the boys interviewed. She conjectures that the girls might well not have used *like* so often if the interviewer had not been one of their own group, a person with whom they felt secure enough to forgo careful preplanning of their speech. They sometimes said things like "I'm trying to think aloud", indicating clearly that they were indeed struggling to express themselves and yet were willing to allow others to witness the struggle directly. Precht's study mentions only *like* + *number*, which she classifies as a downtoner, and where she found a significant sex difference, with men well in the lead.

Sentence-final particles in Japanese

A good deal of the work on Japanese "women's language" focuses on sentence-final particles that add to or mitigate the force of an utterance. For example an assertion such as "I am going" can be expressed plainly, given mild emphasis, or given a more emphatic assertion with the use of particles as follows:

Mild assertion	Neutral	Emphatic assertion
iku wa	iku	iku ze/iku zo

The particles *wa, ze* and *zo* are only three of a fairly large inventory of sentence-final forms that signal the force of statements, questions, requests, and other speech acts. These particles are closely associated with gender, and are commonly identified in the literature as "women's," "neutral," and "men's" particles. (These examples were taken from Okamoto 1995, where they were identified as "feminine," "neutral," and "masculine." Interestingly, as lists get longer, native speakers we have consulted agree less on gender categorization.) Although all the particles occur in the speech of men and of women at one time or another, norms constrain women to use particles that mitigate the force of the utterance in more situations than men. Women are also less free to use the emphatic particles, some of which are nearer in their social value to English speakers' use of profanity for emphasis than to the use of boosters like *so* or *very*. This gendered use of these forms contributes to women's assuming gentle and self-effacing subject positions, men rough and assertive. Elinor Ochs (1996) cites these particles as examples of direct indexes of discourse stances or positions that, by virtue of the strong association between women and a "soft" stance, indirectly index gender. (We discuss indirect indexing of gender in more detail in chapter eight.)

Not surprisingly, real women in Japan often stray far from the normative ideal, and the norms seem to be changing. Shigeko Okamoto and Shie Sato (1992), comparing three age groups, found a decrease in the use of "feminine" forms. The older speakers (45–57 years of age) used "feminine" forms 50 percent of the time, women between the ages of 27 and 34 used them 24 percent of the time, and those between the ages of 18 and 23 used them 14 percent of the time. While it is unclear whether this represents change in usage through time or in the life-span of the speakers, it certainly shows that at least nowadays feminine forms are not favored by younger speakers. In a study of college-age women's use of final particles, Okamoto (1995) found that 65 percent of the forms used were "neutral," 19 percent were "masculine" (!), and 12 percent only were "feminine."

Such changes are bemoaned in the Japanese media as signaling the end of everything that is fine about women – they are becoming less polite, less nice. Some say that the difference between male and female is being erased. But since there have not been empirical studies of the usage of earlier speakers, it is not clear what exactly the status of younger speakers' use is. Yoshiko Matsumoto (2002) has argued that it is possible, even probable, that younger women never used as many of these forms as older women – both because they have not yet learned the delicacies of choice, and because the nature of their social relations is not yet as hierarchically complex. It is also probable, though, that social change is reducing the use of these forms as women enter the marketplace and demand greater equality, but also as girls grow up with different gender expectations and dynamics among their peers. As we will discuss in chapter nine, girls need new linguistic strategies to compete with their male peers, as well as to signal a new kind of youth culture. Women in managerial positions are adopting various linguistic strategies to assume authoritative speaking positions.[15] Recent surveys show the Japanese public will be more than happy to set aside the rule limiting the throne to male occupancy, welcoming the daughter born to the Crown Prince and Princess in late autumn of 2001 as a potential empress. Changing attitudes and practices in Japan outside the linguistic arena go hand in hand with changing gendered norms for speech positioning.

15 Janet Shibamoto Smith (1992) argues that women are importing something like "motherese" into their workplaces in order to sound authoritative while also "feminine", but see Yukako Sunaoshi (1994, 1995) and Miyako Inoue (forthcoming) for further discussion.

Speaking indirectly

Language ideology among dominant white social groups in the US sees directness as a virtue, indirectness as at best a waste of time and often as an impediment to effective communication. The indirection being criticized is often part of politeness, generally aimed at preventing hurt feelings, and it is women who are seen as caring about others' feelings and upholding politeness norms. Not surprisingly, it is women's supposed indirectness that is highlighted for criticism: "Why doesn't she just say what she means and not beat around the bush?"

Directives are requests, commands, and other speech acts that ask the addressee to act in some way specified by the speaker. In part because they generally impose on the addressee and thus threaten the addressee's negative face, it is often considered more polite to issue them indirectly. So one might say "could you pass the salt, please" or "would you mind passing the salt, please" instead of just "pass the salt, please". (Searle 1975 gives an account of some of the many ways in which such "indirect speech acts" can be performed.) The speaker is purporting to assume the position not of director but simply of inquirer, appearing to allow the addressee to decide whether to perform the act the speaker desires.[16] Issuing directives indirectly does not always mitigate the imposition on the addressee. It depends on the situation. For example, instead of directly saying "please set the table" to her child, a mother might say "could you set the table?" or "would you like to set the table?" In the latter utterance, for example, the mother appears to offer the child a choice, appears to respect the child's negative face. She tries to position herself as nonauthoritarian even in cases where she is really not going to let the child get out of table-setting. (Of course the attempt is not always successful. Sally's children, who saw that she was really telling them to set the table and only pretending to let them decide for themselves whether to do so, often responded "no, but I will!") Much of the literature on indirect speech acts deals with directives like these where ostensibly asking about the addressee's ability or desire to do X functions to direct the addressee to do X. Of course, like routine compliments, there are circumstances where the routine attention to negative face implied by an indirect form of a directive

---

16 As Robin Lakoff (1972) pointed out, if the act specified is one that might be assumed to be in the interest of the addressee rather than the speaker, it could be more polite to use the bald imperative: "do have some more cake" is overtly a directive but functions indirectly as an offer, protecting the addressee's positive face by pretending that eating more cake is being done to please the host and not because of the addressee's greediness. In some cases, of course, the addressee may indeed eat more cake just to please the host.

may be expected and welcomed even though everyone knows that the speaker has authority to get the addressee to do what's asked.

There is also the use of statements of one's wants or preferences as a way to direct the other to fill them. Recall the advice to male-to-female transsexuals learning the ways of femininity: avoid the supposedly masculine "I want a Big Mac" and instead say "I'd like a salad". Either of these forms is most likely to be used directively in situations where there is the clear understanding that the addressee is expected to see that the speaker's wants or preferences are attended to – service encounters like those in fast-food establishments are prime examples of cases where this holds. Neither form is an explicit directive: in both cases the server has to supply the unexpressed "give it to me", but both are also quite conventional and easily recognized ways to issue such a directive. The "I'd like" form does seem to suggest "if you have one" or "if you can manage that", not taking for granted quite so strongly as the *I want* that the order will be forthcoming. Positioning oneself as reluctant or hesitant to direct the other by leaving open the possibility that the other will not perform the specified act, can address the negative face needs of that other, and can mitigate the potential damage to social relations done by the directive. Used with peers in situations where the director does not have authority, this kind of indirection – perhaps especially the use of the conventionally "polite" indirect forms – does often have a softening effect. And its routine use in service situations can help maintain an air of civil concern for the server. Whether women actually do use it more in such circumstances is not clear, but it certainly is available for gender positioning, once again drawing on the ideology of women's concern for others. But in some circumstances such "concerned" positioning may be seen as bogus and thus can backfire. Employees may react to a boss's indirection much as Sally's children did to hers (though perhaps less overtly and good-naturedly, just complaining behind the boss's back about what they perceive as the "phony" respect being shown them). Of course, the boss may genuinely be offering employee choices, trying to move the organization toward more nearly egalitarian working modes.

Criticisms are also often presented indirectly. "Oh, you haven't set the table yet" could serve to criticize the addressee for not having set the table as could "Well, I guess I'll have to set the table myself". Or, given certain expectations about appreciative response, criticism of the addressee might be conveyed simply by inadequate or missing positive commentary: consider the boss who when asked "did you read my report?" simply replies "yes". Again, indirection does not always mitigate. None of these examples of indirect criticisms seems to soften the critical blow. Rather they seem to allow the critic to deny having been critical, offering protection against possible complaint from the one criticized. Effectively mitigating criticism, softening its effect, often involves preceding it by noncritical, perhaps complimentary, comments and presenting the criticism in such a way as to seem not to be denigrating the addressee but offering a helpful suggestion. "That was an interesting report – maybe you could add a few charts to help the sales people get your point." Even this genuinely mitigating use of indirection in criticism is seen by some as just a waste of time. A philosopher acquaintance of Sally's recently complained to her about what he sees as the new trend to avoid direct criticism in philosophical debate, a trend he saw as lowering the quality of the debate as well as wasting the debaters' time and energies.

Expressions of one's own desires and preferences when they are being considered along with those of the addressee in some negotiation for joint activity is another kind of move that often leads speakers to position themselves so as to avoid or minimize potential social trouble. Someone might say "well, I could come at nine" in a context where it's clear that to do so would be seriously inconvenient whereas coming at noon would be far preferable. In this case, there's an implicit suggestion that coming at nine would not be good but indicating one's willingness to do so if required is supposed to be an expression of willingness to be as open as possible to others' interests. If the addressee is not tuned in to the fact that the offer to come at nine is really pro forma and the speaker's fervent hope (and concealed plan) is that it be rejected, then the speaker may be quite disappointed in what finally happens. In such situations a partner more accustomed to more direct expression of desires who later discovers the disappointment that's ensued may say "why didn't you SAY that you really wanted to meet at noon rather than nine?"

There are important differences in the extent and kind of indirection expected in different communities of practice. To Europeans, Americans in general often seem overly indirect. Americans, in turn, often hear Japanese as overly indirect. And many analysts have written of women as much less direct than men: this is part of the picture that Lakoff painted of women's hesitating to present themselves forcefully in their speech.[17] It is routine indirection accompanying impositive social moves like directives or criticisms or negotiation over preferences that seems to draw the most attention and criticism, presumably because, as with routine complimenting, some addressees do not

17 Patricia Wetzel (1988) discusses the many ways in which normative Japanese speech (including male Japanese speech) fits with the "powerless" model that Lakoff has proposed for women's speech.

appreciate the figurative character of the pro forma other-respecting positions indirect speakers assume. (And, of course, some addressees resent the work required of them to deal with extreme indirection like that involved in the negotiation over meeting times.)

Indirection is far more pervasive and complex than its use with social moves that impose on the addressee might suggest. Sarcasm and teasing, for example, are indirect, and in the next chapter we will discuss the general phenomenon of implying more or other than what is explicitly said, which is what indirection means. Marcyliena Morgan (1991) has argued that indirection is highly valued in many African American communities of practice and is certainly not always associated with lack of "force." She suggests that language ideology in these communities expects listeners to participate actively in working out possible implications of what speakers say: speakers have neither full responsibility for nor full authority over the meanings that get put into play by their contributions. The practice of *signifying*, for example, involves using clever and sometimes quite subtle allusions, overtly speaking about one thing in order to convey something rather different, which can then be elaborated further by listeners. Claudia Mitchell-Kernan (1969, 1972) offers a particularly cogent discussion of the role of signifying in the co-construction of meaning in the African American community, which we mentioned in the preceding chapter. Signifying and other kinds of teasing sometimes have an aim of correcting the other. Good-humored teasing can mitigate or soften the force of the correction by couching it indirectly and positioning the critic as simply playful; of course, this also makes it more difficult for the object of the teasing to object, given the playful frame. Teasing and humor generally can have a bite but can also often be engaged in for sheer pleasure, including aesthetic pleasure in the verbal skills on which they draw.

Indirectness, then, can be considerate or defensive, part of positioning the self as attending to others' rights and concerns. It can also, however, enter into many other rather different kinds of positioning with very different kinds of effects. In the next chapter we will consider in a bit more detail how people manage to imply so much more than what they explicitly say and see how indirectness depends so heavily on particular expectations about practices within specific communities.[18]

---

18 Rundquist (1992) offers both a discussion of different kinds of indirectness and an empirical study of women's and men's use of one form of indirection. She found differences in how the women and men she studied used this indirection and she found men using it more than women.

CHAPTER 6

Saying and implying

In this chapter we will look more closely at the content of what people communicate as they engage with one another, the substance of the positions they take, especially those that connect directly to gender. Where and how does gender figure in linguistic representations of beliefs, fears, wishes, desires, and plans?

The content of an utterance, its literal meaning, is often thought of as simply what the semantics of the linguistic system being used assigns as the meaning of the linguistic expression that has been uttered, what is directly encoded by the text the speaker has produced. Of course it is important to know what the linguistic expressions used encode, but what is meant and what is communicated seldom end there. For one thing, there are many expressions that need to be interpreted with respect to a particular utterance. To understand, for example, just what is being claimed by an utterance of *she's tall*, we need to know both to whom *she* refers and the approximate standards of tallness that might be at stake in the context in which the utterance is produced. In general, we use stuff beyond the linguistic code like pointing or our assumptions about the height of teenage girls, to help us actually *say* contentful things.

And beyond what we say overtly, we often *imply* much more. In uttering *she's tall*, for example, someone might be conveying that she'll have a hard time finding a suitable boyfriend, drawing on nonlinguistic assumptions about relative heights in heterosexual partnering and also taking it for granted that her finding a boyfriend is important. Covert or hidden messages like these often do more to create and sustain gender ideologies than the explicit messages that are overtly conveyed.

Case study

In the US during the late summer and early fall of 1991, some people wore buttons with the message *I believe Anita Hill*. To know the explicit message conveyed by a particular "utterance" – in this case, a button-wearing – it was necessary to know who was "speaking" – i.e., who was wearing the button – and also to know something about which claims of which person named Anita Hill the wearer was thereby endorsing. This wasn't so difficult. As we mentioned in chapter three, Professor Anita Hill was then testifying during the US Senate hearings that were held as part of the process to confirm Judge Clarence Thomas's nomination to the Supreme Court.

As the hearings were in progress, they were televised to huge audiences and widely reported in other media. In addition, many face-to-face everyday conversations were about the hearings and the issues they raised. Thus lots of adult Americans at that point had access to a shared discursive practice that made it very easy for them to get the explicit message that the button-wearer was claiming to believe Hill's rather than Thomas's account of their earlier interactions. By choosing to wear a button to convey this explicit message, the button-wearer was also making an implicit political statement drawing on the place of wearing such buttons in recent discursive practice in the US. Among other things, the button-wearer implicitly suggested that others might be wearing an identical button and thus that the opinion expressed was not simply that of an individual. So there was the explicit message and the implicit suggestion, provided by the button genre, that the utterer's opinion was shared by other like-minded folks. Notice that the implicit meanings here might not necessarily be generated by other uses of the sentence *I believe Anita Hill*. They arose from the particular discourse contexts, including not only the temporally specific knowledge of the Thomas hearings but also more general assumptions about button-wearing and its purposes.

Around the same time, some people wore a different button, one that said *We believe her*. Here the explicit situated message was essentially the same, except for one important difference. The use of *we* rather than *I* made explicit the suggestion of a collective rather than simply an individual endorsement of Anita Hill's position, a suggestion only implicit in the other button's message. The *we*, of course, did not specify who those others might be, though the implicit suggestion was that they would include those affiliated with the button-wearer, with folks who did not believe Hill assigned to *they*.

Saying *her* rather than *Anita Hill* did not change the explicit content, but it did create some new *implicit* meanings. To use *her* was to assume that the reader could indeed identify the particular female referent, Anita Hill, who was being said to be believed. But more importantly, although *her* in the situations in which the button was being worn clearly referred to Anita Hill, the form itself can refer to any woman.

The implicit suggestion was that the button-wearer and others in the collectivity embraced by *we* were not simply endorsing Hill's particular claims about particular incidents. Rather, the button (implicitly) conveyed the far more general view that when a woman accuses a man of sexually harassing her on the job and he denies the charge, *we* believe *her* rather than the implied *him*. Button readers who wanted to be affiliated with the button-wearer were (implicitly) urged to adopt the view expressed on the button. An implicit suggestion can itself be implicitly qualified: our general policy is to believe her accusations of his harassing her unless there's very strong evidence to suggest that she's untrustworthy or acting maliciously. There was also the suggestion that we take this stance because we believe that sexual harassment of women by men is a widespread and underreported phenomenon.

As we saw in chapter three, many African American women saw the hearings (at least initially) as yet another attempt to frame a black man, and saw Hill's style as signaling an affiliation with European American women and a denial of her own African American heritage. The upshot was that the *we* collectively claiming to *believe her* were seen by African Americans to be primarily middle-class white women. Black women tended to see the implied but absent *him* as black and the *her* in this case and perhaps in all the other evoked cases as white or white-identified.

Were there buttons that said *I believe Clarence Thomas* or *we believe him*? Apparently not. Why the disparity? As we saw in chapter three, Norma Mendoza-Denton (1995) argues that the senators running the hearings tended to position Thomas as more credible in various ways. For example she notes that they offered "pregnant pauses" after his words that attested to the weight they gave those words. But, of course, it was certainly not only the majority of senators who were supporting *him* versus *her*. It was many other men and also many women, both African Americans and others, who distrusted Hill. To be somewhat skeptical of Hill did not, of course, mean a full endorsement of Thomas nor did it mean a blanket rejection of movements against workplace sexual harassment.[1] But the weight of public opinion at the time was with him, not her.

The buttons that were worn thus evoked the buttons not worn, apparently not even made. Perhaps the absence of Thomas-endorsing buttons

---

1 See Morrison (1992), Smitherman (1995a), and other articles in Smitherman (1995b) for more discussion of the complex intertwining of race and gender in this episode and also for some of the ways in which attitudes developed and changed over time. Many women, including many African American women, who initially supported Thomas later joined in efforts to dislodge workplace sexual harassment.

implied most strongly that Thomas's position was politically ascendant, what the powerful endorsed. Buttons typically voice resistance. To wear a button is to take an oppositional stance, implicitly acknowledging that the views enunciated on the button cannot be taken for granted. The *we* on a button are seldom more than a sizable protest voice. The protest in this case did not keep Thomas off the court but it did bring issues of sexual harassment into the public eye, eventually with the support of many who did not identify themselves as believing Anita Hill.

Aspects of meaning in communicative practice

As the Anita Hill buttons illustrate, interpretation is a very complex process. We do not just "understand" other people's utterances – we figure them out, in part, by consulting vast histories of common experience. The focus of this and the next chapter is how gender figures in the content of discourse. What do people say and imply about gender when they talk to one another or produce texts for wider audiences? How are these messages understood and what is their effect? How do gender relations influence the discourse processes that make meaning and vice versa? The next chapter focuses on the categorizing and labeling processes that are fundamental for articulating content. In this chapter, the emphasis is on how texts and the subtexts they imply enter into gendered communicative practice. How do they draw on and change the contexts in which they are uttered?

As we have already noted, it is useful to distinguish three aspects of linguistically conveyed content: what is *encoded*, what is *said*, and what is *implied*. Using Austin's speech act typology, which we introduced in chapter four, what is encoded is a matter of what locutionary act has been performed. That is, what is encoded depends only on the linguistic meaning of the expressions uttered, the words and how they are syntactically combined: what the code assigns to the text produced. What a text encodes does not by itself make a meaningful social move, performance of an illocutionary act. For full meaning in action, we have to consider what is said and what is implied, both of which go beyond what is encoded. And, of course, perlocutionary acts are also critical: what is *accomplished*. What is ultimately taken up, how ideas and feelings are changed, what plans are furthered: all of this is critical to understanding the full significance of ongoing discourse.

Roughly, what is said is a matter of contextual specification or filling out of the encoded meaning as applied on the occasion of a particular utterance. For example, *Anita Hill* on one set of those buttons and *her* on another both referred to a particular person, the law professor from the University of Oklahoma. Knowing this required more than linguistic knowledge. In a different time and place either kind of button would produce bewilderment even in readers with full understanding of the code used: interpreting the buttons depended on access to a rich sociopolitical context in which they were worn. Notice also that what is said need not be fully explicit – for example just exactly what is being said to be believed by the button-wearers is left implicit; nor are the boundaries of the *we* fully specified.

What is implied is, of course, all implicit. What is implied includes all the additional messages that can be conveyed on the basis of what has been said and how it was said in the particular communicative situation, which includes a particular audience. We saw a number of examples of implied messages conveyed by the buttons: for example that one is taking a general stance on allegations of sexual harassment. What is implied need not add to what is said but may restrict or even contradict it; consider, for example, speakers positioning themselves ironically.

Encoding, saying, and implying are what speakers do. Hearers generally both *decode* and *draw inferences* about what speakers are attempting to convey. Often the hearer is really only interested in the total message conveyed, perhaps paying little attention to just which parts were actually said and which were implied. So, for example, someone who has seen a button *I believe Anita Hill* and then encounters a button *We believe her* may (with considerable justification) view them as conveying the same meaning (and may later forget which button was worn by which person). Even where the distinction between what was actually said and what was implied was very relevant in the immediate context for understanding, the hearer may ultimately remember only the end effect, forgetting just how it was accomplished. The distinction between what is said and what is implied is at the heart of indirection, which we discussed at the end of the last chapter. To speak indirectly is to imply rather than say certain things, and the hearer must appreciate the indirection to understand the speaker's positioning. Yet the hearer might simply remember something along the lines of *Mother told me to set the table* when what was actually uttered was *Would you like to set the table?*

In other words, to figure out what was said or what was implied a hearer has to go beyond decoding and draw inferences based not simply on accessing a linguistic code but also on understanding of social practices, of others' motives and strategies and capabilities, and of other particulars about the contexts in which communication is occurring. What is conveyed to a hearer is a total message: what is said plus what is implied. A major mechanism of change in the meanings assigned by a linguistic code is that what is initially (only) implied comes to be conventionally attached to the words used and thus becomes part of what is said (and even of what is encoded). For example, the word *hussy*, which once encoded just 'housewife' but was used to imply more, now encodes the negative evaluation it once just implied.[2] And, of course, the hearer's job is not ended with getting a message: the hearer's response to that message is also critical. Does the hearer set the table or not? Does the hearer complain about being asked to do so? Does the hearer make fun of the way the speaker has phrased the implied directive?

Discursive meaning has many components, and both speaker and hearer (and sometimes others, including unlicensed overhearers) contribute to the ultimate communicative effects of an utterance. What participants contribute, as we have already noted, depends on the positions they occupy in particular communities of practice and social institutions. And gendered stereotypes and power relations can significantly affect how both speaker and hearer approach communication.

Encoded meaning: the language matters

The encoded aspect of the message is what the language system determines. This is roughly the meaning that can be assigned a verbal text independently of its being produced in a particular context. Formal approaches to linguistic semantics have focused primarily on encoded meaning. They have also emphasized what is sometimes called referential or informational meaning even though languages also encode some aspects of affective or expressive meaning. For example, *dame*, *broad*, *lady*, and *woman* encode the same informational meaning in many contexts but differ in the expressive meaning they encode. Expressions like the interjection *damn* or the formulaic *hi* or *bye* or *thanks* encode affect and attitudes rather than information.

When we encounter texts in a language foreign to us, we generally miss most of the content. If we're eavesdropping on conversations in an unfamiliar tongue, we may infer a lot about the participants' attitudes and relations but it is much harder to figure out the content in any kind of detail – and there is plenty of potential to go far astray. Two people may be sitting at a restaurant table looking at a menu and talking with

---

2 See, e.g., McConnell-Ginet (1989) for more discussion of this example and Kearns (forthcoming) for a theoretical account of the role of implication in changing encoded meanings.

one another, pointing to the menu from time to time. An observer who does not understand the language they are using might well be right in thinking that they're talking about what they want to eat (of course, whether they're opting for the squid or the stuffed portobello mushrooms would be harder to figure out). But that observer might equally well be lacking not only detail but also comprehension of the general topic. A multilingual interpreter nearby might volunteer the information that the pair is actually talking about graphic design and discussing critically the font and layout that the menu creators chose. A manual language like American Sign Language can likewise be opaque to onlookers unfamiliar with it even though there are occasional iconic signs like pointing to oneself for self-reference. Usually familiarity with the words and phrases produced is essential to accessing the content of a discourse, no matter how detailed one's nonlinguistic picture of the scene might be.

It is not only that the words and grammatical structures count. Sometimes they seem to count for (almost) everything. As millions of children (and also a sizable number of adults) have recently discovered while reading the *Harry Potter* books, very rich and detailed pictures of interesting people, places, and activities – lots of content – can be created by written texts with little or no help from illustrations. The few pictures in these books are certainly worth far less communicatively than the words that fill the pages. In a letter to his local newspaper in December 2001, a twelve-year-old boy warned that those who encounter only filmed versions of *Harry Potter* will miss much of the depth and richness of the characters and their relations to one another.

In a culture that has become increasingly visual – a lot of the words many of us encounter are surrounded by graphics or computer-generated animation or film of various kinds – it is easy to forget that multimedia is not the only format for entertainment or education. The many devoted readers of romances, science fiction, mysteries, biographies, and other kinds of books have long known that linguistic texts can trigger many varied kinds of thoughts and emotions, can provide transport to different times and worlds, can bring people and other intelligent creatures to life. Notice, however, that what comes in later chapters builds on what has gone before, and later volumes in a series are often better appreciated by those who are familiar with the earlier ones. Texts have a cumulative effect, and earlier sentences contribute to the understanding of those that come later. And even for the first sentence, both reader and writer can count on some general shared expectations about the communication that is beginning, some that come from knowledge of the particular genre (note the button example at the beginning of this chapter and the discussion of genre in chapter three) and others that come from background, culturally prevalent assumptions. In other words, any linguistic text is interpreted as part of ongoing discourse. Still the role of the shared language is enormous. How does this work?

That the actual language used does matter for communication will surprise no one. Few people need to be convinced that words and the syntactic patterns in which they combine are of central importance in conveying and understanding content. Indeed, a popular story about linguistic communication goes something like this. Chris has a thought and wants to share that thought with Kim. To do so, Chris finds appropriate words and ways to combine them, coming up with a sentence that encodes the thought. After Chris utters that sentence, Kim draws on knowledge of the words and grammatical structures Chris has used to decode it and thus retrieve the thought Chris has expressed. When the process works well, it makes Chris's thoughts accessible to Kim and vice versa. Chris and Kim can communicate easily precisely because they share a linguistic code. As we noted in chapter two, a language includes a *lexicon* (something like a mental dictionary), *syntax* (principles for combining lexical items), *semantics* (taking basic meanings and combining them in ways tied to the syntax), and *phonology* (sound patterns). But the code offers only a blueprint: communicative participants have to work together to build real meanings. And of course, they may do it differently: if codes differ on some dimensions, then participants may end up working with somewhat different blueprints.

There is a reason that we identified the code component of meaning with what the speaker encodes. Prima facie, the speaker has authority in shaping the message and the hearer has an obligation to decode as the speaker intended. But speakers also have a responsibility to consider their audience and to design their encoding to assist the hearer both in decoding and in contributing effectively to the other aspects of meaning construction. Not all speakers claim or are accorded encoding authority: "I'm not sure how to say this." And speakers can arrogantly assume that any decoding mismatch is evidence of failure on the part of hearers, rather than of unequal access to particular code resources. Encoding assumes decoding.

Saying/interpreting

Encoding is not enough to determine what is said, even if our interest is solely in informational meaning. To get at what is said, communicative participants need to attach the blueprint provided by the language system to various features of the context in which the text is produced and/or interpreted. For example, when someone utters *Mimi is a cat*, nothing is said unless the utterer is referring to some entity. The interpreter has to figure out to which entity the speaker refers by uttering *Mimi*.

And there can be the question of how to interpret forms for which the code seems to allow multiple meanings. Does *she ran a good race* say that she organized a successful running competition or that she performed well in such a competition? Many English users recognize both of these interpretations as possible ways to understand the text in question. If we say that there are a number of different verbs, each of which is pronounced *run*, then to figure out what is said is to get more information about the encoding. Some analysts, however, propose that the language system – the code – underspecifies the meanings of many words so that the real contribution they make to what is said has to be determined in context. (See, e.g., Green 1995.) That is, the content of some words is not (fully) encoded but must be added in the contextualized *saying*; arguably, this might be the case for *run*. What is said depends then in a number of ways on the situated act of saying, of producing the text.

Fleshing out what is said is subject to a certain amount of vagueness and indeterminacy. Sayer and interpreter inevitably have somewhat different perspectives, and if the different perspectives are not acknowledged and accommodated, there can be a problematic mismatch of saying and interpreting. The elusive *we* is a good example, not only in the button case discussed but in other uses. Just who is included? And who is constituted as *they*?

Implying/inferring

What's implied may simply be added to what is said. "Boys will be boys" doesn't literally say much at all, but it generally implies a kind of light-hearted dismissing of certain problematic aspects of boys' (or adult men's) inconsiderate ways of acting on the grounds of assumptions about the "naturalness" or "inevitability" of such behaviors. A woman who says "I'm not dating any men just now" often implies that she has dated men in the past and that she is not dating anyone just now. But in contexts where lesbian relationships are entertained as live possibilities, a hearer might well infer that she may be dating a woman or women.

What is implied may also shift the slant on what is said, even contradict it. A letter of recommendation that says "she is a lovely person" but does not discuss her job-related skills and achievements will have much the same effect as a letter that says explicitly that the candidate is not qualified for the job. We speak of *damning with faint praise*, indicating that a certain level of appreciation may be expected in certain contexts and its absence can be expected to convey a negative appraisal. Irony and sarcasm often imply something nearly opposite to what is said. A mother who discovers that her unmarried teenage daughter is pregnant may say "that was certainly a smart thing to do" and imply that getting pregnant was indeed very stupid (perhaps also implying that the daughter and not her male partner bears primary responsibility for doing this not very smart thing). A speaker who is joking can also imply something quite different from what is said. Consider the host at a picnic who says "I'm so glad I was able to lure those flies into the soup – they add such a nice little crunch along with the protein." What's implied in this comment may be a light-hearted apology to the guests for the insects buzzing around them and perhaps also a gentle warning to them not to let the bugs bother them too much.

What is implied may be based not just on what is said or not said in some particular exchange but on broader discourse patterns. Wedding announcements in US newspapers these days sometimes include something along the lines of "the bride is keeping her name" but never anything like "the groom is keeping his name." This general asymmetric practice implies that there is still an expectation that brides but not grooms will change their name upon marriage. A tendency to say "John married Mary" rather than "Mary married John" or "Mary and John married" implies a tendency for heterosexual marriage to be seen as gender-asymmetric, with the man's agency as more important than any agency the woman might be exercising.

What is implied may or may not be intentionally implied. Someone who enters a woman's office and says to her, "I want to see the boss," implies that she is not (thought to be) the boss. The person who asks a large unseen audience to "pretend you're homosexual" implies that the intended audience includes only heterosexuals. When brought to the attention of speakers, many such implications come as a surprise, often an embarrassing one.

There are cross-cultural differences in the extent to which speakers are assumed responsible for unintended implications drawn by hearers. Much of the philosophical and linguistic literature, focused on the practices of dominant groups in England and the US, takes the speaker's intentions as delimiting responsibility: the speaker can always plead "I didn't mean that." In contrast, Marcyliena Morgan (1991) argues that African American communities typically hold speakers accountable for what others might infer from what is said. Given that ascertaining others' (and even one's own) intentions can be fraught with difficulties,

US courts have often turned to a standard of what might "reasonably" be inferred from what was said in deciding, for example, whether harassment or intimidation has occurred. But who determines what is reasonable? There used to be a "reasonable man" standard invoked and then there was a move to a "reasonable person." In some recent cases of sexual harassment, courts have appealed to the notion of a "reasonable woman," acknowledging that gender positioning might yield rather different conceptions of what is implied. (See, e.g., Abrams 1989.)

In other words, speakers may or may not always *mean* what they imply in the sense of openly inviting their hearers to draw the available inferences. Philosopher Paul Grice argued that what speaker A means to speaker B depends on what A intends B to figure out (and intends B to realize that the inference is being invited).[3] The corollary is that a speaker may use a single utterance to mean something to some that the speaker does not mean to imply to others. For example someone can say "good work you're doing" in the presence of an onlooker who knows that the speaker really thinks quite poorly of the addressee's work. The speaker may use the insincere message to imply to the onlooker contempt for the addressee. Only the onlooker is supposed to get the sarcasm: the addressee is supposed to interpret the words as if uttered sincerely.

Much of what is called *gaydar*, the ability of gay and lesbian folks to recognize one another without overt communication about sexual preference, depends on implications that work only for audiences actively considering the possibility that the speaker is not heterosexual. The earlier example of a woman's saying "I'm not dating any men just now" is discussed by A. C. Liang (1999), who shows that the possibility of utterances having different implications for different audiences can help lesbians and gay men come out conditionally. They are able to

---

3 In a series of lectures and papers, most of which have been collected in Grice (1989), Grice drew the three-way distinction between what linguistic expressions mean (encoding), what an utterance of them on a given occasion means (saying), and what a speaker means in producing that utterance (implying). He was also the first to try to offer a principled account of how speakers can manage to mean so much more than they say. His notion of conversational implicature, which is basically what the speaker means that is implied but not said, and his theory of how conversational implicatures work have been central to work in pragmatics. His idea was that there are a number of conversational "maxims" such as "be relevant" and "be brief" that operate universally to create expectations against which interpretation proceeds. Levinson (1983) contains an extensive discussion of these maxims, which are also considered in many other texts that discuss linguistic pragmatics. There have been a number of different kinds of attempts to refine Grice's initial account; see Levinson (2000) for a recent neo-Gricean approach and Sperber and Wilson ([1986] 1995) for a more radically altered theory. There is no question that precisely how implicatures work varies significantly cross-culturally, but a number of analysts have argued that we can give accounts that predict the kinds of cross-cultural variation that might occur; this is the thrust of Brown and Levinson's work on politeness, which we discussed in chapter four.

reveal their sexual orientation selectively by saying things that imply it only to audiences who are already predisposed to be gay-affirmative. Notice that if there is a focal stress on "men" – "I'm not dating any MEN just now" – then there is an encoded cue that strongly points to the implication that the speaker is dating a woman or women. Of course, people who are really strongly in the grip of the heterosexual presumption may simply not notice this aspect of the encoding – or else just be perplexed by it.

More generally, what others take to be implied will depend on their appraisal of the speaker. The man who interprets a woman's "no" as implying "maybe" or even "yes but you need to keep coaxing me" does so because of certain assumptions he has about her constraining demureness (and perhaps his own attractions).

Of course, in figuring out what is implied we have more than the words and our prior opinions of the producer of the text being analyzed. Even when we are thinking only about what linguistic actions mean, a speaker's symbolic acts are not confined to producing a particular linguistic text. Every linguistic text has accompanying symbolic material: William Hanks (1996) uses the term *visuals* to cover all the stuff that accompanies or "inflects" the words of a linguistic text. For traditional written texts, visuals can include pictures, graphs, typography, layout, handwriting styles. Newer media provide moving and flashing elements and sound along with the printed word and familiar kinds of graphics. Speech has "tone of voice," facial expressions, and everything that goes under the heading of "body language." In addition, of course, clothing and bodily adornment can have symbolic significance that will affect textual interpretation. The visuals may be a major clue that the linguistic text is being offered in jest.

In addition to visuals, what is used as a basis for drawing inferences includes a history of previous discourse and expectations about future discourse. These involve not just what has been said but what has "typically" been said, along with evaluations of ways of saying things. And, of course, there are general sociocultural assumptions as well as more local ones. These include participants' assessment of themselves and one another as particular "kinds" of people with particular communicative habits and expectations.

Presupposing: gender schemas and ideologies

Sometimes speakers imply messages by presenting them as non-news, as part of the background that they are taking for granted. A teacher mentions to a colleague a student whose exam performance is so far below homework and in-class performance that the teacher thinks that lack of self-confidence in the stress-producing exam situation may be more at issue than academic ability. The colleague says, "Did you advise her to try taking practice exams?" Nothing has been said about the student's sex, but the colleague's choice of the pronoun *her* presupposes, takes for granted, that the referent is female. That presupposition is not licensed by anything said; rather, it is based on general assumptions that come from discursive practice and gender discourses.

The exchange continues. "Actually," the teacher responds, "this student is a guy." This utterance explicitly challenges the content of the presupposition the colleague made and perhaps also implicitly suggests a criticism of the basis for the mistaken assumption (if the colleague knows, perhaps, that this particular teacher is critical of gender stereotypes). The colleague may be somewhat embarrassed and change the topic, recognizing that a presumptive leap was made on the basis of gender schemas. Suppose, however, the teacher replies by saying "No, I hadn't thought of suggesting that but I will when she comes to see me this afternoon." In this case, both the content and the basis of the assumption go unremarked. Neither of the two participants in the discourse need acknowledge or even recognize that the assumption that the student was female was grounded not in the particulars of our exchange but in familiar gender stereotypes. Of course, if the teacher did notice then the assumption could be brought to the colleague's attention. "I didn't say that the student was female. Why did you make that assumption?" On the other hand, most people would be unlikely to do so unless they wanted to force the other person to recognize the dubious nature of the leap that had been made. With silence from the teacher who's commented on the student, the colleague can continue complacently thinking that gender schemas are used only by other "sexist" folks. And the teacher too can fail to notice the leap that they both accepted. In this case, there is further "naturalization" for both participants of views of women and girls as insecure, unable to perform well under pressure. Presuppositions like these are often very powerful, even when the presupposer would sincerely claim at the conscious level that they are wrong.

Do not take us to be maligning those who betray their stereotyped gender assumptions. Listening to ourselves has been humbling. During a phone conversation while we were writing this book, Penny told Sally about taking her very sick cat to the vet. Sally responded "What does he think is wrong?" As it happens, the vet in question was a woman, and, since quotas limiting women's admission to US schools of veterinary medicine were removed in the early 1970s, some 70 percent of newly trained vets have been women. Sally knows perfectly well that many (perhaps now, even most) vets are women and she is committed in general to trying to minimize gender assumptions in her speech, but out they come from time to time.

Start watching and listening and you are likely to find gender assumptions being communicated in many (most?) situations. An Internal Revenue Service representative is interviewing a married couple about their tax returns and directs all questions to the man, ignoring the woman. A guest compliments the woman of a couple on the delicious food that's just been eaten or on the beautiful window coverings. In these cases, it is not the content of what is said but how it is directed that presupposes certain gender stereotypes. And again, if the stereotypes do fit and are not challenged, they are further "naturalized": the man is responsible for a family's finances but the woman is in charge of domestic arrangements such as food and home decor.

Presupposing is not in itself a bad thing. Indeed, it is essential to discursive practice. Without being able to take things for granted, to call on a common background, communities of practice would not function. We'd be forever stuck in the position of strangers with no shared socially significant history. Yet presuppositions that are seldom made explicit, that stay backstage, can be problematic.

The particular presupposition that the feminine pronoun *she* triggers can be expressed explicitly and simply. The presupposition is just that actual or potential referents are classed as female persons. As we saw, that assumption may itself rely on other (tacit) assumptions about characteristics distinguishing females from males. It is not, however, a linguistic convention governing *she* that brings in assumptions about how women and men differ from one another. Rather, such assumptions are often used to underpin gender ascription and hence choice of pronoun. To talk about a specific person without first inquiring about the person's sex (or having a sex-specific name as a guide) English speakers have to use the prescriptively frowned on *they*: choosing either *he* or *she* inevitably imports gender assumptions and, when the assumptions fit, helps further naturalize those assumptions.

A number of expressions, however, indicate explicitly that some rather diffuse and highly context-dependent presupposition is being made. The content of such a diffuse presupposition is often very difficult, perhaps impossible, to state in a fully explicit form. Familiar examples are words like *but* or *even* and constructions like equatives and *when*-clauses. "She's a beautiful blonde but exceptionally intelligent" makes it explicit that the speaker presumes some kind of contrast or tension between a woman's beauty and her intelligence though the precise nature of that contrast is not specified. "Even my mother could understand that book" makes explicit an assumption that the speaker's mother is the least likely of those we might be considering to understand that book, though leaving unspecified just who is being considered and on what basis likelihood of understanding is being judged. "Women are just as intelligent as men" presents men's intelligence as setting the presumptive standard up to which women's may (or may not) measure. "Men are just as intelligent as women" signals a context in which women's intelligence is assumed to be the standard against which men's should be assessed. "When you get married, you'll have to pick up after yourself" assumes that the addressee will get married. And there are many many more English examples of such presupposition-indicating expressions as well as examples from other languages.

We often don't even notice that we have said *but* or *even* or used some other expression that triggers a certain kind of presupposition. That is, such expressions are frequently selected with little or no conscious attention to their significance. Even those who might explicitly (and indeed sincerely) disavow certain kinds of assumptions for themselves may unwittingly reveal the operation of those assumptions through the presuppositions they pack into what they say. "My boyfriend is short, but I really love him" reveals that the speaker assumes that shortness counts against lovability for boyfriends. In using *but* the speaker's boyfriend is being presented as somehow exceptionally managing to overcome the liability of shortness. Yet the speaker may be somewhat chagrined if someone else points out the use of *but*.

Notice that it is difficult to choose a pronoun for referring to the person who uttered this sentiment about the boyfriend without presupposing a gender ascription to that person. The generic *he* is really unavailable for the job here. We might say "the speaker is quite conscious of her boyfriend's deficiencies in height," and you could think we are simply continuing our discussion of some generic utterer of the example sentence. You might have already assumed a female utterer without even noticing that we've said nothing at all about the sex of the utterer. Why would a generic utterer be assumed female? Because there is a powerful presumption of heterosexuality, which is so familiar as to go unnoticed. And that assumption is reinforced by the assumption of preference for heterosexual couples with the male partner taller than the female. In contrast, *his boyfriend* would not sound "generic" but would suggest a romantic relation between two males. (We'll discuss generics in the next chapter.) The presumption of heterosexuality is extraordinarily pervasive. Even those who are fully aware that there are many lesbians, gay men, transsexuals, and others who do not fit the heterosexual or "straight" mold can find themselves speaking in ways that presume heterosexuality – or not noticing that someone else has unwarrantedly so spoken, further reinforcing the assumption.

Talk about sexuality is often about heterosexual desires and activities, again reinforcing the presumption of universal heterosexuality. To ask whether two people *did it* or *went all the way* or *had sex* generally presupposes that one of those people has a penis and the other a vagina and that the answer to the question depends on whether the penis became erect and was inserted into the vagina (with ejaculation generally also presumed). Notice that such presumptions not only ignore erotic activity between people of the same sex but also ignore kinds of erotic activity other than that which might in principle lead to fertilization of an egg. Bill Clinton seemed to rely on such assumptions when he said that he had not ("strictly speaking") *had sex* with Monica Lewinsky. Of course, other ways of putting it would not have gotten him off the hook, even "speaking strictly." He certainly did *engage in sexual activity* with Ms. Lewinsky. Janice Moulton (1981) notes that the general assumption of the primacy of penile penetration makes the male orgasm essentially definitive of (hetero)sexual activity, with female orgasms in heterosexual activity treated as potential but inessential accompaniments. In some contexts *have sex* may not require that it be a vagina into which the penis is inserted, allowing for male homosexuality but not female.

Communication about sexuality often assumes heterosexuality. Even when heterosexuality is not presumed, male sexuality is often assumed essential, with erotic activity between women overlooked or dismissed as "practice for the real thing." Of course, there are ways of speaking about sexual desires and activities that do not carry such heterosexist and sexist presuppositions. But because there are such strong cultural assumptions about canonical sexuality, communication about sex generally tends to reinforce rather than challenge the canonical norms.

It is discursive practice rather than linguistic convention that is ultimately responsible for many (perhaps most) of the sexist and heterosexist presuppositions conveyed when people use language. At the same time, changing patterns of language use in discursive practice can play a role in helping expose and perhaps even dislodge problematic presuppositions.

Assigning roles and responsibility

Languages offer resources for representing situations involving multiple participants playing different roles and assigned differential

responsibility for what is going on. Verbal meanings and word order
are critical cues in English texts to how their producers are interpreting the causal relations in the situations they seek to represent, which
roles they are assigning to which participants. To say "Lee kissed Kim" is
to present Lee as the agent of the kissing, the one causally responsible
for it, and to present Kim as what linguists call the patient of the kissing, an essentially passive recipient. Although subjects are very often
agents, this is not always the case, as we saw in chapter two. Note, for
example, passives like "The cup was broken (by Lee)," where the special
verbal form (the use of *was* plus the past participle form of the verb)
signals that the subject is playing the role played by the object in the
corresponding active sentence and where the agent may or may not
be indicated in a *by*-phrase. While not agents, subjects of passives are
topics – what the sentence is about. With some verbs, things get more
interesting. In "Kim sold Lee a shirt," Lee is the recipient of the shirt
Kim sold; in "Kim sold Lee," Lee seems to be what's sold; in "The shirt
sold," the shirt is not the agent of the selling but its theme – what was
transferred by the selling act – and agency is completely obscured. And,
of course, with some verbs agency is hardly very active: "Kim watched
Lee." In some languages (e.g. German or Finnish), case endings on the
noun phrases are the main formal indicator of who is playing what
role.

   Now consider verbs like *kiss* and *marry* that certainly allow mutuality.
But even though mutuality is not ruled out, to say "Lee kissed Kim" or
"Lee married Kim" evokes a subtext in which it is not also the case that
"Kim kissed Lee" or "Kim married Lee." That is, as subject, Lee is being
assigned the leading, most active role. Looking at grammatical roles
(who is subject, who is object) as well as verb categories (*run* vs. *see*),
Monica Macaulay and Colleen Brice (1997) found a tendency in 1990s
syntax texts to cast males as the active doers, whereas females were
more often the passive recipients of males' actions or the spectators
thereof. As Macaulay and Brice point out, similar findings emerged
from a 1970s study of primary-school textbooks, which also had many
more male characters overall, but a follow-up study at the end of the
1980s suggested a move away from such asymmetries in the school
textbooks, making it even more surprising that they seemed to persist
in most of the syntax texts.[4]

   We do not really know whether popular literature for children (or
adults for that matter) still emphasizes male characters and their

4 See Macaulay and Brice for references to the early textbook studies as well as for
more general discussion.

activities. The *Harry Potter* books, with only a very few interesting female characters (Hermione and Professor McGonagall being the most prominent), suggest this may be the case. Nonetheless there are substantial counter-currents in children's and adult literature. Although Louisa May Alcott's Jo does eventually get married and settle into motherhood and housewifery, she actively engages in life and is no mere spectator of male achievement. Alison Lurie's collection of "modern fairy tales" highlights active and adventurous young female protagonists. Astrid Lindgren's Pippi Longstocking and Robert Munch's "The Paper-Bag Princess" are just a couple of the many relatively recent new brand of adventurous girls young readers encounter. And adult mystery readers know Sue Grafton's Kinsey Milhone, Sara Paretsky's V. I. Warshawsky, Margaret Maron's Deborah Knott, and many other female sleuths as women who take matters into their own hands again and again. There is increasingly available a discourse of girls and women of action, but few completely escape discoursal patterns that highlight male agency.[5]

Yet just where we might expect to find males as actors and responsible agents, they sometimes vanish. Kate Clark (1992) examined reports in British newspapers of male violence against women and girls and notes that in some cases the male perpetrators are hard to find. She quotes the following headline and opening sentence from a December 12, 1986 report in the *Sun*, a high-circulation British daily paper.

GIRL 7 MURDERED WHILE MUM DRANK AT THE PUB
Little Nicola Spencer was strangled in her bedsit home – while her Mum was out drinking and playing pool in local pubs.

The strangling murderer is invisible. His guilt seems to be almost erased by that of the victim's carousing mother. In another report about John Steed, who was sentenced to four life-sentences for raping three women and killing a fourth, the *Sun* focuses not on Steed's acts but on the actions or lack thereof of various women in his life. The headings below seem to blame his girlfriend Sharon Bovil for his crimes because of her failure to inform police about them.

SHARON'S DEADLY SILENCE [headline]
Lover Shielded M4 Sex Fiend [subheading]

---

5 Girls and women often appreciate books featuring boys and men and can frequently identify with the male protagonists, whereas the reverse happens far less often. In a TV clip in the late 1990s, an American male sports hero was shown in a library where he was engaged in encouraging children to read. One young boy showed the sports star the book he'd selected and was told "oh, you don't want that – it's about a girl; let's find something better."

As the first headline illustrates, modifiers like *deadly* can also assign responsibility. In this case, it is Sharon's silence that is characterized as deadly, responsible for terrorizing and killing, whereas John's attacks are not mentioned explicitly at all (though evoked by the label *Sex Fiend*).

Whereas *deadly* assigns responsibility, some modifiers displace or reduce it. Anglo-American law defines rape as involving nonconsensual sexual contact, but in so-called *statutory* rape the absence of (meaningful) consent is attributed to one party's being under the legal "age of consent." Thus someone accused of statutory rape is often assumed to have acted with the consent of the other (young) party, perhaps even to have succumbed to sexual overtures from the younger party and therefore to be at least partly absolved of responsibility for the sexual acts that occurred between them. The sex-neutral language here is misleading: statutory rape is overwhelmingly a matter of an adult man's sexual relations with a female juvenile. A search for *statutory rape* in the *New York Times* archives for 1999 turned up only one instance with a female perpetrator, the widely reported case of teacher Mary Kay LeTourneau, who had sexual relations with a teenage male student (thirteen at the time the relationship first began). What was especially interesting was that the seven other stories that appeared in the *Times* on the same case did not use *statutory rape* at all but spoke instead of her *child rape*, of her "exploiting" of the boy, and also emphasized the youth and vulnerability of the boy involved. These eight stories contrasted with another eight involving adult men (many of them also employed in schools) and much younger females. The term *statutory rape* was repeatedly used in discussion of these cases involving adult men, often figuring in the headline or the first couple of sentences and generally repeated elsewhere in the article.

In contrast to the reports of the LeTourneau case, the young female parties involved were presented less as victims than as willing participants who *had sex with* or *dated* or *had relationships with* the adult males. The term *child rape* appeared in none of the reports involving adult males. The male younger party in the LeTourneau case is generally referred to as *boy*, occasionally as *student*, and never as *young man*. In contrast, the female younger parties are primarily referred to as *students*, a couple of times as *young women* (aged thirteen and fifteen), and less often as *girl*. The contrast in the practices for male and female referents is particularly revealing, given the general tendency for females to get referred to as *girl* at much older ages than males are referred to as *boy*. Such contrasting patterns in a "respectable" newspaper downplay male responsibility for cross-generational sexual contact; they also highlight female responsibility. This highlighting occurs not only in the case where the female is the (appropriately) responsible adult (who is far less likely than her male counterparts to get "off the hook" as a [merely] *statutory* rapist) but also where the female is in fact the vulnerable child (far more likely than her young male counterpart to be assigned at least partial responsibility for heterosexual encounters with an adult – more sensationalist newspapers sometimes dub her *Lolita*).[6] In much the same vein, attractive underage females are often termed *jailbait* in American English.

In a detailed study drawing on a York University (Toronto, Canada) disciplinary hearing dealing with sexual harassment and a Canadian court case dealing with two counts of sexual assault against the same defendant, Susan Ehrlich (2001) shows how gender ideologies frame and help shape the constitution of gendered identities and responsibilities in a sexual assault trial. In her chapter three, she shows how the defendant presents himself through what she calls a "grammar of non-agency" that at best obscures his responsibility for what happened. One strategy implies mutual engagement: "we started kissing," "we were fooling around." He also uses what Ehrlich dubs "the language of love," which stresses mutuality and gentleness, rather than the complainant's language of violence: whereas she says "he grabbed my hair," he says "yeah, I was caressing her hair." When asked explicitly whether he did particular things, he frequently responds "Maybe. I don't remember."

Not surprisingly, agentless passives are another important resource for evading responsibility: "our pants were undone," "our pants were pushed off." There are frequent agentless passives that circumvent the processes of decision making: "It was agreed that," "it was decided that...," "it was established that..." At one point the university lawyer probes the defendant's omission of agency. In response to a question about something he is alleged to have said, the defendant says, "it might have been at one point...uhm...that those words were said." Lawyer: "By you?" Defendant: "Pardon me?" Lawyer: "You said them?" Defendant: "Yes." And the defendant also presents sexual activities as just happening, events without responsible agents. "It started to heat up," "it became increasingly sexual," "it started to escalate." And not only the defendant and his counsel but also the judge speak of the male sexual drive as a force external to the man that is (virtually) irresistible and triggered by a woman's "provocativeness." So male agency

---

6 We thank former Cornell University student Rosemary Timoney for sharing this unpublished research with us.

is minimized. Not only does the male defendant himself work to minimize his responsibility, but to a considerable extent the adjudicators
support this minimization.

In chapter four of her book, Ehrlich explores what she calls the "complainants' discourse of ineffective agency." In the university tribunal
hearings, there was considerable talk about the complainants' "options"
and "choices" and such assertions as "we all have free will" and "why
did you let what you say happened happen?" and "the only appropriate way to protect yourself was to cry out." Questions like "why didn't
you say/do X?" presuppose that the complainants should have said or
done X, and such questions come not only from the defendant's representatives but also from tribunal members in the university hearing
and from the judge in the court case. The complainants are asked
whether this is the "only" effort made, is it "the best you could come
up with," and in various ways told implicitly that they did not ade-
quately resist, that their actions were not what they should have been.
The complainants' expression of fear gets undercut by the questioners,
who seem to discount the fear as an acceptable reason for their lack
of action.

After hearing repeated discounting of their fear, the complainants
do begin themselves to adopt the views tribunal members have advanced of their "ineffectual agency": "I didn't do anything," "I didn't
yell," "I was too busy trying to figure out how to make him stop," "I
kept trying to move away," "I tried to get out of the bed," "I just sat
there." The complainants attribute their lack of effectiveness to their
confused mental state: "I didn't know what to do," "I couldn't really
think straight," "I wasn't sure what to do," "I didn't have a lot of time
to think about what to do," "so many emotions running through me."
Such comments, however, often come in response to leading questions
of various kinds. The women's actual resistance, Ehrlich suggests, is
obscured and underrated by an ideology of a freely acting individual
agent. Operating within this ideological framework, the questioners
ignore or downplay the constraining fear and confusion that the defendant's sexual aggression produced. As the adjudicators in the university
tribunal put it: "[the complainants] clearly set the limits at the very beginning but their resolve became somewhat ambiguous as the night
progressed...their actions at times did not unequivocally indicate a
lack of willing participation...They both agreed that *in hindsight* their
actions were irrational and ineffective" (emphasis added). These characterizations attributed to the complainants arose, however, from questions that presupposed the inadequacy of the complainants' actions
and the "irrationality" of their fears. In many ways, the proceedings

served to chastise the complainants for their "mixed messages" and their failure to show the "utmost resistance" and also served to convince them "in hindsight" of their own ineffectiveness.

Patterns of responsibility assignment for sexual encounters are far more complicated than this brief discussion might seem to indicate. In the United States, a black man is more likely to be assigned full blame than a white one for an apparently forced sexual encounter with a woman who says she did not consent. White William Kennedy Smith and black prize fighter Mike Tyson were both accused of rape by women who acknowledged willingly having accompanied the men to a "private" location late at night. Tyson was sentenced for rape whereas Smith was cleared of the charge. And, as Clark notes, "respectable" women – women who by virtue of marriage or extreme youth or old age are deemed sexually "unavailable" – are much less likely to be assigned responsibility for an assault than other women, who are often judged "loose" or "promiscuous." (Such judgments are also often inflected by race and class.[7])

There are many more ways in which choice of linguistic form promotes (or sometimes coerces) particular views of gendered agency and (relative) responsibility. We will discuss some of these in accounts of naming in the next chapter and some will emerge in the following section on metaphor.

Making metaphors

Metaphors project one field onto another. A linguistic metaphor uses language from one field – for example the sport of baseball – to talk about another different field – for example (hetero)sexual relations. "Did you score with her?" "No, I struck out completely and didn't even get to first base." Or: "Yeah – a home run!" Sexual relations are what is traditionally called the *tenor* of this piece of metaphorical text, or more colloquially, the *subject* or *topic*; recent work on metaphor in cognitive linguistics (see, e.g., Lakoff and Johnson 1980, Lakoff 1987) speaks of the *target* domain. Sports would traditionally be said to provide the *vehicle* for the little discourse about sex above; cognitive linguists talk of the *source* domain. Metaphors often involve labeling something in one

7 Elizabeth Gordon (1997) argues that fear of losing their "respectability," of being seen as sexually "loose," is part of what leads young women to favor pronunciation variants associated with the higher classes. In chapter eight, we discuss variation of this kind and its relation to gender practice, which is very strongly class-inflected.

domain by using a label primarily associated with another domain – for example "that jackass doesn't know what he's talking about." But metaphors are not just about labels. Not only do certain commonplaces about the source get projected onto the topic – for example jackasses are stupid and noisy, scoring is desirable but must be accomplished in the face of difficulty or resistance. There is also, generally, at least the potential for relations among components of the source field to project onto the target – for example striking out precludes even getting to first base, which is the minimum needed to eventually score whereas a home run is the fastest and best way to score. Although we often speak of metaphorical interpretations of a particular word or phrase, metaphor involves much more than this and can extend over substantial texts. Proverbs or fables, for example, are extended metaphors that can push interpreters to adopt new perspectives on or reconceptualize some (often implicit) topic, e.g. morality or practical wisdom. The processes of producing and interpreting metaphors and the discoursal uptake they involve are all critical. This discourse focus leads us also to ask who produces what kinds of metaphors and to what effect.

Some uses of language are clearly metaphorical and others are clearly not. Compare, for example, "she brought out all of her big guns and shot down my argument" with, on the one hand, "she brought out all of her big guns and shot down the bird" and, on the other hand, with "Using authoritative resources and techniques, she established that my argument was fallacious." In most contexts, the talk of guns and shooting in the second sentence is not metaphorical, whereas in the first sentence it is; the third sentence renders nonmetaphorically (approximately) what the first sentence might be used to convey. As Eva Feder Kittay (1987) shows, very few sentences must be interpreted metaphorically or must be interpreted literally. There are, however, often clues in the sentence itself or in the larger text in which the sentence is embedded that point to either literal or metaphorical interpretations.

Even those who see metaphor as central to language generally agree that not every utterance is metaphorical ("The dog is barking" if uttered in reference to the vocalizations being produced by a canine). Nonetheless, there is some dispute as to whether we really can draw a distinction between literal and figurative uses of language, where metaphor is one kind of "figure." Many of our most everyday and apparently "literal" ways of talking almost certainly come to us originally through metaphor. So, for example, we use the language of visual experience to talk about such mental phenomena as understanding: "I *see* what you mean" or "Her memoir offers considerable *insight* into depression."

We use temperature to talk about emotional expressivity: "she's a very *cold* person" or "her *warmth* makes all the new students feel at home immediately." In general, we and our ancestors have looked to concrete experiential domains for resources with which to conceptualize less immediately accessible and more abstract target domains. But this does not mean that for current speakers of English the italicized words in the sentences above function nonliterally. These sentences can be uttered literally because we no longer need detour through vision or temperature to get the expressed messages: *see* and *insight* now connect directly to understanding, *cold* and *warmth* directly to emotional expressivity. In such cases, analysts sometimes speak of "dead" metaphors.

We can't, however, simply ignore dead metaphors, because where the connections are still indicated by the linguistic form, metaphors can be revived. The field mappings originally underlying the now completely standard use of *see* to designate understanding or *cold* and *warmth* to describe emotional expressivity may still be exploited metaphorically: "reading that book really opened my eyes" or "he is a block of ice." In producing and interpreting utterances like these, the domains of vision and temperature do seem to figure. As these examples show, a metaphor's being commonplace (e.g. "opening one's eyes") doesn't necessarily mean that it's "dead." And even dead metaphors can tell us something about the sociocultural patterns of thought and action that underlie them as well as having the potential to contribute to maintaining those patterns. In some cases – for example in interpreting an utterance of an ambiguous sentence like "she's really cold" – language users often access both interpretations (temperature and temperament), albeit briefly.

Sex/gender as the source of metaphor

Sex and gender are widely available as metaphorical vehicles or source domains, not only for speakers of English but also for speakers of many other languages. Helen Haste (1994) argues that what she calls "the sexual metaphor" is central to maintaining sex-gender systems that support male dominance. What she means by "the sexual metaphor" is the striking tendency to use conceptions of female–male difference to structure talk and thinking about a myriad of other contrasts: arts vs. sciences, biology vs. physics, functional vs. formal, qualitative vs. quantitative, poetry vs. mathematics, vowels vs. consonants, peace vs. war, nature vs. civilization, emotion vs. reason, soft vs. hard, body vs. spirit. Different languages have different favored ways of speaking that exploit the overarching sexual metaphor:

DIFFERENCE IS SEXUAL DIFFERENCE.[8] Gender categories are pressed into service for categorizing a host of other domains, and we will discuss the sexual metaphor in somewhat more detail in the next chapter. Apart from the general sexual metaphor for difference, sex and gender serve as metaphorical sources for speaking of a variety of topics.

Male sexuality often provides a way for talking and thinking about weaponry and war. Carol Cohn (1987) mounts a powerful critique of the language of "defense intellectuals," virtually all of whom were male in her study. Their ways of talking, she contends, focus on weapons and their deployment without any reference to the human beings the weapons might kill. The minimization of fundamental matters of damage to human bodies is promoted, she argues, by a kind of sexual charge. There is talk of "thrust" and "(deep) penetration" and "getting rid of your stuff" and being "hard," and she quotes one military advisor speaking of "releasing 70 to 80 percent of our megatonnage in one orgasmic whump" (p. 693, n. 14). The French, she reports, "use the Mururoa Atoll in the South Pacific for their nuclear tests and assign a woman's name to each of the craters they gouge out of the earth" (p. 694). There was contemptuous talk of "nuclear virginity" when New Zealand refused to allow nuclear-armed or nuclear-powered ships to dock at its ports, and India's exploding a bomb was described as the country's "losing her virginity." At the same time, there is a strong hint of homoeroticism: chances to "pat the missile" were eagerly sought. As Cohn stresses, "the imagery itself does not originate in these particular individuals but in a broader cultural context." At the same time, the metaphors have their grounding in the communities of practice in which they are deployed. As Cohn makes clear, there is not simply a larger "cultural context" but a much more specific set of relevant practices that give these metaphors their special significance in the particular community of practice of the "defense intellectual."

Birth and the rest of the reproductive process provide rich material for metaphors of intellectual discovery and invention. A "pregnant" pause (as in the title of Mendoza-Denton's 1995 article) signals the likelihood that the pause is paving the way to a particularly noteworthy thought and its expression. Kittay (1988) reminds us that Plato spoke of the (male) philosopher as a "midwife," who brings forth ideas, and she points to such practices as male initiation rites in which men "give birth" to boys in order to transform them into men. Metaphors

---

8 George Lakoff and Mark Johnson (1980) introduced the use of small capital letters to indicate a general TARGET IS SOURCE connection. In our first example, we could have SEX IS A GAME or, more specifically, SEX IS BASEBALL.

of procreation sometimes put the primary creative force in the paternal role, making the mother's contribution simply one of sheltering the baby. Cohn cites a quote from physicist Hans Bethe: "[Stanislaw] Ulam was the father of the hydrogen bomb and Edward [Teller] was the mother, because he carried the baby for quite a while" (n. 27, p. 700). And she also has a nice quote, which she describes as being offered "self-effacingly," from an unnamed officer giving a briefing on a new satellite system whose technical capabilities he has just "excitedly" described: "We'll do the motherhood role – telemetry, tracking, and control – the maintenance" (p. 700). Motherhood is by no means always used metaphorically as a mere accompaniment to the "main event," but there certainly are some persistent discourse practices that give fathers the starring role in procreation.

Such practices have a long lineage. The English word *seminal* originally derives from metaphorical talk of the male contribution to reproduction. Though a dead metaphor in the sense that most language users process it with no reference at all to the role of semen in producing babies, it has been at least partly revived in recent years. Some feminists who recognized its history, which is undoubtedly predicated on discourse assumptions that the semen-contributor is the one who really matters in creating new beings, have found themselves discomfited by its continued use. Awareness of this problematic history has brought the metaphor back to life for them. Some have suggested *ovular* as a woman-centered alternative, with *germinal* or *generative* offered as more sex-neutral alternatives. But on the other side, some feminists want to use *seminal* to label the work of women who have made groundbreaking contributions in some field in order to highlight those achievements for a wider community, where alternatives to the familiar laudatory *seminal* might weaken or obscure the message. *Seminal* is a nice example of a word that now works quite differently in different communities of practice.

Kittay (1988) has made the interesting argument that women and women's activities are a major source of metaphors through which men construct their sense of a distinct self, their relation to the world, and their relations to one another. Women do not, she argues, draw on men and men's activities in a similar way. We have already seen the birth process, quintessentially women's domain, as a source for talking about creation and creativity. There are many other examples: mother nature with both her bounty and her unpredictable and uncontrollable violence, the poetic muse who inspires but cannot be relied upon, the whore and temptress who symbolizes what "good" men struggle against. Kittay bases her argument on Simone de Beauvoir's insight that men view women as fundamentally Other, an Other sometimes desirable or admirable, sometimes frightening or deplorable, but always profoundly different from themselves. Why don't women view men as Other in much the same way? Because, Kittay argues, of the different ways in which girls and boys form their self-identities in relation/opposition to the mother. Here she draws on work by Nancy Chodorow (1978), who has proposed that females are more "selves-in-relation" and less focused on separation and autonomy because of their predominance in the care of young children.

Although it is true that child-rearing is overwhelmingly in the hands of women and older girls, the universality of Chodorow's picture of psychosexual development and its implications for gendered identities and relations have been challenged. But even if its universality may be dubious, there seem to be particular sociohistorical contexts for which it may offer insight into gender.

We certainly do find metaphorical patterns in line with Kittay's account. For example, literary theorist Annette Kolodny (1980) discusses differences between how relatively prosperous women and men in eighteenth- and early nineteenth-century America talked about the land around them. David Humphreys (1794) spoke of a landscape that "once rustic and rude, now embellished and adorned, appears the loveliest captive that ever befell to the lot of a conqueror." Timothy Dwight (1822) looked to a similar change: "Where nature, stripped of her fringe and her foliage, is now naked and deformed, she will suddenly exchange the dishabille; and be ornamented by culture with her richest attire" (cited in Kolodny 1980, p. 189). These seem to be prime examples of (metaphors of) women mediating men's relationship to something new and profoundly Other. At the same time, Kolodny describes the women finding ways of talking about this new land that assimilate it to what is known and familiar and, perhaps most important, under their own control: they make "gardens" and "nurture" trees and generally focus on domesticating the land around them. As Kolodny puts it, "[t]heir decided preference for evoking an ungendered semi-rural terrain of humble yeoman farms suggests that, within this languagescape only, could they conceive a comprehensible realm of meaningful roles and activities for themselves" (p. 202). The women are taming the landscape in a very different way from the men. Perhaps the American male settlers are not so much evoking woman as Other as they are evoking heterosexual male sexuality as a (familiar) model for conquest of an enticing but resisting goal. That evocation does assume a male-centered worldview, from which perspective women are Other, perhaps even the quintessential Other, yet it also assumes a particular

conception of that Otherness as desirable but also dangerous and in
need of control.

An important question that has been relatively little explored is just
how metaphors of gender/sexuality function in particular communities of practice. Lenora Timm (2000) discusses the prevalence of the
"mother earth" figure in recent discussions of ecology and the future
of our environment. She pays special attention to the so-called Gaia
hypothesis that the earth is a complex self-regulating organism, whose
surface environment depends on interactions among microorganisms,
plants, and animals. Gaia is the name the ancient Greeks gave to their
"earth mother" goddess. What Timm argues is that the Gaia/mother
earth metaphor is problematic on two grounds. First, it seems unlikely
to promote the kind of ecological responsibility that is needed. "The
earth is neither a powerful and bountiful mother nor a sexy goddess
who will take care of 'her' children if they are good and obedient and
love her, or punish them if they misbehave and abuse her" (Timm
2000, p. 113). Using the Gaia metaphor does not, she suggests, promote the kind of thoughtful attention to interconnectedness that is
needed. Women in general and mothers in particular often have been
and continue to be devalued and denigrated. Will "Love Your Mother"
bumper stickers with a Planet Earth graphic really encourage thoughtful respect for the world we share with one another? Might not such a
metaphorical strategy backfire? Second, Timm argues that the continued use of NATURE IS WOMAN metaphors "implicitly sanctions the
view of sex/gender roles as biologically determined."

In contrast, Lisa Perry (2000) argues that traditional Cherokee ways
of talking rely on a conception of gender opposition as genuine complementarity and that the figure of Selu, Corn Woman, is an important
indicator of the way Cherokee thinkers have seen women and men as
harmonious partners. Awi Usdi, her male companion, is chief of the
deer. Together they represent farming and hunting, each of which has
a critical role to play, and each of which needs to be conducted re-
sponsibly, with respect for the earth and for the many creatures that
live together on it. Perry's analysis, which relies heavily on Awiakta
(1993), sees femaleness as functioning metaphorically for the Cherokee in conjunction with maleness to represent such values as balance,
interdependence, mutual responsibility. Paula Gunn Allen (1987) has
also argued that, at the time of their first encounters with European
settlers, a number of American Indian cultures really did embody sexual egalitarianism, even though there was clear gender differentiation.
And she too cites the ritual and symbolic importance of figures like
Corn Woman.

What might look like the "same" metaphor – for example NATURE IS WOMAN – can function very differently in different communities of practice and in different kinds of discourse. The uptake associated with discourses of a mother earth at a conference of ecofeminists may be very different indeed from that produced by similar texts in most other kinds of communities of practice – for example among environmental activists for whom feminist concerns are not an explicit part of the agenda. A picture of the globe with the message "Love Your Mother" is a text pointing to a metaphorical interpretation, but, as with texts generally, the ultimate effects of "uttering" that text will depend on how its production and interpretation get linked to other social practices.

Sex/gender as the topic of metaphor

We started our discussion of metaphors with the example of baseball terminology as the source domain for the topic of (hetero)sexual relations. Note that, although a woman might say "I didn't get to first base with him" (of course the metaphor in this case might well be about some topic other than sexual relations), she would be highly unlikely to describe her having had sexual relations with some guy as having "scored" with him nor would others, male or female, be likely so to describe her. This nonparallelism of usage is just one example of a general tendency in English metaphors that are about (hetero)sexual relations: these metaphors, usually "dead" but still (re)interpretable, often project a picture of a male actively defeating or otherwise harming a female. Examples offered in Robert Baker (1975) include common uses of *screw*, *bang*, and *hump*, which he noted tend to occur with male subjects and female objects. In *screw*, for example, there is the suggestion of force and of damage done to the recipient of the screw – wood into which a screw is inserted is thereafter "ruined," as Stephanie Ross (1981) notes. This subtext of damage done to the patient is found in usage of *screw* in nonsexual domains: *he's been screwed* means that he has been badly treated.[9]

There is a definite tendency in English towards metaphors for heterosexual activity that suggest male force and violence against females, but to stop there would be to miss much of the story. The students whom Baker consulted about usage differed as to whether or not they

9 It is possible that this use of *screw* is itself drawing on the sexual domain rather than directly on the domain of building materials. The parallel usage of *fuck* – "don't fuck with me" or "they really fucked him over" – supports this hypothesis, given that *fuck*, while its etymology may suggest metaphorical sources, is not transparently metaphorical for contemporary English speakers.

would consider applying particular words symmetrically. For example his Wayne State students in the early 1970s did not recognize *Jane laid Dick* as a way to describe things whereas a few years later and with a population that included more white and upper-middle-class students, the respondents did accept female subjects for *lay* and some of the rest of these verbs. And while "we screwed each other" struck Baker's 1970s students as ill-formed, Cornell students in 2000 found such a symmetrical usage quite acceptable though they reported *we screwed around* or *we were screwing*, which lack objects, as more likely. Interestingly, some commented on an imagery drawn not from a screw going into a piece of wood but from the use of *screwing around* to mean something like playing around or having fun in a light-hearted, non-goal-directed way. Precisely how this sort of subtext developed we do not know, but it could come from the sexual intercourse use of *screw* without bringing along the metaphorical source from which that sexual use itself developed. In any case, such a mutual and fun-loving view of heterosexual activity is quite different from the turn of the (male) screw picture associated with the original metaphor.

Ann Weatherall and Marsha Walton (1999) reported a similar "remade metaphor" with the verb *bang*. As with *screw*, contemporary students are more likely to see the possibility of a symmetric kind of usage: not just *Dick banged Jane* but *Dick and Jane banged (each other)*. Discussing the metaphorical basis of *bang* (hammers "bang" nails into wood, e.g.), a New Zealand woman student in their study became quite troubled by her own use of *We were banging last night*. Creatively, she gave the metaphor a quite different twist, drawing on the imagery of a bed banging the wall because of lots of vigorous but mutually very pleasurable activity going on in the bed. In this use, banging is no longer something one person does to another but an effect they collectively produce. After so transforming *bang*, the student reported that she could now use it again quite happily. Reconceptions of *screwing* may similarly have facilitated its transfer to the "playing around" kind of usage, although we have no direct data in support of this conjecture. Stephanie Ross (1981) argues that a primary reason that words like *screw* are objectionable is that their metaphorical origins have helped load them with affect: they are not neutral in the attitudes they convey toward sexual activity.

Michele Emantian (1995) reports that the domains of heat and of eating are used in many cultures to talk about sexual desire and activity. English is, of course, one example. In English, we speak of "steamy" sex scenes and describe lovers as "hot" for each other, as "burning up." We speak of sexual "hunger" ("I'm starved for you") and sexual "appetites" and wanting to "devour" the other. These expressions have a certain sexual symmetry, although women are far more often spoken of as foods for men than vice versa. (See Hines 1999.) Contemporary English speakers also draw on eating to talk about gay male and lesbian sexual activity. Emantian reports that in the language Chagga, spoken on Mount Kilimanjaro in Tanzania, eating metaphors are not just one way of speaking about sex but the primary way. These metaphors are, however, very definitely from the perspective of a heterosexual man, with the desired woman as the food the man wants to "taste" or "eat." Sexual pleasure for heterosexual men is evaluated in terms of the "flavor" of female partners, "good as honey" or "like stale mbege" (yesterday's beer). Chagga also uses heat metaphors but again they are very asymmetric, with men saying "she burns" or "she roasts" or "look at that oven" to describe women who are seen as good sexual partners; a woman may be called "cold" (cf. English "frigid") if she seems to lack a positive attitude towards sex with men. It is not, however, intercourse that is seen as "hot" nor does a lustful man "burn." Emantian does not tell us (and she may well not really know) how women speakers of Chagga talk about heterosexual desire and activity and whether they may conceptualize things somewhat differently. But one of her main points is that, though English and Chagga do draw on similar domains, they do so in quite different (and quite culturally specific) ways.

Menstruation, pregnancy, childbirth, menopause: events associated with female reproductive biology have all been the topics of a host of metaphors in English and in many other languages. Emily Martin (1987) discusses the content of both medical conceptions of women's distinctive experiences and of women's own ways of talking about them. One prominent image in biomedical texts is of a hierarchically organized communication system: "the ovaries...influence, through feedback mechanisms, the level of performance programmed by the hypothalamic-pituitary axis" (quoted in Martin, p. 40). Given this conception, Martin argues, it is hardly surprising that menopause is viewed as what she calls "the breakdown of a system of authority" (p. 42). The hypothalamus begins to give "inappropriate orders" and "the ovaries fail to respond." The medical establishment also, she notes, often turns to the framework of industrial production: menstruation is viewed as failed production, the sad result of the failure of a fertilized egg to implant itself. In menopause the ovaries "fail" to produce "enough" estrogen; the whole system has fallen apart. All this assumes a goal of implanting a fertilized egg so not surprisingly production comes into its own during pregnancy. Childbirth is often seen as the main "point" of women's bodies (and lives?), with medical texts stressing the importance of the proper "management" of "labor" and the important role of medical expertise and technology in making the process more "efficient" and producing a satisfactory "product" (a healthy child). Women's interests and participation are often obscured completely.

Martin was especially interested in how women themselves conceptualized these phenomena. In answer to the question of how to describe menstruation to a young girl who has not experienced it, all of the middle-class women (both white and black) that she talked to, came forth with the "failed production account." They pretty much ignored what menstruation feels like and how to deal with it. In contrast, the working-class women focused on noting a "bodily change" – "you're growing up and becoming a woman"– and dealing with the phenomenology and the practical details. Rarely did they mention what's happening inside the body. Although a wide range of women showed some resistance to the mechanistic views of their bodies offered in standard biomedical accounts and more generally to conditions limiting women's lives, the working-class women were in many ways less enmeshed in the biomedical ideology and were also more likely to see a need for challenging economic and institutional barriers to equality.

There has been considerable discussion of metaphorically inspired labels for referring to women and female genitals, especially as they contrast with those for referring to men and male genitals. Much of what is called *sexist language* is felt to be offensive because problematic attitudes lie behind metaphorical identifications of women and their genitals with, for example, commodities, small animals, and, drawing again on men's eating, with fruit or other desserts. Early discussions of what Muriel Schultz (1975) called the "semantic derogation of women" pointed to the ways in which words with an initially neutral meaning (e.g. *hussy*, originally simply a shortened version of an ancestral form of *housewife*) often acquired negative connotations. In addition, however, many early discussions of sexist language pointed to the problematic nature of the kinds of metaphors that originally supported use of these forms (e.g. Lakoff 1975, [Penelope] Stanley 1977). As we saw in discussing *seminal*, metaphorical etymologies that are no longer transparent – metaphors that are not only dead but also obscured by changes in form – can be interesting evidence of past attitudes but generally do not have a lot to do with the significance of current uses. But transparent metaphors, even if dead and not revivified in some way, can indeed still reinforce the kinds of conceptual connections that motivated their initial uses. In a body of interesting recent work, Caitlin Hines (see esp. 1999) points out that many of the metaphors for female reference are by no means isolated but are systematically connected in various ways. She also finds that there are phonetic consistencies (or at least general phonetic patterns) among various words in the same general metaphorical category.

Metaphor makers

Much of the work on metaphor looks at metaphors divorced from their production and interpretation, not considering who is producing what metaphors and to what effects. But there have been some important observations, especially about the relationship between metaphor makers' experiences and social situations and their choice of metaphorical materials, of sources for talking about a variety of topics. As we noted, Kittay argued that it was men's perspectives on the world that produced metaphors where women and women's activities (e.g. childbirth) were the source domain. She argued that it was precisely the Otherizing of women that made them so attractive as metaphors for men seeking to understand their own (completely "other") concerns. Beginning with the mother, women mediate men's relations to the world and to one another.

Indeed, women themselves and not just words referring to them can symbolize men's relations to one another. Many contemporary US weddings of heterosexual couples still have a ritual "transfer" of the woman from the custody of her father to that of her husband, and name changes often reflect this. When a father answers "who gives this woman to be married?" by saying "her mother and I do," the gender asymmetry of the ritual is reduced but not eliminated. Having each of the couple accompanied down the aisle by both their parents and asking "who gives this man" or eliminating the question about "giving" altogether are ways that some marriage ceremonies challenge the traditional asymmetries. As Kittay notes, the still commonplace phenomenon of wartime rape shows men projecting their conflicts with other groups of men onto the women associated with those "other" men. Wartime rape metaphorically attacks enemy men, but the status of the raped women as symbols does not, of course, reduce their pain and suffering (and in many cultural contexts, their humiliation). What the American press calls a "trophy wife" is another instance of an actual woman as symbol, the youth and beauty of a man's wife testifying to his preeminence among men (his wealth, power, etc.). Linguistic metaphors that project, for example, men's relations to women as mothers or as sexual conquests onto men's relation to the natural world are thus part of more general symbolic practices that seem to depend in some ways on men's "otherizing" of women.

Metaphor making often draws on source domains especially familiar or important to the metaphor maker. In a study of communication in US institutional investing circles, O'Barr and Conley (1992) found a wealth of sports metaphors and also found that men were much more likely to use such ways of speaking than women. Sports metaphors permeate not only business but also political discourse in the contemporary US. In addition, sports itself is often discussed in terms of war and similar kinds of violent conflict, and the same ways of talking are also applied in such male-dominant arenas as business and politics. Women can and do draw on both sports and war ways of talking in speaking of various topics. Doing so can sometimes be a way of constituting oneself a full member of a community of practice that is or has been dominated by men. This suggests that it is not (only) differential familiarity of, say, sports and war, to language users that accounts for why gender seems to matter in producing metaphors that draw on these domains. Sports may be more important in providing gender-weighted symbolic capital than they are in their own right.

In unpublished work at Cornell University, anthropologist Kathryn March has discussed a telling case in which gender expectations seem to play a substantial role in metaphoric uptake – or the lack thereof. The *Therigatha* and *Theragatha* are part of the canon of sacred writings in the Buddhist tradition. They contain ecstatic poetry by both women and men known to have reached enlightenment around the time of the historical Buddha.[10] Writers of each sex draw on imagery from the kinds of experiences of their pre-enlightenment daily lives. So a woman, a Bhikkhuni whose name is unknown to us, writes:

> *Sleep softly, little Sturdy, take thy rest*
> *At ease, wrapt in the robe thyself hast made.*
> *Stilled are the passions that would rage within*
> *Withered as potherbs in the oven dried.*
>
> (Ps. I, p. 9)

A male contemporary named Kula writes:

> *The conduit-makers lead the stream*
> *Fletchers coerce the arrow shaft*
> *The joiners mould the wooden plank*
> *The self 'tis that the pious tame.*
>
> (Ps. XIX, p. 24)

10 *Psalms of the Early Buddhists, I. Psalms of the Sisters* and *II. Psalms of the Brethren*, tr. Mrs. Rhys Davids, London: The Pali Text Society (1909) as Translations Series 1 and 4, respectively; reissued in a single volume, *Psalms of the Early Buddhists*, London: Routledge, 1980.

Each draws on the kinds of things they might have done to talk about the achievement of enlightenment, of working to still the passions and subdue the concerns of ordinary life. Hardly surprising.

What is surprising is the way that much later commentators evaluate the poems. The women are seen as limited, constrained to write just of domesticity and their particular experiences, whereas the men's writings are described as beautifully poetic. The woman above, for example, might be presented as writing about dried potherbs and, incidentally, mentioning the stilling of passions, and the man as using conduit-making, arrow-making, and joinery as powerful metaphors in his talk about stilling the passions. Women are simply assumed by these later commentators to be limited in their capacity for the expression of true religious enlightenment.

Although the commentators do not put it this way, they can be understood as not seeing the women as using metaphors at all. The women's images are more likely to be interpreted as descriptions of mundane concrete experiences, whereas the men's images are seen as tools used to communicate much loftier messages. In part, this is because the images that were picked up and became commonplace in Buddhist texts are those from men's domains: reaping, plowing, digging ditches, making arrows. There is little repetition in later texts (almost all by men) of images of grinding grain, tending to family, burning curries, grieving children's deaths. So later Buddhists encountering these early texts find the men's more familiar-sounding as expressions of religious sensibilities. This is one reason that much later commentary sees the women's texts as showing less genuinely religious sensibility and sophistication – and, concomitantly, less capacity to make metaphors – and thus as inferior religious texts. Some commentators assess the "women's" poems more highly, but then say that they must not actually have been written by women. Of course, there are also more appreciative assessments that do not assume women incapable of using metaphors in the service of religious expression, and there has been a recent resurgence in Buddhist female religious practitioners, especially in Taiwan and Nepal.

Western traditions of "high culture" show some parallel barriers to women's trying to harness metaphor for their own purposes. Drawing on Lacanian psychoanalytic theory, Cora Kaplan ([1986] 1998) has written of the resistance to women's use of the most powerful kinds of language and particularly poetry. She quotes Emily Dickinson: "They shut me up in Prose/As when a little Girl/They put me in the Closet –/Because they liked me 'still'." Science is a very different domain, but there too women have often been seen as limited to careful observation and description and less capable than men of making the theoretical break-throughs that new metaphors often encapsulate. Evelyn Fox Keller's (1983) biography of Barbara McClintock is revealing in this respect, noting the resistance to McClintock's new "language" and her new outlook on genetics. (See also Keller 1987.) Eventually both Dickinson and McClintock have been recognized for their enormous contributions, but that recognition does not erase the muting of their voices and those of other women trying to break new poetic or scientific ground. Of course, there is much more to being a poet or a theoretical scientist than being a metaphor maker, the source of "new" meanings, of reconceptualizations. But metaphor making is one part of the picture.

CHAPTER 7

Mapping the world

We map our world by categorizing its contents and its happenings –
putting together diverse particulars into a single category – and relating the categories they create. One of the basic things language does is
allow us to label categories, making it easier for them to figure in our
shared social life, to help guide us as we make our way in the world.
Gender categories like those labeled by *man* and *woman*, *girl* and *boy*
play a prominent role in the social practices that sustain a gender order in which male/female is seen as a sharp dichotomy separating two
fundamentally different kinds of human beings and in which gender
categorization is viewed as always relevant.

Gender categories do not simply posit difference: they support hierarchy and inequality. We have practices, both linguistic and nonlinguistic, that tend to conflate the gender-specific category labeled *man* with
the generic category of human being, for which English also sometimes
uses the same label, as in book titles like *Man and his place in nature*.
We also have labeling and other categorizing practices that tend to
derogate women as women and to either overlook or disparage sexual
minorities. And both men and women are mapped onto a variety of
other socially important categories, many of which interact significantly with gender. Gender also interacts with just which parts of the
terrain get mapped, which categories get noticed, elaborated, and labeled. This chapter explores some of the complex ways in which categorizing and labeling – along with controversy over categories and
their labels – enter into gender practice.

Labeling disputes and histories

"I'm not a feminist, but ... " Most of our readers have heard and many
may well have uttered these words, often as preamble to the expression
of some sentiment or call to action that might be considered part of
what feminism espouses. (The presupposition that the *but* signals here
is that what follows might be taken as a sign that the speaker is a

feminist.) What follows could be any of a variety of things: "I think women should be paid equally to men" or "you should recognize that what a woman does with her body is no one's business but her own" or "I'm tired of being the token woman on every other committee" or "I'm helping organize a 'Take back the night' march" or "I'm taking a women's studies course this term" or "I've decided to write a letter to the paper about those obnoxiously sexist posters that the XYZ frat used in their recruiting drive this year."

In the US, there have been several studies suggesting that many college students who say that they embrace a basically liberal feminist ideology nevertheless are uncomfortable applying the label *feminist* to themselves.[1] Many of the studies looking at attitudes towards feminism and feminists focus on women. Although many feminisms have room for male feminists there is a widespread belief that feminists are prototypically women and for this and other reasons many fewer men label themselves feminists. Of course, it's not only college students who begin "I'm not a feminist but...": high-school students and middle-aged and older people are also often reluctant to call themselves feminists even though they may in fact agree with much of the agenda advanced by those who do so label themselves. At the same time, there are important generational differences; for example a higher proportion of those fifty or over who embrace gender egalitarianism are willing to call themselves feminists though a lower proportion in this age group does indeed subscribe to explicitly egalitarian goals.

There are a number of reasons why the label *feminist* is often resisted. One has to do with the association of feminists with organized political action and not simply beliefs. It is one thing to express disapproval of sexual harassment and another to organize a movement for anti-harassment policies in one's workplace or school. Some who may not especially disapprove of such activism in the service of women's interests may nonetheless (accurately) not see themselves as taking any role in it. Perhaps they think that activism is no longer needed although it would have been appropriate in some distant past – for example

---

1 See Arnold (2000) for a recent report on some US students' definitions of feminism and the relation of those definitions to whether they labeled themselves feminists. Buschman and Lenart (1996) and Katz (1996) have reported that many college-age women think that there is no longer need to organize for feminist goals, although they also found that those who had experienced gender inequities personally – e.g. being on a women's sports team that had to manage with many fewer resources than the corresponding men's team – often did consider themselves feminists. Twenge (1997) reports that young women today are more likely to subscribe to a broadly "feminist" outlook than was true of women of their mothers' generation even though they are reluctant to call themselves feminists.

in the early part of the twentieth century when women did not have
the vote in the US or in the 1960s when job ads carried "Men only" and
"Women only" headings (with most of the better-paying jobs in the former category and only a handful of positions under "Both") and women
college students had a curfew while their male peers did not. Here, the
general focus in the US on individuals and widespread belief in a meri-
tocracy are relevant: many think that since lots of legal and other institutional barriers to women's achievement have indeed been removed in
the past decades they and those they care most about will not really be
disadvantaged by the gender order. They may be moved by the position
of women elsewhere – for example in Afghanistan under the Taliban –
but just feel lucky that they themselves are not the victims of such
overt female subordination. Or perhaps they think that the price that
they might pay for actively challenging aspects of the current gender
order would be too high. One reason might be that the effort would
take them away from other projects that matter as much or more to
them. Another might be that they think the risks outweigh potential
benefits.

What are seen as risks? The risks have to do with being put in a social
category that is widely disparaged and characterized in very restrictive
and often quite negative ways. Denying the label is a way to avoid being
categorized along with those whom the media in the 1980s began to
deride and caricature, following the example of the antifeminist movement at the beginning of the twentieth century.[2] As novelist Rebecca
West wrote in 1913, "people call me a feminist whenever I express
sentiments that differentiate me from a doormat." Feminists, we've
heard, are "humorless," "rigid and doctrinaire feminazis," "manhat-
ing ballbusters," "ugly cows," "sexually frustrated," "arrogant bitches,"
"whining victims," and, drawing on homophobic discourses, "dykes."
Sources like the *New York Times* used politer language, quoting Ivy
League students in 1982 as saying that feminists were women who
"let themselves go physically" and "had no sense of style." Almost
two decades later, some Cornell students describe feminists as "girls
who don't shave their legs and hate men." Even those who recognize that many (perhaps even most) feminists are quite different from
the sometimes monstrous creatures of the stereotype may (with some
justification) fear that others not so enlightened will take the feminist

2 See Faludi (1991) for an account of the antifeminist backlash in the US of the 1980s;
chapter two draws parallels with earlier periods of active opposition to feminist
activities.

label at its most negative. They may not only reject being so labeled. They may refrain from openly expressing or acting on feminist beliefs because being categorized as a feminist seems so "uncool" (and for many, so potentially dangerous for their success on the heterosexual market).

There are other very different reasons that some women have rejected the feminist label. Black women correctly observed that the US women's movement that began in the late 1960s was focused on issues of primary concern to middle-class white women and was very much run by such women. Poor women and women of color were on the margins, if present at all. Many self-labeled "feminists" hired domestic helpers at very low wages without any job benefits to clean their houses and tend their children. Such jobs were held (and are still held) overwhelmingly by women and disproportionately by African American women and other women of color. Rape and wife-battering were issues around which feminists organized, but it was violence against white women that got the most attention. And many "feminists" did not seem to appreciate how important it was to African American women to fight against racism, not only on their own behalf but for and with their sons, brothers, male lovers, and husbands. When Alice Walker (1983) wrote "womanist is to feminist as purple is to lavender," she helped launch an alternative label and category. Those who identify as womanists generally see themselves as engaged in both antiracist and antisexist struggles, efforts that seem separable only from the perspective of privileged white women.

Of course, for those who start off "I'm a feminist and..." categorizing others as feminists is a very positive thing to do. And refusing to apply the label to certain other would-be feminists is part of shaping what it is one thinks feminists should be like, drawing the boundaries to exclude those who do not meet certain "standards." Some might refuse to allow men into the feminist category; others might want to allow only "women-identified women"; still others might have different criteria. Many academic feminists these days speak of feminisms, thus implicitly recognizing many distinctions among feminists, many subcategories. There is increasing talk in the US of a new category of feminists, third-wave feminists, young women (and men) organizing at the dawn of the twenty-first century around somewhat different gender issues than those that most concerned their parents – and drawing on a somewhat different kind of politics.

Like many labels, *feminist* has a complex and a contested history. How it will figure in social practice in the years ahead remains uncertain.

Category boundaries and criteria

One reason language is so interactionally useful is that it makes it easy for people to develop and refine collectively the category concepts that are so central to social action and inquiry. Languages label many basic categories: linguistic labels group individual objects, persons, or events together in various ways. These groupings abstract from particular things and occurrences to allow us to recognize patterned similarities and structural regularities across the "blooming buzzing confusion" of private phenomenal experience. Categorization does not always require language, but language certainly allows us to use and interact with categories in a host of ways not otherwise possible.

What is it that guides people in assigning distinct entities or occurrences to a single category? On the so-called classical view, there is a set of properties that all and only the individuals belonging to the category share, properties in virtue of which they are category members. A label for the category can then be defined by listing these necessary and sufficient criteria for its application. In his later work, the philosopher Ludwig Wittgenstein challenged this view. He noted that in some categories different members seem to be linked by a web of similarities without there being any property at all essential to all category members. What about games, he asked? Think of soccer, bridge, concentration, hopscotch, marbles, charades, twenty questions, hide and seek, playing house, dodgeball, dungeons and dragons, basketball, tennis, scrabble, monopoly, the farmer in the dell, video arcade games. The category of games seems to involve different criteria, of which only some subset needs to apply. Maybe games are more like a family. Some members may not look much like one another but overall there are "family resemblances."[3]

In the past few decades, there has been a flurry of work on categorization and concepts in psychology, philosophy, anthropology, and linguistics. How do children acquire categorizing concepts? In what ways do cultures map the world differently? How are categories related to one another? How can concepts change? How do categorizing practices facilitate or hinder collective thought and action? Does categorizing in the social domain work differently from categorizing in the biological domain or in the domain of artifacts? Is there a distinction between

---

3 See Wittgenstein (1953). Psychologist Eleanor Rosch and her colleagues in Rosch (1975), Rosch and Mervis (1975), and elsewhere developed the idea of categories as involving family resemblances rather than necessary and sufficient criteria; much other recent empirical work on categories engages with the ideas Rosch formulated.

"defining" and "identifying" criteria? And, of course, how do linguistic labeling practices interact with categorization? There is a vast literature on these and related questions.[4] We will focus on some of the ways in which labeling practices develop and are deployed in social practice.

Patrolling boundaries

In American English we distinguish bowls, cups, and glasses from each other partly on the basis of a set of material properties, ratio of height to width, and possession of a handle. Cups and bowls are commonly (but not always) made of opaque material, glasses of transparent. Cups commonly have handles, bowls and glasses generally do not. Glasses are usually taller than they are wide, bowls are usually wider than they are tall, and cups are about equally tall and wide. As William Labov (1973) showed, manipulating these properties will lead people to be more or less sure of how to draw the boundaries, which terms to apply. We also distinguish these items on the basis of the uses they are put to – whether one serves mashed potatoes, hot coffee, or lemonade in them. While everyone will agree on what a prototypical cup, bowl, or glass is, there will be some disagreement around the edges. For example people will not agree on whether a tall, thin china vessel with no handle is a cup or a glass. If someone serves iced tea in it and thus uses it as a glass, people are more likely to consider it to be a glass. And if it becomes fashionable to serve iced tea in such vessels, the edges of the categories may change for the entire community, or at least for that part of the community that is familiar with this fashion. And fashion itself, of course, does not get established willy-nilly. If a person known for culinary elegance begins to serve iced tea in such a vessel, and/or to call the vessel a glass, the rest of the community is likely to trust her authority and quite possibly to imitate her. If, however, someone with a reputation for inelegance does so it is less likely to catch on. Perhaps that person will be said to be serving iced tea in a cup, or it will be said that she doesn't know a cup from a glass.

Of course, eating/drinking utensils are artifacts. So long as people made vessels so that the material and functional criteria coincided and did not allow overlaps, boundaries were clearly drawn and the categories seemed quite static. Once new kinds of vessels were produced, however, a boundary-drawing issue emerged. Just how such issues

4 In addition to the Rosch research mentioned in the preceding note, see, e.g., Atran (1990), Hirschfeld and Gelman (1994), Keil (1989), Lakoff (1987), Medin (1989), Putnam (1975).

get settled in particular communities of practice will depend on a variety of social factors, an important one of which is the authority with respect to the field in question of different language users in the community. Drawing category boundaries is often an exercise of social power.

But what about other types of categories? People who buy and eat meat often think of various meat cut categories as existing "naturally": rump roasts and tenderloins are simply waiting to be "carved at the joints." Yet as the charts in Figures 7.1 and 7.2 show, butchers in the US and in France draw the boundaries quite differently.

"Naturally" occurring "joints" certainly constrain butchering practices, but there is still plenty of room for different choices to be made as to how to carve up the field into categories. So-called natural kind categories like animal or plant species (see Atran 1990) show somewhat less cross-cultural diversity in boundaries than meat cuts, but even here there are important differences. There are also changes over time in natural kind category boundaries as scientific or other sociocultural practices involving the kind change. We now classify whales as mammals and not as fish, showing a shift from one kind of criterion (living in the water) to another (nursing young). An eggplant is classified biologically as a fruit (because it has internal seeds) but functions culinarily as a vegetable. Where boundaries are drawn for *fruit* and *vegetable* will depend on whether the interests being pursued are those of the botanist or the cook.

Anchoring concepts in discourse

For natural kind terms, philosopher Hilary Putnam (1975) proposed that there is a set of "essential" properties grouping members of a kind together. But Putnam also argued that ordinary people's concepts tend to be based on nonessential criteria, which he called *stereotypes*. The ordinary word *stereotype* suggests negative and discredited beliefs; psychologists more often speak neutrally of *schemas* or *theories* associated with concepts, a set of related hypotheses about members of the category. Putnam also suggested that there is what he called a "linguistic division of labor," which is really an allocation of linguistic authority. Rather than what's in ordinary people's heads, Putnam proposes, it is scientific theories and experts that provide definitive criteria and determine how boundaries are to be drawn. In this approach, it is scientists who "discover" joints at which the natural world is to be carved, and the rest of us are supposed to follow the map that they provide for us.

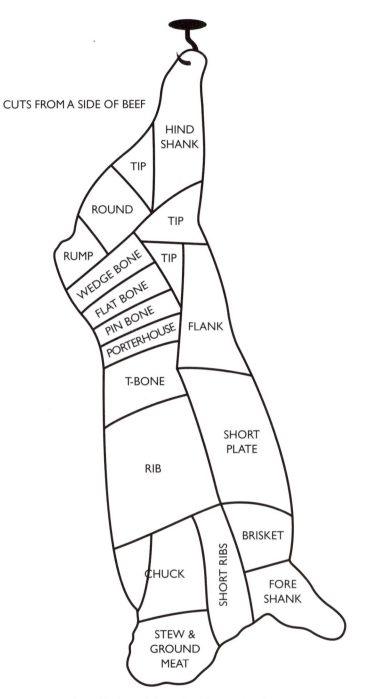

7.1 US cuts of beef (adapted from Rombauer 1998)

Most of us lack the scientists' expertise and base our own categorizations on various kinds of stereotypical properties. At the same time,
we typically believe that there are criteria we may be unable to observe
that sort, for example, species and sexes. Sandra Bem (1993) tells of her

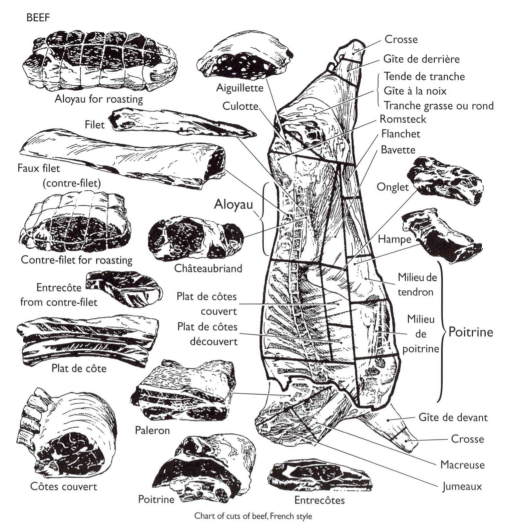

BEEF

Aloyau for roasting

Filet

Faux filet
(contre-filet)

Contre-filet for roasting

Entrecôte
from contre-filet

Plat de côte

Côtes couvert

Aiguillette

Culotte

Aloyau

Châteaubriand

Plat de côtes
couvert

Plat de côtes
découvert

Paleron

Poitrine

Entrecôtes

Crosse
Gîte de derrière
Tende de tranche
Gîte à la noix
Tranche grasse ou rond
Romsteck
Flanchet
Bavette

Onglet

Hampe

Milieu de
tendron

Milieu
de
poitrine

Poitrine

Gîte de devant

Crosse

Macreuse

Jumeaux

Chart of cuts of beef, French style

7.2 French cuts of beef (adapted from Montagné 1961)

son Jeremy's going to nursery school wearing a decorative barrette in his hair. On seeing this, other kids started chanting "Jeremy's a girl – look at his barrette." Having been taught that being a girl rather than a boy had to do only with having a vagina rather than a penis, Jeremy thought he could simply settle the matter. Pulling down his pants, he said, "See, I've got a penis so I'm a boy." But his classmates had an answer for that. "Everyone has a penis, but only girls wear barrettes." The story amuses older children and adults precisely because they do make a distinction between essential and inessential sex differences: the (usually hidden) penis trumps such readily observable characteristics as fastening one's hair in a barrette. As we will see below, however, the "inessential" properties associated with gender categories are by no means always linguistically irrelevant. And, of course, such gender schemas are central to sustaining the gender order.

In recent years, psychologists studying concept formation and change have moved away from a focus on definitional criteria to an emphasis on the place of concepts in the theories or schemas in which they figure. The child eventually comes to recognize that genitalia are relevant to sex in a way that hair decoration is not, that some kind of theory of reproductive biology is central in gender discourse. For purposes of biological investigation, some ways of grouping things are undoubtedly more fruitful than others.

Internal molecular structure has often proved a better guide to biologically interesting properties than behavior or external appearance. So when biological inquiry is what is at stake, it often makes sense for folks to defer to biologists. But as we saw in discussing the concepts designated by *female* and *male* in chapter one, even biological criteria do not always yield sharp boundaries. The three kinds of criteria – chromosomal, endocrinal, and anatomical – sometimes not only fail to coincide, but each can also sometimes fail to determine a perfect two-way sort. There are, for example, some people born with neither the prototypically female XX nor the prototypically male XY chromosomal arrangement. Biologists would reduce the male–female distinction to gamete size – but we have no immediate access to people's gametes. It is our *social* world and not biology that insists on a binary classification and on the permanence of that classification. Social imperatives, not medical or scientific ones, lead doctors to recommend procedures to "normalize" the sex of a baby who does not neatly fall in to one or the other category. In some species, the same individual may readily be male at some points of its life, female at others. In humans, however, changing sex is typically accompanied by surgery and hormonal interventions. Except for such still relatively rare cases, children are right when they conclude that being a girl means a future as a woman.[5]

The important point about concepts is that they do function in particular kinds of discourses, particular background theories and schemas of how things are or should or might be. The "literal" concept of *woman* is grounded in theories of reproductive biology (even though for most of us our grasp of such theories is at best limited). But, of course, what gender discourse is about is connecting the concepts of *woman* and *man* that are grounded in reproductive biological theory and practice to a wide array of other theories and practices.

5 See Fausto-Sterling (2000) for extensive discussion of how bodies are "sexed."

As we observed in chapter one, gender attributions are used far more than most of us realize in predicting people's behavior and in interpreting and evaluating it. Gender categorizations have a profound effect on further categorizations of an individual's behavior, talents, interests, and appearance. Sometimes category-based expectations are very useful, but sometimes they lead observers astray.[6] And especially with children, they can be self-fulfilling, shaping an individual in one direction rather than another.

Highlighting fields

Categorizing always takes place within the bounds of some background field of contrast. A cup, for example, is contrasted with a glass, on the one hand, and a bowl, on the other. Categories are relative to particular fields. To categorize is necessarily to evoke some background field, to highlight it as an area within which certain contrasts are of interest. In mapping the field, making distinctions among kinds in a field, we are highlighting the field itself as something requiring attention, something salient to community life.

The actual fields that one attends to, as well as the ways in which the fields are cut up, can be quite different in different communities of practice. Thus linguists talk about various kinds of sentential structures or verb endings or configurations of the vocal tract, with a host of concepts that organize these fields. Historians can talk about epochs like the Middle Ages or political events like the American Civil War or the movement for female suffrage. Biologists talk about gametes, chromosomes, hormone levels, gonads, brain hemispheres. Some communities of practice talk about movie stars and heavy metal bands, others talk about sexual harassment and date rape, others about homeless people and housing subsidies and the mentally ill, others about post plays and fast breaks and free throws (basketball moves). Becoming part of a particular community of practice generally involves attending to certain kinds of fields and categories. Community members acquire shared categorizing vocabularies and engage in the various discursive practices in which they figure.

Many communities of practice have elaborate categorizing systems for the field of eating utensils, well beyond cups, glasses, and bowls.

---

6 Valian (1998), which focuses on the question of why women are still having so much difficulty achieving in the professions, discusses a host of empirical studies documenting the fact that gender assumptions significantly affect how people interpret their own and others' behavior and capabilities.

Most people in the western world distinguish knives, forks, and spoons. Some people eat primarily with a knife. In some places, eating only with a pocket knife is considered masculine. Then there are more elaborate cutlery choices. Some people have steak knives, butter knives, fish knives, fruit knives; salad forks, dessert forks, fish forks, meat forks; soup spoons, teaspoons, dessert spoons, serving spoons, demitasse spoons. Elaboration of cutlery distinctions is generally associated with class, as is the use of large numbers of pieces of cutlery in each meal. Cutlery itself is an important field for class discourse. What we eat with is part of how we establish ourselves as certain kinds of people.[7] Great attention to cutlery and other eating utensils is associated, in turn, with elaborate eating rituals, which include rules about such things as how to place the utensils on the table, what order to use them in, how to hold and use the utensils, and how and where to place them when one has finished eating. Categorization, then, is part of a larger organization of practice relevant to the field.

Participation in a community of practice involves learning the fields that are salient in the community, and all the knowledge centered around the categorizations. Such knowledge is central to the background discourses that ground concepts. We learn how to use our eating utensils first of all by knowing that the categories of utensils and the manner of their use is salient, then by having plenty of opportunity to observe others as they activate the categories, and having access to direct and indirect discussion as well. If we grow up in a community with elaborate utensil use, we are likely to get direct instruction from parents. We might also hear people comment on someone else's table manners, often disparagingly noting someone's ignorance of the cutlery field and its organization.

Within a community of practice, there may be different forms of membership that are partly constituted by a division of categorizing "labor" and also by differential values attached to certain kinds of categorizing practices. In mainstream American society, for example, women are commonly expected to have more meticulous table manners than men. Certain ways of holding dishes (not only the caricatured sticking out of the little finger but, for example, holding a cup in both hands with fingers extended) are considered feminine. In some circles, men feel the need to joke about small utensils such as a dessert fork or delicate dishes such as thin porcelain teacups. Indeed, men frequently deny detailed knowledge of the category distinctions within the general field of eating utensils and eating practices and make

7 See Bourdieu (1984) for discussion.

fun of women's supposedly more elaborately articulated concepts and beliefs.

Robin Lakoff (1975) claimed that women often have much larger color vocabularies than men and that men often deride women's attention to subtle color distinctions. Color-blindness is in fact a sex-linked secondary trait, and there are far more colorblind men than women. The main social significance of color, however, probably lies in its connections to home decoration and clothing practices. As with eating practices, home decoration and clothing practices are sites for constructing class and gender. Mocking the fine categorizing practices and subtle conceptual distinctions associated with close attention to these fields is one way some men construct themselves as appropriately "masculine." They implicitly downgrade such "feminine" or "effete" fields in comparison to others where they actively participate in highly articulated categorizing and discourse. Sports vocabularies and discourse, for example, are constructed as "masculine." The implication is often that attention to "feminine" fields interferes with effective participation in the putatively more important "masculine" fields. We offer a (true) story of an eight-year-old girl learning to play basketball to illustrate the conflicts, the tension between the practices. Melissa was busily dribbling down the floor when her (male) coach yelled encouragingly "Go, Red." She stopped in her tracks to correct him. "We're not 'Red', Coach, we're 'Maroon'." The anecdote is amusing in part because it's so obvious that female athletes beyond the third grade are virtually never hampered by their devotion to the field of color. Many people of both sexes manage quite successfully to handle color categorizing practices as well as sports.

Social categories in (inter)action

Social categories highlight fields of social identity and are thus of special importance in gender discourse. Adolescence is a good site for the study of social categories for several reasons. First of all, adolescence is a life stage at which a tremendous amount of social work goes on. Adolescents are forging identities in the transition from childhood to adulthood. And in most western industrial societies they are doing it not individually, but as an age cohort, as categorization plays an important role in the social organization of the age cohort. In industrial societies, most adolescents spend much of their time in schools, and most of them in large schools. The larger the population one encounters in the day, the more "anonymous" many encounters are, the more likely one is to rely on ready-made categorizations to make moment-to-moment decisions in behavior. In addition, in a crowded space there is always an issue of territoriality and control. Social categorization in American high schools is not simply about recognition and predictability but about power and social control. In their eagerness to build an age cohort culture, adolescents invest a good deal of energy and passion in the emerging social order. Categorization of salient kinds of deviance becomes one central concern. Learning what constitutes a *geek*, a *freak*, a *nerd*, a *homo* is learning not simply lexical distinctions, but the characteristics that define the boundaries of acceptability.

These overtly normative social categories do not get constructed in the abstract, but primarily in concrete action. People refer to others as geeks or nerds, argue about whether a particular person is a geek or a nerd. They may call someone a geek or a nerd to their face, whether jokingly or as a form of aggression. But the categories get constructed as they get peopled with real exemplars and as people debate whether given individuals actually possess the salient characteristics.

Categories that are overtly about social normativity are only part of the picture, of course. Racial and ethnic categories are important in many high schools: Eckert and McConnell-Ginet (1999) note the emergence of a new *Asian American* category in California schools. In Penny's ethnographic work in Detroit area high schools (1989), a *jock* was a member of the category of those with a positive orientation towards institutionally organized school life, whereas a *burnout* (*burn*) or *jell* was a member of the oppositional category, which oriented toward the neighborhood and the wider community outside the school. As one girl noted, once junior high school started "[A]ll you heard was, 'She's a jock,' 'She's a jell,' you know. And that's all it was. You were either one. You weren't an in-between, which I was." Here the labeling was clearly aimed at establishing oppositional categories that would exhaustively classify the field of individuals attending the school. Such social categories, some of which remain quite salient beyond adolescence, also function normatively but their normativizing function is somewhat more covert. Precisely how any social category is deployed and understood depends on who is using and interpreting it.[8]

Categorizing oneself and others can be an important part of affirming social affiliations, of developing and cultivating a social identity.

---

8 See Eckert and McConnell-Ginet (1995), Bucholtz (1999), Brenneis (1977).

Category relations

Not only is categorizing always done against the background of a field. What matters is the relation among categories within the field.

Kinds of contrast: polar opposites vs. default generics

When we put distinct entities in a single category, we treat them as equivalent, as the same in certain respects. To categorize different individuals as all women is to say that ignoring differences among them is useful for certain purposes, that for those purposes they can be seen as interchangeable. At the same time, we always categorize against the background of some more inclusive or superordinate category or field. This means that members of the category are being contrasted with other entities in the larger field. Women are often being distinguished from other people, though they might be being distinguished from other female animals. Any categorization is partly understood in terms of alternative categorizations within the same field.

Contrasts can be between *polar opposites*: this means that each of the contrasting categories is treated as on a par, complete with its own distinguishing properties. Some linguists call such contrasts *equipollent*. Contrasts are often, however, what analysts sometimes call *privative*: this means that a *generic default* alternative category is defined simply as lacking the distinctive properties that group together the *marked* category (or categories).

Among children, *girl* and *boy* function as polar opposites.[9] Such contrasting categories are generally taken to be mutually exclusive: they do not overlap.

Polarization is the tendency to take contrasting categories as not only mutually exclusive but also jointly exhaustive of some field within which they operate: anything in the relevant field is classed in one or the other of these nonoverlapping categories. Polarized opposites need not be perfectly equivalent. For example, *girl* is applied to adults more often than *boy* is, *girl* is applied insultingly to those whose claimed identity is *boy* whereas the opposite phenomenon is much more limited,

---

9 In its earliest cited uses in Middle English, *girl*, especially as a plural, covered children of both sexes. *Boy* did not apparently designate a male child as such until the later Middle English period, being earlier used to refer to male servants or other males of low rank. Exactly how and when we moved to the present polarized and exhaustive opposition is not clear. This is a striking case of an association of feminine and generic. The background field is one of childhood, and, interestingly, the equation of females and small dependents recurs in other contexts.

and so on. But still, neither *girl* nor *boy* functions as a default for the category designated by *kid* or *child* (as *girl* once did; see note 9). Among adults, the category *woman* is sometimes in polar opposition to the category *man* and, as we saw in chapter one, there is little if any room for individual adults outside one of those two oppositional categories nor is there overlap. In Figure 7.3, we see the background field of humans categorized oppositionally, with gender and age being the two organizing principles.

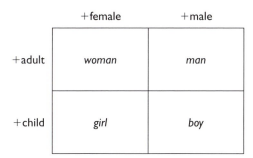

7.3 Polarised oppositions

A field of contrast can, however, be organized privatively so that the marked categories do not exhaustively classify the field, leaving a default background of field membership. *Women* and *children*, for example, may be marked categories against a background that assumes female sex and youth are special properties that the generic human lacks. The generic human is defined privatively in the sense that it is distinguished by what it lacks, what it is "deprived" of, femaleness and youth. Figure 7.4 shows this relationship.

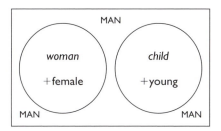

7.4 Default background, marked subcategories

Some years ago a famous anthropologist wrote something along the following lines: "When we woke in the morning we found that the villagers had all left by canoe in the night, leaving us alone with the women and children [who were of course also villagers!]." The following was heard on an NPR broadcast of *Morning Edition* on January 14, 2000: "Over a hundred Muslim civilians were killed, and many women and children." (Perhaps the newscaster meant *including* rather than *and*, but *and* is what he said.) Sometimes it's not only male humans who seem to be taken as default but married male humans, almost certainly assumed to be heterosexual as when a noted linguist urged that linguistics pay more attention to "language as it is used in everyday life by members of the social order, that vehicle of communication in which they argue with their wives, joke with their friends, and deceive their enemies." McConnell-Ginet (1979) argues that cases like this one involve something like personification, giving concrete life to the abstract "member of the social order." Very few personifications fail to be gendered.

Paula Treichler and Francine Frank (1989) call these and similar cases *false generics* and offer many illustrations: for example "the settlers and their wives" and "three Brazilians and a woman" (who in context is revealed also to be a fourth Brazilian). The words themselves don't force the gendered defaults – *villagers, Muslim civilians, members of the social order, the settlers, Brazilians* certainly are not semantically marked as male – but their deployment in discourse supports default (adult) male interpretations.

Conventionally sex-indefinite or generic terms in English can also sometimes be understood as applying only to females, but such uses generally require richer contextual information to work than the male default cases. A woman who was a stewardess on the first commercial transcontinental flight in the US commented during an NPR interview in the spring of 1999 that "back then people stopped working when they got married." Cultural knowledge that there has been no period in recent history in which men resigned their paying jobs upon getting married (plus, perhaps, knowledge that early flight attendants were all female) steers us to limit *people* in this context to women. In occupational fields dominated by women, we can, as we noted in chapter two, also have female defaults: *male nurse*, in the absence of a paired *female nurse*, shows the female default in nursing.

Julia Penelope (1990) argues that most gender-differentiated category labels in Old English (OE) were symmetric polar oppositions, but that gender-differentiated category labels in Modern English (MdE) tend to be organized with male defaults or show some of the other kinds of androcentric or male-centered asymmetries we discuss below. Although it is not clear that such a general claim can be made, the history of the words *woman* and *man* does suggest change from a more generally symmetric opposition to a quite prevalent default organization. The OE form *man*, which was roughly equivalent to *human*, was part of the compound *wifman*, which is the source of MdE *woman*; *wif*, which is historically related to the word *weave*, is the source of MdE *wife*. There was another OE compound, *werman*, which labeled male human beings. The prefix *wer* descends to MdE in *werewolf* and is also historically related to the *vir* of *virile* and *virtue*. At some point, however, the masculine prefix *wer* was lost. Although *man* continued in some contexts to be used to label humans in general, it also came to serve as a masculine form, almost certainly first in the same nonconventional "default" way as the word *villagers* in the anthropologist's report and then eventually as a conventional opposition to *woman*.

In a given situated discourse, *man* is seldom used both to label generic human beings and at the same time to mark off male human beings as a special category among human beings. Yet we do occasionally see what look like such uses: "Man needs food, shelter, [we seem to be using *man* generically here] and sexual access to woman [but here we slip to a more specific sense]." The debate about what Wendy Martyna (1980) dubbed *he-man* language highlights the conventional double use of forms like the pronoun *he* or the noun *man* as both masculine and also generic terms. Not only is the slippage in the example given here potentially problematic. There are also many common contexts in which the sometimes generic forms can only function as masculines. "He doesn't like liver." To say this in reference to a specific person, perhaps someone at whom the speaker is pointing, is to take it for granted that the person is male. Or consider, "There are five men running for the senate seat in North Carolina." If Elizabeth Dole or anyone else assumed to be a woman is on the ballot, then they are not included among the five. In this respect, *man* is different from *cow*, a generic default to the masculine *bull*. In some contexts *five cows* could include a bull (though it also might not – we could speak of *four cows and a bull*).

"Nonsexist" language guidelines generally warn against the use of masculine forms as generics. Empirical research shows that when a form conventionally stands in opposition to a feminine form – can have a "masculine" interpretation – people tend in various ways to interpret the form as masculine rather than simply as a gender-inclusive generic.[10] Interpretations also depend on people's general attitudes towards gender equality. Fatemen Khosroshahi (1989 and further discussed in Bing 1992) found that self-avowed feminists are less likely to use generic masculines for sex-indefinite meanings but are more likely to interpret others' uses of these forms as potentially applicable to women.

Words chosen do matter. But as the false generics we considered first show, the problematic status of generic masculines is by no means

10 See, e.g., Bem and Bem (1973), Schneider and Hacker (1973), Martyna (1980). Frank and Treichler (1989) is a useful general source, which includes not only a number of essays but also a very detailed discussion of strategies for avoiding various problematic but common usages.

simply a matter of linguistic conventions like those involved in using *he* or *man*. There are more general discursive practices and category-marking principles at work.[11] There is a discursive tendency to interpret generics generally so that they exclude those who belong to specially marked subcategories of the genus. Femaleness or youth are not the only marked subcategories of those who might sometimes be thought not (really) people. A particularly chilling example comes from an NPR broadcast in July 2000 on the occasion of the anniversary of the ADA (the Americans with Disabilities Act). The program featured an interview with a woman who is a judge and is herself completely paralyzed below the neck. Commenting on the difficulties she encountered traveling, the judge recalled a flight attendant explaining to her why she would be last off the plane in the event of an emergency: "We have to get the people off first."

Thus although *woman* and *man* can be oppositional categories (in which case *man* is interpreted as positively involving maleness, a distinctive property of some human beings), *woman* may be marked against a default background of *man* (or *villagers* or *Brazilians*), in which case *man* (or *villagers* or *Brazilians*) refers to generic members of the field, with the potential to exclude those who belong to the marked category *woman*. Discursive practices tend often to include as generic members of a field only those who are not specially "marked" – in the case of women, specially marked by their sex. Such practices produce false generics. In the case of *man*, the practice has become institutionalized. Such institutionalizing leads to conventional masculine generics. It is thus misleading to speak of "the" relation between two category labels. In the case of *man* and *woman*, we need to be alert to which relations are operative in particular discursive contexts. And it is not only the label *man* that produces problematically masculine generics: the widespread practice of using category labels to designate only those who are not in certain specially marked subcategories produces much the same effect.

Elaborating marked concepts

As we noted earlier, to put things in the same category is to treat them as more or less equivalent within the background field, as homogeneous. The differences that may exist within a category are seen

---

11 Black and Coward (1981) make this point very effectively in their review of Spender (1980), a book that could be read as locating the problem of masculine generics in particular words.

as much less important than the differences between distinct oppositional categories in the same field or between a marked category and
the background default. There is a tendency to elaborate the picture
of the distinctiveness of marked categories against a background field.

There are two ways this happens: asymmetries in distinctions within
categories, on the one hand, and the erasure of categories when oppositional distinctions and defaults merge, on the other. We look first at
asymmetries and then at erasure.

Category asymmetry

Categories that are used in oppositional relation to one another may
themselves be further categorized in quite different ways, against different background fields. Categorizing women as pretty or beautiful
and men as handsome or good-looking might seem mainly a matter of
different labels for the same categorizing principles against a common
field. But the general field of people's physical appearance is strongly
gender-differentiated in many ways. As we noted in discussing compliments, women's appearance is often commented on in contexts in
which men's is not. But it is not just compliments. A recent example
that we encountered while writing this book comes from a story in the
November 7, 1999, SV Magazine of the *San Jose Mercury News*.

> R. C. Greenwood walks into a dark room lit only by black-light bulbs. The
> 56-year-old chancellor of the 34-year-old University of California-Santa
> Cruz is wearing a peach blouse, slacks, a double strand of pearls and
> sensible heels – an outfit that darkens under the ultraviolet light, while
> her bra glows through the thin material like an X-ray. Greenwood is
> short, her light-colored matronly hair patched by gray at the sides . . .
> (p. 15)

We challenged a group of Stanford students to rewrite this as an introduction to a story about a leading man in the field of university
administration. They tried but found the task difficult. Even for a story
about a woman, mentioning the bra seems astoundingly out of place.
Some of the students proposed to us that a man's undershirt of the sort
that has no sleeves might be a near but imperfect equivalent to the bra.
A label in some circles for such a garment is a *wife-beater*, a name that,
as they pointed out, carries very different connotations than *bra* does.
Not only would a story about a man comparably positioned be unlikely
to pay so much attention to details of appearance, but some of the categories used in describing Greenwood do not have male equivalents: for
example *sensible heels* (men's shoes are assumed to have sensible heels

and thus aren't categorized on the basis of the kinds of heels they have) and *matronly hair*. The man, they noted, might be described as having "light-colored hair, with distinguished silver streaks," but neither they nor we could come up with a concept parallel to *matronly* for categorizing men's appearance or styles. One might describe a man as *fatherly* or, less colloquially, *avuncular*, but neither label also applies to hairdos or clothing styles.

Laurel Sutton (1992) reports a host of slang terms for female reference that also categorize the referent's body size and attractiveness. She encountered virtually no such terms for male reference. One can say that some male is fat and unattractive but a label like *ugly fat slob* can apply just as well to a girl or woman as to a boy or man. Sutton's college-aged consultants reported no prepackaged male labels analogous to *heifer* or *cow*. The focus on women's appearance is by no means simply a matter of language. Although increasing attention is being given to men's appearance, there are still strength but not beauty contests for men. Among some groups, men sit watching women walk by and rate them on appearance ("she's definitely a 10"), but women don't do the same for men. (Or still do so only very rarely.) And, although marital status can certainly categorize both women and men, it is still relied on far more for sorting women. Social titles are one indicator of that as well as the practice of more often commenting on the marital status of a woman in the news than on that of a man. *Ms.* was introduced to try to provide a form parallel to *Mr.*, one that simply did not indicate anything about marital status. Of course, as we noted in chapter two, only if *Miss* and *Mrs.* disappear as options, will *Ms.* be anything like equivalent to *Mr.* Studies of letters of recommendation have also found both appearance and marital status frequently commented on in letters written about women, ignored in letters written about men.[12] Such practices are changing, but categorizations in the fields of appearance and marital status still go on for women far more than for men and in contexts where they would seem to be irrelevant.

Now there certainly are many ways of categorizing men. They can be smart or stupid, strong or weak, kind or mean, rich or poor, fat or thin, generous or stingy, leaders or followers. But these are generally seen as categories that also apply to women. They are principles that sort people. English has very few words for categorizing men as opposed to women on these or other principles. (See, e.g., James 1996 for discussion.) Perhaps the words *prick* or *bastard* might fall in this

---

12 See, e.g., Hoffman (1972), Watson (1987), both cited in King (1991). We have both seen more recent letters that include such comments but do not know how widespread such practices now are.

category. In some ways parallel to the female *bitch*, the expressions do seem to pick out a subgroup of males on the basis of their negatively characterized behavior. Unlike the word *bitch*, however, they don't seem readily to get extended to members of the male sex in general, losing their implications of particular kinds of behavior or personality.

The asymmetry of within-category distinctions is curiously paradoxical. On the one hand, we note that there are fields like personal appearance and sexual availability that are seen as (primarily) applicable to the (marked) female gender category. There are subcategories elaborated specifically for females far more than for males. A nonlinguistic instance of this is dress. In many countries around the world, men have adopted western attire, but women may be expected to wear (at least on certain occasions) some kind of local dress. We will see in chapter eight that in certain communities of practice the females do far more with language to mark social distinctions among themselves than do their male counterparts.

At the same time, there is also a striking and apparently opposite tendency to ignore distinctions among females. Words like *bitch*, *lady*, *girl* have all sometimes been used to apply to females generally, washing out the distinctions of behavior, class, age on which those different labels are (at least originally) based. What is not washed out in such usages is the overarching female–male distinction: the female category just takes over as more important than distinctions within it.

Default (sub)category erasure

The ultimate in marking the distinctiveness of a marked category in a field is the near erasure of the default (sub)category as a category. When queried about whether the *jock* versus *burnout* opposition was still relevant in the last years of high school, one of Penny's interviewees responded: "Burnouts, yes. But jocks – you're not really aware of it." Erasure of the default (sub)category as a category is part of what sustains marking the distinctiveness of the marked category. Jocks become just ("normal") students, men become just ("normal") people, white people don't have a race (that matters), heterosexuals don't have a "lifestyle" or a "sexual preference."

In the US, race is a particularly telling case. Don Terry (2001), a young man whose mother was (classed as) white and whose father was (classed as) black, offers an interesting first-person account of racial categories. He had grown up in Hyde Park, Chicago, a neighborhood that is unusual in having substantial numbers of families that are racially "mixed" and in which he was able to sustain the view promoted by his mother that he belonged to both racial categories. Once he left that (unusual) environment, he was confronted with a forced choice, the strong message being that affiliation with whites was automatically a rejection of his black heritage. Not surprisingly, he embarked on a reconstruction of his sense of himself and his identity so that white was erased and black was highlighted. His is a particular illustration of the general point that in many ways race matters more for those who are classified as black.

Well-intentioned white folks frequently complain among themselves about black people's being so "hung up" on race. "Can't we all just be people? Why should race matter?" In a nonracist society, race would not matter and, indeed, might not even be a categorizing principle. But racial classifications do matter significantly in the US and matter much more for someone classed as black than for someone classed as white. Where there is subordination of a social group, there is at least some default organization of the field against which that group is defined. Belonging to the marked category is generally far more consequential for a person's life opportunities and sense of self than belonging to the often erased default category. The marked category or categories not only come with lots of conceptual and linguistic baggage; they also enter into social practice more overtly than the erased default category, around which notions of what's "normal" cluster.

Of course, the hegemony of default organization is never absolute. In communities of practice in which (most) members identify with the subordinated or marked group, the default concept may well receive fuller elaboration and function more oppositionally than as a default. So the "white" category may be more developed in communities of practice whose own identification is "black" than in mixed or primarily "white" communities of practice. Some communities of practice might even flip defaults, so that it is white folks who are considered "different" and black folks who are "normal." Few, if any, communities of practice in English-speaking societies are completely isolated from institutionalized racism and society-level racist ideologies, but nonetheless partial isolation can promote alternative perspectives on racial categorization.

It's important to remember that default subcategory erasure is not the same as the apparent exclusion of marked subcategory members when we are speaking generically of a larger category. In speaking of villagers, one can exclude the women and children among them. In speaking of people, one can exclude those who are not able-bodied. Similarly, in speaking of women, one can exclude women of color. In speaking of African Americans, one can exclude African American women. Black women have noted their double exclusion from these generics: "All the women are white, all the blacks are men, but some of us are brave" is the title Gloria Hull [now writing as bell hooks] and colleagues gave to a book they edited in 1982 on black women's studies (see Hull *et al.* 1982).

The possibility of the false generic depends in some ways on the erasure of the default subcategory as a category. There are ("ordinary") villagers and then there are the women and the children. Because men as such don't constitute a subcategory, the villagers in general can be equated with those of them who are men. There are ("ordinary") women and then there are women of color. These "specially marked" women get erased in false generic uses of *woman* precisely because whiteness has been erased as a significant subcategory.

Although racism and sexism are similar in some respects, it is important to note that they do not work in exactly the same ways. Significantly, ideologies of complementarity in gender discourse no longer find parallels in racial discourse (at least in the contemporary US). As we noted earlier, maleness does not always function as a default category, with femaleness "marked" in contrast. Sometimes the gender categories are genuinely oppositional. The opposition typically comes with assumptions of exhaustivity – no "in-between" cases. It also comes with rich and elaborated distinctiveness of both categories and not just of the marked one. Thus, in some contexts, we find heavy elaboration of both putative "female" and "male" characteristics, and the polarizing assumption that these various characteristics are incompatible, that they force a binary categorization. In the next section, we will consider how that elaboration works.

Category nesting: gender inside gender

The oppositional (and often complementary) organization of gender categorization might seem to be challenged by category nesting. We don't just have "female" versus "male" or "woman" versus "man" as exhaustive polarizing categories. Within each of those categories, we can apply (almost) the same categorizing principle again. We can split both women and men into (more or less) "feminine" and (more or less) "masculine" people. This is the recursive quality of gender that we mentioned in chapter one, citing the work of Susan Gal and Judith Irvine (1995).

The categorizing principles of "feminine" and "masculine" obviously cannot be exactly the same as those of "female" and "male." We divide each sex in two and thus find "feminine" men and "masculine" women alongside "feminine" women and "masculine" men. But the general assumptions are that (1) "feminine" and "masculine" are oppositional categorizations, and (2) it is only "deviant" people for whom the feminine/masculine sort doesn't coincide with the female/male one. Things are more complicated than this in a number of ways. Feminine and masculine are matters of degree, of more or less. The more masculine a woman might seem, then the more deviant. She's not either in or out of the "normal" category but closer or further from its center. But not only is the feminine/masculine opposition a matter of degree: it's not even (always) an opposition.

As we noted earlier, the categories of feminine and masculine are not just used to classify people. These gender categories classify all manner of things, including abstract entities of various kinds. They classify people primarily through classifying various categorizations we apply to people: personality traits, body shape and demeanor, bodily adornment, clothing, activities, interests, values. As we noted in the preceding chapter, virtually any opposition, any difference, among people can be understood via what Helen Haste calls the sexual metaphor (DIFFERENCE IS SEXUAL DIFFERENCE) as (also) a sort into feminine and masculine.

Throughout the 1950s and 1960s, psychological testing assumed that whatever sorting principles put someone in the feminine category counted against that person's being put in the masculine category and vice versa. In the early 1970s, psychologist Sandra Bem challenged this assumption and developed the Bem Sex Role Inventory (BSRI), which allowed for the same person to score high (or low) on both feminine and masculine scales. (See Bem 1974.) As she pointed out, there is no intrinsic incompatibility between, say, being nurturant (judged a "feminine" trait) and being decisive (judged a "masculine" trait).

In many ways, Bem's approach was liberating. It did not challenge the underlying sexual metaphor that classifies nurturance as feminine and decisiveness as masculine, a metaphor that implicitly suggests gender norms: women "should" be nurturant and men "should" be decisive. But it did challenge the polarizing implication that therefore men should *not* be nurturant, women should *not* be decisive. Indeed, Bem proposed that the psychologically healthiest people were those she dubbed "androgynous": scoring as both very feminine and very masculine. And she did not privilege gender congruence. An androgyny ideal can be seen, however, as simply upping the ante for gender normativity: women should be feminine (and now also masculine), and men should be masculine (and now also feminine). For this reason and also because of its reliance on the basic sexual metaphor, androgyny is no longer widely promoted as an ideal (see Bem 1993).

Gender category nesting can indeed draw on default organization. If we abandon polar opposition, then what is not marked as feminine need not necessarily be marked as masculine. Bonnie McElhinny (1995) found women police officers, who were doing a job that has tradition- ally been categorized as masculine, adopting an emotionally inexpres- sive interactional style. Although the style could not be categorized as feminine, the women themselves did not usually categorize it as mas- culine but rather as *professional*, a (potentially) gender-neutral category. What has been categorized as feminine, having often been treated as off-bounds for men, is harder to shift into a gender-neutral category. When men adopt gender-atypical ways of acting or interests they are often characterized as feminine and thus "deviant."

In the right contexts, however, even once "feminine" characteristics can shift and become interpreted as gender-neutral. New models for good management, for example, call for "people skills" of a sort some- times labeled feminine: listening to others, encouraging others to ex- press themselves, showing an interest in others' ideas. The feminine label can disappear from traits if there are sufficient incentives for men to adopt them. Interestingly, the incentives in the good man- agement case are economic: interpersonally sensitive communicative skills are important to men in managerial positions because they help them retain control over the workforce. So though they are taking on some non-masculine (and often "feminine") characteristics, these men are also showing commitment to some typically "masculine" goals and thus their classification as (real) men need not be appreciably jeopardized.

Somewhat paradoxically then, both women and men may be helped to challenge gender strictures by the very wealth of characteristics that are gender-categorized. A woman who is ambitious and assertive may nonetheless be judged feminine if her general appearance and some other aspects of her behavior can be characterized as feminine. Former British prime minister Margaret Thatcher managed to occupy a mascu- line position of leadership while also satisfying the electorate's expec- tations about her womanliness. She projected herself successfully as a woman even while making literal war in the Falklands and metaphoric war on the home front against the "welfare state" of postwar Britain. Both visual and verbal style contributed to the "femininity" of her self- presentation.[13] Someone who displays enough feminine characteristics may be able to retain her "woman" classification even in the face of many characteristics that are not classified as feminine (and which, in many contexts, are classified as masculine).

---

13 See Fairclough (1987) for analysis of Thatcher's discursive strategies for managing the gender conflict she faced.

Genderizing discourse: category imperialism

Many discursive practices presuppose the pervasive relevance of gender categorizations. We say that discourse is genderized when messages
about gender categorizations are superimposed on the basic content of
the discourse. Genderizing discursive practices can involve particular
linguistic resources – gendered pronouns, grammatical gender agreement, genderizing affixes and other gender-marked lexical items. We
discussed a number of these resources in chapter two.

Genderizing discourse does not always, however, depend on linguistic conventions but may involve such matters as journalistic norms to
mention the nondefault sex in some field. Stories about a woman murderer or child molester or politician will, for example, use the word
woman far more than parallel stories use the word *man*. There are many
cases where users can choose gendered or nongendered terms. The
teacher can say "good morning, kids" or "good morning, students" or
the discourse can be genderized: "good morning, girls and boys." Some
years ago, philosopher Elizabeth Beardsley (1981) argued that referential genderization – cases where sex distinctions seem to be forced,
whether or not they are relevant – problematically encourages gender inequities by making gender categorizations appear to be relevant
where morally they ought not to be.

Pronouns

Many communities of practice take establishing and conveying a (consistent) gender attribution for everyone to be of fundamental importance. In English-using communities, for example, gendered pronouns
make it difficult indeed to talk about anyone other than oneself without presupposing a gender attribution. The late Sarah Caudwell (a pen
name) wrote several novels featuring a protagonist whose gender she
never discloses. How did she pull this off? Well, the character's first
name is Hilary, used for both sexes, and Hilary relates the stories in
the first person, using *I*, which is completely gender-neutral, for self-
reference. Others refer to Hilary using that name or some generic description like "my friend," or address Hilary using the second-person
you, which is also gender-neutral.[14]

Some languages do mark gender in the first- or second-person pronouns. Japanese, for example, has a fairly large array of first-person

---

14 See Livia (2001) for much interesting discussion of literary uses of pronouns to
convey gender messages, and in many cases to challenge standard gender categories.

pronouns, a number of which are gender-marked, as are a number of the second-person pronouns (for speaker and addressee). Interestingly, a considerable number of female Japanese high-school students have now adopted the practice of referring to themselves as *boku*, which is the first-person form boys are expected to use in self-reference and which is also used in reference to very young boys being addressed. Naoko Ogawa and Janet Shibamoto Smith (1997) examined address as well as first- and third-person references used in a documentary film by two gay men in a committed relationship, finding that the two men labeled themselves and the other in much the same ways as do the canonical husband and wife of a traditional Japanese heterosexual marriage.

Pronouns are most often gendered in the third person. As we have already noted, singular English third-person pronouns typically presuppose gender attributions to their (actual or potential) referents. To refer to specific individual human beings pronominally, *it* is seldom used and then it is used either insultingly, to convey that the referent is not conforming properly to gender norms, or in reference to very young babies. Even in reference to babies, *it* can be seen as dehumanizing. In July 2000 the American Academy of Pediatrics cautioned doctors not to use *it* to speak of a baby born with ambiguous genitalia but instead to speak to parents of "your baby" or "your child." This injunction came in the context of a more general reconsideration of the long-standing assumption that all babies should very quickly be assigned to one sex or the other, often with surgery to make genital appearance conform more closely with the assigned sex or with prescriptions for hormonal or other treatment to produce bodies that conform more closely with the polarized sexing assumed by English third-person singular pronouns. "X" is a 1970s story about a child who was going through the early years with everyone but the parents and the doctor who delivered it ignorant of its sex. It is not insignificant that "Baby X" is so dubbed and not given a personal name; it's much easier to repeat "Baby X" or "X" or even to use an *it* than it would be if we had a proper name for the child (Gould [1972] 1983).

Gender attributions conveyed by the pronouns *he* and *she* are explicit, but they are nonetheless backgrounded, presented as taken for granted. Somewhere around the twelfth or thirteenth century, the masculine form (*hē*) and the feminine form (*hēo*) began frequently to sound alike because the unstressed vowel of the feminine form was often just dropped. Had that change simply proceeded in the same way that many similar shifts did, we might now have a single third-person singular personal pronoun, presumably pronounced like modern *he*. In that case, we would have found it easy to talk about Baby X, whose sex we did not know or someone whose sex we did not want to reveal. Some English speakers, however, apparently did not want to lose obligatory genderizing of third-person pronominal reference. The actual history is unclear but one hypothesis is that they began using the word *scho*, ancestor of modern *she*, as a substitute for *hēo*. The suggestion is that this form was imported into English from one of the Scandinavian languages then spoken in the British Isles. The etymology of *she* is still disputed. Whether or not English speakers did import a precursor for *she* from another language, it is clear that there was something more going on than standard phonetic developments, which would have left us with a single third-person pronoun for humans. However it actually happened, it must have been the importance of genderizing to then current discursive practices among English speakers that drove this change in the pronominal system.

English does now have a nongendered pronoun for human referents, namely *they*. Prescriptive grammars restrict *they* to plural contexts, but it has long been used in singular generic contexts of the kind we discuss below in the section on generalizing. But what about nongeneric contexts? Increasingly, we find *they* used when sex is unknown or the speaker wants to avoid genderizing. "Someone called but they didn't leave their name" or "A friend of mine claimed they had met the Beatles." Second-person pronouns in English once distinguished plural from singular, but the originally plural form *you* is now virtually the only choice, even if the addressee is a single individual. It would not be surprising, therefore, if *they* were also to become more widely used in singular contexts. We have used it ourselves in this book at a number of points.

With definite antecedents like *my teacher* or *the photographer*, *they* is still infrequent even colloquially. Definiteness seems to make genderizing of subsequent references hard to avoid. "My teacher promised they would write me a letter of recommendation" still sounds as if the teacher were going to enlist others in the letter writing, and "The photographer forgot to bring their tripod" suggests the tripod is not the photographer's individual property. Still, there are some cases like this where *they* does link to a definite singular antecedent, and such degenderizing may well be spreading. With proper names, however, *they* is still virtually unheard. Discursive practice among English speakers does not yet support interpreting "Chris said they are having their birthday party tomorrow" as Chris's having said that she or he was going to have her or his birthday party tomorrow. Of course there are some nongenderizing options: "My teacher promised to write me a letter of recommendation" or "The photographer forgot to bring the tripod" or "Chris claimed to be having a birthday party tomorrow."

Such alternatives simply eliminate pronouns, but pronoun elimination is not always so easy. Genderizing definite pronominal references is still predominant in the discursive practice of most English speakers though it may begin to wane as more and more speakers use *they* for singular deictic – i.e., "pointing" – references. "What do they think they're doing?" seems unremarkable when one is pointing to a single individual scaling a high rooftop in the distance or referring to a violinist producing unpleasant sounds in the adjacent room. But if used of a bearded individual dressed in high heels and wearing a long dress, earrings and lipstick, it might seem to suggest that the referent is somehow trying to "pass" (and not succeeding), is "really" male though apparently engaging in a feminine self-presentation. Referring to young babies, no matter what their genital appearance, as *they*, might begin to move us nearer to a stage where there are real live options to presupposing gender attribution in English singular third-person reference. Already, many health professionals now routinely use *they* to refer to people in the process of sex/gender change.

Many languages do not mark gender in third-person pronouns. Finnish is one such language. The singular third-person pronoun *hän* can translate either *she* or *he*, and in many contexts where English would require a pronoun Finnish (like many other so-called pro-drop languages) allows its omission. Interestingly, however, in a number of contexts where English speakers would use a singular third-person pronoun, Finnish speakers often choose a gendered noun – for example *tyttö*, which glosses as 'girl.' Thus though third-person pronouns do not force genderization in Finnish, third-person reference is often genderized anyway.

In spoken Mandarin Chinese, there is no gender distinction for third-person pronouns, although writing now does make such a distinction. In transcribing speech, however, there are often no grounds for using *he* rather than *she* (or vice versa) to translate a third-person pronoun into English, and some linguists do now use *he or she* or something similar. For a long time, however, *he* was routinely used, even in contexts where the English form implied maleness and the Chinese being translated did not.

Gender (dis)agreement

As we noted in discussing grammatical gender in chapter two, the first-person pronoun in French is not itself gendered, but adjectives agree with it according to the ascribed sex of its referent, the speaker. The effect, of course, is to genderize first-person discourse. A French-speaking girl, for example, learns to say "je suis heureuse" to express her happiness, whereas a boy learns to say "je suis heureux." Saying *heureuse* rather than *heureux* is one way that one constructs oneself as a girl or a woman, not a boy or a man. The "agreeing" forms impute a sex to the referent of *je*, even though that first-person pronoun does not itself carry grammatical gender. One cannot avoid self-attributions of gender using French first-person discourse as Sarah Caudwell's Hilary could in the English first person. When people talk about themselves in French (or any of a number of other languages with grammatical gender), they must frequently superimpose the message "I am female" or the message "I am male."

At the same time, this gender agreement morphology can be a communicative resource for challenging permanent dichotomous gender assignments. Anna Livia (1997) shows that a first-person narrator in French can play with gender (dis)agreement possibilities to present the self sometimes as female, sometimes as male. She offers examples of transsexuals as well as others resisting conventional gender arrangements by exploiting gender-bending possibilities offered by French grammatical gender. And as we will see in chapter nine, the Hindi-speaking hijras of India use not only gendered pronouns but also gender agreement markers to speak of themselves and others strategically as female or male, according to the situation.[15] Grammatical gender, thus, can be a resource for challenging standard gender binarism.

What happens in a language with gender agreement when plurals are used or a choice that (usually) indicates sex must be made when the referent's sex is unknown? In the Indo-European languages like French and Hindi, the "rule" is to use the masculine in such cases. Again, there is the possibility of playing with this "rule" to express challenges to the dominant gender order. But there is a strong tendency in languages with grammatical gender for the masculine forms to function as defaults. In his extensive discussion of grammatical gender in languages around the world, Corbett (1991) notes this tendency. At the same time, he notes some exceptions to it, languages where females are (linguistically) the default humans and males the special case. Among others, he mentions the Nilotic language Maasai, Iroquoian languages in general, and Seneca in particular, and the Arawakan language Goajiro (spoken by people in the Goajiro peninsula). In Goajiro, one gender is used

---

15 See chapter nine for further discussion of the hijras and their challenges to gender binarism.

for nouns referring to male humans and a very few other nouns (e.g. the words for "sun" and "thumb"), whereas most nouns are in the other gender. This nonmasculine gender includes nouns referring to female humans as well as nouns referring to nonhuman animals, inanimates, and most everything else; it is used whenever sex is not known (pp. 220–221). Unfortunately, we cannot provide any information on the social gender practices in which these (relatively rare) "marked masculine" gender systems have entered into communicative practices. In addition, Corbett notes that some languages offer an alternative to either masculine or feminine agreement in cases where sex is unknown: the Polish neuter, for example, is sometimes used much like the English singular *they* to avoid signaling either femaleness or maleness. In Archi, a Northeast Caucasian language with four genders, two of which are used for human males and human females respectively, one of the other two genders (which normally is used mostly for abstracts) can be used for agreement with nouns like *child* or *thief* if the sex of (potential) referents is unknown, unimportant, or undetermined.

Genderizing processes

As we noted in chapter two, feminizing affixes are found in many different languages, and we discussed the English forms *-ess* and *-ette*. English does not really have affixes that masculinize a generic term nor are such forms easy to find in other languages. This is, of course, a reflection of the "marked" status of femaleness with the generic default tending to be masculine. Among English speakers interested in transforming social gender, there has been a move away from gendered job titles. For example, the people working on airplanes are now quite widely known as flight attendants rather than as stewardesses or stewards. Many women who act call themselves actors rather than actresses. In children's books and on certain official lists of job titles, we now find police officers and firefighters. Gender neutralization is by no means an accomplished fact in such discourse. In most cities in the US, those policing and fighting fires are still overwhelmingly male, and, even though there were a few women among them, media tended to praise the New York City firemen who died while trying to rescue others from the collapsing and burning towers of the World Trade Center on September 11, 2001.

Promoting use of gender-neutral occupational labels is one strategy for challenging labeling practices that support traditional heavily gendered divisions of labor, and it is the strategy used most commonly by speakers of English. A quite different strategy is to find feminine labels for jobs that were traditionally men's so as to highlight the fact that there are now women in such positions. This latter strategy has apparently been the one most used in languages with grammatical gender, probably in part because the gender-neutral strategy is not so easy to implement in such languages, given that any occupational label will carry some gender or other. As we observed in chapter two, gender reformers speaking French and German, for example, have created a number of feminine analogues to the traditional masculine forms for occupational labels. This feminizing strategy not only makes women visible in traditionally male jobs. Reference to such women with feminine pronouns then can obey both gender agreement rules and also conventions for reference to specific individuals. In the Romance languages, finding feminine occupational labels is helped by the fact that there are already many paired masculine and feminine forms that are pretty much symmetric. Italian, for example, has many pairs of proper names where the masculine form ends in *-o* and the feminine in *-a*. Similar alternations are seen in some job titles and other designators. But not all. In an interesting discussion of feminine agentive forms in a number of European languages, mainly from the Romance family, Connors 1971 notes that what might be expected to be feminine agentive forms are already used for machines or instruments or some abstract entity. King 1991 gives a number of examples of this phenomenon. For example, *le trompette* (m.) is a trumpet-player, whereas *la trompette* (f.) denotes the trumpet or (though perhaps not easily) a female trumpet-player; *le médecin* (m.) is the doctor, whereas *la médecine* (f.) is the field of medicine and is not really available to designate women physicians. In fact, historically the feminine form for the field of medicine preceded the masculine agentive used to designate a medical practitioner (and the same may be true for the trumpet, although the historical evidence is less clear). Whatever the historical order, the net result is that what might be a paired feminine agentive is unavailable as a coinage today because the feminine form is already doing another job.

Some argue that even in a language like English, which does not have the gender agreement dilemmas created by grammatical gender, there are dangers in the discourse strategy of neutralizing references, of moving away from genderization towards gender neutrality. Pointing to the false generics we discussed earlier, they note that it is all too easy for *police officer* to be construed as male, whereas using *policewoman* can help make visible the fact that women are indeed moving into and succeeding in this traditionally male domain. There are, of course, other ways of conveying the discourse message that increasing numbers of women function successfully as police officers. But those other ways may require rather more attention than a one-time change in job titles. Others are uncomfortable with coinages like *chairperson* and note that neutral coinages often end up becoming feminized. (See Ehrlich and King 1992.) Not surprisingly, there is no "correct" answer and no guarantee that any particular discourse choice will actually work as intended. This does not mean that processes like gender-neutralization of job titles are not useful in helping change the gendered division of labor. They sometimes are. It does mean, however, that change does not always proceed smoothly. And it also means that there are no linguistic quick fixes.

New labels, new categories

It is characteristic of the development of human thinking that we begin to recognize new patterns that cannot be categorized using our familiar resources. Providing a label for what looks like a newly recognized category can be an important aid to further exploration of those patterns and their significance. Scientific practice is full of examples of the introduction of new concepts – new categories – and their labels, with subsequent refinement of those concepts as inquiry proceeds. But it is not only scientists who look to new ways of categorizing as powerful tools in the development of new modes of thought and action.

As we have seen, categories are relational and connected to theories or schemas. They function in discourses that link them implicitly or explicitly to other categories, both within a single field and across different fields. Thus it is not surprising that new category labels (or new uses of old category labels) often play a role in sharpening and testing ideas. The label *sexism*, for example, was constructed by analogy with *racism*. The first citation is from the mid-1960s,[16] but apparently it was coined independently by a number of different people during that period. That label brought together what had previously been seen as unrelated and random instances of female disadvantage or perhaps had gone unnoticed altogether. The label helped make it easier to talk about patterned systematicity in the disadvantaging of women. As with *feminist* and *feminism*, the categories of *sexism* and *sexist* have been contested in various ways. The important point here is that introducing a label and trying to further understanding of the kinds of phenomena it brings together in a single category have gone hand in hand.

16 See Fred R. Shapiro (1985).

Date rape and *sexual harassment* are both recently introduced category labels that also help people think together about certain patterns that were not really considered earlier. Once category labels are launched, however, their future is uncertain and it is by no means always controlled by the launcher. Ehrlich and King (1992) note that a number of feminist-launched labels are used in nonfeminist discourses in ways that subvert their original purpose.

New social category labels or new practices of using familiar social labels are at the heart of the so-called political correctness (PC) debate. The term *political correctness* originated as a self-mocking label within leftist groups, where those who were too rigid or "holier than thou" were gently teased by their friends and colleagues. (See Cameron 1995 for enlightening discussion of the term and of some of the verbal hygiene practices associated with it.) In recent years, it has been relatively conservative groups who oppose certain kinds of social change who have taken over use of *political correctness*. *PC* is now primarily used to deride concerns over social labels that have arisen in the course of social movements.

The descendants of African slaves brought to the US were called *negroes* in "polite" talk prior to the civil rights movement that really gained momentum in the 1950s. In part because that term was the obvious source of the *nigger* heard from unabashedly racist mouths and in part because there was a desire to claim dark skin color more explicitly as a source of pride rather than shame – recall the "Black is Beautiful" slogan – many people who had once called themselves *negro* now opted to call themselves *Black*. And in part to claim their Americanness in the face of the fact that the default American was a person of European descent, a newer generation turned to *Afro-American* and then *African American* or *American of African descent*. Some now prefer to speak of themselves as Africans or Afrikans. Yet *black* remains a widely used and accepted term within black communities. And rap groups have popularized *niggah*, though many African Americans are uncomfortable with bringing this primarily in-group form into more public discourse contexts. Notice that the rehabilitation of this form is helped by respelling it and insisting on an r-less pronunciation, pulling it further away from the strongly tabooed *nigger*.

Within communities of people with Latin American ancestry, there are similar debates over self-labeling. Some see terms like *Hispanic* as imposed by outsiders and prefer *Latino/a*, along with more specific category labels like *Chicano/a*. Others find *Hispanic* useful for building coalitions across different groups. Most of the communities where self-labeling is a central issue are struggling with a host of social problems and institutionalized racism or other prejudice. Such labeling controversies are always embedded in wider social and political struggles.

Within communities organized around issues of sexual preference, there are also ongoing debates and shifts in labeling. Generally, the move is toward inclusiveness. So, for example, noting that *gay* often functions as a false generic, with lesbians not included, many groups include both *lesbian* and *gay* in their names. Increasingly, other sexual minorities – transgendered and transsexual people, intersex and bisexuals – note that their concerns and even their existence are often overlooked. The growing popularity of the term *queer* for self-reference in these communities stems from the elasticity of its use as a category label, embracing in some uses even those whose erotic preferences are other sex but who want to dis-identify with the dominant heterosexual community.

Like *niggah*, *queer* is an example of a label that has been reclaimed for positive self-reference by (some of) those to whom it has often been negatively applied. *Dyke* and *bitch* are also now fairly frequently heard self-affirmingly, with a positive value. Even *faggot*, which lots of gay men still find a very hurtful label, can be reappropriated for positive purposes. One of Sally's students interviewed a young gay man who used *fierce faggot* as his ultimate stamp of approval, defining it as "someone who is that fabulous and fucking knows it." The same young man also came up with the label *gurl* – "it's spelled with a *u*" – as another way to mark the category of those gay male friends whom he specially admired, the "fierce faggots." Reclaiming labels that have a long history of derogatory use always starts within the designated group, often (as with *fierce faggot*) with obvious ironic humor intended. How widely the revival effort spreads depends on many factors. *Queer* is probably the only one of these reclaimed labels that has wide positive use from people outside its coverage, but even in this case many of those so designated dislike the label, not being able to forget its history of bigoted and demeaning uses.[17]

Those who do not identify themselves with such minority concerns often condescendingly quote the Shakespearean line: "What's in a name? A rose by any other name would smell as sweet." These outsiders find themselves discomfited by their outsider status, by their own ignorance of which names are currently favored by whom. They may grumble about having to watch their words when which label picks out the category has no import: after all, a rose by any other name…But Shakespeare's point is to contrast a rose with a person,

17 See McConnell-Ginet (2002) for further discussion.

for whom names do indeed matter profoundly. *Montague* and *Capulet* were names that brought with them histories of alliances and enmities, histories that ultimately overwhelmed Romeo and Juliet. A woman adopting the family name of the man she marries is symbolically marking her transition from one family category to another. He stays in the same family category, whereas she does not. There are, of course, changes in naming practices: some married couples are jointly adopting a common new name, others are taking the spouse's family name as a middle name, others simply continue with their own earlier names and arrive at some third alternative for their children. The desire for members of the nuclear family to share a name is certainly linked to wanting some way to symbolize the significance of that unit as a social group, a social category.

Of course the place of a social category in social practice cannot be changed simply by changing the labels that designate it. Changing labels can, however, sometimes be part of changing practice centered on the categories labeled. Women have (with some success) tried to stop the practice of using *girl* to designate mature women in subordinate positions. To eschew "have your girl call my girl," the line male executives are supposed to use with one another when suggesting that the secretaries should handle such mundane details as setting up a lunch, can be part of recategorizing office jobs from personal – the office equivalent of the wife who takes care of all of her man's maintenance needs from picking up and washing his socks to buying his ties – to professional, focused on the shared business at hand. That shift in terminology is part of a general pattern of improving women's working conditions: making coffee for the boss or buying his wife's birthday present is no longer standardly assumed part of a secretary's job, which is increasingly professionalized and moved away from the model of a wife's loving care. Getting away from the loving care model makes it clearer that wages and other material rewards for these jobs need to be improved. And the fact that the boss's chair is now sometimes occupied by a woman also often (though not always) helps in improving working conditions for those lower down in the hierarchy.

For people involved in antisexist efforts and for other groups that define themselves in opposition to some kind of dominant oppressive social arrangements, social categories and labels for them do matter. Those who suggest one should worry about wages and not about words offer a false dichotomy. Nobody wants to trade a raise for a respectful form of address, and there is no reason to pay that price. (The same women who were called girls were also addressed by their first name or by such endearments as *honey* and *dear* by men to whom they were expected to use *Mr. Jones* or similar forms. Addressing people is another way of categorizing them.[18])

Changing schemes for categorization and changing labels are part of changing social practice.

18 McConnell-Ginet (forthcoming) considers some of the ways address forms and other social labels enter into gender practices.

CHAPTER 8

Working the market: use of varieties

In earlier chapters our focus has been on how gender interacts with
what people do with the resources provided by the linguistic system
(or systems), and with norms for deploying those resources. We have
noted that the resources themselves may be transformed in the course
of social practice. A form like *Ms.* is introduced and adopted and responded to, and over time the repertoire of English address options
and their significance shift in structured yet unpredictable ways. And
norms for speech get challenged and reshaped: a young woman who
begins to say *shit* in situations that would draw *shucks* from her mother
is helping change the gendered significance of tabooed expletives.

But changes like these are against the backdrop of a speaker's overall
dialect. Speakers can decide to interrupt, avoid apologies, stop swearing, and start talking about women as active sexual agents without
really changing their basic dialect, the system whose resources they
are using to further their various projects. Speakers can do very different things in talking with one another, can pursue quite different
communicative goals, while using essentially the same linguistic variety. As we will see, linguistic varieties are linked to people in a unique
way – they are seen very much as reflecting who people are, where
they come from. They carry a good deal of baggage as a result, and
they figure in the construction of gender in a myriad of ways.

Languages, dialects, varieties

In every culture, learning to talk – like learning to walk – is a part of
growing up. In both cases, the learning seems to happen whether or
not there is explicit instruction. And in both cases, the end product is
a kind of knowledge and facility that operates more or less automatically. Ways of walking are highly constrained by anatomy, but there
are subtle differences from culture to culture – for example, in some
cultures some shuffling may be de rigueur, while in others it may
be frowned upon. And certainly, norms for women's and men's walks

are quite different in many cultures. But in the case of talking, children develop tremendously different activities from one culture to the next, and even from one community to the next. The child learns a particular language – or maybe more than one language. And within that language, the child learns a particular *variety* – an English-speaking child growing up in New York will most likely learn New York English, while an English-speaking child growing up in London will most likely learn London English. And within New York and London there are significant differences in the variety one will learn depending on the specific community within each city. A child growing up in an African American community in New York will most likely learn the New York African American variety, and a working-class Italian American child will most likely develop a more distinctively New York dialect than an upper-middle-class Italian American child.

Children come equipped to learn any language, no matter what the linguistic background of their biological parents or their ancestors. They learn the linguistic variety or varieties of those who take care of them as toddlers and those with whom they spend their time when they are small. A child born to parents who speak Mandarin Chinese will learn English and not Chinese if placed in infancy in an English-speaking household. And a child born to English-speaking parents of long Anglo-Saxon lineage will nonetheless become a native speaker of Chinese if from an early age Chinese is a medium in which caretakers and others regularly engage with it. Early on, the child becomes proficient in certain ways of saying and hearing, but not in others. The child learning Chinese must attend to certain differences in the melodic patterns of syllables (what are called *tones*) that the child learning English or Spanish can ignore. And, of course, it is not just phonology, but morphology and syntax and a lexicon that are acquired. For example children who are beginning to speak Spanish begin early to pay attention to gender marking on adjectives and articles, whereas children learning Chinese or English do not have that to attend to. Those who are fortunate enough to have a diverse set of caretakers and friends in childhood may grow up speaking more than one variety with native-like ease. In many cultures, multilingualism of some kind is the norm.

And within each of those languages that the child learns, he or she learns a specific dialect (or possibly more than one). The differences between two dialects of the same language can be relatively subtle. For instance, many people are not aware that in much of the eastern and midwestern US, speakers make regular use of a construction known as *positive anymore* (Hindle and Sag 1973). In most dialects of English, *anymore* occurs only with negation:

I don't get in a lot of trouble *anymore*

In positive *anymore* dialects, however, it can be used in positive sentences, to mean 'nowadays':

I get in a lot of trouble *anymore*

or even

Anymore, I get in a lot of trouble

In each of these cases, the sentence means 'I get in a lot of trouble nowadays,' and speakers of positive *anymore* dialects are relatively unaware of the fact that this construction does not exist in all dialects of English.

In African American Vernacular English, the verb *be* occurs in invariant form to signal a continuative aspect (Rickford 1999):

He's working hard   meaning 'he's working hard right now.'
He be working hard   meaning 'he's always working hard'.

More common than grammatical differences, though, are the phonological differences by which we distinguish regional dialects. These differences can be quite subtle, or not so subtle. In the New York area and in Chicago, for example, the vowel /æ/ can be pronounced as a diphthong [eᵊ] – and the nucleus of that diphthong can be pronounced even higher in the mouth [iᵊ]. But this does not occur in the same words in the two dialects. In New York, people "raise" /æ/ when it precedes certain consonants – nasals, voiced stops, and voiceless fricatives as in *ham, had,* and *hash* – but not before voiceless stops as in *hat* (Labov 1966). Learning to speak like a New Yorker, then, involves – among other things – knowing which words one can raise /æ/ in, and which words one cannot. In the northern cities dialect area around Buffalo, Cleveland, Detroit, and Chicago, on the other hand, all occurrences of /æ/ have this pronunciation – people in these cities can raise /æ/ in *hat* as well as *had, ham,* and *hash* (Eckert 2000).

In some cases, one dialect may have a phonemic distinction – a contrast in pronunciation that separates distinct words – that another does not. For example in most dialects of English, speakers distinguish between the phonemes /a/ as in *hock, cot, Don* and /ɔ/ as in *hawk, caught, dawn*. In a number of North American dialects (e.g. much of the western US and Canada), however, these two phonemes have merged so that the vowels in *hock* and *hawk, cot* and *caught, Don* and *dawn*, are all pronounced the same. In order for speakers of one of these dialects to acquire a dialect in which the phonemic distinction remains, they would have to learn basically from scratch which words contain /a/ and which contain /ɔ/ – and they'd have to learn it well enough to produce the distinction automatically as they speak.

Compare the chore of learning when to raise /æ/ or learning which words contain /a/ and which contain /ɔ/ with the chore of trying to learn an entirely new language with native-like pronunciation. As we get older, it becomes increasingly difficult to modify our dialect(s) significantly, or to acquire native-like ability in a new language. Jack Chambers (1992), studying Canadian children moving to England, found that those over the age of eight did not learn the distinction well, while their younger siblings did. Many linguists believe that there is a *critical period* beyond which a person can no longer acquire native competence in a new language. This is, however, a matter of some debate. We know that indeed it is difficult to develop such competence, but is it a consequence of biology? Or is it a consequence of the social affordances of different age groups? Or both?[1]

Because of the relative permanence of one's language, and even one's dialect of that language, and the relative difficulty of learning "someone else's" language or dialect, we tend to think of our linguistic variety or varieties as fundamental to who we are. And as a result, dialect differences (to say nothing of differences between languages) carry a good deal of social baggage. Speakers of New York and Chicago dialects can be quite sensitive to the patterns of occurrence of [eə] or [iə] as opposed to [æ], and they are likely to have an attitude about people who use raised /æ/ in the "wrong" words. New Yorkers and midwesterners have stereotypes written indelibly on each other's dialects. The pronunciation of /æ/ is socially significant on the local scene as well, as regional stereotypes give way to local ones. As we will describe later in this chapter, very subtle patterns of variation can relate ways of speaking to class, ethnicity, age, gender, and a range of local groups and types.

We refer to features of language that vary in this way – that essentially offer more than one way of saying "the same thing" – as *variables*. And the study of patterns of use of such variables is referred to as the study of *sociolinguistic variation*. Whether we say [bæg] or [biəg], our hearer knows that we mean the same word – *bag*. But in addition to knowing the general kind of object we're talking about, our hearer can gather some social information from our pronunciation of the variable /æ/ or /ɔ/, or our use of invariant *be* or positive *anymore*.

If our use of variables offers information about who we are, it should also be clear to the reader by now that who we are is never static – and

1 Eve Clark (2000) offers a discussion of this issue. We might add that it is not at all clear what constitutes native competence.

speakers are not likely to simply be defined by the linguistic varieties they learn at home. Access is key to developing competence in a variety, and our greatest access is through our family and friends in our early years. But as we get older, we may move in new circles, gain exposure to new varieties – and we may well find motivation to learn to use those new varieties, or to tone down what makes our old variety distinctive. A New Yorker or a Chicagoan can exaggerate the raising of /æ/ or play it down, for instance, and many people do both – depending on the situation.

Even for those who remain in the same community all their lives, dialect is not static. From our earliest years, we develop a range of variability so that our speech does not simply reflect our fixed place in social space – who we are – but allows us to move around in that space, to do things by exploiting the space of variability open to us. Children growing up in New York do not simply learn to use the phoneme /æ/ in *bag*, but to vary that pronunciation. In other words, children learn the *variable* /æ/, and as their social interactions develop so does their use of that variable. Similarly, children growing up bilingually learn how to use both varieties not just grammatically, but strategically. Each language in a bilingual – and multilingual – community may be associated with particular groups, situations, activities, ideologies, etc. And patterns of language choice are built into the social fabric of the community. Speakers may borrow lexical items from one language to another, they may use different language in different situations and with different people, they may use more than one language in the same conversation – *code-switching* from one turn to another, or within sentences. These strategies make social meaning in much the same way as variation within the same language.[2]

We learn from the beginning to vary our linguistic variety strategically to place ourselves, to align ourselves with respect to others, and to express particular attitudes. We use linguistic variability to move around our initial home communities of practice. At the same time, we can also adapt linguistically to new communities and situations, or we can use language to help us gain access to new communities and situations. Linguistic variability is key to social mobility and the presentation of self, hence to the construction of gender. The story of gender and use of linguistic varieties is to be found in the relation between

2 In the following discussion, we will use the term *dialect* to refer to a speaker's native linguistic system. We will also use *variety* as an intentionally vague term to refer to any linguistic system, in order to avoid problematic distinctions such as *language*, *dialect*, *accent*. Since the dynamics of the linguistic market can have similar characteristics whether the linguistic differences in question are great or small, we opt for this cover term on occasion, in order to be able to talk about several situations at once.

gender and participation in the many communities of practice that make up the diverse social and linguistic landscape.

The linguistic market

In chapter three, we noted Pierre Bourdieu's claim that the value of a person's utterances on the linguistic market lies in the fate of those utterances – in whether they are picked up, attended to, acted upon, repeated. In this chapter, we pick up on Bourdieu's further claim – that the value of an utterance on the market of ideas depends crucially on the language variety in which it is framed. The right linguistic variety can transform an otherwise "worthless" utterance into one that may command attention in powerful circles. Like the right friends, clothes, manners, haircuts and automobiles, the "right" linguistic variety can facilitate access to positions and situations of societal power and the "wrong" variety can block such access. At the same time, although people who speak like Queen Elizabeth or like a US network newscaster may be helped thereby to gain access to the halls of global power, they will have trouble gaining access and trust in a poor community, or participating in a group of hip-hoppers or valley girls. And while each of these communities may not command global power, prestige or wealth, they command a variety of social and material resources that may be of greater value to many. Every linguistic variety, in other words, has positive symbolic value in its own community. For this reason, some sociolinguists (e.g. Sankoff and Laberge 1978, Eckert 2000) speak of opposed linguistic markets – the standard or global language market, in which the value of one's contributions depends on their being uttered in the standard variety, and the vernacular or local language market, in which the value of one's contributions depends on their being uttered in the local vernacular.

Analytic practice in the study of sociolinguistic variation has traditionally emphasized the relation between language variables and socioeconomic class, with a central focus on the socioeconomic stratification of language varieties. The language of societal power – that spoken at the upper end of the socioeconomic hierarchy, commonly referred to as the *standard* – is distinctive above all in its relative invariance across geographic space.[3] As one moves downwards through

---

3 There is more regional variation in the US than in Britain in what is considered standard and, at least traditionally, somewhat more tolerance of regional features in the speech of those who hold power. Nonetheless, even in the US the standard varieties show relatively little regional variation and virtually all of that is in pronunciation rather than in grammatical constructions.

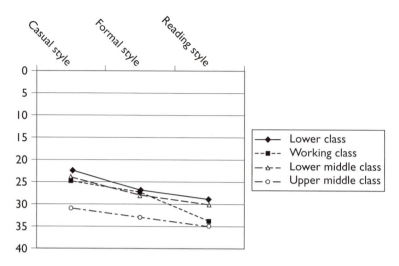

8.1 The social stratification of (oh) in New York City (from Labov 1972c, p. 129)

the hierarchy, one moves away from the standard into an increasing diversity of varieties, varieties whose value lies quite directly in their local distinctiveness. These locally based varieties are commonly referred to as *vernaculars*. This class difference is illustrated in Figure 8.1, which shows the social stratification of /ɔ/ in New York City (taken from Labov 1972c, p. 129). The diphthongization and raising of /ɔ/ (so that *dog* sounds more like *doo-og*) is a well-known feature of the New York accent, and the extent to which a person raises it correlates inversely with the person's socioeconomic status. Each speaker, furthermore, "tones down" this vernacular feature when they're speaking more formally, as shown by the slope of each line in Figure 8.1. Inasmuch as local differences are the result of local changes, local features like this are sometimes evidence of linguistic change, and the class (and gender, and age) differentiation is an indication of the progress of change through the population. Thus people who use the most raised variants of /ɔ/ (or other local features that represent changes in progress) in a community can be said to lead their community in linguistic change.

Depending on the history of the community, vernaculars may be distinct languages from the standard, or they may be alternative varieties of the same language. The social dynamics of language use in either case have a good deal in common, and in the following discussion we will be treating the two kinds of situation similarly. In most bilingual communities, one language is the official or standard language, used in powerful institutions such as government, education, and global business. The other language or languages in the community may be indigenous languages or immigrant languages – but in both cases, they are not the languages of global power in those communities. We will begin with a discussion of the connection between language and institutions of power – the phenomenon of language standardization. We will then go on to consider the alternative linguistic varieties that remain in use in distinction, and often in opposition, to the standard.

The local and the global

We begin our discussion with a few quick examples of the organization of varieties in three communities, in order to provide some context for the kinds of gendered phenomena we are going to present. Each of these examples, in increasing subtlety, illustrates the tension between the local and the global – the vernacular and the standard.

Bilingualism in St. Pierre de Soulan

The Roman Empire brought Latin to the geographic area that is now divided into countries that include Spain, Portugal, France, Switzerland, Andorra, Belgium, Monaco, Luxembourg, Romania, and Italy. Over the centuries, Latin diversified as a result of linguistic changes that began in different places and spread over small and large areas, resulting in a vast linguistic continuum across that geographic area. Until the last century, this rich diversity of modern Latin-based or Romance varieties was alive and well. A hundred years ago, a person walking from Paris to Madrid would have found the language used in daily speech gradually "morphing" from French into Spanish. The differences from one town to the next would have been fairly small, but the accumulation of small differences over a considerable distance would have rendered the varieties at either extreme mutually incomprehensible. But as modern nation states emerged on the old Roman territory, each one laid claim to a distinctive and nationally shared language. The modern standard languages of France and Spain are the local dialects from the area near their respective capitals, owing their new status to the fact that they were in the right place, spoken by the right people, at the right time. These two dialects were elevated to the status of *language*, while the other dialects were demoted, to be viewed as *dialects of* those two languages. Spanish and French were not taken up automatically or through a series of coincidences – their codification and elevation to *standard language* played an important role in the construction of the French and Spanish nations and nationalism, at the expense of all other local varieties.

Soulan, a small commune in the Pyrenees (see Eckert 1980a and b, 1983), is typical of communities throughout France in which the local variety (which we will call Soulatan) is sufficiently different from French that the two are mutually incomprehensible. Soulatan was the only language of the community until the late nineteenth century, when French began to move gradually into the life of the village through nationally controlled institutions. French was the language of global institutions: education, modern medicine, government and finance, social programs, salaried employment, religion and the media. And as these institutions entered the life of the village, they created a contrast with the self-sufficient peasant life that they encountered. The Soulatan language, along with the way of life it served, came to be associated with peasant stereotypes – ignorance, folk medicine, political isolation, a barter economy, poverty, agricultural work, and superstition. Gradually, in the course of the twentieth century, language use shifted from Soulatan to French, as people engaged with increasing regularity in situations and transactions that required French, and as Soulatan became increasingly stigmatized in contrast with French. People began to avoid using Soulatan in public situations so as to avoid humiliation, and to raise their children in French in order to give them a head start into the mainstream economy. The local language may have been useless in the global market, but it was also the language of family, of community, of land and homes, and of an entire way of life that has now all but disappeared. As language use shifted over the years, people's verbal strategies – their choice of French or Soulatan in any utterance – depended on such things as their own status in the community and their ideologies. Their strategies also depended on where they were, who they were addressing and who else was present, the topic, their attitude, their emotions, and any number of other considerations.

Martha's Vineyard

Martha's Vineyard, an island off the coast of Massachusetts, has long been a relatively isolated and fiercely independent island, dominated for many generations by a fishing community of English descent. From the mainland, the Vineyard is considered beautiful, quaint, and a highly desirable vacation spot. It is also known for its distinctive "accent," most notably for its pronunciation of the diphthongs /ay/ and /aw/. The nucleus [a] of the diphthongs is centralized, so that *fight* and *about* are pronounced more like *foit* and *a-boat*. In an ethnographic study of the speech on this island, William Labov (1963) found that the pronunciation of /ay/ was playing a prime role in social changes on the island. The local fishing industry was under pressure from big business fishing from the mainland, and the quiet local community was being encroached upon by a growing tourist industry. Serious conflict had developed within the community between those who wished to maintain their local way of life, and those who embraced the mainland – more *global* – economy. Among the young people, this conflict manifested itself not only in what happened to the island itself, but in whether they would leave the island for college and eventually for mainland adulthoods. Labov found that those who identified most strongly with local island tradition were intensifying the local pronunciation of /ay/, while those who were drawn to the new off-island economy used a pronunciation more like the standard mainland pronunciation. What was striking was that the competition between the local and the global was played out not just in political arguments, but also subtly in every verbal interaction. One might say that there was social meaning in every pronunciation of that particular vowel.

Belten High School

In the suburban area around Detroit, Michigan, there is a series of vowel shifts that constitute a recognizable regional accent.[4] Newest among these shifts is the backing of the vowels /e/ and /ʌ/ so that *flesh* is pronounced like *flush*, and *lunch* is pronounced like *launch*. And these vowel shifts play a subtle but palpable role in the social life of the area. Belten High School, located in a western suburb of Detroit, is like many high schools throughout that area and indeed across the country. It serves an all-white, but socioeconomically diverse, student population. Socioeconomic class plays out in the student social order in the form of two dominant and mutually opposed class-based social categories, which emerge through opposed responses to the school's norms and expectations. The *jocks* are an institutionally-based community of practice, basing their identities, activities, and social networks in the school's extracurricular sphere. In the pursuit of extracurricular careers, they compete for roles and honors, and form a recognized social hierarchy. College bound, jocks develop their friendships as a function of school activities, and expect these friendships to change when they go on to college. The *burnouts*, on the other hand, reject the institution

---

4 The overall pattern of the vowel shifts taking place in Detroit is common to the area described by the northern cities of Buffalo, Cleveland, Detroit, and Chicago, and is referred to as the Northern Cities Shift (Labov, Yaeger, and Steiner 1972; Labov 1994).

as a locus for their social lives, basing their friendships, identities, activities, and social networks in the neighborhoods and public spaces of the suburban-urban area. Headed for the local workforce after high school, burnouts intend that their high-school friendships and activities should continue with them. The jocks and the burnouts constitute middle-class and working-class cultures within the adolescent context, and their practices bring into stark contrast values about friendship, institutional engagement, hierarchy, and the local area. This contrast has all kinds of symbolic manifestations, such as clothing, territory, and musical taste. And it is overwhelmingly manifested in language. Most particularly, the jocks' language is more standard, as befits their institutional orientation, while the burnouts' is both nonstandard and local as befits their antischool stance and local orientation. The burnouts' local orientation is also manifested in their more extreme use of the local vowel shifts affecting /e/ and /ʌ/, whereas the jocks tend to use more conservative variants of these vowels. The different educational orientation is also reflected in the fact that the jocks use overwhelmingly standard grammatical constructions, while the burnouts make far greater use of such forms as nonstandard negation (e.g. *I didn't do nothing*).

Language ideologies and linguistic varieties

In each of these three cases, a variety that has emerged in the local community has come into contact with a nonlocal variety, specifically with a variety associated with institutions and ultimately with the global economy. The opposition between the local and the global is commonly tied up with socioeconomic class, and with power struggles and conflicting interests. Within communities, class differences are generally related to orientation toward and participation in local and global networks, activities, and interests. While members of professional and elite classes are engaged in globalizing institutions (e.g. education, nonlocal government, corporations), the lives of laborers, tradespeople, small business people, etc. are embedded in local communities. While the local language represents membership and loyalty to a local community, and to the practices and relationships that make up life in that community, the standard language represents disengagement from the local.

The notion of the *linguistic market* is based in the fact that one's linguistic variety can ultimately enhance one's chances for material gain. If standard language serves as symbolic capital in the global political and financial markets, vernaculars serve as symbolic capital in local markets by facilitating access to locally controlled resources, which may range from privately owned housing and space, to local jobs and a wide range of services. While the locally based person may have trouble getting around the halls of global power, the nonlocally based person may have trouble gaining access to resources in a local community. Each variety ties its speakers to its community, and to a great extent vernacular-speaking communities are tied to place, while standard-speaking communities are tied to institutions. Bourdieu (1982) emphasizes that it is the association of an individual with the institution that makes that individual's utterances powerful. The power of the utterances resides in the fact that speakers do not speak simply on their own account, but as the "bearer" of words on behalf of the group or institution that provides the basis of power.

The lives of most people do not center around global institutions, but around their local communities. The vernacular ties its speakers to the local community and lends local authority and solidarity. Thus linguistic varieties are not simply linked to communities and ways of life; they are also ideological constructs that carry considerable social weight.

The specific symbolic value of these opposed linguistic resources is embedded in beliefs about their relation to those who speak them. We have seen in chapter one that gender ideology associates male and female gender with specific qualities in such a way as to justify the gender order. Language ideology functions in a similar way, linking supposed qualities of language varieties to supposed qualities of the people or groups that use those varieties. This is a process that Susan Gal and Judith Irvine (1995) refer to as *iconization* – the creation of an apparently natural connection between a linguistic variety and the speakers who use it. We are all familiar with the stereotyping of varieties. Earlier we mentioned that New Yorkers and Chicagoans are likely to have an attitude about each other's dialects – an attitude based in how New Yorkers see Chicagoans (or midwesterners more generally), and how Chicagoans see New Yorkers (or east coast people more generally). The English of the southeastern US is often considered to reflect (depending on who is doing the assessing) the slowness/laziness/gentility of the old south (and sometimes from women's mouths evokes a "southern belle" image). French educators at the turn of the twentieth century argued that the dialects of southern France were evidence of the illogical and confused peasant mind, and a century later many American educators hold an analogous view of African American Vernacular English (AAVE), sometimes called "ebonics".

Since gender is at the center of most social orders, ideologies associated with linguistic varieties can generally be expected to interact in a variety of ways with gender stereotypes. But, as we will see in the following discussion, this interaction may be as varied as the linguistic and gender situations themselves.

Case study: standardization and the Japanese woman

The construction of standard languages is intimately tied to the formation of nation states. And just as the gender dichotomy is constructed through the erasure of differences *among* women and *among* men and the emphasis of differences *between* women and men, the nation state is constructed through the erasure of the history of differences among the population included in it and emphasizing differences between that population and others. Nation-building, then, involves the same processes of naturalization as gender-building. The history of standard Japanese shows how closely these two can be tied.

Japanese people tend to think of Japanese "women's language" as timeless, and as reflecting the essential qualities of Japanese womanhood – qualities that in turn emanate from the special quality of Japanese culture. This is reflected in the following quote from a popular writer: "Japanese womanhood is now being recognized as beautiful and excellent beyond compare with the other womanhoods of the world. Likewise, Japanese women's language is so good that it seems to me that it is, along with Japanese womanhood, unique in the world" (Kyosuke [1942], cited in Inoue [2002]). But as a small number of writers have shown, the connection between Japan, the qualities of Japanese women, and Japanese women's language is neither natural nor enduring. Miyako Inoue (1994) has argued that these ideological constructs emerged in recent history, in the building of the modern Japanese nation. Japan was made up of feudal autonomous regions until the late nineteenth century, at which time, with the advent of industrial capitalism, there were tremendous social and political changes. The Meiji restoration brought about a centralized government and a centralized society as mass communication, transportation, and compulsory education allowed the population of the new nation to perceive themselves as participants in an imagined community (Anderson 1983). But engaged in wars with China and Russia on the one hand, and moving into overseas markets on the other, the emerging Japan was faced with a tension between nationalism and modernization. Associated with the world outside Japan, particularly the west, modernization posed an economic opportunity, but it also posed a threat to Japan's authenticity. This threat was met through an appeal to Confucianism. Appealing to the association of Confucianism with Japanese tradition, the state was able to achieve social control and authentication by making the Confucian ideal part of the new national identity.

An important part of this ideal was the enforcement of a patriarchal family structure that enlisted the cooperation of women as well as men, elevating a woman's role as wife, mother, and homemaker. Women's education was instituted to fulfill this ideal. For the first time, girls were sent to school, where they received education in homemaking and the female arts. The liberation of girls from their traditional confinement to their home for the purposes of learning feminine arts linked these arts to freedom and agency. The womanly arts, then, and education went together and were no doubt seen as liberating. As Inoue puts it (2002, pp. 396–397), "This contradictory conjuncture, inherent in – but not unique to – Japan's experience of modernity, was the overdetermined context in which 'women' increasingly became targeted as a national and social issue. Women, here as elsewhere, came to embody the shifting boundary between tradition and modernity, and gender became a key site where this irrevocable binary was negotiated."

Language standardization was key to uniting a country marked by tremendous dialectal variety, and the Japanese state-makers set out to construct and enforce a standard language, based on Tokyo dialect. The invention of women's language, Inoue argues, brought together the new attention to language and to women, creating both as new subjects for control and study. Women's language was part and parcel of the invention of modern Japan, a modern Japanese language and literacy, and the modern Japanese woman. And in the process, the inventors laid on the new Japanese woman the responsibility for holding up the new/traditional values of the nation as Japanese femininity became a national treasure.

This woman's language, also claimed as a national treasure, is in fact associated with urban life and particularly urban elites. Dominant ideology says that the ways of speaking that constitute Japanese women's language are a natural reflection of the Japanese woman's unique, virtuous, and quintessentially feminine character. If this is true, then the majority of Japanese women probably fall short of the ideal, for as Yukako Sunaoshi (1995) has shown, once one leaves urban centers for provincial and rural areas, there is very little gender difference in linguistic practice. The national project attempted to homogenize widely different dialects, and widely different gender practices, into something that appeared to suit an urban lifestyle.

Central to the nation-building project, this new woman, this new language, and this new unitary Japanese-ness was presented as anything but new. But where did it come from? Elements of women's language are attributed to the speech of *court ladies* as far back as the fourteenth century, and of the cultured *play ladies* of the Edo period (1603–1867). Risako Ide and Tomomi Terada (1998) argue that certain forms were part of these women's "occupational language" and were then transformed to "gender language." While it is clear that the sources of the modern forms are heterogeneous, one question that lies in the foreground is how the language of play ladies, or geisha – forms that were apparently stigmatized at the time – came to be feminine norms. Geisha, as professionals in the womanly arts, may well have served an important role in the construction and dissemination of the womanly arts. Although many women did not inhabit the geisha quarter by choice, but were sold there by families in need of money, it was a female-dominated community, and the geisha profession was the one route for women to achieve economic independence. And as a relatively independent, male-centered but female-dominated milieu, this quarter may well have served as inspiration to young girls seeking to construct themselves as modern women through the development of the womanly arts. Ide and Terada argue that the play ladies had a certain covert prestige,[5] and that their language – which was gendered by virtue of association with them – was disseminated through popular culture.

Inoue (2002) concurs that popular culture was the main vehicle of dissemination, but focuses on written genres, arguing that the same genres that disseminated women's language also helped construct it. Comparing dialogue in popular fiction of the early and late nineteenth century, Inoue (1994, 2002) found that while most of the forms that appear as women's language in the later works do occur in the earlier work, their gender specialization emerges only in the later works. She traces the emergence of modern fiction during the late Meiji era, and particularly the new genres that portrayed "real" modern life. Aimed at girls and women, these genres minted and gave voice to the new women's language, and their readers – both in reading and in participating in the lives they portrayed – came to participate in the language. In doing so, they were not, Inoue argues, striving for femininity, but for participation in the modern nation. In this way, Inoue says: "language

5 The notion of covert prestige was introduced by Peter Trudgill (1972) to refer to the prestige associated with things (and actions and people) that are considered admirable by standards other than global prestige norms. Particularly, he attributed the force of working-class language among men to the covert prestige associated with physical masculinity.

does not wait until the category it refers to or indexes is 'out there.'...
The case of the development of women's language [shows] that index-
ical practice was involved with the construction of modern Japanese
women right from its inception" (2002, p. 412).

The story of Japanese "women's language" is a particularly dramatic
example of the role of language manipulation in the construction of
a single society and its gender order – and of the intimate relation between language ideology and gender ideology. As we will see in chapter
nine, the construct of women's language has played a central role in
current social change in Japan as well.

Gender and language ideologies

The ideologies associated with standards and vernaculars unfold from
the particular histories in which they emerge. Nonetheless, there are
certain properties of standard and vernacular that emerge from the
very process of standardization. Standards, as languages of global institutions, are associated with different communities and concerns from
vernaculars, the languages of local communities. By association with
these communities, a range of stereotypes come to be associated with
the two types of varieties.

Because of their role in nation-building, standards are designed to
unite diverse populations – not only by providing a common language
or lingua franca but by symbolizing homogeneity. Through codification
and institutionalization, successful standardization ultimately erases
the local origin of the standard and the heterogeneity that it is intended to supplant. The codified status of standard language renders
it apparently unchanging and invariable, "immune" to the vagaries of
time and locality. This allows the language to symbolize its speakers'
(supposed) subordination of their own personal or local interests to
those of particular institutions, and ultimately to those of society at
large. The conservative nature of the standard thus allows it to be associated with rationality and stability. Furthermore, this association of
standard language with impersonal and formalized communications
and with rationality offers a contrast with the personal and affective
engagement associated with the vernacular.

Standard and vernacular are also associated with different kinds of
knowledge and authority. The association with institutions of education allows the standard variety to symbolize "objective" knowledge
from global, unimpeachable sources, which entitles people to act on
behalf of others. At the local level, on the other hand, knowledge and

judgment function in a different realm. Locally based working- and lower-middle-class people are the ones who keep the physical infrastructure together. In this context, the technical knowledge associated with such things as plumbing, cleaning, secretarial work, electricity, and carpentry is highly valued. And closely related to the maintenance of the infrastructure are the knowledge of, and the ability to work with, local networks and resources. Engagement in the local community, then, is crucial not only to daily life, but to the accomplishment of professional goals. The display of this kind of knowledge and connection commands the same kind of authority in the local context that the display of institutional knowledge and connection commands in the institutional or global context.

By virtue of its association with elites, standard language is also associated with refinement. The time and financial resources required to manufacture a refined self and to engage in refined behavior, and the incompatibility of refinement with physical work, are an important component of the symbolic value of refinement. Refinement distances a person from the physical world, and in a working-class environment, it is the ability to work with the physical world that is valued – physical strength, mechanical know-how, the ability to make and repair the things of everyday life, and the ability to defend oneself. The opposing pole to refinement, then, is physicality, practical knowledge, roughness and toughness.

The reader will recognize that these oppositions: global vs. local concerns, objective vs. subjective reasoning, theoretical vs. practical knowledge, refinement vs physicality simultaneously link language to class and to gender stereotypes. Dominant ideologies paint women and the working class as concerned primarily with personal interests and relationships, and as more inclined to be emotionally volatile and irrational. And at the same time, women (especially of the privileged social classes) are expected to exhibit refinement.

The discussion that follows will explore some of the ways in which the use of standard and vernacular varieties – and elements of these varieties – interacts with gender. There is no simple relation between gender and varieties, and as we will see, the various connections among gender and class can interact to produce a variety of dynamics.

Gender and the use of linguistic varieties

Use of any variety requires, first of all, access to participation in the communities of practice in which the variety is used, and the right to actually use it in situations. Use also requires desire. Speakers will not accept linguistic influence from people they do not value – their linguistic varieties indicate movement in the direction of desired identities, of communities of practice in which they desire to participate. Given that our lives involve participation in multiple communities of practice, our linguistic practice involves a certain amount of heterogeneity. We may use one language in one situation, another in another; we may use a stronger local accent in one situation, a weaker one in another. Depending on where we are, what we're doing, who is in our audience, what we're talking about, how we're feeling about the situation – and any other of a number of things – we call upon resources to adapt our variety to our immediate needs.

An important aspect of the gendered use of varieties is the relation of language to the structure of opportunity for material success, which importantly includes employment outside of the home and, for some, marriage to a partner with good economic prospects. Employment opportunity structures gendered language development in a variety of subtle ways. Jobs often require particular kinds of language skills – whether it's simply because of the community in which they are located, or because of the actual kind of work. And the jobs themselves may differentially attract women or men because the work is gender-specific or because there are local or temporary reasons for women or men to be attracted to them. The gendered availability of employment works on linguistic norms in more ways than one. On the one hand, the actual work may not require specific language skills, but being in the workplace may provide greater access to certain varieties. On the other hand, the differential linguistic requirements of jobs attracting (or specifying) male or female employees may motivate men and women to develop different linguistic skills. In either case, the effect on community norms could be profound, as the anticipation of entering gendered jobs may motivate differential language development in childhood. Marriage opportunities may also play a role in motivating language development in a world in which girls are socialized to focus on marriage as a means of advancement. To have a chance of marrying a prince, a young girl had better be able to talk like a princess.

The role of industrialization and urbanization has been powerful in language change and language shift, as people have moved away from their local agricultural communities into larger towns and cities, leaving small farming for salaried work, particularly in factories. This commonly entails a shift from one's local variety to a more global variety – whether a regional or a national standard. The gender pattern of this shift depends on the local details of social change, but a common development is for women to leave the farm fastest, and hence to lead in the shift from the vernacular. Susan Gal's (1978, 1979) ethnographic study of a Hungarian-speaking village in Austria documents a case of this sort in detail. Gal found that women's linguistic choices in the community of Oberwart were influenced not so much by the availability, but by the preferability, of occupations (and marriage opportunities) that required the standard language, German. In this community, Hungarian was the language of a peasant life that did not offer the same advantages to women that it did to men. Men inherited and controlled households and land, while women did both agricultural work and all of the domestic work on their husbands' property. Modernization tended to affect farm work before it affected housework, tying women in farm households to long hours of hard physical labor while their husbands' burden in the field was lightened by modern farm equipment. Gal found that women were leading the men in the shift from Hungarian to German in this community, because many of them were attracted to the factory jobs available in the nearby German-speaking town. These jobs offered greater autonomy and a town lifestyle that involved an easier domestic life than that of the Hungarian woman in a farming household. Few of them were willing to marry the Hungarian peasant men with whom they grew up, many opting instead for marriage to German-speaking factory workers and the town life that these marriages entailed.

Jonathan Holmquist (1985) found a similar situation in the village of Ucieda in the Cantabria mountain region of northern Spain. Once a very poor community, the modern cash economy that followed the Franco era has improved the economic situation in Ucieda considerably, and brought about considerable social change. The traditional mountain agricultural life consisting of shepherding native stock (ponies, long-horned cattle, sheep, and goats) has given way over the past couple of generations to factory work in the nearby town, and to dairy farming, which can be managed in addition to a factory job. The local vernacular of this village was a Romance dialect closely related to Castilian Spanish, but with significant differences. Holmquist focused on word-final /u/, which corresponds to Castilian /o/. Thus, for example, in a quote from an older person in the village speaking of young men and their new way of life, Holmquist records (p. 197):

el traba**ju** del cam**pu** no lo saben   'field work, they don't know it'

which in Castilian would be:

el traba**jo** del cam**po** no lo saben

Table 8.1. *Lowering of /u/ in Ucieda (from Holmquist 1985, p. 197)*

	males	females
Mountain agriculture	2.27	1.86
Dairy farming	1.78	1.12
Workers	.79	.79

As people in the village moved away from the traditional mountain agricultural way of life, they began to lower this vowel to conform more closely to the standard Spanish [o] pronunciation, assimilating linguistically as they assimilated culturally to the national cash economy. And as in Oberwart, young women have found factory work preferable to agricultural work, even dairy farming (as Holmquist says [p. 200], they don't want to be "stuck at home with the cows"), while many young men continue to engage in dairy farming. The fate of word-final /u/ is closely linked to the fate of the agricultural way of life, as shown in Table 8.1, which shows a numerical value for the height of this vowel. The numerical value is the average of all pronunciations on a scale of 0 to 4, where 0 is the lowest [o] pronunciation, and 4 is the highest (most conservative) pronunciation [u]. As this table shows, factory workers are the most likely to lower this vowel and those who engage in the mountain animal economy are the least likely, with dairy farmers in the middle. And in all agricultural groups, furthermore, women are more likely to use the lowered pronunciation than men, suggesting their attraction to town life. Only among those working solely in factories – those whose pronunciations are consistently low – does the gender difference disappear.

In these two cases, one would not say that the jobs that were drawing women into the standard language market were themselves particularly gendered. Many of the cases in which we see gendered shifts in language use, though, do involve the gendering of work. For example in a study of a Gullah-speaking African American island community in South Carolina, Patricia Nichols (1983) found that in general the variety spoken by women was closer to standard English than that spoken by men. This difference corresponded to the different employment opportunities open to women and men on this island. The men were able to make good money as laborers on the mainland – jobs that required physical skill, but that did not depend on the way they spoke. The women, on the other hand, found the best jobs as teachers or as maids in wealthy homes or hotels – all settings in which they were expected to use more standard language. In this case, it was the place of gendered jobs in the language market that led to gender differences in speech.

David Sankoff *et al.* (1989) have argued that gendered roles in the workplaces of western society tend to engage women more than men in the standard language market. Women in their traditional work roles are often what Sankoff *et al.* have called "technicians of language." Employment as governesses and private tutors was an early extension of middle-class women's domestic role into the workplace, allowing educated women to make a living, while keeping them out of the public sphere. This employment mixed raising children with providing education. Some governesses taught academic subject matter, but all of them taught manners and refinement, of which linguistic propriety was an important component. While governesses provided private instruction to children of the elite, other women were playing a similar role as classroom teachers of somewhat less privileged children. As primary school teachers, women were responsible for providing children who did not have access to private instruction with both "moral" and intellectual education, including access to "correct" or standard grammar.

As more women have moved into the workplace, many of the jobs accessible to them have been as front women, whose role is either exclusively or primarily to embody and give voice to corporate standards to outsiders: receptionists, hostesses, phone operators, flight attendants, secretaries. These jobs require technicians of language not because language qualifies a person as directly able to handle the practical demands of the job, but because it serves as the cultural capital necessary to be the "kind of" person who is qualified to occupy that position. In order to be a receptionist in the front office of corporate headquarters, one needs to be able not only to communicate with one's employer and those who come in the door, but to represent the company's desired image. In this sense, the receptionist's command of standard language is not only part of that individual's cultural capital but also part of the company's cultural capital.

In her study of the language of corporate managers in Beijing, Qing Zhang (2001) examined a prime example of women providing cultural capital for their company, as different work trajectories shaped women's and men's use of Mandarin. Zhang compared the speech of managers in two kinds of business: traditional state-owned businesses, and new foreign-owned financial enterprises. All of these people, male and female, had entered their businesses with the same high level of education. In the state-owned businesses, women's and men's career trajectories were the same. In the foreign-owned businesses, however, the men moved directly into sales positions and quickly into management, whereas the women were initially given secretarial jobs from which they only gradually moved into management positions. Hired primarily for their linguistic skills, these women's initial value to their companies was their ability to represent the company in other languages as well as in other varieties of Chinese, and to present a cosmopolitan image for the company. These women, therefore, developed a style of Chinese that was more "cosmopolitan" – less locally "Beijing" – as befits a globally based enterprise. This variety was notably different from that employed by the men in the same businesses, while the speech of managers in the state-owned businesses showed very little gender difference. We will discuss this further in chapter nine.

Employment is only one way in which the gendering of activity leads to gender differences in the development and use of linguistic varieties. For women who do not work in the public marketplace, linguistic needs and preferences will depend on the nature of their private lives. Women themselves constitute capital that is regularly deployed by individual men as well as by institutions. The expression *trophy wife* refers to just such a practice, with the emphasis on the woman's physical properties and on her ability to consume with refinement. A cultured and well-spoken wife, even one who lacks the physical accoutrements of the trophy wife, bespeaks a man of refinement and substance. Standard language, therefore, has often been emphasized as an important part of a woman's capital on the marriage market. Building on a tradition in which women do not compete in the financial market, a woman may well use standard language in the social market.

Women's and men's social networks may also lead to differential linguistic patterns. In a study of the English spoken in Belfast, Lesley Milroy (1980) found that the use of vernacular language was reinforced in close locally based social networks. Density (the number of connections among the members of a network) and multiplexity (the number of kinds of connections among these members) of networks is quite closely related to class. In working-class communities, people tend to live near, and spend leisure time with, relatives – and to make friends through neighbors and relatives. They also tend to find jobs through those same connections. As a result, there tend to be connections among more of the people in a working-class network, and these connections tend to cover more domains (e.g. work, church, activities). Milroy found that because of the poor employment situation for women, though, women's networks tended to be less dense and multiplex than those of their male peers. Correspondingly, their vernacular usage was lower than that of their male peers. In one neighborhood

Milroy studied, however, it was women rather than men who were employed and who were involved in more dense and multiplex networks. In that situation, the women's vernacular usage was on many measures ahead of that of their male peers.

In a study of migrants from rural communities to Brazlandia, a satellite city near Brazilia, Stella Maris Bortoni-Ricardo (1985) found that men adapted their rural dialect more readily to the urban variety than women. The apparent reason was that men found work opportunities in Brazlandia that gave them access to social networks in which the urban variety was used. The women, on the other hand, were restricted to the neighborhoods where they lived. Since these neighborhoods were populated by others who had migrated from the same rural areas, they had little access to the urban variety. She did find four exceptions to this pattern, who turned out to be four women who belonged to large nuclear families, and who were exposed to many interactions with school-aged people in the home, providing considerable exposure to urban culture and language.

Access

As these examples have suggested, access to varieties is as gendered as access to the situations and networks in which varieties are used. But there is more – access also involves one's right to use a particular variety. Inasmuch as varieties are associated with groups or categories of people, those who are not members of those groups or categories may be unable to gain access to the varieties. But even for those who are capable of using a variety, gatekeeping can impose serious constraints on its use. On the one hand, the "owners" of the variety may not be receptive to hearing an outsider use it. On the other, there may be considerable sanctions within one's own group for using an "outside" variety. For example, in Soulan before World War II, since French was the language of intrusion, the villagers considered speaking French unnecessarily (i.e., when there were no monolingual French speakers present) disloyal. This applied to women and men alike, but there were subtle differences. Since French was associated with administrative power, men's use of French was associated with access to power. Women's use of French, on the other hand, was more often associated with pretension.

Jane Hill (1987) describes a situation in a Mexicano-speaking community in Mexico, in which women's use of both Mexicano and Spanish is constrained by their position in the social order. People in this community are bilingual to varying degrees in the national language, Spanish, and the Native American language, Mexicano (the general name for the Native American language Nahuatl). Language use in the community is shifting to Spanish, and Mexicano is undergoing significant Spanish influence (such as lexical borrowing). Community members consider that "pure" Mexicano is a thing of the past, but Mexicano remains highly valued, associated with local and ethnic solidarity. The local domains with which it is associated, and the activities in which it is most often used, however, are male dominated – particularly the system of family alliances called *compadrazco*, and male friendships. Spanish, meanwhile, is associated with activities and situations of power, particularly the system of community offices – also dominated by men. Hill found that although they had access to both languages, women's usage avoided either pure Spanish or pure Mexicano, since each was male linguistic territory, associated as it was with domains of male power. The women tended to adopt what might be called "modest" linguistic practices, to the extent that they lay claim neither to political power nor to community status, following a fairly narrow and nonstandard range of both languages.

Jack Sidnell (1999) found an analogous case in a village in Guyana. The linguistic repertoire in this community comprises a classic *creole continuum* ranging from Guyanese English-based creole to a local variety of English. Creolists call the variety that is closest to the standard (in this case English) the *acrolect*, and the variety that is the farthest from the standard the *basilect*. Sidnell found that while men moved around fairly freely from basilect to acrolect, women stayed within a fairly narrow range that neither carried the stigma of the basilect nor claimed the prestige of the acrolect. Sidnell's detailed analysis of the pronominal system sheds light on the complex ways in which identity and linguistic form interact in this community. The first-person singular subject pronoun, for example, has the basilectal variant *mi* and the acrolectal variant *ai*. As shown below (p. 381), as a woman recites a prayer, both variants can appear in the same sentence:

> *mi* mos see oo gad *ai* wanch yuu protek mii.
> 'I must say, "Oh God, I want you to protect me."'

The use of the acrolectal variant signals that the speaker is using a more prestige variety – and hence can be seen as constituting a claim to personal status. But in addition, referring to oneself in that variety, bestows prestige on the speaker as the referent of the pronoun (it renders the speaker an *acrolectal subject*). It is this latter claim, according to Sidnell, that enters into gender differences in the use of pronouns. Men use *ai* in a variety of situations in which they wish to project a middle-class cosmopolitan identity, or to index authority and respectability. This strategy is commonly invoked by men flirting with women by calling out to them on the road (p. 381):

> heloo, *ai* lov yuu beebii wats op … *ai* laik di wee yuu wak
> 'hello, I love you baby, what's up … I like the way you walk'

Women, on the other hand, use this form more rarely because, according to Sidnell, such self-presentations are more likely to backfire for women than for men. While such uses on the part of a man may go unnoticed or be evaluated as playful, women are more likely to be judged as snooty or pretentious. Sidnell gives the example (p. 383) of a young woman taking secretarial courses in the village, who called out to her friend:

> hai darling, *ai* goin in, *ai* gon sii you leeta
> 'hi darling, I'm going in, I'll see you later.'

A group of young men nearby mocked her for being presumptuous:

> hai hai *ai* goin in *ai* goin in of leson *ai* komin out leeta
> 'hi, hi I'm going in I'm going in for my lessons, I'm coming out later.'

The general language used in Egypt, modern Egyptian Arabic, is not the institutional standard. The standard is, rather, Classical (Koranic) Arabic, which is no one's native language. Classical Arabic is used regularly in Islamic religious practice, and also in national institutions such as government and universities. However, in these institutions, it is used only in certain situations – although it might be used in a lecture, it would not be used in a discussion about the lecture or a casual conversation after class. In a study of variability in the Arabic of Cairo, Niloofar Haeri (1997) noted the role of access to religious practice in gender difference. In Classical Arabic, *qaf*, a voiceless uvular stop, is a distinct phoneme from glottal stop. In modern Egyptian Arabic, however, these two have merged as a glottal stop. By virtue of its association with education and with Classical Arabic, the use of *qaf* in modern Egyptian Arabic is a well-known marker of prestige. Its correct use, however, requires not simply being able to pronounce it, but (as in the case of English /a/ and /ɔ/ discussed above) knowing which occurrences of glottal stop in modern Egyptian Arabic correspond to a classical glottal stop and which ones correspond to *qaf*. Not surprisingly, the use of *qaf* increases with higher levels of education – among both men and women. However, even among speakers with the same education, Haeri found that men used *qaf* more than women. She attributed this to the fact that although women have the same access to education as men, they do not have the same access to religious linguistic practice, in which the Classical language is regularly used.

In a study of the Arabic spoken in Tunis, Chedia Trabelsi (1991) found that male speakers had completely abandoned the local pronunciation [aw] and [ay] for the more cosmopolitan monophthongal pronunciation [u:] and [i:]. In more recent generations, with schooling and greater participation outside of domestic settings, women have followed in this change. Thus while older women exclusively use the traditional diphthongs and younger women exclusively use the more cosmopolitan monophthongs, middle-aged women show their in-between status with considerable switching between the two. According to Trabelsi, which variants women in this age group use depends on who they are speaking to, and particularly, where their interlocutor falls with respect to social change. When addressing an older woman who identifies with the traditional way of life they are more likely to use the diphthongal pronunciation, whereas when addressing a younger woman who identifies with the modern values that include greater freedom for women, they are more likely to use monophthongs. This change, clearly associated with modern urban life for the entire community, indexes women's problematic relation to that life as well.

Although it is the men in Tunis who engage more with the modern societal context, Ayala Fader (forthcoming) found the reverse situation in her study of Orthodox Jews in New York City. In Orthodox Jewish communities, Jewish languages such as Hebrew and Yiddish serve as important cultural capital, associated as they are with Jewish history and texts, and with the focal activity of the community – the study of Jewish texts. This scholarly activity, pursued in Yiddish, is reserved primarily for men, while women act as the interface between the Jewish community and the surrounding English-speaking community. Men and women, therefore, have different dominant languages. This represents an interesting gender inversion as Jewish linguistic practices have changed in recent years. A century ago, Yiddish was the home language for many Jewish families in the US and Europe, and was thus associated with women while Hebrew, the religious language, was associated with men. Today US Jews generally speak English at home. But in certain religious communities, the use of Yiddish in male-dominated religious activities makes it now a "men's" language.

In a less linguistically extreme community in northern California, Sarah Benor (2001) has traced the centrality of religious learning activity to differences in the English of young Orthodox Jewish boys and girls. Benor found that the boys were more likely than girls to use Hebrew and Yiddish words in their English. This, she found, was related to the fact that boys engage in Talmudic study in a way that girls do not, and as they approach adolescence, boys leave home to study in a Yeshiva, while girls generally stay home and attend the local Orthodox school. On the one hand, this gives boys greater access to such words. But more important, in so far as Talmudic study is crucial to the construction of masculinity in this community, the use of Hebrew and Yiddish words has come to be a mark of masculinity. While the use of Yiddish and Hebrew words has a clear connection with Talmudic study, another linguistic difference in this community has a more subtle connection. In common North American English, the final /t/ in a word like *that* is not released when it is followed by a pause as in "I didn't say that" – the tongue stays closed against the teeth. It is common practice in the Orthodox Jewish community, however, to release this /t/ – to pull the tongue away, emitting a small audible burst of air. Benor found that within the Orthodox community, men release /t/ more than women, and boys release it more than girls. Furthermore, she found that this pronunciation occurs particularly when the speakers are making authoritative statements. In other words, released /t/, like Yiddish and Hebrew borrowings, is associated with Talmudic study and knowledge, and as a result is an index of gender as well. We will return to this particular variable in chapter nine.

Whose speech is more standard?

As these examples show, the relation between gender and linguistic varieties is directly related to local history and conditions. And given differences in these histories and conditions, generalizations about the relation between gender and the use of standard or vernacular features will be highly problematic. Nonetheless, such generalizations abound in the sociolinguistic literature. In the face of conflicting evidence, it is commonly claimed that women's speech is regularly more standard than men's – a claim that Deborah Cameron (1998a) has held up as a prime example of the hall of mirrors.

Let us consider how we interpret statistics. If a comparison of a large heterogeneous sample of the speech of women and of men shows women's use of grammar to be more standard, we might seem to be justified in saying that women's grammar is more standard than men's. This is the pattern that indeed has emerged in what comparisons there have been of grammatical patterns in western industrial culture. But appealing to a monolithic construct such as "being male" or "being female" skirts the issue of why the statistical pattern emerges. Rather than relating variability to social categories directly, interpreting them as "markers" of social address, therefore, we turn to the notion of *indirect indexing* of social categories.

Elinor Ochs (1991) has argued that linguistic behaviors are seldom associated directly with social categories such as class or gender. A linguistic choice can index a social category indirectly because its primary level of meaning is something that enters into the practices that construct that social category. So, for example, if it is considered refined to stick out one's little finger while drinking tea, and if women are more inclined than men to act refined, then more women will stick out their little fingers while drinking tea. The reason they do so will be not to show they're women, but to show they're refined. In chapter five, we noted the role of honorifics in constructing a feminine speaking position for Japanese women. Skillful use of the complex honorific system does not, however, directly mark a Japanese woman's femininity, but her refinement. Refinement in turn enters centrally into the construction of ideal Japanese femininity and thus honorific usage indirectly indexes femininity. But there are plenty of unrefined women in Japan, as elsewhere.

Once we view linguistic resources as indexing aspects of social practice that constitute social categories rather than the categories themselves, we are ready to consider that not all of the resources that indirectly index a particular category do so in the same way. For example, not all features that we consider standard are standard in the same way. The belief in a monolithic standard is what has led William Labov to designate as a paradox (1991, 2001) the fact that while women's grammar is more standard than men's, women tend to lead men in sound change (i.e., they use more of the vernacular variants that represent changes in progress), moving away from standard pronunciations faster than men. This constitutes a paradox only if we believe that nonstandard grammar and innovative pronunciations have the same social meaning.

We begin with the data on grammar. It is in fact clear that studies show women on the whole using more standard grammar than men. Walt Wolfram's study (1969) of the English of African Americans in Detroit compared the speech of women and men at four socioeconomic levels. Wolfram found a regular stratification of grammatical usage according to class – the higher the socioeconomic status the fewer AAVE grammatical features – and he found, within each social stratum, that women used fewer of these features than men. Thus women were less likely than men to use invariant *be* (*he be singing in the street*); absence of final /s/ on third singular verbs and possessive and plural nouns (*she run to school every morning, that's John dog, I went there five time*), and zero copula (*he bad*). The extreme stigmatization of these patterns is a testimony to racism in the US, and it is possible that the gender difference at all levels here is a reflection of the degree of social risk presented by their use. It is also possible that educational patterns and the gendering of occupations that puts women in the standard language market more than men have contributed to such strict gender differences in the African American speech.

The observation that women's grammar is statistically more standard than men's has given rise to a variety of explanations. Peter Trudgill (1972) has proposed that because they have been excluded from advancement in the employment marketplace, women have relied on symbolic capital for social advancement. He has also proposed that men are more likely to value nonstandard language because of its association with working-class masculinity. As we have already noted, Sankoff *et al.* (1989) have argued that women's employment opportunities tend more than men's to require standard language. Margaret Deuchar (1989) has argued that as the weaker participant in many interactions, women must be attending to the face of their interlocutors. Using standard language, she argues, allows a woman to elevate her own status while showing respect for her interlocutor, thus constituting a safe strategy. Chambers (1995) has argued that women's greater use of the standard is a result of their greater inherent linguistic skill (another hall of mirrors).

Some of these explanations undoubtedly have some force. But the relation between grammar and refinement and obedience, which has been little discussed, is also undoubtedly very salient. The fact that grammar attracts overt attention in the family and in school makes it an object of discipline. Using nonstandard grammar in school is not only considered uneducated, it is considered rebellious. Indeed, in some circles, "bad grammar" merges with other kinds of "bad language." Inasmuch as rebelliousness is tolerated and even valued in boys, but not in girls, one might expect that the same would apply to nonstandard grammar. In that case, one might speculate that women and girls will be more circumspect in their use of grammar while making free with their phonology. We might ask, then, whether rebellious girls use nonstandard grammar more than nonrebellious girls, and whether they use it as much as rebellious boys.

Data from Belten High suggest that indeed they do. The reader will recall from earlier in this chapter that burnouts use overwhelmingly

Table 8.2. *Percent negative concord among jocks, burnouts, and burned-out burnout girls.*

jock girls	jock boys	burned-out burnout girls	other burnout girls	burnout boys
2	19	50	40	45

more nonstandard negatives than jocks. However, this class/category difference is far greater among the girls than among the boys. Among the jocks, there is only one girl who uses any nonstandard negatives at all, while almost all of the burnout girls use at least some nonstandard negatives, and some use them almost exclusively. And as Table 8.2 shows, although there is a considerable difference between boys and girls among the jocks, there is almost no difference among the burnouts. It is apparent that the jock girls are using super-standard grammar, and that the burnout girls are speaking with the same grammatical standard as the burnout boys. But in addition, while the burnout girls and boys use nonstandard negatives at about the same rate, by far the greatest users of these forms are a group of burnout girls who pride themselves on their wild lifestyle and who are commonly referred to as the "burned-out burnouts." As shown in Table 8.2, these girls use more negative concord than any other speakers in the school, male or female.

Edina Eisikovits (1987), in a study of adolescents in Australia, found a clear gender difference in the use of grammar in encounters with authority. Comparing kids' use of nonstandard linguistic features in conversation among themselves and in conversations with her, she found that while the girls' speech became more standard when speaking with her, the boys' became less standard. She interpreted the boys' behavior as an active rejection of her institutional linguistic authority. While the precise dynamics remain unclear, there is little question that the boys were showing some linguistic defiance, whether to Eisikovits as an authoritative adult or as an authoritative female adult. Either way, it is the act of defiance that is meaningful. The crucial fact is that the boys' linguistic behavior corresponds to the generally greater expectation and tolerance for boys to flout authority.

The relation between nonstandard language and toughness and defiance shows up also in bilingual situations. The linguistic situation in the Spanish region of Catalonia is a particularly interesting one. While Castilian is the standard language of Spain, Catalan (a variety much like that spoken in Soulan) is the regional variety of Spain's wealthiest region. Because of their economic power, the Catalonians have been able to give Catalan official status in the region, and Catalan has its own considerable prestige. People moving to Barcelona from poorer regions of Spain in search of employment are expected to learn Catalan, and their children are expected to learn Catalan in school. For many of them, Catalan is the language of wealthy employers, and associated with institutional authority. In an ethnographic study of adolescents in Barcelona, Joan Pujolar i Cos (1997) found that teenagers whose families had come to Barcelona from Andalusia associated Catalan with institutional authority (particularly the school), and associated the native Andalusian variety of their parents with machismo and an anti-institutional stance. Pujolar i Cos makes the important observation that the meaning associated with a language variety depends on one's particular experience with it.

This pattern of working-class defiance is not limited to adolescents. Almost all of the evidence that women's grammar is more standard is based on studies that group socioeconomic classes (Wolfram's study, discussed above, is an exception). But in other cases in which the classes are separated out, the picture corresponds to the facts found in Belten High. Labov's data on negation in Philadelphia (2001, p. 265) shows the greatest gender difference in the upper middle class, where men clearly lead women in the use of nonstandard negative concord. But as shown in Figure 8.2, this difference continues as we move downward in

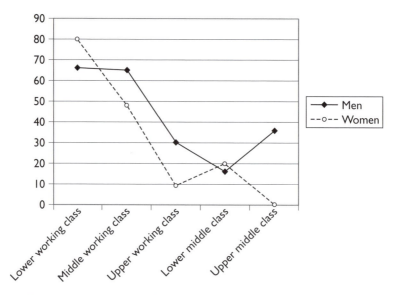

8.2 Percent negative concord in Philadelphia by class and gender (casual speech) (from Labov 2001, p. 265)

the socioeconomic hierarchy, until we reach the lower working class. There, we find that women in fact lead men in the use of negative concord.

If we consider phonological variation, we get an interesting and mixed picture. Some phonological variables are common to many dialects, and are considered to be stable (that is, not to be changes in progress – see Labov 2001). Others are more clearly the product of the progress of changes yielding regional differentiation. These groups of variables show somewhat different patterns. Two well-studied stable phonological variables show patterns similar to negative concord. One is the alternation between the standard interdental fricative dental sounds [θ] and [ð] and the dental stops [t] and [d], as in the pronunciations *ting* and *dis* for *thing* and *this*. The other is the alternation between *-ing* and *-in* (as in *walkin'* and *talkin'*).

The stop variants of /θ/ and /ð/ appear to occur more in urban areas, and to be associated with immigrant groups (e.g. Italians in Chicago and New York, Poles in Detroit, Chicanos in California). No doubt originally arising from native language interference (Italian, Polish, and Mexican Spanish do not have such dental fricatives), these variants have now been adopted into native English as a social resource. In two unpublished studies, one by Walter Edwards in a Polish neighborhood of Detroit and one by Penny Eckert in an Italian neighborhood in Chicago, the use of these variants was greatest among those who were the most integrated into the ethnic community. In his studies of both New York City (1966) and Philadelphia (2001), William Labov found these two variables to be used more at the lower end of the socioeconomic hierarchy and more by males than females. North American speakers of English associate these variants unequivocally with urban toughness, and it is probable that the class/gender pattern that links this variable to negation arises from a similar social meaning. While the New York data do not separate out socioeconomic class, the Philadelphia data do (Labov 2001, p. 265). The Philadelphia data (see Figure 8.3) show the same crossover effect as in the case of negative concord, with men leading in the nonstandard form at the top of the socioeconomic hierarchy, and women leading at the bottom.

Throughout the English-speaking world, the reduction of *-ing*, as in *walkin'*, *talkin'*, *fishin'*, is associated with informality, casualness, or insouciance. John Fischer (1958) carried out a study on the reduction of *-ing* among New England school children. He found that boys used more reduction than girls, that the more rough and tumble boys used more than "model" boys (i.e., teacher's pets), and that boys and girls both used more reduction among themselves than in interviews with

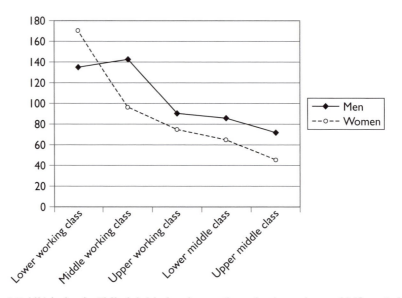

8.3 (dh) index in Philadelphia by class and gender (casual speech) (from Labov 2001, p. 265)

an adult. Unfortunately, Fischer did not distinguish the bad girls from the good girls. Studies of New York in the US and Norwich in England (Labov 1966, Trudgill 1974) show this variable to be stratified by gender (with women overall showing less reduction) and class (with increased reduction at the lower end of the socioeconomic hierarchy). Labov's Philadelphia data (2001, p. 265), which separate gender and class, however, show social stratification of this variable only among women, with a substantial male lead in the upper middle class, dwindling down to virtually no gender difference at the lower end of the socioeconomic hierarchy (see Figure 8.4). It should be clear to any English speaker that this variable has a somewhat different significance from negative concord or the fortition of /θ/ and /ð/.

The patterning of these variables can tell us something about the interaction between gender and class. As we mentioned earlier in this chapter, women in general are expected to be more refined than men. However, this can be exaggerated. Inasmuch as refinement is associated with elites, and contrasts with physicality and a practical approach to life, it runs counter to many of the values of working-class women as well as men. Trudgill has argued that men in general value working-class masculinity for its toughness, but this toughness is not just the property of men. Working-class women take pride as well in being able to take care of themselves and to cope with a difficult environment. Thus, it stands to reason that at the lower end of the socioeconomic

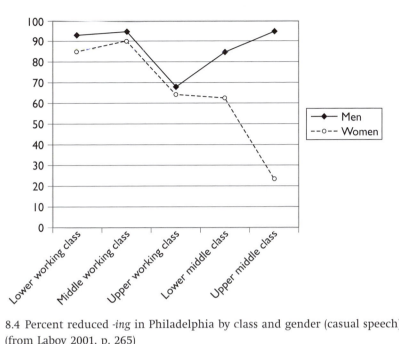

8.4 Percent reduced *-ing* in Philadelphia by class and gender (casual speech)
(from Labov 2001, p. 265)

hierarchy, we will find women who rival men in toughness and in the
use of vernacular features.

But the use of linguistic variants associated with the local market is
certainly not restricted to the rough 'n' tough. It is also associated with
a more general construction of locally based authority. While refinement is an expectation for women in the middle class, moral authority
seems to be more important in the working class. Susan Harding's discussion (1975) of women's role in the Spanish peasant village of Oroel,
which we mentioned in our discussion of gossip in chapter three, emphasizes the construction of moral authority in women's verbal interaction. This is also an important aspect of conversation among Soulatan
women, who emphasize women's role in maintaining the local order.
This is illustrated by a story told by one woman of an occasion on
which the women of a nearby village punished a local man who had
been sexually harassing a young woman. At the instigation of the older
women, the young woman in question made an assignation with this
man in a meadow. When he arrived in the meadow, the older women
of the village jumped out from behind a bush, undressed him, plucked
all his pubic hairs and sent him back to the village naked. One would
certainly not say that this is a story of refinement, but it is a story
of the exercise of fierce moral authority. The woman who told this
story was in fact a prominent figure in the village, one feared and

admired by the entire population. And she was one of the people in the village who proudly used Soulatan regularly in public as well as private situations. Her moral authority included a defiance of outsiders (monolingual French speakers) who might denigrate the local variety.

In a study of a Welsh mining village, Beth Thomas (1988) found that a distinctive feature of local Welsh (the use of [ɛː] where other dialects of Welsh have [aː]) was only used by women over fifty, all other residents having assimilated their pronunciation to the more widespread dialect. Thomas attributed this maintenance of the conservative pronunciation to the fact that these women are the only group in the community who continue to base their lives locally – most particularly around church. She attributed their use of the local feature to the tightness of their network, following Lesley Milroy's claim (1980) that the use of local variables is directly associated to the density and multiplexity of one's social network. While the nature of their network is clearly important, it may be an abstract fact that reflects their status and orientation as a local force. These women's language may well be part of their construction of strong claims to local authority.

In addition to these stable phonological variables, the vast majority of phonological variables that have been studied have been regional variables and viewed as changes in progress. When we consider phonological variables that are clearly changes in progress, any male lead disappears altogether. These variables stratify by class, with innovation appearing to originate in the working class, and move outward; and in a vast number of phonological changes, women simply lead men in innovation. In other cases, there is a crossover similar to that found for negation and for the fortition of /θ/ and /ð/. In the crossover cases, women at the upper end of the hierarchy lag behind their male peers in the sound change, while women at the lower end of the hierarchy lead. This is illustrated by a particularly dramatic example in Figure 8.5,[6] showing the raising of the nucleus of /ay/ among jocks and burnouts in Belten High.

This change is fairly new in the Detroit area, and is somewhat similar to the variable that Labov studied in Martha's Vineyard. The tendency to pronounce *fight* as [foyt] and *right* as [royt] is strongest at the urban end of the Detroit suburban area, and correspondingly among burnouts. But as Figure 8.5 shows, the biggest jock–burnout difference in Belten

---

6 The numbers on the y axis represent the output of Goldvarb, a linear regression program for the measure of constraints on linguistic variability. The input value is the overall average rate of rhotacization (i.e., about 70%) for all of the speakers. The numbers represent the degree to which each group of speakers show more (if the value is over .500) or less (if the value is under .500) than the input value.

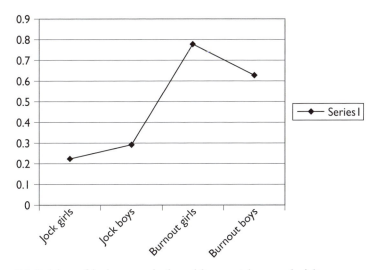

8.5 Raising of /ay/ among jock and burnout boys and girls

High is among the girls – the girls' pronunciation of this vowel creates the envelope within which the male burnouts and jocks distinguish themselves.

Figure 8.6, adapted from Labov (2001, p. 298), shows a change in progress in Philadelphia. This figure shows the raising of /æ/ before s (e.g. *class*) according to a hierarchy of occupational categories, ranging from unskilled laborers to professionals. The major gender differences occur at each end of the occupational hierarchy, with men using fewer standard forms than women at the upper end and more standard forms at the lower end. In these cases, while there is no overall relation between standardness and gender, there is an overall relation between gender and the steepness of the class correlation: the socioeconomic difference is greater among women than among men.

What explains the different gender patterns among sociolinguistic variables? We are inclined to think that the differences reflect differences in the nature of the variables themselves – and in the communities being studied. Some variables have overt social meaning, in which the vernacular form is highly stigmatized in the standard language market. In these cases, it is those who are most willing to defy the norms of this market who will accentuate the use of the vernacular. Others, like *-ing*, are not so clearly stigmatized, but convey a more specific meaning – in this case, something like casualness. And one's willingness to use this will depend on one's eagerness to convey a casual persona. On the other hand, while saying *dis* and *dat* for *this* and *that* may sound casual, it is also emphatic. And in the ethnic communities in which it is used most commonly, it is no doubt associated

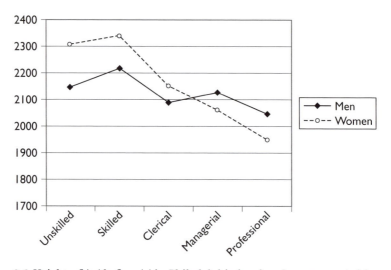

8.6 Height of /æ/ before /s/ in Philadelphia by class (as represented by occupational group) and gender (from Labov 2001, p. 298)

with certain kinds of personae. Are these personae equally available to women and men? To middle-class women and working-class women?

Untangling the gender question in variation is far more complex than figuring out who's more standard than whom. There are doubtless many layers of explanation, but those layers are all related to the relation between variables and the personae that they contribute to. We observed in chapter one that it is men and boys who are the primary keepers of the gender order, and Miriam Meyerhoff (1996) has emphasized that social psychological research has shown that gender is in many ways more salient to men than to women. According to Meyerhoff, while one might expect men to be differentiating themselves from women in their speech, women are more likely to be focused on other aspects of social identity. One might want to explain these patterns, then, by saying that women are using language more to construct social differences among themselves while men are avoiding extreme usages (perhaps such usages might seem flamboyant). This would certainly explain a good deal of the data we have discussed in this chapter (as well, perhaps, as the fact that it is generally male linguists who insist that linguistic variables mark gender directly). Further, as we discussed in chapter one, girls and women are far less constrained about crossing gender boundaries than boys and men. So that although the vernacular might seem to be masculine linguistic terrain, there are fewer constraints against a working-class woman stepping boldly onto that terrain, leaving girls and women freer to make full use of all linguistic resources, while boys and men stay carefully within fairly conservative bounds. But if this is so, it is culturally specific, for it is quite directly contradicted by some of the non-US studies we have discussed. As Jack Sidnell has pointed out (1999), this interpretation assumes the freedom to cross boundaries, and as he and Jane Hill have shown, women in some communities are constrained to avoid making "inappropriate" linguistic claims. In both of these cases, it is the men who are in a position to make flamboyant use of linguistic resources, and women who stay carefully within fairly conservative bounds. The quite direct opposition of these two sets of data is similar to the attribution of politeness and indirection to women in European cultures and to men in Madagascar (Keenan 1974).

These cross-cultural considerations make it clear that the relation between gender and the use of varieties depends on a wide range of local practices, and ultimately will come down to the nature of the claims that different categories of people are entitled to make through the use of language. The issue of entitlement is quite central to the gender issue. In the halls of academe or government, one is more likely to find men projecting a folksy demeanor than women. This is no doubt because women are more easily disqualified in the professional marketplace, and cannot afford to muddy the waters by talkin' about huntin' and fishin' or, heaven forbid, quiltin'. They can't afford to seem too casual – they need to show that they know the rules. Men, on the other hand, can show their entitlement by flaunting the rules. By a similar token, men in these venues are more likely than women to use nonstandard grammar for effect. If in doing so they evoke toughness or down-homeness, they evoke something that is favorably evaluated in men and can add these qualities to the other qualities that presumably got them into the halls of power. But toughness and down-homeness are more likely to detract from a woman's persona in the same halls. Geneva Smitherman (1995) argues that it is precisely this imbalance that gave Clarence Thomas the rhetorical edge over Anita Hill in the congressional hearings on her allegations of sexual harassment. Thomas was able to make himself appear more sympathetic by calling upon African American rhetorical strategies – strategies that might well have disqualified Hill as a professional whose claims could be trusted. Women in institutional positions of authority generally enhance their images by appearing more educated, more meticulous, more ethical, more serious. But adopting this strategy lost Hill support, especially among African American women, many of whom saw her as "stuck-up."[7]

7 See n. 1, ch. 6.

What's missing in our study of linguistic varieties is the textured view of speakers' lives. The claims that people make with language are not simply claims about class or about jobs; they are claims about who they are more broadly. People use language to construct whole personae – to lay claim to a place in the social landscape, to make social meaning of themselves. They struggle to bring together – or to keep apart – the personae that they can construct in their different communities of practice. And these personae embody gender, along with class, race, and every other thing that is significant to selves in a particular time and place. This work of construction requires all of the linguistic resources that we have discussed in this book so far – and more. And this work of construction is what we will turn to in chapter nine.

CHAPTER 9

Fashioning selves

Throughout this book, we have been emphasizing that gender is not part of one's essence, what one is, but an achievement, what one does. Gender is a set of practices through which people construct and claim identities, not simply a system for categorizing people. And gender practices are not only about establishing identities but also about managing social relations.

All of the linguistic practices we have discussed in the previous chapters can be thought of as constituting a conventional toolbox for constructing gender identities and relations. We have outlined the range of choices a speaker has at the moment of any utterance, the kinds of constraints there are on those choices, and the possibilities of interpretation and reception once that utterance is launched into the discourse. One can look upon gender as a set of constraints that one embraces or simply accepts, that one struggles within, or that one struggles against. But these constraints are not set for all time, and it is people's day-to-day actions that make them change. And as the constraints change, so do the resources in the toolbox. Up until now, we have talked separately about different aspects of linguistic practice. In this, the final chapter, we will consider how people, working within the constraints imposed by a gender order and by the linguistic practices of their communities, assemble the various resources in this linguistic toolbox to fashion selves that they can live with. For it is in this process of fashioning that we bring about change. Each person uses the toolbox in their own way, mixing and matching linguistic resources such as lexical items, grammatical gender marking, syntactic constructions, metaphors, discourse markers, speech acts, intonation contours, segmental variables. And the toolbox also includes other communicative resources such as pregnant pauses, overlapping speech, rhythm and speed, tone of voice, gaze and posture, facial expression. Some of these uses may be automatic – the product of long-ingrained habit – some of them may be quite consciously strategic. The outcome is a communicative style, which combines with other components of style such as dress, ways of walking, hairdo, and so on to constitute the presentation of a persona, a self. This presentation may place the individual squarely within a well-known category, or it may constitute a claim to a somewhat novel identity. Communicative style is sometimes thought of as the external wrapping inside which the meaningful substance is found, the how it is said as distinct from what is said. But this picture is profoundly misleading. What and how are inextricably linked, and the styles people develop have as much to do with what they (typically) say and do as with how they say it. Elite young women in the American south being prepared for cotillions that present them to society are still receiving instruction on table manners, makeup, posture and carriage, and not only how to speak but what to speak about (avoid religion and politics, they are told). And although there isn't overt instruction in how to talk or what to say, members of men's varsity teams at elite universities often adopt a "locker-room" style that includes not only lots of profanity but also ways of talking disparagingly about women and about other men who don't measure up to certain norms of masculinity. Style combines what we do and how we do it. It is not a façade behind which the "real" self stands but it is the manifestation of a self we present to the world.

A person's style is not static – it emerges in social practice, and involves an ongoing history of stylistic moves. The first time a girl puts on eyeliner, the first time a boy adds some flair to his basketball toss may be momentous moves for them. Each time they repeat these moves, they become increasingly part of their style, part of a claimed persona. And a given individual may develop alternative styles, presenting different personae in different communities of practice. A male athlete who presents a somewhat misogynistic and homophobic persona to his teammates may present quite a different persona in the orchestra in which he also participates. In the earlier chapters, we spoke of moves primarily with respect to advancing personal agendas as relationships unfolded. Here we will focus on stylistic moves, which are indeed made with respect to our personal agendas and relationships, but which also carve out new social possibilities for the kinds of personae that we present, and for the kinds of personae that can inhabit our communities.

Stylistic practice

Our place in the gender order constrains our acts, but at the same time it is our acts (and those of others) that place us in the gender order and that bring the different aspects of gender into being. While social structure and available resources provide constraints, it is people who decide just how constrained they will allow themselves to be. And these decisions are not made simply with reference to gender, but with reference to all the other aspects of our being that interact – often unknown to us – with gender. For example, the prescriptive norm against females' use of profanity is constantly invoked, often obeyed, but at least as often "broken." And when it is broken, a rebuke may take the form of a gender-based admonishment, such as "that's not ladylike!" But the decision to use profanity is more likely to be on the level of whether one wants to be "nice" or not, whether one is sufficiently provoked, or whether one wants to be cool, modern, in-your-face, etc. Furthermore, the decision is not necessarily made at the level of "shall I start using lots of profanity?" – but interaction by interaction, in a particular situation, as one decides at that moment to use some profanity. And with each choice to swear or not to swear, the next choice is weighted by one's experience with the previous one – how was it received? How did one feel afterwards? Often, perhaps even usually, there is not the kind of self-conscious deliberation involved that the word *choice* seems to suggest, but the important point is that people speak in certain ways rather than others for reasons even though they may be unable to articulate those reasons. Over time patterns will emerge (and the decision process is likely to become more and more automatic), and the use (or nonuse) of profanity in certain situations becomes part of a person's *style*.

Such decisions are not made in a vacuum, but always with reference to, and collaboratively within, our communities of practice. The early adolescent girl who starts inserting profanity into her discourse does so with respect to those she interacts with. She may be showing autonomy from her teachers or other adults who are the main norm enforcers for her age group, or perhaps distinguishing herself from her more "goody-goody" peers. Or she may be showing affiliation with her mother who swears, or her friends who swear. She may see swearing as grown-up, as rebellious, as assertive, as angry, as autonomous, as roustabout, or as a combination of these and other things. Maybe she and her friends are beginning to fashion themselves as tough or maybe she is pulling away from her friends and moving towards some tougher people. Whatever the local dynamics, she is modifying her persona, however slightly, and placing herself slightly differently with respect to her communities of practice and the rest of the world. And depending on what those modifications are, she may or may not be changing other things about herself – possibly other parts of her language use. For example if she is trying to get rebellious or tough, she may be using more nonstandard grammar as well. She may be adopting threatening tags, or uttering threats. She may be changing the way she dresses, the way she moves, the places she hangs out, the way she does her hair, the things she talks about. In other words, she is changing her *style*. And the style she develops may be exactly like some existing style, or it may be slightly different. She may add her own twist. As she does this, she is not just making a personal move, but changing the balance of social meaning in her communities of practice, and ultimately in her school and so on. One more girl who swears is one more drop in the gender bucket, and one little modification of style puts a slightly new meaning out into the discourse. Thus what is a momentary interactional move for one girl can become part of a more long-term stylistic move. And this, in turn, makes a slight change in the stylistic landscape that this individual girl participates in. And enough similar stylistic moves will carry potential for societal change as girls are more inclined to use pro-fanity, and as they carry their profanity into adulthood. Perhaps with greater use the profanity will lose some of its power; but at the same time, girls will move one step away from constraints of delicacy and niceness.

When we talk about style, we are talking about a process that con-nects combinations of elements of behavior with social meaning. If a girl takes up swearing, the swearing itself does not constitute a style, but it combines with all the other things she does to constitute a style. Depending on the resources she combines with her swearing, she may project a style that's slutty or tough, quirky, preppy but "different," free-thinking intellectual, etc. The reader might stop to think about how combinations of grammar, lexicon, intonation, voice quality, segmen-tal phonology, discourse markers and speech act types – for example – would combine with swearing to constitute quite different personae. It is these personae, whole stylistic packages, that change social meaning and reconfigure the social landscape, not the swearing by itself.

People are continually engaging in stylistic practice. Every act is by definition a stylistic act, and our continual invention of ourselves is a continual stylistic enterprise. Dick Hebdige (1984) presents style as a process of *bricolage*. People take already available elements and com-bine them to make something new. Our understanding of the social world is based in, and facilitated by, a stylistic landscape. We recognize landmarks in that landscape such as *Valley Girl*, *Orthodox Jewish Male*, *Suit*, *Teeny-Bopper*, *Zoot Suiter*, *Sloanie*, *Flapper*, *Punk*, *Hood*, *Cholo*. Some of these are located regionally, all are located socially, and all are located in time. All of them invoke some place in social-stylistic time-space, and all of them are composed of many elements. It is the multiplicity of elements that allows for variation among different people orienting, self-consciously or not, towards a common stylistic landmark. And as we will see, the multiplicity of elements also makes it possible to populate the stylistic landscape with socially significant new configurations, producing new landmarks. In chapter eight, we discussed the shift from Hungarian to German in Oberwart, Austria, and young women's move away from the peasant lifestyle. Hungarian and German were stylistic resources for these women – and each language choice went no doubt with a way of dressing, of behaving, of doing their hair. The choice was not simply between speaking in Hungarian and speaking in German, but between being rural women and being townies.

The difference in use of linguistic variables by jocks and burnouts, as discussed in chapter eight, is only a small part of the stylistic work that goes into the creation of difference between the two mutually opposed categories. Jocks and burnouts have distinct territories – the jocks hang out at lunchtime in the cafeteria hall, where they sell tickets to events and hold sales of various sorts, while the burnouts hang out in the school smoking area. They wear different clothing. In the early eighties when this study was done, the jocks wore preppy clothes in pastel colors with straight-legged jeans, while the burnouts wore dark colors, rock concert tee shirts and bell-bottom jeans. They had different hairstyles – the burnouts (male and female alike) had long hair, and the girls wore their hair straight; the jock boys and some of the jock girls had short hair, while the jock girls with long hair wore it in a "feathered" style. The girls wore different makeup – the jocks wore pastel colors, while the burnouts wore dark eye makeup. The burnouts flaunted the use of controlled substances (particularly cigarettes) while the jocks participated in antismoking activities in the school. The burnouts wore urban symbols such as wallet chains and Detroit or auto plant jackets, while jocks wore school symbols such as varsity and school jackets and sweaters. They listened to different music, went to different places, did different things. The symbolic differences were endless, and almost every component of these two styles was viewed as directly related to the core meaning of being a jock or a burnout. And each side viewing the other interpreted the display of any element of the other's style as a direct expression of that core. These two communities of practice, defining the social extremes of the school, represented stylistic landmarks for the rest of the school. (This is not to say that the jocks and the burnouts were the source of stylistic elements, but that their use of these elements lent prominence and visibility to them.) The many people who considered themselves "in-between" often mixed elements from jock and burnout style to indicate exactly where in the continuum between the two poles they placed themselves. One symbol in particular – the width of jeans legs – was especially iconic. The wider the bell, the more burned-out a message the wearer sent.

A similar iconicity was visible in the makeup worn by the Chicana gang girls that Norma Mendoza-Denton (1996) studied. One crucial feature of the gang look was long eyeliner, which is taken to signal the intention and willingness to fight. This kind of symbolism reaches into action, since a girl with long eyeliner is not only expected to be tougher – she is more likely to be called on to fight. As one girl put it: "When I wear my eyeliner, me siento mas macha (I feel more macha), I'm ready to fight." Mendoza-Denton (forthcoming) emphasizes the combination of such things as hair, lipstick, eyeliner, and clothing in creating a "look" – and the combination of this look with an interactive style – as described by one gang girl:

> Think about all the shit.
> You're hard.
> Nobody could fuck with you,
> you got power.
> People look at you,
> but nobody fucks with you.
> So when you walk down the street,
> you got the special walk, [begins to walk deliberately,
>   swinging her upper body]
> you walk like this,
> you walk all slow,
> just checking it out.
> I look like a dude, ¿que no? ('don't I?')
> I walk, and then I stop.
> I go like this [tilts head back – this is called looking "in"]
> I always look in, I always look in,
> I never look down.
> It's all about power.
> You never fucking smile.
> Fucking never smile.
> We never wear earrings,
> just in case we get in a fight.
> It's not our style to wear earrings, ¿me entiendes? ('you know?')
> Don't ever smile.
> That's the weak spot.
> Don't ever smile.

While the style does its work as a whole, its meaning draws on the meanings of its elements. And it is in the creative use of these elements that we modify old styles, and create new ones. An example of this process was described by two white high-school girls in northern California in 1985 (Eckert 2000, p. 214). These two best friends were part of a preppy crowd in their school, but they prided themselves on being a little more open-minded and daring, a little less willing to be dominated by the "school thing" than their friends. They symbolized this by modifying specific elements of their clothing to show a small similarity to another place in the local social landscape – the new-wave crowd in the high school, whom these two girls considered to be desirably independent, but a bit too far out. The prominent style then current among the new wavers featured black pegged pants. Clothing color is an important stylistic element in this school – indeed among adolescents in general, and adults as well. The dark eye makeup and clothing of the new wavers is quite commonly associated with "fast" sophistication, whereas the preppies' pastels are commonly associated with a clean-cut image. To adopt the dark colors of the new wavers would have been too strong a stylistic statement, because "nice girls" don't wear black. What these two girls adopted was the distinctive cut of the pegged pants: they pegged their blue jeans. They were able to articulate that this stylistic move placed them exactly where they wanted to be in the local social-stylistic map. And to the extent that these particular girls were moving a bit towards the "daring" new wavers, they were redefining what it means to be a preppy (and a new wave) girl and any other kind of girl (and non-girl). They were making a ripple in the landscape.

In such ways, people interpret the stylistic landscape and attribute meaning to stylistic elements by contrasting a variety of styles; and they build modifications and new styles through the creative segmentation, appropriation, and recombination of these elements. In the process, they make social meaning. This process is relatively apparent in clothing, but it also takes place in language, and linguistic styles are commonly part of larger styles that include clothing. In this way, people construct selves in a process that is deeply embedded in the social world, and this process of construction constructs the world itself. One person's stylistic move enters into the larger discourses of gender, race, ethnicity, class, age, body type, and so on. In theory, no stylistic move leaves anything unchanged. At the same time, no stylistic move comes out of nowhere. If convention is a resource in this activity, it is also a constraint, as the value of a stylistic move depends on its comprehensibility to others – just as a stylistic move must be creative, it must also be recognizable. Styles cannot start with all new material, but owe their success to the fact that they are based on elements that have been used before, over and over again. This is what Jacques Derrida (1991) refers to as *iterability*. The significance of pegged blue jeans relies on the already existing significance of jeans, of black clothing, of pegged pants. It also relies on the place of the preppy girls and the new wavers in the local social order – for much of the meaning of this move would be lost if it were made, for instance, by a stoner (the local equivalent of a burnout) or by a teacher.

Qing Zhang has illustrated the importance of the history of stylistic elements in their contribution to meaning. In chapter eight, we discussed Zhang's study (2001) of Beijing business managers, comparing the language of men and women in state-owned and foreign-owned businesses. In that discussion, we focused on the way in which men's and women's job trajectories affected their use of linguistic variables. Here we will return to Zhang's work, but with a slightly different emphasis. With China's entrance into the global capitalist market in recent years, there has emerged a new social category of young people working in foreign financial enterprises. These people, who are embracing a new level of materialism and consumption in a society that has been materially egalitarian for several generations, are commonly referred to as "Chinese yuppies." The conditions in which the yuppies work are radically different from those of their peers in traditional state-owned businesses. While the state-owned businesses emphasize functionality in both decor and dress, the yuppies' business headquarters are elegant, and the yuppies are expected to display a similar kind of global elegance on their persons. Thanks to considerable salaries, the yuppies pursue an elegant cosmopolitan lifestyle, introducing a completely new way of life to the mainland. Along with the rest of their style, which includes clothing, home decor, electronics, and leisure activities, their language is changing to conform to their global personae. Specifically, the yuppies are moving away from features that are typical of Beijing speech, developing a more "cosmopolitan" speech style in contrast with the quite local Beijing style of managers in state-owned businesses. In constructing new styles, the yuppies draw on age-old and almost mythical types that can be found in literature as well as in everyday parlance. One of these types is a classic Beijing male, the "smooth talker" – a survivor, a glib character who can talk anybody into anything. Beijingers commonly associate with this style a phonological variable that is characteristic of the Beijing dialect of Mandarin. This variable, a rhotacization of intervocalic fricatives and of syllable-final vowels, amounts to putting an /r/ at the end of the syllable – a sound that Beijingers hear

Table 9.1. *Use of Beijing rhotacization (input = .699, p = .000)*

Female yuppies	Male yuppies	Female state managers	Male state managers
.105	.457	.737	.699

as giving a kind of rolling, "smooth" quality to speech. As shown in Table 9.1,[1] Zhang found that this feature is common in the speech of both men and women in the state-owned business, that male yuppies retain this local feature in their speech to some extent, and that female yuppies avoid it. As we can see, the female yuppies' speech is not entirely devoid of rhotacization, but almost. The male yuppies' moderate use of rhotacization appears to yield a style that is "toned down," but that nevertheless carries some smooth-talker flavor.

Zhang argues that while the smooth-talker image may add to a high-flying businessman's image, it would be risky for a woman with global aspirations to try to make it in the same way. This brings us back to the fact that we cannot simply compare males and females in similar positions, since the two are constrained to perform very differently in those positions. A yuppie businesswoman may have to be smooth, but there is a certain trickiness and aggressiveness about a wheeling-and-dealing smooth talker that is still judged "inappropriate" in a woman.

Zhang also found that both male and female yuppies are adopting a tone feature from non-mainland dialects of Chinese as spoken in Hong Kong, Taiwan, and Singapore – the Chinese-speaking regions that dominate in the global market. In Beijing Chinese, unstressed syllables lose their distinctive tone, becoming "neutral," while in non-mainland dialects, the syllables are more stressed and retain their own tone. This tone feature gives the non-mainland dialects a staccato quality, and the adoption of this feature into Mainland Mandarin has a similar effect. While both male and female yuppies are using this tone feature, which is overwhelmingly associated with the global market, the women use it considerably more than the men. Zhang notes that the female yuppies in general sound more careful and articulate than the men, due primarily to their avoidance of rhotacization and a few other variables

1 The numbers in this table represent the output of Goldvarb, a linear regression program for the measure of constraints on linguistic variability. The input value is the overall average rate of rhotacization (i.e., about 70%) for all of the speakers. The numbers in the table itself represent the degree to which each group of speakers show more (if the value is over .500) or less (if the value is under .500) than the input value.

that contribute to this sound (and that show similar distributions) and their use of the non-mainland tone feature. This meticulous-sounding style, according to Zhang, enhances their overall image as competent businesswomen. Partially explaining women's care to construct a meticulous global speech style is the fact that men and women have very different career trajectories in the foreign financial sector, which impose different kinds of language use as they build careers. As we mentioned in chapter eight, the women served as part of the business's global symbolic capital, and presumably their desire to be recognized for their technical knowledge as well constrained them to use as global a variety as possible. Note that the Beijing yuppies' stylistic work is part of a major social change, as they made selective use of local and non-local features to construct particular gendered personae that moved them into a new social niche. And the effect of their use of these features built on the history of the features and the social types they had come to be associated with.

The history of a linguistic resource can be cross-linguistic as well. We mentioned above the importance of makeup to the Chicana gang girl style that Norma Mendoza-Denton has studied (forthcoming). A prominent linguistic resource that enters into this style is the pronunciation of /i/ as in *thing* – Chicano English includes a raised (i.e., higher in the mouth) pronunciation of this vowel that matches the Spanish pronunciation, as in *seep* rather than the English pronunciation as in *sip*. While this feature clearly emerged as a result of Spanish–English bilingualism, it is no longer a "foreign" feature, but an integral part of a native English dialect that indexes Chicano identity. Different groups of girls show quite different uses of this feature. Members of the two rival gangs, the Norteñas and the Sureñas, use the raised pronunciation 43 percent and 42 percent of the time respectively. Chicanas who are engaged in school, on the other hand – the jocks – use it only 18 percent of the time. But in addition, this feature is most pronounced when it appears in *and everything*. This is a common stylistic element in Chicana speech, and Mendoza-Denton argues that it serves to invoke in-group implications. For example in a gang girl's discussion of how girls from different gangs look at each other in order to pick a fight (Mendoza-Denton 1995, p. 120):

> Well I guess it depends on the person because one person will look at you *and everything*, but they'll kind of be scared at the same time. Cause they'll probably say, oh, look at her *and everything*, and if the girl turns back *and everything* they could either back down or back up, and go, "hey, what's on," you know? Then she can look at you up and down *and everything*, you know, go around you know?

Mendoza-Denton points out that in these uses, *and everything* refers to actions and scenarios that only an insider could fill in – one has to be familiar with gang confrontations to know what else happens besides saying "look at her," turning back, and looking someone up and down. Thus the vowel itself takes on increased symbolic value as it participates in a larger stylistic structure.

Stylistic resources can be appropriated from different genres as well. In an analysis of sports talk shows, Daniel Lefkowitz (1996) has shown how the hosts of these shows construct a hypermasculine style through the appropriation of the intonation patterns of play-by-play sports announcing. In play-by-play speech, announcers maintain high pitch during long stretches with only occasional – but dramatic – drops in pitch. Lefkowitz argues that this maintenance of high pitch in fast-paced talk conveys a quality of "liveness" – a quality that the male sports-show hosts achieve by the same means in their talk with callers.

Inasmuch as people feel that their way of speaking defines them, the development of linguistic style is a central part of identity work. Style is about creating distinctions (Irvine 2001), and how people talk expresses their affiliations with some and their distancing from others. It expresses their embrace of certain social practices and their rejection of others – their claim to membership (and to particular forms of membership) in certain communities of practice and not in others. And within communities of practice, the continual modification of common ways of speaking provides a touchstone for the process of construction of forms of group identity – of the meaning of belonging to a group (as a certain kind of member). Stylistic practice is a resource for the orientation of the community and its participants to other nearby communities and to the larger society, a resource for constructing community members' relation to power structures, locally and more globally.

Style and performativity

What we are referring to as stylistic practice is at the crux of gender performativity, a notion we discussed briefly in chapter four. Judith Butler argues (1990, p. 25) that gender is "constituting the identity it is purported to be. In this sense, gender is always a doing, though not a doing by a subject who might be said to preexist the deed...There is no gender identity behind the expressions of gender; that identity is performatively constituted by the very 'expressions' that are said to be its results." Butler is arguing against the notion of a "core" self, a "core" gender identity that produces one's gendered activities. Rather, Butler argues, it is those very activities that create the illusion of a core. And it is the predominance of certain kinds of performances that support the illusion that one's core is either "male" or "female." From a linguistic perspective, those expressions of gender are deployments of linguistic resources. The effect of any resource depends on the manner in which it is deployed – on the situation, and on the broader style within which it is embedded. This style involves both the other cooccurring stylistic elements and the history of the speaker's stylistic activity. Butler emphasizes the laying down of performances over time, and at the heart of this history is the combined history of individual speakers' performances. Here we emphasize the importance of viewing styles as set down over series of interactions.

The notion of a gendered core surfaces in much of the work on language and gender, as "habitual" behaviors are attributed to fundamental differences between male and female people. For example, as we have pointed out in earlier chapters, the view of men as hierarchical and competitive, and women as egalitarian and connection-seeking, dominates a good deal of thinking about gender and about language and gender (e.g. Tannen 1990, Trömmel-Plötz 1982). This allows analysts to make connections between speech moves and strategies on the one hand, and character and dispositions on the other. Thus, one observing a man being competitive in a particular situation may associate that demeanor with men's supposed greater general competitiveness, and then with their supposed hierarchical mode of viewing the world. But there is a great distance between a person's behavior in a given situation – or even a type of situation – and their more general character. There are also multiple strategies for competing, and for ensuring one's place in a hierarchy, and there are multiple reasons for competing in a given situation that may be unrelated to longer-term hierarchical aspirations.

Individuals or communities of practice may engage frequently, or habitually, in particular patterns of moves and activities, yielding a discursive style. It is at the level of style that people are judged friendly or mean, competitive or argumentative, pushy or passive. And the repeated engagement in those discursive strategies may connect the strategies to people as personal dispositions. If people are viewed as making regular complaint moves, or engaging regularly in complaint sessions, they may be viewed as complainers. If they engage regularly in one-up moves or one-up sessions, they may be viewed as competitive. If they engage regularly in disagreeing or in arguments, they may be seen as contentious. Note that these perceived strategies are situated.

So if someone engages regularly in complimenting they may be seen as polite or as suck-ups depending on the situated nature of their compliments – most specifically whom they compliment and about what. It is when these styles are associated with some overarching category – a gender category, or an ethnic category – that they take up residence in the social landscape. Categories of people get marked as aggressive, as complainers, as sycophantic, as competitive, as empathetic. And the moves associated with those styles are more quickly "recognized" in people known or believed to be members of those categories. And with each recognition, the category story is reinforced.

Consider, for example, the now famous claim that men are more reluctant than women to ask directions (Tannen 1990). The explanation offered is that men are more hierarchical than women, and asking directions would put them in a one-down position. There is no evidence that there is in fact such a difference in behavior. And one might well imagine a quite different gender story – that women are more reluctant than men to ask directions because it puts them in a potentially dangerous situation. Either way, once tossed into the gender ring, the gender story takes on a life of its own. Every occasion for asking directions becomes an occasion for gender commentary – if behavior follows the gender story, it is taken as confirmation; if it doesn't, there may be jokes about exceptions to the "rule" – or some may even worry that there's something wrong with them. Either way, it is the gender story that gets reproduced.

Although these views of language and gender are not essentialist in the sense of attributing these character types to biology, they do attribute the linguistic behavior to an underlying character type. A different perspective, however, might be to attribute character types to the regular engagement in particular types of performance. Consider, for example, the process of moving from childhood into adolescence. Much of gender development is experienced as simply getting older – as doing older things. And in doing older things one transforms oneself into someone older. In her elementary school ethnographic work, Penny noted that kids transformed themselves into adolescents through the gradual accumulation of adolescent acts. Consider Trudy, for instance, who is discussed at some length in Eckert (1998). Over the course of fifth and sixth grades in Hines Elementary, Trudy projected herself into the leading mover and shaker in her age cohort's heterosexual market. As the cohort moved into sixth grade, the boys in the heterosocial crowd took to playing football, and the girls replaced vigorous physical playground activity with observing, heckling, and occasionally disrupting boys' games, and with sitting or walking around in small and large groups. The practice of sitting or walking around, and talking, had in itself symbolic significance. Moving away from the crowd and walking around slowly, intensely engaged in conversation drew attention to those who did it, by contrasting with the fast movements of their peers, with play, with the larger groups engaged in games, and with the louder tone of children's talk. This walking, furthermore, was a visible occasion on which girls engaged in intense social affiliation activities, negotiating heterosexual pairings and realigning friendships.

Trudy was at the forefront of this activity. One day, as Penny walked out of the lunchroom onto the playground, Trudy and her friend Katya, who normally played Chinese jump-rope at recess, rushed over and invited her to come with them. Penny had been out of town for a week, and Katya informed her of a new development: "We don't always play at lunchtime anymore," she said. "Sometimes we just talk." She said "just talk" with a conspiratorial hunch of her shoulders, and widening of her eyes. She added, as if the two facts were connected, that Trudy had a boyfriend. Penny, Trudy, and Katya then went over to some picnic tables near where other girls were playing hopscotch and Chinese jump-rope. After sitting awkwardly on the tables for a bit, Trudy and Katya "talked." Once again, that conspiratorial look, a hesitation and a giggle, and Trudy whispered to Penny behind her hand that Carlos was her boyfriend. And that he had kissed her on the cheek. After a few brief comments about this, and a brief pause, Trudy straightened up and announced, "Now we can go play." And the two girls and Penny threw themselves into the game of hopscotch.

This conversation was a small move in the gradual construction of Trudy as the "fastest" girl in her class – as a leader in the heterosexual market and the wisest about teenage things. What made the conversation a socially significant *move* was not so much what was said, but the simple fact that they sat and talked. Little girls play; teenage girls talk. Moving across the playground to sit on the table, and engaging in talking, were visible moves witnessed by the rest of the cohort. And, of course, the credibility of these moves was enhanced by the general knowledge that Trudy had a boyfriend to talk about. "Talking" started out as the adoption of someone else's behavior – Trudy was "acting like" a teenager. But in doing so, she moved herself one more step towards being a teenager. When she returned to the hopscotch game, she was that much different from the girls who had started playing the minute they left the lunchroom. And she brought the change not only to her own persona, but to her cohort. There was a new distinction in the cohort, based on "talking." Both Trudy's place in the cohort and the cohort's definition of itself changed ever so slightly.

This day-to-day assumption of new behaviors mixes seamlessly with kid behaviors, and is experienced as whim – as a choice of options. One day, Trudy reached into her low-slung baggy jeans to show Penny her new sexy lace underpants, saying, "Yesterday I wore kid pants" (meaning cotton pants). She said this with a childlike giggle, but with the clear understanding that the wearing of these sexy underpants was intended as a move towards a sexy style. Over the following year, Trudy emerged as a stylistic icon: she had more boyfriends (serially) than anyone else, she was more overt in her relations with her boyfriends, she dressed with greater flair, she was sexier, tougher, louder, more outgoing, more innovatively dressed, and generally more outrageous than any of her peers. The highly prominent style that became Trudy's hallmark was simultaneously an individual and a group construction. The heterosexual crowd supported Trudy's activities, providing the social landscape, the visibility, and the participation necessary to make them meaningful. At the same time, Trudy made meaning for the crowd and for its members individually and severally, her actions drawing others into the adolescent world, taking risks in their name.

After school one day in sixth grade, a small group of girls fussed over Trudy, who was crying because her boyfriend had told someone that he didn't want to "be with" her anymore. The assembled group of admiring and sympathetic girls criticized the boyfriend. "That's what he always does," said Carol. Sherry said, "He just uses girls." Trudy sniffled, "I like him so: much." In her heartbreak, Trudy established herself as way ahead in the heterosexual world – as having feelings, knowledge, and daring as yet unknown to most of her peers. At the same time, she gave Carol and Sherry the opportunity to comfort her, to talk knowingly about her boyfriend's perfidy – to participate in the culture of heterosexuality. In this way, her flamboyance propelled Trudy and those who engaged with her into a new, older, sphere. But at what point did Trudy begin to feel the heartbreak? We would argue that her heartbreak did not simply begin in her heart and then manifest itself in speech. Engaging in the discourse of heartbreak also helped transform Trudy into a person capable of heartbreak.

Trudy and her friends knew the moves that it took to get from childhood to adolescence. The style that Trudy developed was built on a style already set out and well known – she had only to add her own twist. While some of the stylistic knowledge she built on was out in the media, her stylistic activity was locally based. Trudy's crowd was a local crowd, and the models she looked to were local models – older girls and women, older crowds, and the people they talked about. And the stylistic resources she learned locally set her and her friends apart from other crowds. Trudy's was a predominantly Latino crowd, and their particular style was quite distinct from that of, for example, the predominantly European American crowd in nearby Grant Elementary. While the norm among the Latinas of Hines Elementary was to develop attitude, the notable European American girls of Grant Elementary developed a somewhat childlike "cute" style for public displays. Trudy and her friends used a variety of features of Chicano English to heighten their style, while the girls in Grant Elementary delved into a more prototypically white California style. Girls' backroom machinations at Grant had their equivalent at Hines in up-front challenges and occasional fights. Both groups of girls were doing femininity, but they were doing different femininities.

Legitimate and illegitimate performances

What do people generally mean when they say that someone has "style"? It seems to mean that a person is good at manipulating resources to construct an impression. It usually indicates approval of the particular style as well. When we say that someone does something with style, we mean that they have some kind of *savoir-faire*. Style, in the end, is a display of the "right" knowledge. But there is always an implication that stylistic displays – although they may reflect someone's know-how – are somewhat superficial. Style can "hide" a person's "real self."

Similarly, the popular notion of performance commonly suggests a conflict with the "real" self. Actors perform personae other than their own, people "put on performances" in an attempt to affect others' views of who they are. A sense of prevarication pervades the term *performance*. In Butler's use of the term, the way in which we have been using it here, gender performances do not imply prevarication, which assumes a core self to be lying about.

We are not saying that people do not lie in their performances, or in the manipulation of style. Lying is a fundamental human ability: we do sometimes perform so as to mislead others, projecting personae that we do not identify with. It is not, however, just to deceive others that our acts might present a persona that we do not full-heartedly claim as our own. Many of our stylistic acts are aimed more at what we hope to become than at what we think we are. But it is through these stylistic acts that we have a chance of becoming what we hope to be. By the same token, we may present a persona we at some level dislike but that nonetheless on some occasions we want to display to others. In this case, repeated stylistic practice can transform us into someone we might have said we hoped not to be.[2] Most people have at least somewhat different multiple personae, different ways of acting in the world (and thinking about those actions) that they draw on. Often it is absurd to say that one of these selves is the "true" one, all the others false. Most people feel the tug of conflicting forces and motives for action, and shifting selves (even very slightly) is one way we deal with such conflicts.

Our belief in our own performances is fluid. As we noted in chapter one, emotional responses to situations are as much of our learned gender behavior as our walks and our grooming: girls learn to cry as much as boys learn not to. Yet down the line, these emotional responses become a fundamental part of ourselves. In saying that gender is performance, we are not saying that it is not real. We are saying, rather, that this personal reality comes not from within, but from our participation in the global performance that is the social order.

We notice performativity in cases when we believe that a person's linguistic behavior in some fairly dramatic way clashes with, or misrepresents, what we take to be their "core" selves. Thus the performance of a transgendering individual may be seen as not unlike a child enacting Superman, while the performative aspects of the new parent cooing at his or her baby, or of the corporate executive giving a powerful and confident presentation, are missed altogether. The reason is that the parent and the executive are engaged in legitimized performances of legitimized identities – that is, performances of conventional identities by the kinds of bodies that are recognized as legitimate possessors of those identities. And to the extent that they are conventional, the performers have considerable opportunity and support to engage in them.

As these examples suggest, the fact that most of our performances are of embodied selves places substantial constraints on the personae we can readily project. "Aha," some still skeptical readers might say, "bodies do matter," implying that this observation spells doom for the performative view of gender.[3] Of course bodies matter in everyday performances just as they do in the acting profession (where, for

2 Dorothy Parker makes this point vividly in "The Waltz," a 1933 short story that Paula Treichler (1981) discusses. "The Waltz" alternates the protagonist's "inner" and "outer" voices. We begin by thinking that the "inner" voice expresses her "real" self whereas the "outer" is pure sham, a style she has assumed just to hide the true self. By the end of the story, however, that neat dichotomy has been completely undermined. The story, only four pages long, is reprinted in Parker (1995); it eloquently shows the complexities of gender performativity.
3 It was such comments that prompted Judith Butler to write *Bodies That Matter*, her second book on gender performance. See Angier (1999) on women's bodies.

example, women in older bodies or in fat or disabled bodies find it rather difficult to land any roles at all, especially film roles). But our bodies are not just there. They are subjected to various socially imposed disciplines as well as other environmental vicissitudes (slaps and more extreme physical violence, sexual maturation, pregnancy and child-birth, nursing, aging, rape, weight-lifting, playing football, disease and accidents), and such matters make it much easier to fashion certain kinds of selves than others. New technologies change the force of bod-ily constraints on the selves we can fashion: babies can drink from bottles, eggs can be fertilized in test tubes, a fetus created with an egg from one woman can be embedded in another woman's uterus, people can take hormones and undergo surgical procedures to change their bodies to ones more characteristic of the other sex, fitness machin-ery and body-altering chemicals change athletic potential, hormone re-placement therapy is available for menopausal women, diet and other regimens affect the aging process, and so on. And of course informa-tion technologies in modern societies – reading and writing, film and video, phones and radios, the internet – supplement face-to-face en-counters not only in conveying possibilities for ordinary face-to-face performances but also in allowing for people to engage in (relatively) disembodied performances for audiences unable to judge the "legiti-macy" of those performances.

Kira Hall (1995) interviewed women who earn their money by engag-ing in paid verbal sexual encounters on the telephone. Their linguistic performances are a product that they develop and sell on the phone market.[4] They intentionally use elements of language to construct ver-bal styles that the men who call find sexually stimulating, varying the styles (i.e., performing quite different personae) depending on what their clients like or want. These are purely verbal performances, with the voice their only "bodily" sign. The phone sex workers engage in this activity because it pays well and gives them flexibility, and it allows them to do other things – such as washing the dishes – while they are engaged in their work. Some of them are also proud of their linguistic virtuosity and enjoy the creativity of the work. They almost certainly do not fit their clients' imaginings.

Many of the workers Hall interviewed are graduate students, the majority of them lesbians, and one man. Shielded from identification or physical contact by a call-back system, they do not have to deal with the apparent mismatch between the identities they claim for

4 Judith Irvine (1989) has argued that there are times when language products themselves are immediately exchangeable on the market – this is clearly one of them.

themselves outside of work and those they perform for their male
callers. People may find it odd, perhaps even titillating, that sexually
unengaged female phone sex workers should put together sexualized
performances of "other" females. But they are unlikely to find it
completely strange. Perhaps this is because an assumption that these
women do themselves sometimes engage in sex (with men)[5] leads to
the feeling that they are at some level doing "native" performances –
just displaced ones. Furthermore, people (particularly women) are
often encouraged to experiment and perform new sexual personae
for the pleasure of their partners. Aside from the fact that they
are not physically engaged, in what way are the phone workers'
performances different from those of the prostitute, or the girlfriend
or the wife, who feigns sexual arousal and satisfaction? But more
crucially, in what way are they different from those of male phone
sex workers who put together similar female performances for men
who call the fantasy lines? Or suppose the participants in a senior
citizen center were to raise money in a similar activity? Whether
women or men, the elderly are often assumed to be asexual. It is only
young (presumptively heterosexual) women who are authorized to do
"female" sexual performances. Any others answering the fantasy lines
would be people performing "unauthorized" performances.

Hall comments on how her male consultant, a 33-year-old Mexican
American bisexual whom she calls "Andy," performed his female roles:

> To convince callers of his womanhood, Andy style-shifts into a higher
> pitch, moving the phone away from his mouth so as to soften the
> perceived intensity of his voice. This discursive shifting characterized by
> the performance of the vocal and verbal garb associated with the other
> sex, might more appropriately be referred to as *cross-expressing*. (p. 202)

Both Andy and another of Hall's consultants noted the "dismay of
callers who for some reason came to suspect that the voice on the
telephone was not the beautiful young blonde it presented itself to be"
(p. 207). In support of their conjecture that many of the male callers
viewed their interactions with the operators as reality rather than fantasy, Hall offers a telling anecdote (n. 19, p. 213):

> [M]y next-door neighbor... told me about "all the sexy women" he had
> seen in the 900-number advertisement of *Penthouse*. When I later told him
> that all the women in my study [apparently she did not tell him that
> there was also a man] had been hired by voice alone and had never met

5 Or, perhaps, that they would if they could. So strong is the presumption of
heterosexuality that some people do not believe that lesbians lack desire for men in
any fundamental way but just that they have been rejected by men.

[and thus never been seen by] their employers, he responded in disbelief. "What? You mean it's all a scam?"

In a very different cultural context, Kira Hall has also explored "highly unauthorized performances" in the linguistic construction of the hijras, India's "third sex."[6] Hijras have a ritual place in India, where they are paid for dancing and singing at birth celebrations – an activity that is said to offer protection for the newborn. They are sometimes described as eunuchs and sometimes as hermaphrodites. Many hijras have had their genitals removed as part of their passage into the community; some have been born with ambiguous genitals. Although generally brought up as boys, they embrace an identity that is in many ways neither male nor female. Entering the hijra community involves a process of socialization by which the individual learns to dress and speak "like a woman" and to speak to other hijras as they would speak to women. In Hindi, the primary language being used by the hijras whom Hall studied, one thing this involves is using feminine gender agreement in self-reference and in addressing other members of the community.[7] But being a hijra is not about being a woman, so much as about living on the edge of the male–female dichotomy. The use of gendered forms of self-reference is one indication of this, as hijras tend to refer to themselves in the past tense in the masculine, and in the present tense in the feminine. By extension, feminine and masculine reference seem to signal something like in-group and out-group status. For example, Hall and O'Donovan (1996) give examples of hijras' use of masculine reference to signal anger at another hijra, to deny a hijra's appropriateness or legitimacy in the community, as well as simply to signal distance. The hijras constitute an extreme claim on the performativity of gender. In discussing Sulekha, one of the hijras, Hall and O'Donovan note (1996, p. 7) that "[i]n Sulekha's opinion, a speaker will be identified as a hijra precisely because of this versatility, her alternations of femininity and masculinity signaling to outsiders that she is allied with neither camp." This perspective is apparently not shared by all hijras, and indeed, given the number of hijras and the number of hijra communities across India, there is no doubt considerable diversity of gender ideology, with some hijras insisting on their unwavering claim to female gender.

6 Some of this work was done in collaboration with Veronica O'Donovan; see Hall and O'Donovan (1996) as well as Hall (1997).
7 See chapter two for general discussion of grammatical gender and chapter seven for mention of its potential as a resource for those offering nonlegitimated gender performances. With respect to grammatical gender, Hindi works almost exactly like French, the language we discuss in most detail in those passages.

Rudolf Gaudio (1996, 1997) studied the Hausa-speaking 'yan daudu, or "men who act like women" in Nigeria. Although many of them are husbands and fathers, the 'yan daudu live "as women" in certain ways – but in locations somewhat distant from where they live with their wives and children. They engage in "women's" activities – specifically cooking and serving food for a living – and in a variety of other feminine behaviors, including elements of linguistic style associated with women. Rhetorical skill is highly valued among the 'yan daudu, and is important capital for status within the community, for attracting "boyfriends," and for navigating the dangerous territory between their world and the straight world. The 'yan daudu pursue much of their joint lives in public places, and inasmuch as their gendered and sexual behavior is highly stigmatized in their Muslim culture, they are at considerable odds with the mainstream and at the same time need to protect themselves. Their verbal performances include the use of two "indirect" speech resources (Gaudio 1997), *karin magana* (proverbs) and *habaici* (innuendo, insinuation). The strategies for use of these resources are complex, and while *karin magana* is a valued strategy throughout the culture, *habaici* is generally stigmatized by its association with women. Through the association of in-group meanings with *karin magana* and *habaici*, the 'yan daudu are able to carry on in public in a relatively outrageous fashion, but protected by the ambiguity and indirection of the speech forms they use. They are exploiting the possibility of implying rather than explicitly saying in order to expand the scope of their options for presenting themselves in the world. Although *habaici* is associated with women, the 'yan daudu have given it their own quite distinctive twist.

One small step

It is precisely the laying down of dichotomous convention that determines which performances will be viewed as authentic, and which will not. While the hijras and the 'yan daudu illustrate this in a spectacular way, smaller claims make it clear that within a culture the dichotomy not only excludes other options, but restricts the range of variability that will be tolerated within the two authorized gender categories. The delicacy of gender performances is made particularly clear by the volume of self-help literature aimed at advising women how to produce credible verbal performances. Indeed, what are touted as the most legitimate performances are not left to unfold on their own. Deborah Cameron (1995, p 204) reminds us of an old feminist poster that said

"If being a woman is natural, stop telling me how to do it." Indeed, the media are full of advice for women, who apparently cannot cope with the most mundane situations without explicit instruction. When we were teenagers, the teen magazines told girls how to make conversation with boys – how to draw them out, make them feel smart, important, and in charge. Nowadays, there is a new emphasis on helping women and girls be assertive – to garner power in a man's world. The implication is that as women move into new arenas, they will need new verbal skills – that traditionally legitimated activities of woman in society have not called for authoritative speech behavior. Of course, women have often used authoritative linguistic forms – for example with children and, in the case of elite women, with servants. It is seldom linguistic skills that are really the issue, though getting used to deploying them in new contexts may be difficult, calling for assuming new personae. Even where those new personae do not meet overt resistance, as they often do, women can sometimes find it hard to present themselves as authoritative in unfamiliar contexts. But most successful women report more problems from the stumbling blocks erected by men who want to keep women out of their preserve than from their own lack of experience. Nonetheless there is a substantial industry that sets out to help women overcome their "deficiencies."

While writers and people running self-improvement workshops are getting rich telling women how to change, the real progress is being made "on the ground," as people expand the range of tolerance with small moves. Mary Bucholtz (1996) provides an example of a group of girls who use style to lay claim to a piece of male cultural territory. These girls were students at a northern California high school who wished to distance themselves from their peers' concerns with coolness, and from what they viewed as demeaning norms of femininity. These girls prided themselves on their intelligence and their freedom from peer-imposed constraints, and based their common practice in intellectual pursuits, and in the construction of a joint independent intellectual persona. They did well academically, but considered their intellectual achievement to be independent of the school, priding themselves in catching their teachers' errors. These girls lay claim to a female "geek" identity – an identity that is prototypically male. Their linguistic style was an important resource for the construction of their more general joint intellectual persona, and it involved a choice not unlike that made by the Beijing yuppies discussed above.

Living in northern California, their peers – particularly their "cool" peers – make high stylistic use of current California sound changes – the fronting of back vowels /u/ as in *dude* (pronounced [dɪwd] or

[dyd] – sounding more like the vowel commonly heard in *feud* than that in *food*), and /o/ as in *boat* (pronounced [bɛwt]). According to Bucholtz, these girls moved away from the "cool California" style by avoiding these pronunciations. On the other hand, they made use of an additional stylistic resource. We discussed the release of word-final /t/ as an American stylistic resource in chapter eight, as it is used among Orthodox Jews as a symbol of articulateness. These girls used the same variable, releasing /t/ at the ends of words regardless of what follows, as in *you nut* or *what's that?*, or *at a*. These girls also heightened the performance of articulateness by aspirating /t/ word medially between vowels. In American English, /t/ is generally pronounced the same as /d/ when it occurs between two vowels as in *butter*. In British English, on the other hand, it is generally released or aspirated: [bʌtʰ]. This aspirated pronunciation of /t/ served as an important stylistic resource for the geek girls' style. By aspirating many of their occurrences of /t/, they marked themselves as "articulate," in keeping with the American stereotype of the British and their speech. The geeks were quite consciously using conservative and prestige features of English to construct a distinctive style – not so much to claim social status within the adolescent cohort as to disassociate themselves from the adolescent status system altogether, and what they clearly saw as trivial adolescent concerns. In so doing, they were pushing the envelope, extending the range of possible "girl" styles beyond those currently available to them.

A more highly visible example of pushing the boundaries is in young Japanese women's departure from prototypical "women's language." "Women's language" is the subject of a vast sociolinguistic literature, and figures prominently in language pedagogy, as foreign men and women strive to achieve gender correctness in their new language. As we have discussed in previous chapters, Japanese women's language is not a distinct variety but mostly a way of using linguistic resources for signaling politeness, especially respect and deference. As we discussed in chapter five, there are two main kinds of resources involved: the elaborate system of honorifics that indicate how speakers are positioning themselves relative to other participants in a discourse and utterance-final particles that indicate the position the speaker is adopting towards what the rest of the utterance says. Although there are indeed gender differences to be found in the use of these forms, the resources are available to all speakers of Japanese and are used by both women and men. It is the public and academic discourse in which Japanese women's language is constructed that is in fact the most interesting thing about it.

The use of deferential language is symbolic of the Confucian ideal of the woman, which dominates conservative gender norms in Japan. This ideal presents a woman who withdraws quietly to the background, subordinating her life and needs to those of her family and its male head. She is a dutiful daughter, wife, and mother, master (or mistress?) of the domestic arts, gentle, mature, and self-possessed. The prototypical refined Japanese woman excels in modesty and delicacy, "treads softly in the world," elevating feminine beauty and grace to an art form.[8] As we observed in chapter eight, geisha were often taken to be experts in the feminine arts; in thinking about gender performance, it is interesting to note that young geisha were often sent to observe (male) kabuki actors to learn how best to perform femininity.

Nowadays, it is commonly observed that young women are not conforming to the feminine linguistic ideal. They are using fewer of the very deferential "women's" forms, it is said, and even using the few strong forms that are known as "men's." This, of course, attracts considerable attention and has led to an outcry in the Japanese media against the defeminization of women's language. Indeed, we didn't hear about "men's language" until people began to respond to girls' appropriation of forms normatively reserved for boys and men. There is considerable sentiment about the "corruption" of women's language–which of course is viewed as part and parcel of the loss of feminine ideals and morality – and this sentiment is crystallized by nation-wide opinion polls that are regularly carried out by the media (Inoue 2002, forthcoming).

As we mentioned in chapter five, Yoshiko Matsumoto has argued (2002) that young women probably never used as many of the highly deferential forms as older women. This highly polite style is no doubt something that young women have been expected to "grow into" – after all, it is a sign not simply of femininity, but of maturity and refinement, and its use could be taken to indicate a change in the nature of one's social relations as well. One might well imagine little girls using hyper-polite forms when playing house or imitating older women – in a fashion analogous to little girls' use of a high-pitched voice to do "teacher talk" or "mother talk" in role play (Anderson 1990).

---

8 The ideal Japanese woman has been extolled not only for her elegant acceptance of subordination, but for her beauty and grace, her physical and social delicacy – all of which appear to be separate from her domestic and subordinate role. This refinement is associated with breeding, carrying social value in the class hierarchy, and class differences are reflected in the degree to which women display these behaviors. The construction of femininity, therefore, is also part and parcel of the construction of the wider hierarchy within which women are subordinated not only to men, but to other women, and in which men are also subordinated to men.

The relation between development and style emerges in an interest-ing twist in Matsumoto's (1996) discussion of the portrayal of gender in the Japanese media. The Confucian ideal of the mature and self-effacing woman is now sharing the stage with a new "cute" femininity. Matsumoto illustrates this style with an ad for Kikkoman soy sauce, which features a pert gamine-ish housewife greeting her husband at the door asking him what he wants for dinner. In doing so, she does not use normative women's language, but in fact uses forms that are tra-ditionally labeled as "masculine." Yet, Matsumoto argues, her manner is anything but masculine; on the contrary, it is eminently feminine – and childlike. It is the language of someone who has not yet "learned" to use mature "women's language." This new feminine image contrasts with the mature and gentle femininity of the Confucian ideal, replac-ing it with a modern youthful playmate ideal. The two femininities are equally subservient, one by virtue of acceptance of the adult fe-male role, the other by virtue of acceptance of a perpetual child's role.

The fact that young Japanese women are using less deferential language is a sure sign of change – of social change and of linguistic change. But it is most certainly not a sign of the "masculinization" of girls. In some instances, it may be a sign that girls are making the same claim to authority as boys and men, but that is very different from saying that they are trying to be "masculine." The simplification of the styles involving honorifics and sentence-final particles to male and female choices obscures the more interesting use that people can be making of these forms. In the younger age group, there appears to be emerging a gendered cult of youth. Katsue Reynolds (1990) has argued that girls nowadays are using more assertive language strategies in order to be able to compete with boys in school and out. Social change also brings not simply different positions for women and girls, but different relations to life stages, and adolescent girls are participating in new subcultural forms. Thus what may, to an older speaker, seem like "masculine" speech may seem to an adolescent like "liberated" or "hip" speech.

The linguistic changes are not something that have simply washed over the younger generation; they are the result of girls' finding ways of constructing kinds of selves that were not available to earlier gener-ations. They are the result of social and linguistic strategies. In other words, this linguistic change is part of identity work – of finding new ways of being in the world – of creating new meanings for themselves. Young Japanese women who use stronger forms may be seen by some as speaking like men, and their motives may be attributed to their try-ing to be more "like men." From the perspective of practice, however, one needs to ask what kinds of meaning are being made with the use of these forms? How are girls constructing a new kind of self – a new female possibility – with these particular linguistic strategies? One might view this usage as a way of changing the category itself – as expanding possibilities for a girl. Perhaps she is affirming her right to be assertive. And perhaps she is not thinking of assertiveness so much as being "cool." Perhaps life stage is as salient to her as gender, and she is projecting a new adolescent image.

Laura Miller (1998, 2000) discusses an even more wild, in-your-face new Japanese urban femininity. The *Ko-Gal* is a current version of what the Japanese media have called the "Three Negatives Girl" – she doesn't work, doesn't get married, and doesn't bear children. Referring to them as "disturbers of the cultural peace," Miller describes the Ko-Gals as flamboyantly rejecting a variety of norms, interrupting discourses of racial purity (through, e.g., the appropriation of ethnic dress and in-tense use of tanning salons) as well as femininity. These Ko-Gals not only flout traditional feminine norms, but quite openly display their sexuality and their contempt for (horny and repressed) older men. The particular target of their contempt is the postwar *salaryman*, who toes the line in his company year after year, working long hours at a dull job for relatively little reward. Ko-Gals' language is as flamboyantly dif-ferent as the rest of their style, not only including taboo language, but a variety of shortenings. While the media focus on the contrast between Ko-Gals and feminine ideals, their significance is more impor-tant to the construction of current youth. As the diametric opposite of the salaryman, one might say that the Ko-Gal represents the ultimate disenfranchised youth. The diametric opposition between Ko-Gals and salarymen – to say nothing of the fact that these young women can play on the older men's weaknesses – emphasizes the extent of the threat that they pose. On the one hand, hegemonic gender ideologies would have these young women maximally contrasting with salarymen by virtue of their modest demeanor. By this very fact, they have the most to work with stylistically. While they run greater risk, they can also probably do more to shock, more to assert their autonomy than their male counterparts. In this way, Ko-Gals may well be becoming the quintessential new Japanese youth.

Where are we headed?

Fifty years ago, no one would have dreamed that so many women would be working out in gyms today – that there would be female weightlifters and professional basketball players, or that young women would be attending US universities with athletic scholarships. Fifty years ago, no one would have dreamed that gay marriage would be an important political issue, or that single motherhood would be an everyday thing. Fifty years ago, no one would have dreamed that some men would opt to stay home and care for children while their wives went out to earn the family's keep. Fifty years ago, no one would have dreamed that the courts would debate the right for a person to choose their own gender, or that a large group of people would parade publicly and shout "we're here, we're queer, get used to it." Fifty years ago, no one would have dreamed that a show called *The Vagina Monologues*, incorporating material from interviews with many different women about their vaginas and including a section on proud reappropriation of the word *cunt* (as well as many other comments on terminology for female genitalia), could even be produced let alone prove a hit in venues around the world.

The selves being fashioned at the beginning of the twenty-first century are different in many ways from selves of the middle of the twentieth century. But the picture is complex. In Ciudad Juarez, located in Mexico near the Texas border, many young women have become workers at assembly plants of foreign companies (*maquiladoras*) and, along with financial independence, have gained freedom from the traditional supervision of fathers, brothers, and husbands. Yet over a period of nine years, nearly 300 of these young women have been murdered. The predominant theory is that the murderer (or murderers) is striking back, enraged both by the new-found independence of these young women and by the economic impact on middle-aged men of women's willingness to work for lower wages and without unions and other benefits. Most responses to people's fashioning selves in new ways are not murderous, but there are always reactions of some kind from other selves and those reactions are often far from supportive of those whose choices challenge traditional gender arrangements.

Nonetheless, along with fashioning new individual selves, people have been reshaping institutions and developing alternative gender ideologies. So, for example, even in Ciudad Juarez there is a rape counseling center and a number of other advocacy groups organizing to protest what they see as police incompetence or even collusion in the string of murders of young women workers. It is striking that in many different settings, women whose counterparts fifty years ago were silent in the face of violence against women, are now speaking out forcibly and actively working to counter such violence in its many different forms, sometimes alongside sympathetic men.

Language figures in all of these developments. But language is never the whole story. Because the linguistic toolbox is so rich and varied, no single kind of linguistic choice (e.g. the use of profanity or the avoidance of generic masculines) can determine the effect produced, either in a particular interaction or more generally in the kind of persona being projected and the projects being pursued. Not only does each particular choice work in concert with other choices (e.g. use of very careful articulation or the choice of conventionally polite forms). But linguistic choices also go with all the other stylistic choices a person makes. And, of course, personal choices are played out in the social world, in communities of practice and the larger institutions to which they connect us. All we can confidently say about where we are headed is that gender and language will continue to change. And they will continue to be intertwined in social practice, perhaps in ways we do not now foresee.

Bibliography

AAUW. 1992. *Shortchanging Girls/Shortchanging America*. Washington DC: American Association of University Women.

Abrams, Kathryn. 1989. Gender discrimination and the transformation of workplace norms. *Vanderbilt Law Review*, 1183–1203.

Allen, Paula Gunn. 1987. *The Sacred Hoop*. Boston: Beacon Press.

Andersen, Elaine Slosberg. 1990. *Speaking With Style: The Sociolinguistic Skills of Children*. London: Routledge.

Anderson, Benedict. 1983. *Imagined Communities: Reflections on the Origin and Spread of Nationalism*. London: Verso.

Angier, Natalie. 1999. *Woman: An Intimate Geography*. Boston and New York: Houghton Mifflin.

Aries, Elizabeth. 1976. Interaction patterns and themes of male, female, and mixed groups. *Small Group Behavior*, 7:7–18.

Aries, Elizabeth and Johnson, Fern L. 1983. Close friendship in adulthood: conversational content between same-sex friends. *Sex Roles*, 9:1185–1196.

Arnold, Lorin Basden. 2000. "What is a feminist?": students' descriptions. *Women and Language*, 23:8–18.

Atran, Scott. 1990. *Cognitive Foundations of Natural History: Towards an Anthropology of Science*. New York: Cambridge University Press.

Austin, J. L. 1962. *How to Do Things with Words*. Oxford: Oxford University Press.

Awiatka, Marilou. 1993. *Selu: Seeking the Corn-Mother's Wisdom*. Golden, CO: Fulcrum.

Baker, Robert. 1975. "Pricks" and "chicks": a plea for "persons." In *Philosophy and Sex*, ed. by Robert Baker and Frederick Elliston, 45–64. New York: Prometheus Books.

Baron, Dennis E. 1986. *Grammar and Gender*. New Haven: Yale University Press.

Basso, Keith H. 1972. "To give up on words": silence in Western Apache culture. In *Language and Social Context*, ed. by Pier Paolo Giglioli, 67–86. London: Penguin.

Bauman, Richard. 2001. The ethnography of genre in a Mexican market: form, function, variation. In Eckert and Rickford 2001, 57–77.

Bauman, Richard and Sherzer, Joel. 1974. *Explorations in the Ethnography of Speaking*. Cambridge: Cambridge University Press.

Beardsley, Elizabeth. 1981. Degenderization. In Vetterling-Braggin 1974, 155–160.

Belenky, M. F.; Clinchy, B. M.; Goldberger, N. R.; and Tarule, J. M. 1986. *Women's Ways of Knowing.* New York: Basic Books.

Bellinger, D. and Gleason, Jean Berko. 1982. Sex differences in parental directives to young children. *Journal of Sex Roles,* 8:1123–1139.

Bem, Daryl J. 1996. Exotic becomes erotic: a developmental theory of sexual orientation. *Psychological Review,* 103:320–335.

Bem, Sandra L. 1974. The measurement of psychological androgyny. *Journal of Consulting and Clinical Psychology,* 42:155–162.

  1993. *The Lenses of Gender: Transforming the Debate on Sexual Inequality.* New Haven: Yale University Press.

Bem, Sandra L. and Bem, Daryl J. 1973. Does sex-biased job advertising "aid and abet" sex discrimination? *Journal of Applied Social Psychology,* 3:6–18.

Benor, Sarah. 2001. The learned /t/: phonological variation in Orthodox Jewish English. In *Penn Working Papers in Linguistics: Selected Papers from NWAV 29,* ed. by Tara Sanchez and Daniel Ezra Johnson, 1–16. Philadelphia: University of Pennsylvania, Department of Linguistics.

Benor, Sarah; Rose, Mary; Sharma, Devyani; Sweetland, Julie; and Zhang, Qing (eds.). 2002. *Under Construction: Gendered Practices in Language.* Stanford: CSLI Publications.

Berger, Joseph; Fizek, M.; Hamit, M.; Norman, Robert Z.; and Zelditch, Morris, Jr. 1977. *Status Characteristics and Social Interaction.* New York: Elsevier.

Bergvall, Victoria L.; Bing, Janet M.; and Freed, Alice F. (eds.). 1996. *Rethinking Language and Gender Research: Theory and Practice.* London and New York: Longman.

Biemans, Monique. 2000. *Gender Variation in Voice Quality.* Utrecht: LOT.

Biernat, Monica; Manis, Melvin; and Nelson, Thomas. 1991. Stereotypes and standards of judgment. *Journal of Personal and Social Psychology,* 60:485–499.

Bilious, Frances R. and Krauss, Robert M. 1988. Dominance and accommodation in the conversational behaviors of same- and mixed-gender dyads. *Language and Communication,* 8:183–194.

Bing, Janet M. 1992. Penguins can't fly and women don't count: language and thought. *Women and Language,* 14:11–14.

Black, Maria and Coward, Rosalind. 1981. Linguistic, social and sexual relations. *Screen Education,* 39:111–133.

Blackless, Melanie; Charuvastra, Anthony; Derryck, Amanda; Fausto-Sterling, Anne; Lauzanne, Karl; and Lee, Ellen. 2000. How sexually dimorphic are we? Review and synthesis. *American Journal of Human Biology,* 12:151–166.

Blackstone, Kathryn R. 1998. *Women in the footsteps of the Buddha: Struggle for Liberation in the Therigatha.* Richmond, Surrey: Curzon Critical Studies in Buddhism.

Bodine, Ann. 1975. Androcentrism in prescriptive grammar: singular "they," sex-indefinite "he," and "he or she." *Language in Society,* 4:129–146.

Bolin, Dan. 1993. *How to Be Your Daughter's Daddy: 365 Ways to Show Her You Care.* Colorado Springs: Navpress.

Bolin, Dan and Sutterfield, Ken. 1993. *How to Be Your Little Man's Dad: 365 Things to Do with Your Son*. Colorado Springs: Navpress.

Bornstein, Kate. 1998. *My Gender Workbook: How to Become a Real Man, a Real Woman, the Real You, or Something Else Entirely*. New York and London: Routledge.

Boroditsky, Lera. Forthcoming. Not-just-grammatical gender: effects of grammatical gender on meaning. In *Language in Mind: Advances in the Study of Language and Cognition*, ed. by Dedre Gentner and Susan Goldin-Meadow. Cambridge, MA: MIT Press.

Bortoni-Ricardo, Stella Maris. 1985. *The Urbanization of Rural Dialect Speakers*. Cambridge: Cambridge University Press.

Bourdieu, Pierre. 1977a. The economics of linguistic exchanges. *Social Science Information*, 16:645–668.

   1977b. *Outline of a Theory of Practice*. Cambridge: Cambridge University Press.

   1982. *Ce que parler veut dire*. Paris: Fayard.

   1984. *Distinction: A Social Critique of the Judgement of Taste*. Cambridge, MA: Harvard University Press.

   1991. *Language and Symbolic Power*. Cambridge, MA: Harvard University Press.

Brenneis, Donald. 1977. "Turkey," "wienie," "animal," "stud": intragroup variation in folk speech. *Western Folklore*, 36:238–246.

Briggs, Charles. 1992. "Since I am a woman I will chastise my relatives": gender, reported speech, and the (re)productions of social relations in Warao ritual wailing. *American Ethnologist*, 19:337–361.

Britain, David. 1992. Language change in intonation: the use of high rising terminals in New Zealand English. *Language Variation and Change*, 4:77–104.

Brouwer, Dédé. 1982. The influence of the addresser's sex on politeness in language use. *Linguistics*, 20:697–711.

Brouwer, Dédé; Gerritsen, Marinel; and De Haan, Dorian. 1979. Speech differences between women and men: on the wrong track? *Language in Society*, 8:33–50.

Brown, Penelope. 1980. How and why are women more polite: some evidence from a Mayan community. In McConnell-Ginet, Borker, and Furman 1980, 111–136.

   1990. Gender, politeness, and confrontation in Tenejapa. *Discourse Processes*, 13:123–141.

Brown, Penelope and Levinson, Stephen. 1987. *Politeness: Some Universals in Language Usage*. Cambridge: Cambridge University Press.

Brown, Roger and Ford, Marguerite 1961. Address in American English. *Journal of Abnormal and Social Psychology*, 62:375–385.

Brown, Roger and Gilman, Albert. 1960. The pronouns of power and solidarity. In *Style in Language*, ed. by Thomas A. Sebeok, 253–276. Cambridge, MA: MIT Press.

Brumberg, Joan J. 1997. *The Body Project: An Intimate History of American Girls*. New York: Random House.

Bucholtz, Mary. 1996. Geek the girl: language, femininity and female nerds. In Warner, Ahlers, Bilmes, *et al.* 1996, 119–131.

1999. "Why be normal?": language and identity practices in a community of nerd girls. *Language in Society*, 28:203–224.

Bucholtz, Mary; Liang, A. C.; Sutton, Laurel A.; and Hines, Caitlin (eds.). 1994. *Cultural Performances: Proceedings of the Third Berkeley Women and Language Conference*. Berkeley: Berkeley Women and Language Group.

Bucholtz, Mary; Liang, A. C.; and Sutton, Laurel A. (eds.). 1999. *Reinventing Identities: The Gendered Self in Discourse*. New York: Oxford University Press.

Buschman, J. K. and Lenart, Silvo. 1996. "I am not a feminist, but...": college women, feminism, and negative experiences. *Political Psychology*, 17:59–75.

Butler, Judith. 1990. *Gender Trouble: Feminism and the Subversion of Identity*. New York and London: Routledge.

1993. *Bodies That Matter: On the Discursive Limits of Sex*. New York and London: Routledge.

Cameron, Deborah. 1985. *Feminism and Linguistic Theory*. London: Routledge. Revised 2nd edition, 1992.

1995. *Verbal Hygiene*. London and New York: Routledge.

1996. The language gender interface: challenging cooptation. In Bergvall, Bing, and Freed 1996, 31–53.

1997. Performing gender identity: young men's talk and the construction of heterosexual masculinity. In Johnson and Meinhof 1997, 47–64.

1998a. Gender, language and discourse: a review essay. *Signs: Journal of Women in Culture and Society*, 23:945–973.

(ed.). 1998b. *Language: The Feminist Critique*, 2nd edition. London: Routledge.

2000. *Good to Talk?: Living and Working in a Communication Culture*. London and Thousand Oaks, CA: Sage Publications.

Cameron, Deborah; McAlinden, Fiona; and O'Leary, Kathy. 1988. Lakoff in context: the social and linguistic function of tag questions. In Coates and Cameron 1988, 74–93.

Campbell-Kibler, Kathryn; Podesva, Robert J.; Roberts, Sarah J.; and Wong, Andrew (eds.). 2002. *Language and Sexuality: Contesting Meaning in Theory and Practice*. Stanford, CA: CSLI Press.

Chambers, Jack. 1992. Dialect acquisition. *Language*, 68:673–705.

1995. *Sociolinguistic Theory*. Oxford: Blackwell.

Cheshire, Jenny. 2000. The telling or the tale? Narratives and gender in adolescent friendship networks. *Journal of Sociolinguistics*, 4:236–262.

Chodorow, Nancy. 1978. *The Reproduction of Mothering*. Berkeley: University of California Press.

Christie, Christine. 2000. *Gender and Language: Towards a Feminist Pragmatics*. Edinburgh: Edinburgh University Press.

Clark, Eve. 2000. *First Language Acquisition*. Cambridge: Cambridge University Press.

Clark, Kate. 1992. "The linguistics of blame": representations of women in *The Sun*'s reporting of crimes of sexual violence. In *Language, Text, and*

Context: Essays in Stylistics, ed. by Michael Toolan, 208–226. London and New York: Routledge.

Clark, Herbert H. and Gerrig, Richard J. 1984. On the pretense theory of irony. *Journal of Experimental Psychology: General*, 113:121–126.

Clift, Rebecca. 1999. Irony in conversation. *Language in Society*, 28:523–553.

Coates, Jennifer. 1988. Gossip revisited: Language in all-female groups. In Coates and Cameron 1988, 94–121.

   1993. No gap, lots of overlap: turn-taking patterns in the talk of women friends. In *Researching Language and Literacy in Social Context*, ed. by David Graddol, Janet Maybin, and Barry Stierer, 177–192. Cleveland: Multilingual Matters.

   1996. *Women Talk: Conversation Between Women Friends*. Oxford: Blackwell.

Coates, Jennifer and Cameron, Deborah (eds.). 1988. *Women in Their Speech Communities: New Perspectives on Language and Sex*. London and New York: Longman.

Cohn, Carol. 1987. Sex and death in the rational world of defense intellectuals. *Signs: Journal of Women in Culture and Society*, 12:687–718.

Condry, John and Condry, Sandra 1976. Sex differences: a study in the eye of the beholder. *Child Development*, 47:812–819.

Connell, Robert W. 1987. *Gender and Power: Society, the Person and Sexual Politics*. Stanford, CA: Stanford University Press.

   1995. *Masculinities*. Berkeley: University of California Press.

Connors, Kathleen. 1971. Studies in feminine agentives in selected European languages. *Romance Philology*, 24:573–598.

Corbett, Greville. 1991. *Gender*. Cambridge Textbooks in Linguistics. Cambridge and New York: Cambridge University Press.

Corson, David. 2000. *Language Diversity and Education*. Mahwah, NJ: Lawrence Erlbaum.

Cos, Joan Pujolar I. 1997. Masculinities in a multilingual setting. In Johnson and Meinhof, 86–106.

Crawford, Mary. 1995. *Talking Difference: On Gender and Language*. Gender and psychology: feminist and critical perspectives. London, Thousand Oaks, and New Delhi: Sage Publications.

Crystal, David. 2001. *Language and the Internet*. Cambridge: Cambridge University Press.

Dalby, Liza. 1983. *Geisha*. Berkeley: University of California Press.

Damasio, Antonio R. 1994. *Descartes' Error: Emotion, Reason, and the Human Brain*. New York: G. P. Putnam.

Delph-Janiurek, Tom. 1999. Sounding gender(ed): vocal performances in English university teaching spaces. *Gender, Place and Culture*, 6:137–153.

Derrida, Jacques. 1991. Signature event context. In *A Derrida Reader: Between the Blinds*, ed. by Peggy Kamuf, 80–111. New York: Columbia University Press.

Deuchar, Margaret. 1988. A pragmatic account of women's use of standard speech. In Coates and Cameron 1988, 27–32.

Dill, Bonnie Thornton. 1979. The dialectics of black womanhood. *Signs*, 4:543–571.

Dreger, Alice Domurat. 1998. "Ambiguous sex" – or ambivalent medicine? *The Hastings Center Report*, 28 (May/June):24–35.

Dreifus, Claudia. 2001. A conversation with Anne Fausto-Sterling. The *New York Times*, January 2.

Dubois, Betty Lou and Crouch, Isabel. 1975. The question of tag questions in women's speech: they don't really use more of them, do they? *Language in Society*, 4:289–294.

Duckett, John and Baskin, Laurence. 1993. Genitoplasty for intersex anomalies. *European Journal of Pediatrics*, 152:S80–S84.

Duncan, Starkey. 1972. Some signals and rules for taking speaking turns in conversations. *Journal of Personality and Social Psychology*, 23:283–293.

   1974. On the structure of speaker–auditor interaction during speaking turns. *Language in Society*, 2:151–180.

Dundes, Alan; Leach, Jerry W.; and Özök, Bora. 1972. The strategy of Turkish boys' verbal dueling rhymes. In Gumperz and Hymes 1972, 130–160.

Durkheim, Emile. 1915. *The Elementary Forms of the Religious Life*. London: George Allen and Unwin.

Eagleton, Terry. 1991. *Ideology: An Introduction*. London and New York: Verso.

Eckert, Penelope. 1980a. The structure of a long-term phonological process: the back vowel chain shift in Soulatan Gascon. In *Locating Language in Time and Space*, ed. by William Labov, 179–220. New York: Academic Press.

   1980b. Diglossia: separate and unequal. *Linguistics*, 18:1053–1064.

   1983. The paradox of regional language movements. *Journal of Multilingual and Multicultural Development*, 4:289–300.

   1989. *Jocks and Burnouts: Social Categories and Identity in the High School*. New York: Teachers College Press.

   1990. Cooperative competition in adolescent girl talk. *Discourse Processes*, 13:92–122.

   1996. Vowels and nailpolish: The emergence of linguistic style in the preadolescent heterosexual marketplace. In Warner, Ahlers, Bilmes, et al. 1996, 183–190.

   2000. *Linguistic Variation as Social Practice: The Linguistic Construction of Social Meaning in Belten High*. Oxford: Blackwell.

Eckert, Penelope and McConnell-Ginet, Sally. 1992. Think practically and look locally: language and gender as community-based practice. *Annual Review of Anthropology*, 21:461–490.

   1995. Constructing meaning, constructing selves: snapshots of language, gender and class from Belten High. In Hall and Bucholtz 1995, 469–507.

   1999. New generalizations and explanations in language and gender research. *Language in Society*, 28:185–202.

Eckert, Penelope and Newmark, Russell. 1980. Central Eskimo song duels: a contextual analysis of ritual ambiguity. *Ethnology*, 19:191–211.

Eckert, Penelope and Rickford, John (eds.). 2001. *Stylistic Variation in Language*. Cambridge: Cambridge University Press.

Edelsky, Carole, 1979. Question intonation and sex roles. *Language in Society*, 8:15–32.
  1981. Who's got the floor? *Language in Society*, 10:383–421.
Edelsky, Carole and Adams, Karen. 1990. Creating inequality: breaking the rules in debates. *Journal of Language and Social Psychology*, 9: 171–190.
Ehrlich, Susan. 2001. *Representing Rape: Language and Sexual Consent.* New York and London: Routledge.
Ehrlich, Susan and King, Ruth. 1994. Feminist meanings and the (de)politicization of the lexicon. *Language in Society*, 23(1):59–76.
Eisikovits, Edina. 1987. Sex differences in inter- and intra-group interaction among adolescents. In Pauwels 1987, 45–58.
Ely, Richard; Gleason, Jean Berko; Narasimhan, Bhuvaneswari; and McCabe, Allyssa. 1995. Family talk about talk: mothers lead the way. *Discourse Processes*, 9(2): 201–218.
Emantian, Michele. 1995. Metaphor and the expression of emotion: the value of cross-cultural perspectives. *Metaphor and Symbolic Activity*, 10:163–182.
Epstein, Cynthia Fuchs. 1988. *Deceptive Distinctions: Sex, Gender, and the Social Order.* New Haven and New York: Yale University Press and Russell Sage Foundation.
Eskilson, Arlene and Wiley, Mary Glenn. 1976. Sex composition and leadership in small groups. *Sociometry*, 39:183–194.
Esposito, Anita. 1979. Sex differences in children's conversations. *Language and Speech*, 22:213–220.
Fader, Ayala. Forthcoming. Controlling knowledge and languages: literacy, bilingualism, and gender in a Hasidic community in Brooklyn. *Linguistics and Education.*
Fagot, B. I.; Hagan, R.; Leinbach, M. D.; and Kronsberg, S. 1985. Differential reactions to assertive and communicative acts of toddler boys and girls. *Child Development*, 56:1499–1505.
Fairclough, Norman. 1987. *Language and Power: Language in Social Life.* London and New York: Longman.
Faludi, Susan. 1991. *Backlash: The Undeclared War Against American Women.* New York: Doubleday.
Fausto-Sterling, Anne. 2000. *Sexing the Body: Gender Politics and the Construction of Sexuality.* New York: Basic Books.
Fidell, L. S. 1975. Empirical verification of sex discrimination in hiring practices in psychology. In *Woman: Dependent or Independent Variable?*, ed. by R. K. Unger and F. L. Denmark, 774–782. New York: Psychological Dimensions.
Fischer, John. L. 1958. Social influences on the choice of a linguistic variant. *Word*, 14:47–56.
Fishman, Pamela. 1980. Conversational insecurity. In *Language: Social Psychological Perspectives*, ed. by H. Giles, W. P. Robinson and P. Smith, 127–132. Oxford: Pergamon Press.
  1983. Interaction: the work women do. In Thorne, Kramarae, and Henley 1983, 89–102.

Forgas, Joseph (ed.). 2000. *Feeling and Thinking*. Cambridge: Cambridge
    University Press.
Foucault, Michel. 1972. *The Archaeology of Knowledge and the Discourse on
    Language*. New York: Pantheon Books.
Fox, H. E.; White, S. A.; Kao, M. H.; and Fernald, R. D. 1997. Stress and
    dominance in a social fish. *Journal of Neuroscience*, 17:6463–6469.
Frank, Francine Wattman and Treichler, Paula A. 1989. *Language, Gender,
    and Professional Writing: Theoretical Approaches and Guidelines for
    Nonsexist Usage*. New York: Modern Language Association.
Friedrich, Paul. 1972. Social context and semantic features: the Russian
    pronominal usage. In Gumperz and Hymes 1972, 270–300.
Gal, Susan. 1978. Peasant men can't get wives: language change and sex
    roles in a bilingual community. *Language in Society*, 7:1–16.
   1979. *Language Shift: Social Determinants of Linguistic Change in Bilingual
    Austria*. New York: Academic Press.
Gal, Susan and Irvine, Judith T. 1995. The boundaries of languages and
    disciplines: how ideologies construct difference. *Social Research*,
    62:967–1001.
Garb, Tamar. 1993. The forbidden gaze: women artists and the male nude
    in late nineteenth-century France. In *The Body Imaged: The Human Form
    and Visual Culture since the Renaissance*, ed. by Kathleen Adler and
    Marcia Pointon, 33–42. Cambridge: Cambridge University Press.
Gardner, Carol Brooks. 1980. Passing by: street remarks, address rights,
    and the urban female. *Sociological Inquiry*, 50:328–356.
   1989. Analyzing gender in public places: rethinking Goffman's vision of
    everyday life. *The American Sociologist*, 20:42–56.
Gaudio, Rudolf P. 1994. Properties in the speech of gay and straight men.
    American Speech, 69:30–57.
   1996. Funny Muslims: humor, faith and gender liminality in Hausa. In
    Warner, Ahlers, Bilmes, *et al.* 1996, 261–267.
   1997. Not talking straight in Hausa. In Livia and Hall 1997, 642–662.
Gervasio, A. H. and Crawford, Mary. 1989. Social evaluations of
    assertiveness: a critique and speech act reformulation. *Psychology of
    Women Quarterly*, 13:1–25.
Gilligan, Carol. 1982. *In a Different Voice*. Cambridge, MA: Harvard
    University Press.
Gilligan, Carol; Lyons, Nona P.; and Hanmer, Trudy J. 1990. *Making
    Connections: The Relational Worlds of Adolescent Girls at Emma Willard
    School*. Cambridge, MA: Harvard University Press.
Gleason, Jean Berko. 1973. *Code Switching in Children's Language. Cognitive
    Development and the Acquisition of Language*, ed. by T. Moore. New York:
    Academic Press.
Gleason, Jean Berko and Greif, Esther Blank. 1983. Men's speech to young
    children. In Thorne, Kramarae, and Henley 1983, 140–150.
Gleason, Jean Berko; Perlmann, R.Y.; Ely, D.; and Evans, D. 1994. The baby
    talk register: parents' use of diminutives. In *Handbook of Research in
    Language Development Using CHILDES*, ed. by J. L. Sokolov and C. E.
    Snow, 50–76. Hillsdale, NJ: Lawrence Erlbaum.

Goffman, Erving. 1967. On face work. In *Interaction Ritual*, 5–45. New York: Doubleday.

1974. *Frame Analysis.* New York: Harper and Row.

1976. Gender advertisements. *Studies in the Anthropology of Visual Commmunication*, 3:69–154.

1977. The arrangement between the sexes. *Theory and Society*, 4:301–332.

1979. Footing. *Semiotica*, 25:1–29.

Goodwin, Marjorie Harness. 1980. Directive-response speech sequences in girls' and boys' task activities. In McConnell-Ginet, Borker, and Furman 1980, 157–173.

1990. *He-Said–She-Said: Talk as Social Organization among Black Children.* Bloomington: Indiana University Press.

1994. "Ay chillona!": stance-taking in girls' hopscotch. In Bucholtz, Liang, Sutton, and Hines 1994, 232–242.

2000. Constituting the moral order in girls' social organization: language practices in the construction of social exclusion. Paper presented at IGALA1 (Conference of the International Gender and Language Association), Stanford.

Gordon, Elizabeth. 1997. Sex, speech, and stereotypes: why women use prestige forms more than men. *Language in Society*, 26(1):47–63.

Gould, Lois. 1983. X: a fabulous child's story. In *Stories for Free Children*, ed. by Letty Cottin Pogrebin. New York: McGraw-Hill.

Graddol, David and Swann, Joan. 1989. *Gender Voices*. Oxford: Blackwell.

Gramsci, Anton. 1971. *Selections From the Prison Notebooks*. London: Lawrence and Wishart.

Green, Georgia M. 1995. Ambiguity resolution and discourse interpretation. In *Semantic Ambiguity and Underspecification*, ed. by Kees van Deemter and Stanley Peters, 1–26. Stanford: CSLI Press.

Grice, H. Paul. 1989. *The Ways of Words.* Cambridge, MA: Harvard University Press.

Gumperz, John J. 1982. *Discourse Strategies.* Cambridge: Cambridge University Press.

Gumperz, John J. and Hymes, Dell (eds.). 1972. *Directions in Sociolinguistics: The Ethnography of Communication.* New York: Holt, Rinehart, and Winston.

Guy, G.; Horvath, B.; Vonwiller, J.; Daisley, E.; and Rogers, I. 1986. An intonational change in progress in Australian English. *Language in Society*, 15:23–52.

Haeri, Niloofar. 1997. *The Sociolinguistic Market of Cairo: Gender, Class, and Education.* London: Kegan Paul International.

Haiman, John 1990. Sarcasm as theater. *Cognitive Linguistics*, 1:181–205.

Hall, Kira. 1995. Lip service on the fantasy line. In Hall and Bucholtz 1995, 183–216.

1997. "Go suck your husband's sugar cane!": Hijras and the use of sexual insult. In Livia and Hall 1997, 430–460.

Hall, Kira; Bucholtz, Mary; and Moonwomon, Birch (eds.). 1992. *Locating Power: Proceedings of the Second Berkeley Women and Language Conference.* Berkeley: Berkeley Women and Language Group.

Hall, Kira and Bucholtz, Mary (eds.). 1995. *Gender Articulated: Language and the Socially Constructed Self.* New York and London: Oxford University Press.

Hall, Kira and O'Donovan, Veronica. 1996. Shifting gender positions among Hindi-speaking hijras. In Bergvall, Bing, and Freed 1996, 228–266.

Hanks, William F. 1996. *Language and Communicative Practices.* Boulder, CO: Westview Press.

Harding, Susan. 1975. Women and words in a Spanish village. In *Toward an Anthropology of Women*, ed. by Rayna R. Reiter, 283–308. New York: Monthly Review Press.

Hardman, M. J. and Taylor, Anita (eds.). *Hearing Many Voices.* Creskill, NJ: Hampton Press.

Haste, Helen. 1994. *The Sexual Metaphor.* Cambridge, MA: Harvard University Press.

Heath, Shirley Brice. 1983. *Ways With Words.* Cambridge: Cambridge University Press.

Hebdige, Dick. 1984. *Subculture: The Meaning of Style.* New York: Methuen.

Henton, Caroline. 1989. Fact and fiction in the description of female and male speech. *Language and Communication,* 9:299–311.

Herbert, Robert K. 1990. Sex-based differences in compliment behavior. *Language in Society,* 19(2): 201–224.

Herdt, Gilbert. 1996. *Third gender: Beyond Sexual Dimorphism in Culture and History.* New York: Ozone Books.

Herring, Susan. 1994. Politeness in computer culture: why women thank and men flame. In Bucholtz, Liang, Sutton, and Hines 1994, 278–294.

Hill, Jane. 1987. Women's speech in modern Mexicano. In *Language, Gender, and Sex in Comparative Perspective*, ed. by S. U. Philips, S. Steele and C. Tanz. Cambridge: Cambridge University Press, 121–160.

Hindle, Donald and Sag, Ivan. 1973. Some more on "anymore." In *Analyzing Variation in Language*, ed. by Ralph W. Fasold and Roger W. Shuy, 89–110. Washington DC: Georgetown University Press.

Hines, Caitlin. 1999. Rebaking the pie: the "woman as dessert" metaphor. In Bucholtz, Liang and Sutton 1999, 145–162.

Hinton, Leanne. 1992. Sex difference in address terminology in the 1990s. In Hall, Bucholtz, and Moonwomon 1992, 263–271.

Hirschfeld, Lawrence A. and Gelman, Susan A. (eds.). 1994. *Mapping the Mind: Domain Specificity in Cognition and Culture.* Cambridge: Cambridge University Press.

Hoffman, Nancy Jo. 1972. Sexism in letters of recommendation. *Modern Language Association Newsletters,* Sept.: 5–6.

Holmes, Janet. 1982. The functions of tag questions. *English Language Research Journal,* 3:40–65.

   1984. Hedging your bets and sitting on the fence: some evidence for hedges as support structures. *Te Reo,* 27:47–62.

   1986. Functions of "you know" in women's and men's speech. *Language in Society,* 15:1–22.

1995. *Women, Men and Politeness.* London and New York: Longman.

2001. A corpus-based view of gender in New Zealand English. In *Gender Across Languages. The Linguistic Representation of Women and Men*, Vol. I, ed. by Marlis Hellinger and Hadumod Bussman, 115–136. Amsterdam: John Benjamins.

Holmquist, Jonathan C. 1985. Social correlates of a linguistic variable: a study in a Spanish village. *Language in Society*, 14:191–203.

Houghton, Carolyn. 1995. Managing the body of labor. In Hall and Bucholtz 1995, 121–142.

Howes, C. 1988. Same- and cross-sex friends: implications for interaction and social skills. *Early Childhood Research Quarterly*, 3:21–37.

Hull, Gloria T.; Scott, Patricia Bell; and Smith, Barbara. 1982. *All the Women are White, all the Blacks are Men, but Some of Us are Brave: Black Women's Studies.* Old Westbury, NY: Feminist Press.

Hymes, Dell. 1972. Models of the interaction of language and social life. In Gumperz and Hymes 1972, 35–71.

1974. *Foundations in Sociolinguistics: An Ethnographic Approach.* Philadelphia: University of Pennsylvania Press.

Ide, Sachiko. 1982. Japanese sociolinguistics: politeness and women's language. *Lingua*, 57:357–385.

Ide, Sachiko and McGloin, Naomi Hanaska (eds.). 1990. *Aspects of Japanese Women's Language.* Tokyo: Kurosio Publishers.

Ide, Risako and Terada, Tomomi. 1998. The historical origins of Japanese women's speech: from the secluded worlds of "court ladies" and "play ladies". *International Journal of the Sociology of Language*, 129:139–156.

Inoue, Miyako. 1994. Gender and linguistic modernization: historicizing Japanese women's language. In Bucholtz, Liang, Sutton, and Hines 1994, 322–333.

2002. Gender and linguistic modernity: towards an effective history of Japanese women's language. *American Ethnologist*, 29(2):392–422.

Forthcoming. Vicarious Language: The Political Economy of Gender and Speech in Japan.

Irvine, Judith. 1974. Status manipulation in the Wolof greeting. In Bauman and Sherzer 1974, 167–191.

1989. When talk isn't cheap: language and political economy. *American Ethnologist*, 16: 248–267.

2001. "Style" as distinctiveness: the culture and ideology of linguistic differentiation. In Eckert and Rickford 2001, 21–43.

James, Deborah. 1996. Derogatory terms for women and men: a new look. In Warner, Ahlers, Bilmes, *et al.* 1996, 343–354.

James, Deborah and Clarke, Sandra. 1993. Women, men and interruptions: A critical review. In Tannen 1993, 231–280.

James, Deborah and Drakich, Janice. 1993. Understanding gender differences in amount of talk: a critical review of research. In Tannen 1993, 281–312.

Johnson, R. C. and Medinnus, G. R. 1969. *Child Psychology: Behavior and Development.* New York: Wiley.

Johnson, Sally and Meinhof, Ulrike Hanna (eds.). 1997. *Language and Masculinity.* Oxford: Blackwell.

Jones, Deborah. 1980. Gossip: notes on women's oral culture. In *The Voices and Words of Women and Men,* ed. by Cheris Kramarae, 193–198. Oxford: Pergamon Press.

Kalčik, S. 1975. "...like Ann's gynecologist or the time I was almost raped": personal narratives in women's rap groups. *Journal of American Folklore,* 88:3–11.

Kaplan, Cora. [1986] 1998. Language and gender. In Cameron 1998b, 54–64.

Katz, P. A. 1996. Raising feminists. *Psychology of Women Quarterly,* 20:323–340.

Kearns, Kate. Forthcoming. Implicature and semantic change. In *Handbook of Pragmatics,* ed. by Jef Verschueren, Jan-Ola Östman, Jan Blommeart, and Chris Bulcaen.

Keenan, Elinor. 1974. Norm-makers, norm-breakers: uses of speech by men and women in a Malagasy community. In Bauman and Sherzer 1974, 125–143.

Keil, Frank C. 1989. *Concepts, Kinds, and Cognitive Development.* Cambridge, MA: MIT Press.

Keller, Evelyn Fox. 1983. *A Feeling for the Organism: The Life and Work of Barbara McClintock.* New York: W. H. Freeman.

   1987. The gender/science system: or is sex to gender as nature is to science? *Hypatia,* 2(3): 37–50.

Kerbrat-Orecchioni, C. 1987. La description des échanges en analyse conversationnelle: l'exemple du compliment. *DRLAV – Revue de Linguistique,* 36–37:1–53.

Kessler, Suzanne J. and McKenna, Wendy. 1978. *Gender: An Ethnomethodological Approach.* New York: Wiley.

Khosroshahi, Fatemeh. 1989. Penguins don't care, but women do: a social identity analysis of a Whorfian problem. *Language in Society,* 18:505–525.

Kiesling, Scott Fabius. 1997. Power and the language of men. In Johnson and Meinhof 1997, 65–85.

Kindaichi, Kyosuke. 1942. *Zoku kokugo kenkyû* (Studies of national language, additional supplement). Tokyo: Yakumoshorin.

King, Ruth (ed.). 1991. *Talking Gender: A Guide to Nonsexist Communication.* Toronto: Copp Clark Pitman.

Kissling, Elizabeth Arveda. 1991. Street harassment: the language of sexual terrorism. *Discourse and Society,* 2:451–460.

Kissling, Elizabeth Arveda and Kramarae, Cheris. 1991. "Stranger compliments": the interpretation of street remarks. *Women's Studies in Communication,* 14:77–95.

Kittay, Eva Feder. 1987. *Metaphor: Its Cognitive Force and Linguistic Structure.* Oxford: Oxford University Press.

   1988. Woman as metaphor. *Hypatia,* 3:63–86.

   1998. *Love's Labor: Essays on Women, Equality and Dependency.* New York: Routledge.

Kollock, Peter; Blumstein, Philip; and Schwartz, Pepper. 1985. Sex and power in interaction: conversational privileges and duties. *American Sociological Review*, 50:34–46.

Kolodny, Annette. 1980. Honing a habitable languagescape: women's images for the new world frontiers. In McConnell-Ginet, Borker and Furman 1980, 188–204.

Kondo, Dorinne. 1990. *Crafting Selves*. Chicago: University of Chicago Press.

Kortenhoven, Andrea. 1998. Rising intonation in children's narratives (ms).

Kroch, Anthony S. 1978. Toward a theory of social dialect variation. *Language in Society*, 7:17–36.

Krupnick, Catherine G. 1985. Women and men in the classroom: inequality and its remedies. *On Teaching and Learning: Journal of the Harvard-Danforth Center*, 1 (May):18–25.

Kuczmarski, Robert J.; Ogden, Cynthia L.; Grummer-Strawn, Laurence M.; Flegal, Katherine M.; Guo, Shumei S.; Wei, Rong; Mei, Zugou; Curtin, Lester R.; Roche, Alex F.; and Johnson, Clifford L. 2000. CDC growth charts: United States. Advance data from vital and health statistics. Report 314. Hyattsville, MD: National Center for Health Statistics.

Kuhn, Elizabeth D. 1992. *Gender and Authority: Classroom Diplomacy at German and American Universities*. Tübinger Beitrage zur Linguistik, 373. Tübingen: Narr.

Kuiper, Koenraad. 1991. Sporting formulae in New Zealand English: two models of male solidarity. In *English Around the World: Sociolinguistic Perspectives*, ed. by Jenny Cheshire, 200–209. Cambridge: Cambridge University Press.

Labov, William. 1963. The social motivation of a sound change. *Word*, 18:1–42. Reprinted in Labov 1972c, 1–42.

1966. *The Social Stratification of English in New York City*. Washington, DC: Center for Applied Linguistics.

1972a. *Language in the Inner City*. Philadelphia: University of Pennsylvania Press.

1972b. Rules for ritual insults. In Labov 1972a, 297–353.

1972c. *Sociolinguistic Patterns*. Philadelphia: University of Pennsylvania.

1973. The boundaries of words and their meanings. In *New Ways of Analyzing Variation in English*, ed. by Joshua Fishman, 340–373. Washington DC: Georgetown University Press.

1991. The intersection of sex and social class in the course of linguistic change. *Language Variation and Change*, 2:205–251.

1994. *Principles of Linguistic Change: Internal Factors*. Oxford: Blackwell.

2001. *Principles of Linguistic Change: Social Factors*. Oxford: Blackwell.

Labov, William; Yaeger, Malcah; and Steiner, Richard. 1972. *A Quantitative Study of Sound Change in Progress*. Philadelphia: US Regional Survey.

Ladd, D. Robert, Jr. 1980. *The Structure of Intonational Meaning. Evidence from English*. Bloomington: Indiana University Press.

1996. *Intonational Phonology*. Cambridge and New York: Cambridge University Press.

Ladner, J. 1971. *Tomorrow's Tomorrow: The Black Woman*. Garden City, NJ: Doubleday-Anchor.

Lakoff, Robin. 1972. Language in context. *Language*, 48:907–924.

1975. *Language and Woman's Place*. New York: Harper and Row.

Lakoff, George. 1987. *Women, Fire and Dangerous Things: What Categories Reveal About the Mind*. Chicago: University of Chicago Press.

Lakoff, George and Johnson, Mark. 1980. *Metaphors We Live By*. Chicago: University of Chicago Press.

Langlois, J. H. and Downs, A. C. 1980. Mothers, fathers, and peers as socialization agents of sex-typed play behaviors in young children. *Child Development*, 62:1217–1247.

Lapadat, Judy and Seesahai, Maureen. 1977. Male versus female codes in informal contexts. *Sociolinguistics Newsletter*, 8(3):7–8.

Lave, Jean and Wenger, Etienne. 1991. *Situated Learning: Legitimate Peripheral Participation*. Cambridge: Cambridge University Press.

Lefkowitz, Daniel. 1996. On the mediation of class, race and gender: intonation on sports radio talk shows. *UPenn Working Papers in Linguistics*, 3:197–211.

Levinson, Stephen. 1983. *Pragmatics*. Cambridge: Cambridge University Press.

2000. *Presumptive Meanings: The Theory of Generalized Conversational Implicature*. Cambridge, MA: MIT Press.

Lewis, David K. 1974. Languages, language, and grammar. In *On Noam Chomsky: Critical Essays*, ed. by Gilbert Harman, 253–266. New York: Anchor Press.

Liang, A. C. 1999. Conversationally implicating lesbian and gay identity. In Bucholtz, Liang, and Sutton 1999, 293–310.

Livia, Anna. 1997. Disloyal to masculine identity: linguistic gender and liminal identity in French. In Livia and Hall 1997, 349–368.

2001. *Pronoun Envy: Literary Uses of Linguistic Gender*. Studies in Language and Gender. Oxford and New York: Oxford University Press.

2002. *Camionneuses s'abstenir*: Lesbian community creation through the personals. In Campbell-Kibler, Podesva, Roberts, and Wong 2002, 191–206.

Livia, Anna and Hall, Kira (eds.). 1997. *Queerly Phrased: Language, Gender and Sexuality*. Oxford and New York: Oxford University Press.

Lloyd, Genevieve. 1984. *The Man of Reason: "Male" and "Female" in Western Philosophy*. Minneapolis: University of Minnesota Press.

Lutz, Catherine. 1990. Engendered emotion. In *Language and the Politics of Emotion*, ed. by Catherine Lutz and Lila Abu-Lughod. Cambridge: Cambridge University Press.

Macaulay, Ronald K. S. 1977. *Language, Social Class and Education: A Glasgow Study*. Edinburgh: University of Edinburgh Press.

1978. The myth of female superiority in language. *Journal of Child Language*, 5:353–363.

Macaulay, Monica and Brice, Colleen. 1997. Don't touch my projectile: gender bias and stereotyping in syntactic examples. *Language*, 73:798–825.

Maccoby, Eleanor E. 1998. *The Two Sexes: Growing Up Apart, Coming Together*. Cambridge, MA: Harvard University Press.

2000. Perspectives on gender development. *International Journal of Behavioural Development*, 24(4): 398–406.

2002. The intersection of "nature" and socialization in childhood gender development. In *Psychology at the Turn of the Millennium*, Vol. II, *Social, Developmental, and Clinical Perspectives*, ed. by C. VonHoften and P. Blackman, 37–52. Hove: Psychology Press.

Maccoby, Eleanor E. and Jacklin, Carol N. 1974. *The Psychology of Sex Differences*. Stanford: Stanford University Press.

1987. Gender segregation in childhood. In *Advances in Child Behavior and Development*, ed. by H. Reese. New York: Academic Press.

Maltz, Daniel N. and Borker, Ruth A. 1982. A cultural approach to male–female miscommunication. In *Language and Social Identity*, ed. by John J. Gumperz, 196–216. Cambridge: Cambridge University Press.

Manes, Joan. 1983. Compliments: a mirror of cultural values. In *Sociolinguistics and Language Acquisition*, ed. by Nessa Wolfson and E. Judd, 96–102. Rowley, MA: Newbury House.

Manes, Joan and Wolfson, Nessa. 1981. The compliment formula. In *Conversational Routine*, ed. by Florian Coulmas, 115–132. The Hague: Mouton.

March, Kathryn. 1975. Therigatha and Theragatha: a comparison of imagery used by women and men recluses in their early Buddhist poetry (MS, Cornell University).

2002. *"If Each Comes Halfway." Meeting Tamang Women of Nepal*. Ithaca, NY: Cornell University Press.

Martin, Emily. 1987. *The Woman in the Body: A Cultural Analysis of Reproduction*. Boston: Beacon Press.

Martin, M. Kay and Voorhies Barbara. 1975. *Female of the Species*. New York and London: Columbia University Press.

Martyna, Wendy. 1980. The psychology of the generic masculine. In McConnell-Ginet, Borker, and Furman 1980, 69–78.

Matsumoto, Yoshiko. 1996. Does less feminine speech in Japanese mean less femininity? In Warner, Ahlers, Bilmes, *et al.* 1996, 455–468.

2002. Gender identity and the presentation of self. In Benor *et al.* 2002, 339–354.

McCarthy, D. 1953. Some possible explanations of sex differences in language development and disorders. *Journal of Psychology*, 35:155–60.

McConnell-Ginet, Sally. 1975. Our father tongue: essays in linguistic politics. Diacritics, 5(4):44–56.

1978. Intonation in a man's world. *Signs*, 3:541–559.

1979. Prototypes, pronouns, and persons. In *Ethnolinguistics: Boas, Sapir, and Whorf Revisited*, ed. by Madeline Mathiot, 63–83. The Hague: Mouton.

1983. Intonation in a man's world. In Thorne, Kramarae, and Henley 1983, 69–88.

1984. The origins of sexist language in discourse. In *Discourse in Reading and Linguistics*, ed. by S. J. White and V. Teller, 123–135. Annals of the New York Academy of Sciences.

1989. The sexual (re)production of meaning: a discourse–based theory. In Frank and Treichler 1989, 35–50.

2002. "Queering" semantics: definitional struggles. In Campbell-Kibler *et al.* 2002, 137–160.

Forthcoming. "What's in a name?": social labeling and gender practices. In *The Handbook of Language and Gender*, ed. by Janet Holmes and Miriam Meyerhoff. Oxford: Blackwell.

McConnell-Ginet, Sally; Borker, Ruth A; and Furman, Nelly (eds.). 1980. *Women and Language in Literature and Society*. New York: Praeger.

McElhinny, Bonnie S. 1995. Challenging hegemonic masculinities: female and male police officers handling domestic violence. In Hall and Bucholtz 1995, 217–244.

McElhinny, Bonnie; Hols, Marijke; Holtzkener, Jeff; Unger, Susanne; and Hicks, Claire. Forthcoming. Gender, publication and citation in sociolinguistics and linguistic anthropology: the construction of a scholarly canon. *Language in Society*.

McGurk, H. and MacDonald, J. 1976. Hearing lips and seeing voices. *Nature*, 264:746–748.

McLemore, Cynthia. 1992. *The Interpretation of L *H in English*. Linguistic Forum 32, ed. by Cynthia McLemore. Austin: University of Texas Department of Linguistics and the Center for Cognitive Science.

McMillan, J. R.; Clifton, A. K.; McGrath, D.; and Gale, W. S. 1977. Woman's language: uncertainty or interpersonal sensitivity and emotionality? *Sex Roles*, 3(6):545–549.

Medin, Douglas L. 1989. Concepts and conceptual structure. *American Psychologist*, 44:1469–1481.

Mendoza-Denton, Norma. 1995. Pregnant pauses: silence and authority in the Anita Hill–Clarence Thomas hearings. In Hall and Bucholtz 1995, 51–66.

1996. "Muy macha": Gender and ideology in gang girls' discourse about makeup. *Ethnos: Journal of Anthropology*, 61:47–63.

1997. Chicana/Mexicana identity and linguistic variation: an ethnographic and sociolinguistic study of gang affiliation in an urban high school. Ph.D. dissertation, Stanford University.

Forthcoming. *Homegirls: Symbolic Practices in the Making of Latina Youth Styles*. Cambridge: Blackwell.

Meyerhoff, Miriam. 1992. "We've all got to go one day, eh": powerlessness and solidarity in the functions of a New Zealand tag. In Hall, Bucholtz, and Moonwomon 1992, 409–419.

1996. Dealing with gender identity as a sociolinguistic variable. In Bergvall, Bing, and Freed 1996, 202–227.

Miller, Laura. 1998. Bad girls: representations of unsuitable, unfit, and unsatisfactory women in magazines. *US–Japan Women's Journal*, 15:31–51.

2000. Ko-Gals, B-Girls and Miss Surf: enactment and assessment of
   trendy Tokyo types. Paper presented at the annual meeting of the
   American Anthropological Association, San Francisco.
Mills, Sara. 1995. *Feminist Stylistics*. London: Routledge.
Milroy, Lesley. 1980. *Language and Social Networks*. Oxford: Blackwell.
Milroy, James and Milroy, Lesley. 1985. Linguistic change, social network
   and speaker innovation. *Journal of Linguistics*, 21:339–384.
Mitchell-Kernan, Claudia. 1969. Language behavior in a Black urban
   community. Ph.D. dissertation, University of California at Berkeley.
   1972. Signifying and marking: two Afro-American speech acts. In
   Gumperz and Hymes 1972, 161–179.
Modaressi, Yahyah. 1978. A sociolinguistic analysis of modern Persian.
   Ph.D. dissertation, University of Kansas.
Montagné, Prosper. 1961. *Larousse Gastronomigue*. New York: Crown
   Publishers.
Moore, T. 1967. Language and intelligence: a longitudinal study of the
   first eight years. Part I: patterns of development in boys and girls.
   Human Development, 10:88–106.
Morgan, Marcyliena. 1991. Indirectness and interpretation in African
   American women's discourse. *Pragmatics*, 1:421–451.
Morrison, Toni (ed.). 1992. *Race-ing Justice, En-gendering Power: Essays on Anita
   Hill, Clarence Thomas, and the Construction of Social Reality*. New York:
   Pantheon Books.
Moulton, Janice. 1981. Sex and reference. In Vetterling-Braggin 1981, 100–115.
   1983. A paradigm of philosophy: The adversary method. In *Discovering
   Reality*, ed. by Sandra Harding and Merrill B. Hintikka, 149–164.
   Dordrecht: Reidel.
Mowrer, O. H. 1952. Speech development in the young child: 1. Autism
   theory of speech development and some clinical applications. *Journal
   of Speech and Hearing Disorders*, 17:264–268.
Mukama, Ruth. 1998. Women's discourses as the conservators of cultural
   values in language. *International Journal of the Sociology of Language*,
   129:157–165.
Murray, Thomas E. 1997. Perceptions of *Ms.*-titled women: evidence from
   the American midwest. *Onomastica Canadiana*, 79:73–96.
Newman, Michael. 2001. "I represent me": identity construction in a
   teenage rap crew. Paper presented at Symposium about Language in
   Society – Austin (SALSA) IX, Austin, TX.
Nichols, Patricia C. 1983. Linguistic options and choices for black women
   in the rural south. In Thorne, Kramarae, and Henley 1983, 54–68.
Nochlin, Linda. 1992. Why have there been no great women artists?
   Heresies, 7:38–43.
O'Barr, William M. and Atkins, Bowman K. 1980. "Women's language" or
   "powerless language"? In McConnell-Ginet, Borker, and Furman 1980,
   93–110.
O'Barr, William M. and Conley, John M. 1992. *Fortune and Folly: The Wealth
   and Power of Institutional Investing*. Homewood, IL: Business One Irwin.

Ochs, Elinor. 1991. Indexing gender. In *Rethinking Context*, ed. by Alessandro Duranti and Charles Goodwin, 335–358. Cambridge: Cambridge University Press.

    1996. Linguistic resources for socializing humanity. In *Rethinking Linguistic Relativity*, ed. by John J. Gumperz and Stephen Levinson, 407–437. Cambridge: Cambridge University Press.

Ochs, Elinor and Taylor, Carolyn. 1995. The "father knows best" dynamic in dinnertime conversations. In Hall and Bucholtz 1995, 97–120.

Ogawa, Naoko and Smith, Janet Shibamoto. 1997. The gendering of the gay male sex class in Japan: a case study based on "Rasen no Sobyo". In Livia and Hall 1997, 402–415.

Okamoto, Shigeko. 1995. "Tasteless" Japanese: less "feminine" speech among young Japanese women. In Hall and Bucholtz 1995, 297–325.

Okamoto, Shigeko and Sato, Shie. 1992. Less feminine speech among young Japanese females. In Hall, Bucholtz, and Moonwomon 1992, 478–488.

Ortner, Sherry. 1996. *Making Gender: The Politics and Erotics of Culture*. Boston: Beacon Press.

    1990. Gender hegemonies. *Cultural Critique*, 14:35–80.

Ortner, Sherry and Whitehead, Harriet. 1981. *Sexual Meanings: the Cultural Construction of Gender and Sexuality*. New York: Cambridge University Press.

Parker, Dorothy. 1995. *Complete Stories*, ed. by Colleen Breese and introduction by Regina Barreca. New York: Penguin.

Pauwels, Anne (ed.). 1987. *Women and Language in Australian and New Zealand Society*. Mosman, NSW: Australian Professional Publications.

    1998. *Women Changing Language*. London: Longman.

Penelope, Julia. 1990. *Speaking Freely: Unlearning the Lies of the Fathers' Tongues*. New York: Pergamon Press.

Perry, Lisa R. 2000. Cherokee generative metaphors. In Hardman and Taylor 2000, 221–232.

Phillips, Melanie A. 1989–2000. Transgender support site. http://www.heartcorps.com/journeys/voice.htm.

Podesva, Robert J.; Roberts, Sarah J.; and Campbell-Kibler, Kathryn. 2002. Sharing resources and indexing meanings in the production of gay styles. In Campbell-Kibler, Podesva, Roberts, and Wong 2002, 175–190.

Pollock, Griselda. 1988. *Vision and Difference: Femininity, Feminism, and the History of Art*. London: Routledge.

Poole, J. 1646. *The English Accidence*. Menston, England: Scolar Press Facsimile.

Precht, Kristen. 2002. Gender differences in affect, evidentiality, and hedging in American conversation. Paper presented at the annual meeting of the Linguistic Society of America, San Francisco.

Propp, Kathleen. 1995. An experimental examination of biological sex as a status cue in decision-making groups and its influence on information use. *Small Group Research*, 26(4):451–474.

Putnam, Hilary. 1975. The meaning of "meaning." In *Mind, Language, and Reality: Philosophical Papers*, Vol. II, ed. by Hilary Putnam, 215–271. New York: Cambridge University Press.

Radway, Janice. [1984] 1991. *Reading the Romance: Women, Patriarchy and Popular Literature,* revised edition. Chapel Hill, NC: University of North Carolina Press.

Reisman, Karl. 1974. Contrapuntal conversations in an Antiguan village. In Bauman and Sherzer 1974, 110–124.

Reynolds, Katsue. 1990. Female speakers of Japanese in transition. In Ide and McGloin 1990, 127–144.

Rickford, John. 1986. Concord and contrast in the characterization of the speech community. *Sheffield Working Papers in Language and Linguistics,* 3:87–119.

   1999. *African American Vernacular English: Features, Evolution, Educational Implications.* Malden, MA: Blackwell.

Risch, Barbara. 1987. Women's derogatory terms for men: that's right, "dirty" words. *Language in Society,* 16:353–358.

Roger, Derek B. and Nesshoever, Willfried. 1987. Individual differences in dyadic conversational strategies: a further study. *British Journal of Social Psychology,* 26:247–255.

Rombauer, Irma von Starkloff. 1998. *The Joy of Cooking.* New York: Scribner.

Rosch, Elinor. 1975. Cognitive representations of semantic categories. *Journal of Experimental Psychology: General,* 104:192–232.

Rosch, Elinor and Mervis, Carolyn B. 1975. Family resemblances: studies in the internal structure of categories. *Cognitive Psychology,* 7:573–605.

Rose, Robert; Gordon, Thomas; and Bernstein, Irwin. 1972. Plasma testosterone levels in the male rhesus monkeys: influences of sexual and social stimuli. *Science,* 178:634–645.

Ross, Stephanie. 1981. How words hurt: attitudes, metaphor and oppression. In Vetterling-Braggin 1981, 194–216.

Rubin, Joan. 1992. Nonlanguage factors affecting undergraduates' judgments of nonnative English-speaking teaching assistants. *Journal of Higher Education,* 33:511–531.

Rubin, J. Z.; Provenzano, F. J.; and Luria, Z. 1974. The eye of the beholder: parents' view on sex of newborns. *American Journal of Orthopsychiatry,* 44:512–519.

Rundquist, Suellen. 1992. Indirectness: a gender study of flouting Grice's maxims. *Journal of Pragmatics,* 18:431–449.

Sacks, Harvey; Schegloff, Emanuel; and Jefferson, Gail. 1974. A simplest systematics for the organization of turn-taking for conversation. *Language,* 50:696–735.

Sadker, Myra and Sadker, David. 1985. Sexism in the schoolroom of the 80s. *Psychology Today,* March: 54–57.

Sankoff, David and Laberge, Suzanne. 1978. The linguistic market and the statistical explanation of variability. In *Linguistic Variation: Models and Methods,* ed. by David Sankoff, 239–250. New York: Academic Press.

Sankoff, David; Cedergren, Henrietta J.; Kemp, William; Thibault, Pierre; and Vincent, Diane. 1989. Montreal French: language, class and ideology. In *Language Change and Variation,* ed. by Ralph W. Fasold and Deborah Schiffrin, 107–118. Amsterdam: John Benjamins.

Schegloff, Emanuel. 1972. Sequencing in conversational openings. In
   Gumperz and Hymes 1972, 346–380.
Schegloff, Emanuel and Sacks, Harvey. 1973. Opening up closings.
   Semiotica, 8:283–327.
Schiffrin, Deborah. 1984. Jewish argument as sociability. *Language in
   Society*, 13:311–335.
   1987. *Discourse Markers*. Cambridge and New York: Cambridge University
   Press.
   1994. *Approaches to Discourse*. Oxford: Blackwell.
Schneider, Joseph and Hacker, Sally. 1973. Sex role imagery and the use
   of generic "man" in introductory texts. *American Sociologist*, 8:12–18.
Schultz, Muriel R. 1975. The semantic derogation of women. In Thorne
   and Henley 1975, 64–75.
Searle, John. 1969. *Speech Acts*. Cambridge: Cambridge University Press.
   1975. Indirect speech acts. In *Syntax and semantics*. Vol. III, *Speech Acts*,
   ed. by Peter Cole and Jerry Morgan, 30–57. New York: Academic Press.
Selnow, Gary W. 1985. Sex differences in uses and perceptions of
   profanity. *Sex Roles*, 12:303–312.
Seremetakis, C. Nadia. 1991. *The Last Word: Women, Death, and Divination in
   Inner Mani*. Chicago: University of Chicago Press.
Shapiro, Fred R. 1985. Historical notes on the vocabulary of the women's
   movement. *American Speech*, 60(Spring):1–16.
Sheldon, Amy. 1992. Preschool girls' discourse competence: managing
   conflict. In Hall, Bucholtz, and Moonwomon 1992, 528–539.
Sheldon, Amy and Johnson, Diane. 1994. Preschool negotiators: gender
   differences in double-voice discourse as a conflict talk style in
   early childhood. In *Research on Negotiation in Organizations*, Vol. IV, ed.
   by B. Sheppard, R. Lewicki, and R. Bies, 25–57. Greenwich, CT: JAI
   Press. Reprinted in *The Sociolinguistics Reader* 1998. Vol. II, *Gender and
   Discourse*, ed. by J. Cheshire and Peter Trudgill, 76–99. London:
   Edward Arnold.
Sherwood, Kaitlin Duck. 1994. Women in the engineering industry.
   www.webfoot.com/advice/women.in.eng.html.
Sidnell, Jack. 1999. Gender and pronominal variation in an Indo-Guyanese
   creole-speaking community. *Language in Society*, 28:367–400.
Siegel, Muffy. 2002. "Like": the discourse particle and semantics. *Journal of
   Semantics*, 19, 35–71.
Smith, Janet Shibamoto. 1985. *Japanese Women's Language*. New York:
   Academic Press.
   1992. Women in charge: politeness and directives in the speech of
   Japanese women. *Language in Society*, 21:59–82.
Smith, Philip M. 1985. *Language, the Sexes and Society*. Oxford: Blackwell.
Smith-Lovin, L.; Skvoretz, J. V.; and Hudson, C. J. 1986. Status and
   participation in six-person groups: a test of Skvoretz's comparative
   status model. *Social Forces*, 64:992–1005.
Smith-Lovin, Lynn and Robinson, Dawn T. 1992. Gender and
   conversational dynamics. In *Gender, Interaction and Inequality*, ed. by
   Cecilia L. Ridgeway, 122–156. New York: Springer-Verlag.

Smitherman, Geneva. 1995a. Testifyin, sermonizin, and signifyin: Anita
    Hill, Clarence Thomas, and the African American verbal tradition. In
    Smitherman 1995b, 224–242.

(ed.). 1995b. *African American Women Speak Out on Anita Hill–Clarence
    Thomas.* Detroit, MI: Wayne State University.

Snow, M. E.; Jacklin, Carol N.; and Maccoby, Eleanor E. 1983. Sex-of-child
    differences in father–child interaction at one year of age. *Child
    Development*, 54:227–232.

Spender, Dale. 1980. *Man Made Language.* London: Routledge and Kegan
    Paul.

Sperber, Dan and Wilson, Deirdre. 1981. Irony and the use–mention
    distinction. In *Radical Pragmatics*, ed. by Peter Cole, 295–318. New
    York: Academic Press.

1986. *Relevance: Communication and Cognition.* Oxford: Blackwell.
    Reprinted (with new preface), 1995.

Stanley, Julia Penelope. 1977. Paradigmatic woman: the prostitute. In
    Papers in Language Variation, ed. by D. L. Shores and C. P. Hines.
    Tuscaloosa: The University of Alabama Press.

Staples, R. 1973. *The Black Woman in America: Sex, Marriage and the Family.*
    Chicago: Nelson Hall.

Stein, Edward. 1999. *The Mismeasure of Desire: the Science, Theory and Ethics of
    Sexual Orientation.* Oxford and New York: Oxford University Press.

Stocker, Michael. 1996. *Valuing Emotions.* Cambridge: Cambridge University
    Press.

Strand, Elizabeth. 1999. Uncovering the role of gender stereotypes
    in speech perception. *Journal of Language and Social Psychology*,
    18:86–99.

Strand, Elizabeth and Johnson, Keith. 1996. Gradient and visual speaker
    normalization in the perception of fricatives. In *Natural Language
    Processing and Speech Technology: Results of the 3rd KONVENS Conference,
    Bielefeld, October 1996*, ed. by D. Gibbon. Berlin: Mouton.

Sturken, Marita and Cartwright, Lisa. 2001. *Practices of Looking: An
    Introduction to Visual Culture.* Oxford: Oxford University Press.

Sunaoshi, Yukako. 1994. Mild directives work effectively: Japanese
    women in command. In Bucholtz, Liang, Sutton, and Hines 1994,
    678–690.

1995. Japanese women's construction of an authoritative position in
    their communities of practice. Master's Thesis, University of Texas at
    Austin.

Sutton, Laurel A. 1992. Bitches and skanky hobags: the place of women in
    contemporary slang. In Hall and Bucholtz 1995, 279–296.

Swacker, Marjorie. 1975. The sex of speaker as a sociolinguistic variable.
    In Thorne and Henley 1975, 76–83.

Swann, Joan. 1988. Talk control: an illustration from the classroom of
    problems in analysing male dominance of conversation. In Coates
    and Cameron 1988, 123–140.

Swann, Joan and Graddol, David. 1988. Gender inequalities in classroom
    talk. *English in Education*, 22:48–65.

Talbot, Mary. 1995. A synthetic sisterhood: false friends in a teenage magazine. In Hall and Bucholtz 1995, 143–165.

  1998. *Language and Gender: An Introduction*. Cambridge: Polity Press; Malden, MA: Blackwell.

Tannen, Deborah. 1981. New York Jewish conversational style. *International Journal of the Sociology of Language*, 30:133–139.

  1984. *Conversational Style: Analyzing Talk Among Friends*. Norwood, NJ: Ablex.

  1989. Interpreting interruption in conversation. Paper presented at the 25th annual meeting of the Chicago Linguistics Society. Part 2: Parasession on Language and Context, University of Chicago.

  1990. *You Just Don't Understand: Women and Men in Conversation*. New York: William Morrow.

  1993. *Gender and Conversational Interaction*. New York: Oxford University Press.

  1994. The relativity of linguistic strategies: rethinking power and solidarity in gender and dominance. In *Gender and Discourse*, ed. by Deborah Tannen, 19–52. Oxford: Oxford University Press.

  1998. *The Argument Culture: Stopping America's War of Words*. New York: Ballantine Books.

Terry, Don. 2001. Getting under my skin. In *How Race is Lived in America: Pulling Together, Pulling Apart*, ed. by Correspondents of the *NY Times*, 269–284. New York: Henry Holt.

Thomas, Beth. 1988. Differences of sex and sects: linguistic variation and social networks in a Welsh mining village. In Coates and Cameron 1988, 51–60.

Thomason, Richmond. 1990. Accommodation, meaning and implicature: interdisciplinary foundations for pragmatics. In *Intentions in Communication*, ed. by Philip Cohen, Jerry Morgan, and M. Pollack, 325–263. Cambridge, MA: MIT Press.

Thorne, Barrie. 1993. *Gender Play*. New Brunswick, NJ: Rutgers University Press.

Thorne, Barrie and Henley, Nancy (eds.). 1975. *Language and Sex: Difference and Dominance*. Rowley, MA: Newbury House.

Thorne, Barrie; Kramarae, Cheris; and Henley, Nancy (eds.). 1983. *Language, Gender, and Society*. Rowley, MA: Newbury House.

Threadgold, Terry. 1997. *Feminist Poetics: Poiesis, Performance, Histories*. London: Routledge.

Timm, Lenora A. 2000. Romancing the earth: Feminized maternal/erotic metaphors in recent eco-environmental literature. In Hardman and Taylor 2000, 105–118.

Trabelsi, Chedia. 1991. De quelques aspects du langage des femmes de Tunis. *International Journal of the Sociology of Language*, 87:87–98.

Treichler, Paula A. 1981. Verbal subversions in Dorothy Parker: "Trapped like a trap in a trap." *Language and Style*, 13:46–61.

  1989. From discourse to dictionary: how sexist meanings are authorized. In Frank and Treichler 1989, 51–79.

Treichler, Paula A. and Frank, Francine Wattman. 1989. Guidelines for nonsexist usage. In Frank and Treichler 1989, 137–278.

Trömmel-Plötz, Senta. 1982. *Frauensprache – Sprache der Veränderung.* Frankfurt-am-Main: Fischer.

Trudgill, Peter. 1972. Sex, covert prestige, and linguistic change in the urban British English of Norwich. *Language in Society,* 1:179–195.
  1974. *The Social Differentiation of English in Norwich.* Cambridge: Cambridge University Press.

Twenge, J. M. 1997. Attitudes toward women, 1970–1995. *Psychology of Women Quarterly,* 21:35–51.

Valian, Virginia. 1998. *Why So Slow?: Women and Professional Achievement.* Cambridge, MA: MIT Press.

Veblen, Thorstein. [1899] 1994. *Theory of the Leisure Class.* New York: Penguin.

Vetterling-Braggin, Mary (ed.). 1981. *Sexist Language: A Modern Philosophical Analysis.* Totowa, NJ: Littlefield, Adams.

Vincent, Diane. 1982. *Pressions et impressions sur les sacres au Québec.* Quebec: Gouvernement du Québec, Office de la langue française.

Vygotsky, L. S. 1962. *Thought and Language.* Cambridge, MA: MIT Press; New York: Wiley.

Walker, Alice. 1983. *In Search of Our Mothers' Gardens: Womanist Prose.* New York: Harcourt Brace Jovanovich.

Wareing, Shan. 1996. What *do* we know about language and gender? Paper presented at eleventh sociolinguistic symposium, Cardiff, September 5–7.

Warner, Natasha; Ahlers, Jocelyn; Bilmes, Leela; Oliver, Monica; Wertheim, Suzanne; and Chen, Melinda (eds.). 1996. *Gender and Belief Systems: Proceedings of the Fourth Berkeley Women and Language Conference.* Berkeley: Berkeley Women and Language Group.

Watson, Carol. 1987. Sex-linked difference in letters of recommendation. *Women and Language,* 10:26–28.

Weatherall, Ann and Walton, Marsha. 1999. The metaphorical construction of sexual experience in a speech community of New Zealand university students. *British Journal of Social Psychology,* 39:479–498.

Wenger, Etienne. 1998. *Communities of Practice.* New York: Cambridge University Press.

West, Rebecca. 1982. *Selections of Rebecca West's Writings, 1911–1917. The Young Rebecca,* ed. by Jane Marcus. London: Macmillan.

West, Candace and Zimmerman, Don. 1987. Doing gender. *Gender and Society,* 1:125–151.

Wetzel, Patricia J. 1988. Are "powerless" communication strategies the Japanese norm? *Language in Society,* 17:555–564.

Wharton, Edith. 1905. *House of mirth.* New York: Charles Scribner's Sons.

Whiting, B. B. and Edwards, C. P. 1988. *Children of Different Worlds: The Formation of Social Behavior.* Cambridge, MA: Harvard University Press.

Wierzbicka, Anna. 1987. *English Speech Act Verbs: A Dictionary*. Sydney: Academic Press.

Williams, Raymond. 1977. *Marxism and Literature*. Oxford and New York: Oxford University Press.

Wilson, T. 1553. *Arte of Rhetorique*. Gainsville: Scholars Facsimiles and Reprints, 1962.

Wittgenstein, Ludwig. 1953. *Philosophical Investigations*. New York: Macmillan.

Wolfram, Walt. 1969. *A Sociolinguistic Description of Detroit Negro Speech*. Washington DC: Center for Applied Linguistics.

Wolfson, Nessa. 1984. "Pretty is as pretty does": a speech act view of sex roles. *Applied Linguistics*, 5:236–244.

Wolfson, Nessa and Manes, Joan. 1980. "Don't 'dear' me!" In McConnell-Ginet, Borker, and Furman 1980, 79–92.

Wong, Andrew. 2001. The evolution of a genre, the emergence of a community: Coming-out stories and the gay imaginary (ms).

Woolard, Kathryn. 1985. Language variation and cultural hegemony. *American Ethnologist*, 12:738–748.

Woolf, Virginia. 1966. *Collected essays*, Vol. II. London: Hogarth Press.

Wright, Saundra and Hay, Jen. 2002. Fred and Wilma: a phonological conspiracy. In Benor *et al.* 2002, 175–192.

Zhang, Qing. 2001. Changing economics, changing markets: a sociolinguistic study of Chinese yuppies. Ph.D. dissertation, Stanford University.

Zimmerman, Don and West, Candace. 1975. Sex roles, interruptions and silences in conversation. In Thorne and Henley 1975, 105–129.

Index